Law and Philosophy Library

Volume 148

The Law and Philosophy Library , which has been in existence since 1985, aims to publish cutting edge works in the philosophy of law, and has a special history of publishing books that focus on legal reasoning and argumentation, including those that may involve somewhat formal methodologies. The series has published numerous important books on law and logic, law and artificial intelligence, law and language, and law and rhetoric. While continuing to stress these areas, the series has more recently expanded to include books on the intersection between law and the Continental philosophical tradition, consistent with the traditional openness of the series to books in the Continental jurisprudential tradition. The series is proud of the geographic diversity of its authors, and many have come from Latin America, Spain, Italy, the Netherlands, Germany, and Eastern Europe, as well, more obviously for an English-language series, from the United Kingdom, the United States, Australia and Canada.

Kevin M. Clermont

A General Theory of Evidence and Proof

Forming Beliefs in Truth

Springer

Kevin M. Clermont
Law
Cornell University
Ithaca, NY, USA

ISSN 1572-4395 ISSN 2215-0315 (electronic)
Law and Philosophy Library
ISBN 978-3-031-66551-6 ISBN 978-3-031-66552-3 (eBook)
https://doi.org/10.1007/978-3-031-66552-3

This Springer imprint is published by the registered company Springer Nature Switzerland AG
The registered company address is: Gewerbestrasse 11, 6330 Cham, Switzerland

Contents

Chapter 1
Introduction

***Stuart:** Oh, Sheldon, I'm afraid you couldn't be more wrong.*
***Sheldon:** More wrong? Wrong is an absolute state and not subject to gradation.*
***Stuart:** Of course it is. It's a little wrong to say a tomato is a vegetable, it's very wrong to say it's a suspension bridge.*
—The Big Bang Theory (The Big Bang Theory: The Hofstadter Isotope (CBS television broadcast Apr. 13, 2009); see Russell (1947) ("When one admits that nothing is certain one must, I think, also admit that some things are much more nearly certain than others.").)

Abstract This book analyzes and explicates the logical process of forming beliefs in truth. Section 1.1: The book first introduces the example of legal factfinding. Section 1.2: Then the book will explain uncertainty and the theories of bivalent probabilities and multivalent beliefs. It will apply the theories to understand how the legal factfinder should and does process evidence and evaluate proof. It will finally extend the theories to all kinds of attempts by humans to decide what they will treat as truth in an uncertain world. Section 1.3: This book is an original take on an important problem that has long impeded comprehension of decisionmaking under uncertainty.

How do we humans undertake establishing truth about the world? We must do this constantly, in order to guide the decisions made in living our lives. One method is to consider the available evidence, then form a belief, and finally treat the belief as true if it meets some standard. The methodology has *broad* significance, as we utilize it in all corners of life.

Simple enough? But what makes the topic *deep* is that we live in a world of uncertainty. Of course, in contemplating uncertainty, there is a role played by what we see as randomness, the inexplicable and irreducible variation in outcomes that the universe hides from even the all-knowing person. Yet more importantly, there is the role played by all the unknown things in the part of the world that we view as

K. M. Clermont, *A General Theory of Evidence and Proof*, Law and Philosophy Library 148, https://doi.org/10.1007/978-3-031-66552-3_1

nonrandom. First, the evidence is almost always incomplete, inconclusive, ambiguous, dissonant, or unreliable. Second, the issue almost always involves concepts and expressions that are vague, entailing all kinds of borderline cases. Third, we never know the extent of what we do not know, a residue of unknown unknowns.

Remarkably little knowledge, and not even much careful conjecture, exists on how we humans *do* go from evidence to beliefs in truth. Perhaps more astounding is that little work has been done on how we *should* go about establishing truth in the real world of real uncertainty. To the extent that any of us think about the subject, we tend at most to encapsulate our theorizing in some sort of statement like "I am at least 51% sure of such-and-such proposition." The point of this book is that such thinking is fundamentally maladapted to many decisions made in the real world. The failing lies in the use of probability, which recognizes only randomness. The cure lies in using a logic that handles all relevant kinds of uncertainty.

Prefatory Summary Okay, take a step back and consider the trip this book will take in challenging the hegemony of probability. The book starts with the ground already laid: two leading methods compete to guide decisionmaking in an uncertain world. There is probabilist theory, and there is belief theory. Humans very readily employ one or the other when seeking uncertain truth.

- First, although probability arrived later on humanity's scene, it proved so useful and amenable to theoretical sophistication that it has become, for those thinking about decisionmaking, the default theory of uncertainty. Traditional probability assumes everything is either true or false ("bivalence"); but after conceding that truth might be uncertain, probability theory allows people to assert that the odds of truth are such-and-such, and the odds of falsity are then 1 minus truth's odds ("additivity"). We often find truth to exist when the odds of truth exceed that measure of falsity.
- Second, a method frequently invoked by intuition, since long ago, is more focused on evidential proof. Belief theory does not divide the factfinder's state of mind into two, but rather into three multivalently gradated concepts: belief, conceivably knowable unknowns, and disbelief. We often find truth to exist when belief exceeds disbelief, where these concepts measure the degree to which the proposition and its opposite have been fully proved by reliable means. But retention of uncommitted belief to reflect unknowns requires the use of nonadditive multivalent mathematics (such as the belief in a and b equals the lesser of the belief in a and the belief in b).

Different mathematics mean different answers. Different answers mean that we must choose between the two methods, based on their appropriateness for the task at hand. Probability might seem the more natural and promising alternative to try for handling uncertainty, but it has proved to be a highly imperfect fit for legal factfinding. The fault is not the law's. Probability is just the wrong model for truth-finding.

Route Taken This book's amazing conclusion will be that, by intuition rather than by theory, we humans usually and rightly deploy belief theory in everyday life, science, law, and elsewhere. The book provides the missing theoretical argument in support of what we do in practice by proceeding in the next five chapters through these five points:

- In analyzing truth-finding, the predominant approach has been to assume every proposition about the world is either true or false, that is, to utilize classical binary logic. Any uncertainty is accommodated by traditional probability theory alone, which treats the truth or falsity as subject only to randomness. That is, traditional probability theory assumes whatever is known includes all that is conceivably knowable, so that everything else can be treated as random and hence unpredictable variation. (The term for randomness is aleatory uncertainty.)
- I contend that this is a strange way to conceive of, say, factfinding, which is always subject to gaps in our knowledge attributable to imperfect evidence and such. Failing to account for these gaps leads to the many problems, puzzles, and paradoxes that trouble theorists endlessly. (The term for this kind of uncertainty is epistemic uncertainty.)
- We need instead a measure of truth that expresses the degree of belief in the proposition's truth, as proven by the evidence. It would indicate where our sureness falls between full falsity and full truth. Multivalent logic, which jettisons the assumption that all is either true or not true, was developed for just this kind of situation. It is more general than classical logic. It yields classical logic as a special case if binariness is assumed. Multivalent logic is accepted as valid for handling partial measures, such as partial truths. It is fully developed as a theory, and it has produced astonishingly sophisticated refinement and application.
- Also, we need a measure of truth that recognizes both aleatory and epistemic uncertainty. That needed measure could be a multivalent belief function with a scale from 0 to 1 that allocates belief between an affirmative belief and a disbelief both subject to aleatory uncertainty, and that retains an uncommitted remainder of belief to express epistemic uncertainty. The result of belief and disbelief not adding to 1 critically affects the mathematics for combining beliefs.
- The present book shows how using multivalent beliefs clarifies legal factfinding profoundly. But it goes further to illuminate much decisionmaking outside the realm of law and facts.

1.1 Legal Factfinding

Law I shall detail this argument by using the law as initial exemplar, before stretching out toward the horizon. Why use the law? Besides being something I know about, law gives great illustrations for thinking about the subject of decisionmaking. Much more pertinently, legal theorists have thought more about practical truth-finding than other theorists. Legal academics have spawned a hotly contested but informative literature. Perhaps the reason for their interest is that judges have to explain publicly to laypersons how to measure truth. Much more likely, the reason for academic contemplation is that forming beliefs in truth is central to the operation of law.

The principal task of law's actors is decisionmaking.[1] Decisionmaking necessarily takes place in a world of uncertainty.[2] That combination explains why a legal decisionmaker must know in every step along the way not only what the present issue is, but also how sure he or she must be to decide it in a particular way.

Legal procedure aims to improve that decisionmaking.[3] Indeed, much of this procedure aims at facilitating optimal decisionmaking in the face of uncertainty. A central and critical task of procedure, then, is to facilitate for each kind of issue the proper way to process the relevant considerations and then to evaluate the output against the applicable standard of sureness.

Fact Effective decisionmaking most often requires taking an accurate position on what is true. Accuracy requires processing evidence and evaluating it as proof of truth. For clarity of exposition, I shall narrow my initial focus from decisionmaking in general to factfinding, or how a factfinder decides that a contestable fact exists. However, I refer to "fact" in its broad sense, as covering anything that a court, other institution, or person subjects to the evidential proof process in order to establish what the system or person will treat as being true.

Because factfinding itself remains so broad, however, this book will further narrow its initial focus to law's procedural method of evidential proof. Happily, it is nicely representative of all factfinding. Still, the subject of legal factfinding extends far beyond the jurors' task that springs to mind. I have mined civil, criminal, and administrative procedure for doctrines on factfinding. The subject includes not only yes-or-no facts but also vague and partly normative terms like "fault" and many other applications of law to fact; it includes a variety of nonbinary[4] opinions,[5] as well

[1] "So thoroughly immersed is law in the business of decision that one might easily be tempted to say that decision is its sole activity." Cowan (1963), p. 507.

[2] "Most legal decision making, like that in many other areas of complex activity, is done under conditions of uncertainty." Saks and Kidd (1981), p. 126. One can play with the notion of uncertainty, of course. For example, "to be certain of uncertainty ... is to be certain of at least one thing," Dawes (1986), p. 131, or "it is not certain that everything is uncertain," Pascal (1670), no. 387 (edited out by Pascal); cf., e.g., Gabler (2011) (announcing as the "elusive big idea" that we are in a post-idea era). The philosophically inclined can do more than play with the notion, however. See, e.g., Greco (2013) (objecting to the view that what we know has a probability of one); Lawson (1992), pp. 871–874 (discussing possible Cartesian arguments regarding uncertainty). For some propositions in closed systems, uncertainty will seem rather thin, except in the metaphysical sense that nothing is absolutely certain. But in almost all circumstances calling for legal factfinding, uncertainty will be a palpable concern. See Twining (2006), p. 104 (rebutting "the myth of certainty"); Tang and Foley (2014) (showing the importance for lawyers to accept uncertainty).

[3] "Legal procedure is the methodology of the law, and it is by understanding and improving this methodology that we can best hope to make our justice system more reliable and fair." Lind (1982), p. 14.

[4] See infra Chap. 6 (treating nonbinary decisions).

[5] For example, what criminal sentence does the defendant deserve? But I am not hereby wading into the debate on the fact/value distinction. See Mulligan and Correia (2017) ("Facts, philosophers like to say, are opposed to theories and to values . . . ."). It would take us into cognate theoretical fields, such as moral uncertainty, which studies how to make decisions in the face of uncertainty about

as odd kinds of "facts" such as the prediction of an event[6] or legislative and historical facts.[7]

Truth My concern will be with legal factfinding only as an *accurate* way to uncover truth.[8] Justice is law's more inclusive goal, where truth is but one of multiple values.[9] Those other values, I put aside here. Viewing legal factfinding as aimed solely at truth will allow my later analysis of decisionmaking to extend broadly. As I have already indicated, I shall eventually go not only beyond the realm of law but also beyond factfinding.

---

what we should morally do. See Cox (2023) (providing a nice introduction to moral uncertainty's relation to legal decisionmaking). Instead, I use a broad definition of "fact" so as to include all matters subjected to a proof process. Cf. Mulligan and Correia (2017), § 2.4 (distinguishing fact and proposition).

[6] Furthermore, prediction of an event may involve odd kinds of events. For an example, a court has to gauge the sureness of a future imprecise event when determining, for pretrial detention of juveniles, whether a serious risk of future criminal conduct exists. See Schall v. Martin, 467 U.S. 253, 278 (1984). Also, the Supreme Court contemplated the likelihood of a conjectural event—uncovering tainted evidence in another way—when it ruled that in order to avoid the exclusionary rule, the prosecution had to establish by a preponderance the evidence's "inevitable discovery," rejecting both a lower and a higher "quantum of proof." Nix v. Williams, 467 U.S. 431, 444 & n.5 (1984). The oddity in these examples springs from what some call an iterated epistemological operator. See Haack (2012), p. 212 (giving as an example that "the Texas death-penalty statute requires prosecutors … to prove *beyond a reasonable doubt* that *there is a probability* that the defendant will be dangerous in future ('definitely maybe,' as my students say)" (footnote omitted)).

On the one hand, when trying to determine how likely an event is likely, the solution lies in collapsing the iterations into a single measure. See Hagerty v. L & L Marine Servs., Inc., 788 F.2d 315, 319 ("we conclude that a plaintiff can recover only where he can show that the toxic exposure more probably than not will lead to cancer" (emphasis omitted)), modified on other grounds, 797 F.2d 256 (5th Cir. 1986).

On the other hand, sometimes the questions do not collapse and so the standard of proof applies in ordinary fashion to a compound proposition, as when a judge has to decide how sure it was that reasonable minds could differ. See Wampler v. Indianapolis Colts, 902 F. Supp. 2d 1143, 1151–52 (S.D. Ind. 2012) ("Moreover, during her pre-hire interview, Ms. Wampler *arguably* lied about posing nude. Whether it was *actually* a lie depends on your conception of nudity. If a person uses latex body paint to cover his or her private parts, does that constitute nudity? Perhaps reasonable minds could disagree on this issue. (And the answer may turn on the quality and opaqueness of the paint at issue.) The relevant point is that the Club reasonably construed Ms. Wampler's statement as a lie.").

The distinction between the two preceding paragraphs lies in whether the cumulative likelihoods contribute to predicting one proposition's existence or whether the factfinder is trying to determine two propositions' coexistence.

[7] See Williams (2024).

[8] See Enoch et al. (2021) (arguing that accuracy in terms of truth, rather than other epistemological goals, is the paramount aim of legal factfinding). But see Ho (2008), pp. 127, 155–156, 171 (arguing that legal factfinding must aim for more than truth).

[9] See Field et al. (2023), pp. 1774–1784, 1826–1832 (exploring the multiple values).

Surprisingly, how humans should process and evaluate evidence as part of any proof process aimed at truth remains largely unexplored and misunderstood. Humans just somehow do it, having performed this basic mental process since the dawn of human time.

For legal factfinding's vehicle that moves toward truth, there has been a contest between probability and some alternative such as belief. To resolve that contest, a bit of overview is necessary. The starting point is realizing that the major difference between probabilities and beliefs lies in how they treat uncertainty. That point necessitates some preliminary explaining.

The order of explaining a complex thesis is all-important. The optimal explanatory line might sometimes appear circuitous, even if it is steadfastly careful. So I begin here by considering how the two vehicles handle uncertainty.

1.1.1 Uncertainty and Probability Theory in Legal Factfinding

Why the lack of study and understanding about evidential proof? The big impediment has been that our prevailing logic fails to contemplate the full range of uncertainty. Classical binary logic assumes that everything is or will be either true or false, 1 or 0. It operates in a black-and-white world.

Eventually, theorists developed so-called classical probability as a supplement to binary logic.[10] It expressed the chance of an outcome as 1 divided by the number of possible outcomes. With more time, probability came to employ frequentist and then subjective measures. If the issue is whether a drawn ball will be black, when taken from an urn containing 100 balls of which 60 are black, then probability is ready to work its magic in dealing with random, or aleatory, uncertainty.

But what if the issue is whether a certain culprit was in fact Dave? As we shall see,[11] mathematical probability did not reach the kind of uncertainty that is far more important for the theory of evidential proof: uncertainty about the strength of the evidence, about the relevant matters that are vague in conception, and about the matters we do not even know that we should be considering. This kind of uncertainty is called epistemic uncertainty.

The percentage probability represents the factfinder's estimate of how often the proposition would turn out to be true in a long run of trials, or the factfinder's subjective view of the odds for betting on it being true upon this particular trial. It is not a promise of outcome. Any particular outcome will be the product of mysterious

[10] See Howson (2009), p. 178 (combining probability with logic and quoting De Finetti (1936), p. 1: "It is beyond doubt that probability theory can be considered as a multi-valued logic (precisely: with a continuous range of values), and that this point of view is the most suitable to clarify the foundational aspects of the notion and the logic of probability.").

[11] See infra Sect. 3.1.3 (elaborating how traditional probability hides epistemic uncertainty).

variation. Some of the variation might be truly random, but some may reflect the working out of conceivably knowable unknowns. Probability's critical move is then to assume that the unknowns will work out just like the knowns that are subject to randomness. So the percentage probability will remain unaffected by the epistemic unknowns. Then we have no more need to measure the epistemic unknowns than the aleatory uncertainty, because all epistemic unknowns are assumed to have no predictable effect. The percentage probability remains the best guess. In other words, the probability process buries all the epistemic uncertainties, by treating them as if they were aspects of randomness. It yields betting odds that express an expected outcome supposedly subject only to the effect of random variation.

So what? After all, in most cases, factfinding ultimately comes down to a yes-or-no answer. Probability seems to provide that sort of answer, via a percentage likelihood that the culprit was Dave.[12] The difficulty is that in evidential proof, epistemic uncertainty matters. Here is an example that shows the importance of keeping track of epistemic uncertainty when factfinding:

> Assume that the evidence on fact *a*'s existence, say, Dave's identification as the culprit, remains weak after hearing all the available, but very imperfect, evidence (based on weak eyewitness identification). The factfinder *somehow* gauges a showing of likelihood that it was Dave at around 16%, perhaps using a gauge of full proof that ticks up as proof comes in. Nonetheless, this affirmative evidence definitely outweighs the evidence that the fact does not exist, which the factfinder gauges at around 4% (based on very weak exculpatory evidence). Through no one's fault, no other evidence exists. If you were forced to bet on whether accepting the identification is the right course and you wanted to use odds to express the proof, then perhaps you would say Prob(*a*) = 80% and Prob(*not-a*) = 20%. That is, even though your belief one way or the other is fairly weak, if you had to allocate all your belief to either yes or no, you would formulate odds of 80/20.[13]

The law must decide on the available evidence.[14] I think its factfinders would and should normally consider *a* to be proved in this situation, in a civil suit where the plaintiff has carried the burden of production.

Does the 16% probability tell us anything other than that there was not much evidence? Does the absence of evidence tell us that the probability it was not Dave is 84%? No. It suggests only that the factfinder would prefer not to decide upon the state of this evidence. But the factfinder must decide.

---

[12] In statistical terminology, "likelihood" (the chance that the data would be observed, given a hypothesis as true) is not wholly equivalent to "probability" (the chance that a hypothesis is true, given the observed data). See Royall (1997), pp. 5–6, 28. But for most people, likelihood means probability. I use likelihood here in that popular way, with perhaps the connotation of an intuitive measure of probability. The popular way has the benefit of conforming to the common legal, and probabilistic, usage of "more likely than not" as a standard of proof.

[13] See infra Sects. 3.2.2, 3.2.3 and 4.3.3.2 (returning to this example).

[14] See Laudan (2007), pp. 304–305 ("The trier of fact cannot say, 'Although plaintiff's case is stronger than defendant's, I will reach no verdict since neither party has a frightfully good story to tell.' Under current rules, if the plaintiff has a better story than the defendant, he must win the suit, even when his theory of the case fails to satisfy the strictures required to qualify his theory as the best explanation.").

Is the 80/20 figure, all alone, an accurate representation of your state of mind as to the existence of *a*? In terms of state of mind, an 80% chance on airtight evidence of a frequentist sort is very different from an 80% chance on thin evidence. Can the factfinder safely treat the 80% thin finding about Dave as equivalent to more solid findings on the case's other issues? It is natural to suspect that probability theory would introduce a source of error by discarding epistemic uncertainty and converting the weak showing on *a* to a simple and powerful 80%.

Traditional probability's elision of epistemic uncertainty might still allow it to render the final answer in a legal case (where the only issue was whether Dave did it), but not to perform other functions. Using probability at interlocutory steps of factfinding would introduce all sorts of errors. Errors might arise when the factfinder needs to work with the interlocutory probability, as when combining it with findings from other evidence. The need to combine arises in connection with (1) linking uncertain inferences from a piece of evidence to reach a conclusion, (2) aggregating the probative force of several pieces of evidence that bear on a single conclusion, and (3) combining separate conclusions. When the factfinder combines findings subject to epistemic uncertainty, it will often arrive at a different answer if it accounts for epistemic uncertainty rather than ignores it.

1.1.2 Uncertainty and Multivalent Logic in Legal Factfinding

Fortunately, there is a feasible way to account for epistemic uncertainty when factfinding. It involves the use of multivalent logic rather than binary (or bivalent) logic. This alternative way allows variables, like belief, to take values between 0 and 1. We can then view the factfinder's belief system as including, after hearing the evidence, (1) a belief in *a* as a partial truth, (2) a disbelief in *a* as another partial belief, and (3) the remaining unallocated belief on the issue as a container of uncertainty. In Dave's case, the smallish belief it was Dave would overcome the even smaller disbelief. This newish brand of logic is accepted as valid for handling partial truths. It is fully developed as a theory, and it has produced a plethora of insights.

Multivalent logic is not in tension with probability theory. Multivalent logic is a generalization of bivalent logic and its traditional probability. If one were to assume bivalence, so that everything could only be completely true or completely false, and if one were to assume away epistemic uncertainty, so that everything conceivably knowable is known, then multivalent logic would reduce to the theoretical systems we are used to. That is, multivalent logic produces bivalent logic and traditional probability as special cases.

Moreover, one need not stick with bivalent logic to handle aleatory uncertainty. There are versions of multivalent logic that can handle facts exhibiting both aleatory and epistemic uncertainty.

Percentage probabilities can be converted into multivalent beliefs. They feed into the construction of the multivalent belief in the fact and the corresponding disbelief.

But this translation into beliefs is no easy task. The probability will have to be connected up with the issue by a series of permissible but uncertain inferences; also, the evidence may have to be discounted for defects in credibility; and so on—in short, epistemic uncertainty would have to be accounted for, as the probability is converted into a belief.

Still, both the probabilities and the beliefs/disbeliefs rest on evaluating the knowns. Also, both systems ultimately disregard higher-order aleatory uncertainty, because it tells us nothing, randomness being the absence of information. The difference between probabilities and beliefs/disbeliefs is that multivalent belief theory retains a measure of the epistemic unknowns as uncommitted belief, making the committed beliefs into more honest and revealing measurements. Epistemic uncertainty, consisting of the conceivably knowable unknowns, is not devoid of information. It allows the computation of how well a fact is proven. It shows the distinction between strong and weak proof. It thereby delivers a more accurate combination of findings.

As we shall also see,[15] some other theorists claim that this move to multivalent beliefs is all sleight of hand. They say that I cannot change reality by switching logic systems. Of course I cannot. But I can measure different aspects of reality more accurately by sometimes switching logical tools. Traditional probability assumes that everything must be either true or false and that there is only randomness, which is an odd step to take when handling imperfect evidence in a proof system that regularly produces outputs falling partway between true and false. Multivalent beliefs measure the outputs with many gradations, include comprehensive measures of uncertainty, and come with simple operators to combine these more complex beliefs. My argument for multivalent beliefs is the analogue of saying that calculus will give different and better answers than multiplication rules when one faces a problem of instantaneous rates of change.

In short, I am not switching realities. I am only urging use of different metrics for stories' believability as contrasted with sequences' odds. *I argue for the natural but subtle course of measuring how well proven a fact is. I argue against taking the further step of converting that natural measure into the artificial measure of the probability of truth, a conversion that requires discarding any sense of epistemic uncertainty.*

Furthermore, my argument does not require reform. Instead, it explains the current law. Law was one of the first of society's endeavors in which things routinely appeared as neither completely true nor completely false. Multivalent beliefs mark the route to accurate decisionmaking in a real world dominated by shades of gray. The law, long ago, intuited multivalent beliefs from natural language and daily life. Thus, our law came naturally to conform to multivalent logic.[16]

---

[15] See infra Sects. 4.5.4.2 and 4.5.5 (refuting those theorists who view using different logical tools for different tasks as a magic trick).

[16] Cf. Nichols (2021) (arguing that humans formulate and learn moral rules from experience by a rational process).

True, the law still does not explicitly acknowledge its reliance on multivalent beliefs. The law does not do so because the theoretical understanding of multivalent logics is a recent development. Nevertheless, multivalent beliefs explain so much about the law that we can today infer that the law has long utilized them implicitly. The law knew where it was going all along. As a result, if the law were openly to embrace multivalent beliefs, its approach to evidence and proof would need no drastic rethinking or reconception—but we would end up understanding the law much better.

1.2 Book's Coverage

This book's subject has long intrigued me. It has led me over the years to think hard, read widely, and write periodically, which yielded a prior book on the standards of proof[17] and a series of articles on factfinding more generally.[18] In this new book, I

[17]The book was Kevin M. Clermont, Standards of Decision in Law: Psychological and Logical Bases for the Standard of Proof, Here and Abroad (2013). In the current book I generalize the prior book. I examine the parts of evidential proof that precede and follow application of the standard of proof. I summarize the prior book's lessons on standards of proof in Sect. 5.2 of this new book. The two books thus stand as companion pieces that complement one another.

[18]The principal articles were (1) Kevin M. Clermont, Procedure's Magical Number Three: Psychological Bases for Standards of Decision, 72 Cornell L. Rev. 1115 (1987); (2) Kevin M. Clermont & Emily Sherwin, A Comparative View of Standards of Proof, 50 Am. J. Comp. L. 243 (2002), translated in 47 China L.J. 117 (2002), reprinted in Kuo-Chang Huang, New Perspective of Civil Procedure Theory 19 (2005); (3) Kevin M. Clermont & Emily Sherwin, A Comparative Puzzle: Standards of Proof, in Law and Justice in a Multistate World 629 (James A.R. Nafziger & Symeon C. Symeonides eds., 2002); (4) Kevin M. Clermont, Standards of Proof in Japan and the United States, 37 Cornell Int'l L.J. 263 (2004), translated in 33 J. Japanese Inst. Int'l Bus. L. 611, 779 (2005), reprinted in Theories of American Civil Procedure 139 (Masahiko Omura & Koichi Miki eds. & trans., 2006); (5) Kevin M. Clermont, Jurisdictional Fact, 91 Cornell L. Rev. 973 (2006); (6) Kevin M. Clermont, Standards of Proof Revisited, 33 Vt. L. Rev. 469 (2009); (7) Kevin M. Clermont, Aggregation of Probabilities and Illogic, 47 Ga. L. Rev. 165 (2012); (8) Kevin M. Clermont, Death of Paradox: The Killer Logic Beneath the Standards of Proof, 88 Notre Dame L. Rev. 1061 (2013); (9) Kevin M. Clermont, Trial by Traditional Probability, Relative Plausibility, or Belief Function?, 66 Case W. Res. L. Rev. 353 (2015); (10) Kevin M. Clermont, Conjunction of Evidence and Multivalent Logic, in Law and the New Logics 32 (H. Patrick Glenn & Lionel D. Smith eds., 2017); (11) Kevin M. Clermont, Common Sense on Standards of Proof, 48 Seton Hall L. Rev. 1057 (2018); (12) Kevin M. Clermont, The Silliness of Magical Realism, 23 Int'l J. Evidence & Proof 147 (2019); (13) Kevin M. Clermont, Staying Faithful to the Standards of Proof, 104 Cornell L. Rev. 1457 (2019); (14) Kevin M. Clermont, Rules, Standards, and Such, 68 Buff. L. Rev. 751 (2020); (15) Kevin M. Clermont, The Logic of Uncertainty in Law and Life, 19 Law Probability & Risk 181 (2020); (16) Kevin M. Clermont, A Theory of Factfinding: The Logic for Processing Evidence, 104 Marq. L. Rev. 351 (2020); (17) Kevin M. Clermont, A Theory for Evaluating Evidence Against the Standard of Proof, 127 Penn St. L. Rev. 345 (2023); (18) Kevin M. Clermont, Beliefs and Probabilities: The Errors That Remain Are Mine Alone, 15 Wash. U. Juris. Rev. 273 (2023); and (19) Kevin M. Clermont, Skirmishing Toward a General Theory of Evidence and Proof (2024), https://ssrn.com/abstract=4865804.

integrate all this journal work with the prior book's lessons to expand the subject far beyond the standards of proof.

Here is the order followed in the book. The initial chapters will analyze the factfinding process. That is, Chap. 2 will treat the phenomenon of uncertainty. Chapter 3 will turn to the theory of probability, exposing all the shortcomings of traditional probability when used for factfinding. Chapter 4 will develop the case for using "multivalent belief theory," the most suitable variant of multivalent logic for factfinding. Chapter 5 will apply multivalent beliefs to explicate, first, the legal factfinder's mental work in processing the evidence and, second, the legal factfinder's evaluation of the evidence against the applicable standard of proof.

The true importance of this work lies in Chap. 6. It briefly makes two points. First, the methods of legal factfinding extend to many other areas of law, such as proving law. Second, the methods of legal factfinding extend not only far beyond law but also far beyond factfinding. Decisionmaking under uncertainty constitutes a major feature of life both inside and outside the law. The same methods are employed across all human endeavors whenever decisions need to be made in a way that accounts for epistemic uncertainty. One can speak of decisions on whether to go out to the movies tonight. Or whether to marry this particular person. A mistake on going to the movies might not be serious, but a false positive, or negative, in marriage can be extraordinarily costly. We should strive to understand the decisionmaking process in order to optimize its output.

This bigger point is that my subject is far from parochial. Although I start the discussion in the realm of legal factfinding, my concerns are universal. This book will take the subject well beyond the borders of the law and facts, and will do so by heavily utilizing logic and psychology. My ultimate concern is with how people should, can, and do think.

Such a concern with how people think seems a bit presumptuous for a professor of law. But this book does not aim at pioneering refinements for logic theory or discovering truths about cognitive psychology. I use law as an exemplar. I build out from my expertise in law, utilizing accepted philosophical and psychological learning developed by the experts. This program allows my conclusions as to the law to have significance beyond law's realm. This study can thus loftily aim at enhancing our general understanding of decisionmaking under uncertainty.

1.3 Book's Significance

Decisionmaking under uncertainty has spawned an enormous literature, of course.[19] Yet that literature has charted only a part of the subject. The literature emphasizes the need to consider all the consequences that various decisional choices among multiple options might bring about. It champions techniques like additive weighting and expected utility theory.[20] It utilizes sophisticated mathematical tools and increased computing power in the pursuit of optimization.

When the literature turns toward the more basic problem of treating factual uncertainty, it provides much less help. The reason is that these theorists have remained wedded to bivalence and its treatment of aleatory uncertainty by traditional probability theory.[21] Because their tools bury the epistemic uncertainty that is almost ubiquitous, they do not contribute to understanding proof based on available evidence.

The distinction between the existing literature and this book is not the literature's complex decisions versus factfinding's straightforward decisions. It is between relying on probability to handle uncertainty and trying to account seriously for epistemic uncertainty. Because the literature glosses over the latter task, the state of the art in understanding evidence and proof remains stagnant. A myriad of problems persist in theory and practice, all resulting from the widespread failure of the current art to account intelligibly for epistemic uncertainty.

For an easily perceived example, think of inferring from a piece of evidence to a conclusion. Multiple and uncertain inferences are always involved. Probability's product rule then implies decreasing likelihood along the inferential chain,[22] potentially leading to a skepticism that believes nothing.[23] Yet, in real life, one would almost never think to employ the product rule for such inferences upon inferences.

Multivalent belief theory, which can account for epistemic uncertainty, teaches not to apply the product rule to inferences.[24] Nonetheless, to date, no one has applied multivalent logic to the relatively mundane task of inferring facts. Nor have the legal

---

[19] See, e.g., Bell and Schleifer (1995); Kochenderfer (2015); Scholz (1983); cf. Marchau (2019) (treating epistemic uncertainty about the future as "deep uncertainty," which must be handled by a "monitor and adapt" paradigm).

[20] See infra Chap. 6 (discussing simple additive weighting).

[21] Significant exceptions here include Denœux (2019) (giving general review) and Halpern (2017) (developing his "plausibility measures").

[22] See Morgan (1950), pp. 943–945 (surmising the logical method jurors supposedly use to process evidence, and incorrectly saying: "Now it must be obvious that the value of item A as probative of F varies inversely with the number of inferences between A and F.").

[23] See Anderson et al. (2005), p. 102 (arguing that repeated applications of the product rule up the chain of reasoning "cumulatively seem like an invitation to extreme skepticism. It regularly provides strong ammunition for attacking an opponent's argument and for questioning one's own. So many generalizations seem so vulnerable in so many respects that one may be led to the conclusion that all arguments about evidence are built on shifting sands.").

[24] See infra Sect. 5.1.1 (elaborating the process of inferential reasoning).

theorists who write about factfinding, including even those who fault traditional probability, justified any normatively logical and practically feasible methodology as a potential alternative to multivalent beliefs.[25] Not being able to explain inferential reasoning is a huge and fatal defect in theorizing.

Taking legal factfinding as the initial exemplar for applying multivalent logic, this book's key innovation is to treat the steps involved in factfinding as producing multivalent beliefs rather than probabilities. This move provides justification for all of the law's departures from the dictates of traditional probability, such as law's putting aside the product rule for factfinding. Moreover, the book can explain how the law should and does proceed in factfinding: inferring from evidence, aggregating different evidence into proof, and reaching a decision. Moreover, the key innovation rationalizes the current doctrine attendant on burdens and standards of proof. Finally, the book suggests that multivalent belief theory illuminates decisionmaking under uncertainty generally. The bottom line will be that much of the decisionmaking all of us have long performed, with which we intuitively feel comfortable, actually makes theoretical sense when viewed through the lens of multivalent beliefs.

As the previous paragraph implies, the book's emphasis is on the normative, this being the appropriate initial inquiry into factfinding. Stating that norm has eluded us all until now. The book's primary aim is to expose the normative method, in the hope of determining its feasibility and use.

However, this emphasis does not further imply that the descriptive is of no concern in the book. The normative approach turns out to be feasible for ordinary people to perform. Moreover, the normative seems to be what people do in reality. Now, I am not so foolish as to contend that people abide by all my theoretical details. People certainly are prey to heuristics, emotions, and biases. Nevertheless, in general, people apparently conform to the normative approach by intuition, at least in an approximate and nonquantified way. Just as the theory advises, they form degrees of belief in facts, while retaining a sense of epistemic uncertainty, and they apply standards of proof by comparing belief to disbelief. Normative theory thus has practical lessons.

Indeed, theory's primary lesson for factfinding is that the commands of law and the practices of factfinders make sense. Please do not read my appeal to theory as an academic pipe dream. I do not suggest that my mathematical and somewhat mechanical prescriptions carry over to control or alter practice. The flow is the other way. I use theory to argue that the practice holds up to scrutiny.

In final summary, I want to take the established tools of logical theory and combine them with our knowledge of psychology, in order to understand how legal actors and others should, can, and do perform the processes of factfinding

[25] By far, the most valiant effort came from the brilliant L. Jonathan Cohen, a philosopher who tackled legal factfinding in Cohen (1977). He converted traditional probability into his new "inductive probability" scheme, ending up with conclusions equivalent to the ones that I derive by multivalent logic. However, his path is challenging to follow, as explained infra Sect. 3.4. See Spohn (2009), p. 217 ("His presentation is a bit imperspicuous . . . .").

and other decisionmaking in the face of epistemic uncertainty. This work has not been done before. It is important work to do.

Book's Point—in One Paragraph

If everything were known about a required decision other than the outcome of random chance, then traditional probability would provide adequate tools to calculate the chance that the answer is yes and the complementary chance it is no: incidentally, these premises mean mathematically that a conjunction of independent facts is as likely as the product of their chances. But if the evidence leaves more matters unknown, then we need a more general measure, such as the one provided by multivalent logic, of how far a fact is believed to be fully proven: accordingly, a conjunction of partially proven facts is proven to the extent that the weakest constituent was proven. This multivalent measure allows factfinders to ask, after an imperfect showing that left some belief uncommitted, whether the fact in dispute was proven to be more (or much more) true than proven to be false. Law, in fact, has long intuited procedures based on multivalent beliefs of this sort. With that realization, legal factfinding and the rest of decisionmaking under uncertainty finally make sense. We finally know why the plaintiff should win even when the plaintiff has made a very weak but reasonable showing, as long as we believe the plaintiff's account perceptibly more than we disbelieve it.

PS: This book's point may sound rather dryly technical, but it is not. If one accepts the point, then one is accepting that we have for centuries been theorizing incorrectly about assessing uncertain truth. We have leaped to an ingrained logical approach that is bivalent. We accordingly have tended to invoke traditional probability to deal with real-world unknowns. But this probability is an inappropriate measure when facing epistemic uncertainty.

We consequently make errors. Experience fails to correct those errors. When the uncertainty is resolved, if ever it is, we do not perceive error in our analysis. An erroneous conclusion can always be attributed to randomness or to some evaluation error. And so probabilities continue to reign far beyond their proper realm.

References

Anderson T, Schum D, Twining W (2005) Analysis of evidence, 2nd edn. Cambridge University Press, New York

Bell DE, Schleifer A (1995) Decision making under uncertainty. Duxbury Press, Belmont

Clermont KM (1987) Procedure's magical number three: psychological bases for standards of decision. Cornell Law Rev 72:1115

Clermont KM (2004) Standards of proof in Japan and the United States. Cornell Int Law J 37:263, translated in 33 J. Japanese Inst. Int'l Bus. L. 611, 779 (2005), reprinted in Theories of American Civil Procedure 139 (Masahiko Omura & Koichi Miki eds. & trans., 2006)

Clermont KM (2006) Jurisdictional fact. Cornell Law Rev 91:973
Clermont KM (2009) Standards of proof revisited. Vt Law Rev 33:469
Clermont KM (2012) Aggregation of probabilities and illogic. Ga Law Rev 47:165
Clermont KM (2013) Death of paradox: the killer logic beneath the standards of proof. Notre Dame Law Rev 88:1061
Clermont KM (2015) Trial by traditional probability, relative plausibility, or belief function? Case West Res Law Rev 66:353
Clermont KM (2017) Conjunction of evidence and multivalent logic. In: Glenn HP, Smith LD (eds) Law and the new logics 32
Clermont KM (2018) Common sense on standards of proof. Seton Hall Law Rev 48:1057
Clermont KM (2019a) The silliness of magical realism. Int J Evidence Proof 23:147
Clermont KM (2019b) Staying faithful to the standards of proof. Cornell Law Rev 104:1457
Clermont KM (2020a) Rules, standards, and such. Buff Law Rev 68:751
Clermont KM (2020b) The logic of uncertainty in law and life. Law Prob Risk 19:181
Clermont KM (2020c) A theory of factfinding: the logic for processing evidence. Marq Law Rev 104:351
Clermont KM (2023a) A theory for evaluating evidence against the standard of proof. Penn St Law Rev 127:345
Clermont KM (2023b) Beliefs and probabilities: the errors that remain are mine alone. Wash Univ Juris Rev 15:273
Clermont KM (2024) Skirmishing toward a general theory of evidence and proof, https://ssrn.com/abstract=4865804
Clermont KM, Sherwin E (2002a) A comparative view of standards of proof. Am J Comp Law 50: 243, translated in 47 China L.J. 117 (2002), reprinted in Kuo-Chang Huang, New Perspective of Civil Procedure Theory 19 (2005)
Clermont KM, Sherwin E (2002b) A comparative puzzle: standards of proof. In: Nafziger JAR, Symeonides SC (eds) Law and justice in a multistate world 629
Cohen LJ (1977) The probable and the provable. Clarendon Press, Oxford
Cowan TA (1963) Decision theory in law, science and technology. Rutgers Law Rev 17:499–530
Cox CM (2023) The uncertain judge. Univ Chic Law Rev 90:739–811
Dawes M (Summer 1986) Multiordinality: a point of view. ETC 128–132
De Finetti B (1936) La logique de la probabilité. In: 4 Actes du congrès international de philosophie scientifique. Hermann, Paris, pp 1–9
Denœux T (2019) Decision-making with belief functions: a review. Int J Approx Reason 109:87–110
Enoch D, Fisher T, Spectre L (2021) Does legal epistemology rest on a mistake? On fetishism, two-tier system design, and conscientious fact-finding. Phil Issues 31:85–103
Field RH, Kaplan B, Clermont KM, Clopton ZD (2023) Materials for a basic course in civil procedure, 14th edn. Foundation, St Paul
Gabler N (14 Aug 2011) The elusive big idea. NY Times (Sunday Review) 1
Greco D (2013) Probability and prodigality. Oxford Stud Epistemol 4:82–107
Haack S (2012) The embedded epistemologist: dispatches from the legal front. Ratio Juris 25:206–235
Halpern JY (2017) Reasoning about uncertainty, 2nd edn. MIT Press, Cambridge
Ho HL (2008) A philosophy of evidence law: justice in the search for truth. Oxford University Press, New York
Howson C (2009) Can logic be combined with probability? Probably. J Appl Logic 7:177–187
Kochenderfer MJ (2015) Decision making under uncertainty. MIT Press, Cambridge
Laudan L (2007) Strange bedfellows: inference to the best explanation and the criminal standard of proof. Int J Evidence Proof 11:292–306
Lawson G (1992) Proving the law. Nw Univ Law Rev 86:859–904
Lind EA (1982) The psychology of courtroom procedure. In: Kerr NL, Bray RM (eds) The psychology of the courtroom. Academic Press, New York, pp 13–37

Marchau VAWJ et al (eds) (2019) Decision making under deep uncertainty. Springer Science +Business, Heidelberg
Morgan EM (1950) Introduction to evidence. In: Scott AW, Simpson SP (eds) Cases and other materials on civil procedure. Little Brown, Boston, pp 941–1031
Mulligan K, Correia F (2017) Facts. In: Zalta EN (ed) Stanford encyclopedia of philosophy. https://plato.stanford.edu/entries/facts/
Nichols S (2021) Rational rules: towards a theory of moral learning. Oxford University Press, Oxford
Pascal B (1670) Pascal's pensées. Dutton, New York (1958)
Royall RM (1997) Statistical evidence: a likelihood paradigm. Chapman and Hall, London
Russell B (1947) Am I an atheist or an agnostic? https://scepsis.net/eng/articles/id_6.php. Accessed 11 Sep 2023
Saks MJ, Kidd RF (1981) Human information processing and adjudication: trial by heuristics. Law Soc Rev 15:123–160
Scholz RW (ed) (1983) Decision making under uncertainty. North-Holland, Amsterdam
Spohn W (2009) A survey of ranking theory. In: Huber F, Schmidt-Petri C (eds) Degrees of belief. Springer Science+Business, Heidelberg, pp 185–228
Tang S, Foley T (2014) The practice of law and the intolerance of certainty. Univ N S W Law J 37: 1198–1225
Twining W (2006) Rethinking evidence, 2nd edn. Cambridge University Press, New York
Williams RC (2024) Historical fact. Notre Dame Law Rev 99

Chapter 2
Kinds of Uncertainty

[I]n our reasonings concerning matter of fact, there are all imaginable degrees of assurance, from the highest certainty to the lowest species of moral evidence. A wise man, therefore, proportions his belief to the evidence.
—David Hume (David Hume, An Enquiry Concerning Human Understanding 80 (Peter Millican ed., Oxford Univ. Press 2007) (1777).)

Abstract To understand decisionmaking under uncertainty, one should begin by dissecting uncertainty. Section 2.1: Uncertainty includes both the aleatory kind, which probability and multivalent logic recognize, and also epistemic uncertainty, which traditional probability cannot handle but multivalent logic can. Aleatory uncertainty refers to the kind that comes from a process that appears random to us. Epistemic uncertainty refers to the kind that comes from the ignorance left by incomplete, inconclusive, ambiguous, dissonant, or unreliable evidence, from the indeterminacy produced by the vagueness of our concepts and expressed perceptions of the real world, and from the limits on our imaginative powers as to what we do not know. Section 2.2: For accurate factfinding, we need to utilize a method that can handle both kinds of uncertainty.

As already observed, decisionmaking necessarily takes place in a world of uncertainty. Two distinguished British economists recently turned out *Radical Uncertainty*,[1] a well-reviewed[2] book that landed on the best-seller lists.[3] It is worth

[1] Kay and King (2020a) (544 pages).

[2] See, e.g., Arevuo (2020) ("Kay and King's book is a thoughtful and welcome call for economists and policymakers to accept 'radical uncertainty' and start rethinking their models."); Kenneally (2020) ("Their book is demanding, and at times difficult, but it is also an elegant and careful guide to thinking about personal and social economics, especially in a time of uncertainty.").

[3] The book was, inter alia, #1 on Amazon's Risk Management list. It received 4.1 out of 5 stars in Customer Reviews. Amazon (2020).

K. M. Clermont, *A General Theory of Evidence and Proof*, Law and Philosophy Library 148, https://doi.org/10.1007/978-3-031-66552-3_2

discussing here both because it conveys a majorly important insight and because it goes off the tracks in a majorly instructive way.

2.1 Radical Uncertainty

Their book's central idea is that in large part the world is way too complicated for probabilistic analysis. There are just too many factors we cannot reduce to a meaningful percentage, as well as way too many factors we do not even know exist.[4] This ignorance produces what the authors call "radical" uncertainty, as opposed to "resolvable" uncertainty about stuff that feasibly can be verified or can be described with precision by probabilities.[5] This distinction is commonly reconceived as epistemic uncertainty versus aleatory uncertainty.[6]

Uncertainty is a many-colored thing.[7] But as an initial cut, aleatory versus epistemic is a sound and instructive division.[8] Most other varieties of uncertainty can be seen as subvarieties of epistemic uncertainty that divide up what we do not know about reality.[9]

2.1.1 Aleatory Uncertainty

This brand of uncertainty we are used to. Aleatory uncertainty comes from any process that appears random to us, like flipping coins under ideal conditions. By its nature, this randomness is a built-in part of existence. It, along with any free will, is what keeps us, at the present time at least, from seeing the universe as wholly deterministic. Of course, our view of what is random has shrunk over the centuries.

We might know the distribution of outcomes from the random process. Aleatory uncertainty could thus show a tilt, like the urn drawing where 60% of the balls are

---

[4]See Kay and King (2020a), p. 14 ("Radical uncertainty has many dimensions: obscurity; ignorance; vagueness; ambiguity; ill-defined problems; and a lack of information that in some cases but not all we might hope to rectify at a future date.").

[5]See id. (defining resolvability as "uncertainty which can be removed by looking something up . . . or which can be represented by a known probability distribution of outcomes").

[6]*Radical Uncertainty* also phrases its radical/resolvable distinction as uncertainty versus risk, mysteries versus puzzles, wicked versus tame problems, and epistemic versus aleatory uncertainty. See id. at 12–13, 19–23.

[7]See generally Liu et al. (2011), p. 6; Dubois and Prade (2012).

[8]See, e.g., Fox and Ülkümen (2011) (distinguishing aleatory from epistemic uncertainty as the first cut in classifying uncertainties).

[9]See, e.g., Squair (2009) ("Ontological uncertainty lies at the far end of our continuum and represents a state of complete ignorance. Not only do we not know, but we don't even know what we don't know.").

black. But beyond that tilt, aleatory uncertainty about the order of outcomes conveys no information and shows no patterns, because patterns would mean that there is more nonrandom information extricable from the data. Aleatory uncertainty is irreducible, in the sense of our thinking that accessible information would not remove it; even if everything we conceive as knowable about a situation were known, we would still be left with that aleatory uncertainty.

Frequentist probability is compatible with this aleatory uncertainty. But frequentism is used for more. It is used to recognize all kinds of uncertainty by assuming whatever is known includes all that is conceivably knowable, and then treating all unknowns as random variation. The outcome distribution would be derived by extending the hypothesized probability to all those unknowns. If you thereby feel you know everything except random variation, you can say that the chance of an event is x% and mean that if the scenario were replayed 100 times the event would occur, on average, x times and only x times. And complete knowledge means that it will not occur, on average, 100−x times. You thus claim to know everything but the random order of the outcomes.

Think of a drawing from the urn containing a hundred balls. What is the probability of blindly drawing one of the sixty black balls? It is 60%, a number generated from information on the balls' distribution between black and non-black. If the probability is 60%, then there is a 40% chance that the drawn ball will be non-black. Which ball is picked will reflect the randomness of a hand's doing the drawing, if the hand's performance reflects no biased proclivities. So, in practical terms, we can settle on a percentage of likelihood that is admittedly subject to aleatory uncertainty.

A newcomer to the scene, happening upon the urn and now about to draw, would have tried to gather information on the total number of black balls. Ever better information would improve the newcomer's numerical estimate of the odds, maybe even ending up at 60/40. But even perfect information would not remove the random variation.

The person who counted the balls as they went into the urn and the newcomer who merely guessed a 60/40 ball distribution might employ the same odds. Traditional probability recognizes only the ball distribution and the randomness factor provided by the hand's ball selection. Those odds contain no measure of the oddsmaker's depth of knowledge that lies beneath the prediction. Traditional probability buries the additional sources of uncertainty that spring from ignorance, by treating them as if they were random. The difficulty is that unknowns are indeed unknown, and treating them as a known probability will introduce computational errors down the line, as the next chapter will elaborate. Still, for making a prediction of the ball color to be revealed, traditional probability works very well.

2.1.2 Epistemic Uncertainty

The idea of the two economists, Kay and King, is very simple: besides random uncertainty, there are other effects about which we know a lot or a little, and additionally there are many effects on outcome that we have not even imagined. Theirs is not a new idea: the authors attribute[10] the aleatory/epistemic distinction to Frank Knight[11] and John Maynard Keynes.[12] The distinction seems to be enjoying a new moment of fashion.[13] Nevertheless, Kay and King's surely sound idea is still often overlooked.

Their insight teaches that a full understanding of uncertainty must cover both aleatory and epistemic uncertainty, which differ fundamentally. Aleatory uncertainty expresses the uninformative uncertainty that results from a system that behaves in an apparently random way. Traditional probability just sets aside this kind of uncertainty when giving guidance to the bettor. But there can also exist epistemic uncertainties coming from the ignorance left by incomplete, inconclusive, ambiguous, dissonant, or unreliable evidence, from the indeterminacy produced by the vagueness of our concepts and expressed perceptions of the real world, and from the limits on our imaginative powers as to what we do not know. By definition, epistemic uncertainties are conceivably knowable unknowns that, because of our limited knowledge, do not make a particular outcome more or less probable. For that questionable reason, traditional probability sets aside this kind of uncertainty too.

As Donald Rumsfeld put it when tangling with epistemic uncertainty, "There are known knowns; there are things we know we know. We also know there are known unknowns; that is to say we know there are some things we do not know. But there are also unknown unknowns—the ones we don't know we don't know."[14] His unknowns need some expansion as to their sources.

First, much epistemic uncertainty comes from imperfect evidence that leaves the factfinder partially ignorant. Any conclusion based on evidence is necessarily uncertain for five reasons: "Our evidence is 'never complete', is usually 'inconclusive', is frequently 'ambiguous', is commonly 'dissonant' to some degree and comes to us from 'sources having imperfect credibility'."[15]

[10] Kay and King (2020a), pp. 12–15.

[11] Knight (1921), p. 20 (distinguishing risk from uncertainty, with risk being the measurable likelihood of nonoccurrence).

[12] Keynes (1936), p. 162.

[13] Kay and King (2020a), pp. 509–511, cites recent books with very similar themes: Binmore (2009), Blastland (2019), and Taleb (2010).

[14] See Kay and King (2020a), p. 7 (quoting Donald Rumsfeld's 2002 press conference).

[15] Schum (2009), p. 216 (quoting Carnap (1966), p. 51).

Second, an important source of epistemic uncertainty is that the almost ubiquitous vagueness of our language produces indeterminacy.[16] The fuzziness of any category involves a type of unknown and hence its own epistemic uncertainty.

Modern philosophy, beginning with Bertrand Russell's work, has struggled with this problem of vagueness.[17] Work on vagueness addresses such matters as the famed sorites paradox of ancient Greece ("sorites" comes from the Greek word for heap):

- Premise 1: if you start with a billion grains of sand, you have a heap of sand.
- Premise 2: if you remove a single grain, you still have a heap.
- Conclusion: If you repeat the removal again and again until you have one grain of sand left, then you will by logic still have a heap.
- Paradox: There is still a heap. But there is no heap. Thus, heap equals non-heap. Two true premises yield an absurd conclusion. (Or—to picture the paradox in another common way—start with Tom Cruise's full head of hair, and continue plucking hairs, yet Tom will by logic never become bald.)[18]

At some point the heap undeniably became a non-heap. Was there a fixed boundary? No, this is not a way out—at least according to most philosophers.[19]

A different path taken in the attempt to avoid the sorites paradox leads to the embrace of multivalent logic. This form of logic boldly declines the simplification offered by bivalent logic, which is built on a foundation of true/false with an excluded middle. Multivalent logic instead recognizes partial truths, measured by gradations between true and false. Then, both a statement and its opposite can be true to a degree. In other words, sometimes you have neither a heap nor a non-heap, but

[16] See Sorensen (2018) ("a term is vague to the extent that it has borderline cases"). Some theorists find attributes of vagueness beyond language, as in perception, mental imagery, objects, or the real world. See id. § 9 ("Perhaps vagueness is just one face of indeterminacy."). But I need not take a position. To the extent that other forms of vaguity exist and bear on legal factfinding, they would only be other sources of uncertainty that multivalent belief theory could take into account.

[17] See Russell (1956), p. 180 ("Everything is vague to a degree you do not realize till you have tried to make it precise, and everything precise is so remote from everything that we normally think, that you cannot for a moment suppose that is what we really mean when we say what we think."); Russell (1923); Russell (1918), pp. 511–512, 517–518 (applying his point that all language is vague to the word "Piccadilly").

[18] Another way to see the problems that bivalence entails is to ponder the liar's paradox, represented by a sentence like "This sentence is false." Because bivalent logic insists that the sentence be either true or false, one inevitably ends in a loop of contradiction and hence paradox. See generally Beall (2003); Clermont (2023), p. 288. For an overview of proof paradoxes, to which this book will soon turn, see Spottswood (2021).

[19] Compare Williamson (1996) (viewing vagueness as a form of ignorance, there being an exact point that a heap ceases to be a heap), with Field (2003) (countering the Williamson view), Field (2016) (incorporating ideas similar to multivalent logic), and Field (2000), p. 20 (referencing work on belief functions).

something that falls between, with the statement "this is a heap" being both true and false.[20]

There are obvious applications of vagueness theory to law, as where a jury tries to determine fault vel non, even though degrees of fault are the reality. Analogous would be causation, consent, coercion, good faith, intent, and a host of other legal issues. Many, many legal concepts are inherently vague, in that they draw indistinct lines, most often unavoidably—and many of these vague concepts are subjected to proof in litigation.[21] After all, remember that Bertrand Russell saw all of natural language as vague.

Third, as a source of epistemic uncertainty, there is also what "we don't know we don't know" or, as they are sometimes called, "unk-unks."

> We are emphasising the vast range of possibilities that lie in between the world of unlikely events . . . and the world of the unimaginable. This is the world of uncertain futures and unpredictable consequences, about which there is necessary speculation and inevitable disagreement—disagreement which often will never be resolved. . . . Before the wheel was invented (by the Sumerians, ancient Iraqis, around 3500 BC) no one could talk about the probability of the invention of the wheel, and afterwards there was no uncertainty to discuss; the unknown unknown had become a known known.[22]

Maybe the way to sum up these three sources of epistemic uncertainty is to draw a contrast: probabilities express a first-order estimate of which way things will turn out subject to an apparently random variation in the order of outcomes, while epistemic uncertainty comprises the unknowns that are conceivably knowable. Of course, there can be higher-order uncertainties about the estimated location of the line demarking the probability.[23] But there can also be higher-order uncertainties about the strengths of a belief and a disbelief, strengths that do not add to 1. Both of these higher-order uncertainties are what we mean by epistemic uncertainty. It comes from the

---

[20] Multivalent logic gives a pretty good answer to the sorites paradox, by allowing a response to "heap vel non?" in terms of a degree of heapness rather than a yes-or-no response. See Beall and Van Fraassen (2003), pp. 131–145; Kosko (1993), pp. 94–97; Sainsbury (2009), pp. 56–63. But it is not a perfect answer, being more of a circumvention than a solution. See Sainsbury and Williamson (1997), pp. 475–477 (saying that multivalence does not do justice to higher-order vagueness, or borderline-borderline cases); Smith (2011) (similar). But see Endicott (2000), pp. 77–136; Schiffer (2003), pp. 178–237 (providing a "psychological" solution to the paradox).

[21] See Endicott (2000) (arguing that vagueness plays a significant role in law, a role not owing solely to the vagueness of language); Katz (2011), pp. 139–156 (cataloging examples of vague concepts); Lanius (2019), pp. 1–61 (discussing types of vagueness); Marmor (2014), pp. 85–106 (articulating the different types of vagueness in law, beyond those entailing only a simple sorites sequence); Soames (2012) (treating vagueness in law by bridging between legal philosophy and philosophical logic). As a result of the law's vagueness, legal scholars are increasingly using multivalent logic. See Nguyen (2008), p. 1261 (listing examples).

[22] Kay and King (2020a), pp. 14, 39. But see Standage (2021), pp. 2–5 (agreeing as to time but not place for the wheel, citing new evidence to place its invention in the Carpathians).

[23] See Schum (1986), p. 868 (distinguishing belief functions from second-order probability, which he defined narrowly as "my uncertainty about the uncertainty reflected in my precise estimate").

ignorance left by imperfect evidence, from the indeterminacy produced by vagueness, and from the limits on our imaginative powers.

Now, traditional probability treats epistemic uncertainty as if it were aleatory uncertainty. But given the nature of epistemic uncertainty, for which by definition we could know the distribution of outcomes, the intuition arises that the decisionmaker should instead recognize it somehow.

2.1.3 Faulty Solution for Radical Uncertainty

With their central idea of radical uncertainty in hand, Kay and King proceed to draw a proper lesson in the form of a long rant[24] that some mathematical techniques have escaped their proper realm and now dominate analysis of all sorts of problems plagued by epistemic uncertainty. Theirs is a broadside on modern economics, but they actually fire in all directions. Their interest, like mine, extends to all decisionmaking, technical or everyday. Their well-taken point is that experts frequently use mathematical probability to hide the epistemic uncertainty.

Their proposed substitute as a problem-solving technique is, however, disappointing. They do not propose an actual method to analyze difficult problems.[25] Instead, they counsel that one should address all cases of epistemic uncertainty by asking, "What is going on here?"[26] What they mean is that one should get a holistic sense of the problem and its uncertainty (of course, only after seeking more information, if possible, and discussing and challenging various perspectives), and then take a stab if at all doable. They are not limiting this prescription to those problems

[24] Sandbu (2020) ("An eloquent, highbrow, entertaining and enlightening rant, but a rant all the same.").

[25] See Kennedy (2020) ("This book is not, in itself, a primer for good decision-making and there is no attempt to create a model for such a process."). Nor are the authors suggesting that we learn to live with uncertainty. See Jackson (2023). In law and elsewhere, the decisionmakers need to resolve difficult problems now.

[26] Kay and King (2020a), p. 10. "To cope with radical uncertainty we try to form a coherent and credible answer to the question 'What is going on here?'" Id. at 218. True, they mention other techniques—reference narratives, id. at 122–124, abduction, id. at 138, satisficing, id. at 149–152, 175, fast and frugal heuristics, id. at 152, and narrative and contextual reasoning, id. at 215–231—but they treat these techniques as equivalents of "What is going on here?" They edge toward the more relevant technique of inference to the best explanation when discussing legal reasoning. Id. at 210–214. "In civil proceedings, the narrative must be a good one [as measured by the twin criteria of coherence (consistency) and credibility (believability)], better than any alternative narrative. If so, the claimant succeeds on the balance of probabilities." Id. at 211–212. But they misunderstand ranking methodology and so miss its possible contribution, a shortcoming that produces misstatements: "The further requirement of 'balance of probabilities' or 'preponderance of the evidence' is then that the best explanation is *significantly* better than any alternative explanation. ... Reasoning by elimination is sustainable *only* if the complete set of possibilities is known." Id. at 212 (emphasis added); infra Sect. 4.4.1 (discussing inference to the best explanation) and Sect. 4.4.3 (discussing ranking theory).

that are so ill-defined and so riddled by unmanageable uncertainty that they defy analysis, ones where mathematical analysis will do much more harm than good and where nothing but a stab or a refusal to answer is possible—such as "What is the meaning of life?" No, they are also addressing countless practical problems that would appear to benefit from more rigorous thought—such as "What should we do about the coronavirus?"[27]

A puzzlement then ensues concerning how their simple thesis could grow into book form.[28] The answer is that they use the device typical of modern popular nonfiction: the book provides endless illustrations and theoretical detours, which are intended to be entertaining.[29] But its illustrations also expose where the book went dangerously wrong. That mistake lies, of course, in its proposal on how we should handle all those practical problems that involve epistemic uncertainty.

---

[27] Their book did not foresee the pandemic. See Sandbu (2020) ("Or the burning issue du jour: how should we make policy in the face of coronavirus? Kay and King would rightly dismiss the notion of an objective, knowable probability distribution of epidemiological and economic outcomes. But surely any responsible approach includes tentatively putting numbers on these and the likelihood that they will ensue under different policies."). The authors have since addressed the pandemic, concluding that their book's lesson of taking a stab at what is going on fully applies to this new problem. Kay and King (May 2020b).

[28] See Dougharty (2020) ("This book presents some thought-provoking ideas. The problem is it takes five hundred plus pages to do what could have been done in thirty.").

[29] Many of the illustrations and theoretical detours, however, are uninformative, irrelevant, or contestable.

First, the authors identify good and bad decisionmakers, like the respective pairs of Churchill in World War II and Napoleon in the Russian campaign, see Kay and King (2020a), pp. 3–4, 24–26, 433; Steve Jobs at Apple and Stephen Ballmer at Microsoft (or the early Steve Jobs, for that matter), see id. at 27–31, 227; and the railroader Leland Stanford and the Gold Rush's John Sutter, see id. at 48–49. But these illustrations of persons who properly applied the authors' stab method seem to emerge mainly from picking past winners who may have just stumbled to the right side of history. See id. at 169–170, 266, 269 (conceding the predominant role of chance in Churchill's and Jobs's successes). By the way, in his 2005 Stanford Commencement address, Steve Jobs said of his actual approach to decisionmaking: "You can't connect the dots looking forward; you can only connect them looking backwards. So you have to trust that the dots will somehow connect in your future. You have to trust in something—your gut, destiny, life, karma, whatever. This approach has never let me down, and it has made all the difference in my life." BrainyQuote (2022).

Second, the book includes frequent discussions of probability paradoxes, some of which, like the two-envelope problem, actually have solutions. Compare Kay and King (2020a), pp. 107–108, with Wikipedia (2022) ("The probability theory underlying the problem is well understood, and any apparent paradox is generally due to treating what is actually a conditional probability as an unconditional probability."). Indeed, most of them, like the boy-girl puzzle, merely make the good point that any probability question should be carefully specified. Compare Kay and King (2020a), pp. 76–78, 98, with Lynch (2011).

Third, the authors denigrate subjective probability, while disregarding its usefulness in bringing the power of probability theory to bear on single events. See Kay and King (2020a), pp. 111–114, 435–444; infra Sect. 3.1.2 (discussing subjective probability). Other detours include unnecessarily bashing behavioral economics, with Daniel Kahneman and Amos Tversky as the unlikely victims. See Kay and King (2020a), pp. 135–153. Another detour reflexively embraces evolutionary psychology, arguing that evolution provided cave people with the stab method, which therefore still serves us well today. See id. at 154–177.

The authors' favorite illustration, President Obama's 2011 decision to take out Osama bin Laden in Pakistan,[30] is a very bad illustration for them, one that exposes the big hole in their approach. The question for the President was whether to "approve the proposed raid by US Navy SEALs on the Abbottabad compound."[31] His advisers varied from 30% to 95% on the probability that bin Laden was in the compound. There were other uncertainties, such as whether the helicopters would even get there, whether the SEALs would prevail on the ground, whether the team would be able to get back out, and how Pakistan would react to the infringement of its sovereignty. Should Obama have tried to analyze the problem rigorously? No. "Obama understood that he had to arrive at a decision on the basis of limited information, and made what, with hindsight, proved a good call. He did so not by probabilistic reasoning but by asking 'What is going on here?'"[32]

Wow, that prescription for presidential decisionmaking will not help me sleep at night. I would think that Obama should at least have been making a determination of the probability of a successful round trip that found bin Laden in residence and then seeking to factor in the expected costs of the political considerations somehow.[33] The outcome would eventually become known to all. The situation seems to be calling on him to place a bet on how events will turn out. At the very least, a bettor should make an assessment of the odds of each necessary condition. For example, Obama might come up with a p for the probability that bin Laden was in the compound, with $1-p$ being the probability he was absent. Then p could be combined with the other conditions' odds, yielding the preliminary odds that going in would be a good idea rather than a bad idea. He could then try to account for the remaining factors like the political considerations, by combining separate and necessary beliefs with the odds.[34]

In his new book, *A Promised Land*, Barack Obama describes the actual decisionmaking process.[35] The gathered intelligence was thin. Whether bin Laden was there was put at 50/50 by Obama himself.[36] Although the military was "highly confident" about getting there and prevailing, their view was that getting out "might be a little more 'spotty.'"[37] Based on the quality of the men who would conduct the raid, however, Obama "trusted that the SEALs would find a safe way out of

[30] See Kay and King (2020a), pp. 8–12, 118–120, 122–123, 174–175, 298.

[31] Id. at 8.

[32] Id. at 9–10. But cf. id. at 262–263 (attributing Obama's success to luck).

[33] The authors seem to concede the usefulness of an as-rigorous-as-you-reasonably-can-be approach when praising the problem-solving of aerospace engineers who break a problem into parts. See id. at 352–356.

[34] See Fox and Ülkümen (2011), pp. 21–22 (analyzing Obama's bet).

[35] Obama (2020), pp. 676–688.

[36] See id. at 685.

[37] Id. at 682.

Abbottabad."[38] The Pakistani reaction was a source of great concern.[39] Then, alone at night in the Treaty Room (and, a bit disturbingly, while watching a pro basketball game), Obama reached his decision. "Everything I did or had done involved working the odds, quietly and often late at night in the room where I now sat. I knew that I could not have come up with a better process to evaluate those odds or surrounded myself with a better mix of people to help me weigh them. … And while I couldn't guarantee the outcome of my decision, I was fully prepared and fully confident in making it."[40]

A very different one of the economists' illustrations of when we should throw up our hands and take a stab was the disappearance of the American brigantine *Mary Celeste* in 1872.[41] It was found largely intact but abandoned off the Azores. The lifeboat and the ten persons aboard were missing, never to be found. "What happened?" was the question. "No sea mystery has ever received more attention. … Even though there is an answer, we will never know what it is. The claim of the modern science of decision theory is that most mysteries can be reduced to puzzles by the application of probabilistic reasoning. Such reasoning can provide solutions to puzzles, but not to mysteries."[42] Here the authors have a point. Probabilities were of little help. But we would not have wanted the decisionmaker in the resultant salvage-court hearings to just shrug off an "I don't know," which in this case is the authors' preferred response.[43] We would instead want the decisionmaker to deal, based on the evidence, in beliefs that retain all senses of uncertainty while proceeding to find the best explanation conceivable.

Although their book correctly saw the distinction between aleatory and epistemic uncertainty as a boundary between decisional methodologies, the mistake that the authors made, as revealed by these two illustrations, was to give up when facing epistemic uncertainty. Probabilities work for puzzles of aleatory uncertainty, but the authors contend that a mystery's epistemic uncertainties counsel switching to asking, "What is going on here?" That is false. Sure, decisionmakers, and those who require the decisions to be made, should attend to the difference between aleatory and epistemic uncertainties. If aleatory, then probabilism is the way to go. But if epistemic, they must think further about the optimal methodology for deciding.

For legal factfinding, the case of the *Mary Celeste*, which seems to call for belief analysis, turns out to be the relevant illustration. Admittedly, legal actors face some other kinds of decisions, which might have more the structure of the Obama bet.[44] For the law, however, the economist authors reject any such nuanced view of methodologies dependent on the nature of the decision, saying: "The job of the

[38] Id. at 688.

[39] See id. at 682–683.

[40] Id. at 688.

[41] See Kay and King (2020a), pp. 33–34.

[42] Id. at 34.

[43] See id. at 11–12, 64, 82.

[44] For examples, see infra Sect. 4.6.2 (discussing the standard for reviewing another's decision).

court is always to establish 'what is going on here' in a unique case."[45] That view is not only false, but always false.

2.2 Path Forward

The range of popular methodologies for handling epistemic uncertainty extends from probabilism to "What is going on here?" Maybe some decisions made under radical uncertainty, like Obama's, could see some benefit from probabilistic reasoning in placing the bet. However, at some point, probabilities will surely become more misleading or obscurative than helpful. Yet that eventuality does not argue for throwing up one's hands. Other methodologies, ones that go beyond shrugging, exist for handling complex problems.

Indeed, for most problems, imposing some methodological rigor will bear benefit. It is the nature of the question to be answered, which must be carefully specified, and the extent of information in hand that will determine the appropriate methodology. For example, some problems, like the maritime mystery the key to which will in all likelihood never be revealed, are well handled by belief analysis.

Clearly, the ideal logic for evidential proof is worth inquiry. But is the quest for the logical ideal even possible? In past writing, I concluded about the ideal: "Logicians have not managed to agree on how evidence should get processed."[46] Now, I assert that the logicians' failure was not inevitable. It resulted from inapt premises, which led inevitably to a roadblock. That is, virtually every logician has proceeded on the basis of classical logic and its derivative of traditional probability. With those tools, understanding proof by typically uncertain and incomplete evidence is an impossible task.

In this book, I propose to address the evidential proof problem with an alternative to that constrained logic and its probability scheme. That move will allow me to complete the task that the economists' book and logicians' efforts leave undone. To show how decisionmakers can better deal with epistemic uncertainty, I devote the next four chapters.

First, I shall agree with the economists that probability theory does not carry the load, but I see the situation as requiring a turn to multivalent logic. Second, I shall introduce the belief function concept, an established method for expressing the strength of multivalent beliefs and also for expressing the degree of uncertainty by means of uncommitted belief. Third, having combined the concept of belief functions with the tools of multivalent logic to create an alternative decisionmaking methodology, I shall explain and validate the current system for legal factfinding.

---

[45] Kay and King (2020a), p. 204.

[46] Clermont (2019), p. 1465 (citing Symposium (2001) (working on the need to formalize evidence processing for application of "computational intelligence") and Franklin (2012), p. 245 (taking a pessimistic view on formalizing common reasoning)).

Fourth, I shall show how this "multivalent belief theory" applies to huge swaths of legal, scientific, and other thinking.

References

Amazon (2020) Risk management list. https://www.amazon.com/Radical-Uncertainty-Decision-Making-Beyond-Numbers-dp-1324004770/dp/1324004770/ref=mt_hardcover?_encoding=UTF8&me=&qid=1588094294. Accessed 28 Apr 2020

Arevuo M (2020) Book review. https://iea.org.uk/radical-uncertainty-decision-making-for-an-unknowable-future-book-review/. Accessed 13 Dec 2021

Beall JC (ed) (2003) Liars and heaps. Oxford University Press, Oxford

Beall JC, Van Fraassen BC (2003) Possibilities and paradox: an introduction to modal and many-valued logic. Oxford University Press, Oxford

Binmore K (2009) Rational decisions. Princeton University Press, Princeton

Blastland M (2019) The hidden half: how the world conceals its secrets. Atlantic Books, London

BrainyQuote (2022) Steve Jobs quotes. https://www.brainyquote.com/quotes/steve_jobs_416875. Accessed 2 Jan 2022

Carnap R (1966) An introduction to the philosophy of science. Basic Books, New York

Clermont KM (2019) Staying faithful to the standards of proof. Cornell Law Rev 104:1457–1512

Clermont KM (2023) Beliefs and probabilities: the errors that remain are mine alone. Wash Univ Juris Rev 15:273–289

Dougharty LA (2020) Customer book review. https://www.amazon.com/Radical-Uncertainty-Decision-Making-Beyond-Numbers-dp-1324004770/dp/1324004770/ref=mt_hardcover?_encoding=UTF8&me=&qid=1588094294. Accessed 14 Dec 2021

Dubois D, Prade H (2012) A unified view of uncertainty theories. http://legal1.cit.cornell.edu/private/Dubois&Prade.pdf. Accessed 13 Dec 2021

Endicott TAO (2000) Vagueness in law. Oxford University Press, Oxford

Field H (2000) Indeterminacy, degree of belief, and excluded middle. Noûs 34:1–30

Field H (2003) No fact of the matter. Australas J Phil 81:457–480

Field H (2016) Vagueness, partial belief, and logic. In: Ostertag G (ed) Meanings and other things. Oxford University Press, Oxford, pp 172–189

Fox CR, Ülkümen G (2011) Distinguishing two dimensions of uncertainty. In: Brun W et al (eds) Perspectives on thinking, judging, and decision making. Universitetsforlaget, Oslo, pp 21–35

Franklin J (2012) How much of commonsense and legal reasoning is formalizable? A review of conceptual obstacles. Law Prob Risk 11:225–245

Jackson M (2023) Uncertain: the wisdom and wonder of being unsure. Prometheus, Guilford

Katz L (2011) Why the law is so perverse. University of Chicago Press, Chicago

Kay J, King M (2020a) Radical uncertainty: decision-making beyond the numbers. Norton, New York

Kay J, King M (May 2020b) The radical uncertainties of coronavirus. Prospect Mag. https://www.prospectmagazine.co.uk/magazine/coronavirus-model-uncertainty-kay-king. Accessed 14 Dec 2021

Kenneally C (5 Apr 2020) The mind. NY Times (Sunday Book Review) 22

Kennedy L (Apr 2020) Book review. IPE Mag. https://www.ipe.com/comment/book-review-radical-uncertainty-by-john-kay-and-mervyn-king/10044493.article. Accessed 14 Dec 2021

Keynes JM (1936) The general theory of employment, interest and money. Harcourt Brace, New York

Knight FH (1921) Risk, uncertainty and profit. Houghton Mifflin, Boston

Kosko B (1993) Fuzzy thinking: the new science of fuzzy logic. Hyperion Books, New York

Lanius D (2019) Strategic indeterminacy in the law. Oxford University Press, Oxford

Liu S, Forrest J, Yang Y (2011) A brief introduction to grey systems theory. In: 2011 IEEE international conference on grey systems and intelligent services, Nanjing, pp 1–9. https://ieeexplore.ieee.org/xpl/conhome/6035840/proceeding. Accessed 13 Dec 2021
Lynch P (2011) The two-child paradox: dichotomy and ambiguity. Irish Math Soc Bull 67:67–73. https://irishmathsoc.org/bull67/2011-6-1.pdf
Marmor A (2014) The language of law. Oxford University Press, Oxford
Nguyen MT (2008) The myth of "lucky" patent verdicts: improving the quality of appellate review by incorporating fuzzy logic in jury verdicts. Hastings Law J 59:1257–1284
Obama B (2020) A promised land. Crown, New York
Russell B (1918) The philosophy of logical atomism. Monist 28:495–527
Russell B (1923) Vagueness. Australas J Psychol Phil 1:84–92
Russell B (1956) Logic and knowledge. Allen and Unwin, London
Sainsbury RM (2009) Paradoxes, 3rd edn. Cambridge University Press, Cambridge
Sainsbury RM, Williamson T (1997) Sorites. In: Hale B, Wright C (eds) A companion to the philosophy of language. Blackwell, Oxford, pp 458–486
Sandbu M (16 Mar 2020) Book review. Fin. Times. https://www.ft.com/content/0b2dcf46-6538-11ea-a6cd-df28cc3c6a68. Accessed 14 Dec 2021
Schiffer S (2003) The things we mean. Oxford University Press, Oxford
Schum DA (1986) Probability and the processes of discovery, proof, and choice. Boston Univ Law Rev 66:825–876
Schum DA (2009) A science of evidence: contributions from law and probability. Law Prob Risk 8: 197–231
Smith NJJ (2011) Fuzzy logic and higher-order vagueness. In: Cintula P et al (eds) Understanding vagueness: logical, philosophical and linguistic perspectives. College Publ'ns, Rickmansworth, pp 1–19
Soames S (2012) Vagueness in the law. In: Marmor A (ed) The Routledge companion to philosophy of law. Routledge, London, pp 95–108
Sorensen R (2018) Vagueness. In: Zalta EN (ed) Stanford encyclopedia of philosophy. https://plato.stanford.edu/entries/vagueness/
Spottswood E (published as Mark) (2021) Paradoxes of proof. In: Dahlman C et al (eds) Philosophical foundations of evidence law. Oxford University Press, Oxford, pp 317–331
Squair M (2009) Epistemic, ontological and aleatory risk. https://bit.ly/3ykSUgu. Accessed 30 Oct 2022
Standage T (2021) A brief history of motion. Bloomsbury Publ'g, New York
Symposium (2001) Artificial intelligence and judicial proof. Cardozo Law Rev 22:1365–1851
Taleb NN (2010) The black swan: the impact of the highly improbable, 2nd edn. Random House, New York
Wikipedia (2022) Two envelopes problem. https://en.wikipedia.org/wiki/Two_envelopes_problem. Accessed 2 Jan 2022
Williamson T (1996) Vagueness. Routledge, London

Chapter 3
Bivalent Probabilities

[T]he rational man, who attaches to each proposition the right degree of credibility, will be guided by the mathematical theory of probability when it is applicable. *The concept "degree of credibility," however, is applicable much more widely that that of mathematical probability . . .*
.—Bertrand Russell (Bertrand Russell, Human Knowledge: Its Scope and Limits 399 (1948) (emphasis in original).)

Abstract The aim is to understand evidence and proof, and thereby ensure more accurate factfinding. A possible route to that end is probability theory. The traditional probability with which we are all familiar is actually built on assumptions that are much less familiar. Its logical basis assumes bivalence, so that everything is either true or false and so that the probabilities of truth and falsity add to one. This assumption leads inevitably to all the logical problems we encounter when using probability to explain factfinding, problems such as the law's strange willingness to accept weak evidence on both sides and the seemingly asymmetrical burden put on plaintiffs to prove a whole series of elements. After critiquing all of probability's problems, this chapter, whose length merits a separate Analysis of its sections, concludes that probability theory is not the way to understand evidence and proof.

Section 3.1: Traditional probability systems are built on bivalent logic, with an excluded middle, so that any proposition must be either true or false. The systems are additive in the sense that the chances of truth and falsity add to one. The most useful of those systems for factfinding is subjective probability, which relies on the image of the factfinder's willingness to bet on the disputed fact. Section 3.2: However, the use of any system of traditional probability for factfinding runs into six major problems, which all result from its failure to account for epistemic uncertainty: resorting to an unrealistic way to express how humans measure proof; fumbling in its advice when there is weak evidence on both sides; allowing the argument to be made that infinite possibilities prevent proving anything to be more likely than not; lacking accurate tools for combining uncertain evidential items or found facts; creating the appearance of asymmetries in the treatment of plaintiffs and defendants; and failing conceptually to capture what we intuitively think of as adequacy of legal proof. Section 3.3: Law professors also anguish over, or revel in, the use of naked

K. M. Clermont, *A General Theory of Evidence and Proof*, Law and Philosophy Library 148, https://doi.org/10.1007/978-3-031-66552-3_3

statistical evidence and its resulting paradoxes, such as finding a bus company liable for an injury solely because it owns 80% of the buses running that route. Although there are hazards of improper use of mathematics in evidence, statistical evidence is not unique in nature. And in the law's treatment of statistical evidence, there is no real logical problem. Section 3.4: Over the decades, the problems of traditional probability have become obvious to theoreticians, leading some of them to alter probability in ways that account for epistemic uncertainty. They have produced a variety of dazzling but clumsy ways for probability to do what multivalent logic does easily and clearly. These ways include so-called logical, imprecise, and inductive probability theories.

Evidence and proof are simple concepts, unless you stop to think about them. At the least, the law is quite clear in stating the factfinder's task.[1] Here is a pattern civil jury instruction, where "element" means a finding necessary for a claim or defense to succeed under the substantive law:

> Plaintiff has the burden in a civil action, such as this, to prove every essential element of plaintiff's claim by a preponderance of the evidence. If plaintiff should fail to establish any essential element of plaintiff's claim by a preponderance of the evidence, you should find for defendant as to that claim.[2]

Doing their job, academics have stopped to think about evidence and proof. What is a "preponderance"? The courts told them it means more likely than not, which to most modern academics means more probably true than false, which thus calls for use of probability theory.[3] The academics' output appears in Fig. 3.1 as it is routinely taught. It shows the initial steps in the pull and haul of the trial evidence on a

[1] See Allen and Jehl (2003), pp. 897–904 (criticizing Nance (1986), pp. 949–951, for finding the pattern jury instruction ambiguous).

[2] O'Malley et al. (2011), § 104.01 (also defining "preponderance" as "evidence, which as a whole, shows that the fact sought to be proved is more probable than not"); see In re Corrugated Container Antitrust Litig., 756 F.2d 411, 416–17 (5th Cir. 1985) (requiring proof of each element to a preponderance); cf. People v. Newman, 385 N.E.2d 598, 599–601 (N.Y. 1978) (holding that the trial court violated In re Winship, 397 U.S. 358 (1970), and committed reversible error by failing to instruct the jury that the prosecution must prove each element beyond a reasonable doubt). This pattern jury instruction also verbalizes the process imposed implicitly on the judge when acting as factfinder.

[3] See, e.g., Brown v. Bowen, 847 F.2d 342, 345 (7th Cir. 1988) ("[T]he trier of fact rules for the plaintiff if it thinks the chance greater than 0.5 that the plaintiff is in the right."); Eggleston (1983) (embracing probability fully); Miceli (2017), pp. 302–303 (giving a straightforward and uncritical account of the probabilistic approach); Rowe et al. (2020), p. 36 (saying, in a casebook: "The usual burden of persuasion in a civil case is 'fair preponderance of the evidence,' a less exacting standard that requires a party with the burden to persuade the factfinder that the evidence 'more likely than not' supports its view. . . . Thus, for a plaintiff to win on a claim, the factfinder must be persuaded to a slightly more than 50% degree of confidence that the plaintiff's evidence supporting the claim is credible[, that is, a >50% chance the plaintiff 'is right']."); Cheng (2013), p. 1256 ("As every first-

Fig. 3.1 Prevailing image of proof and evidence

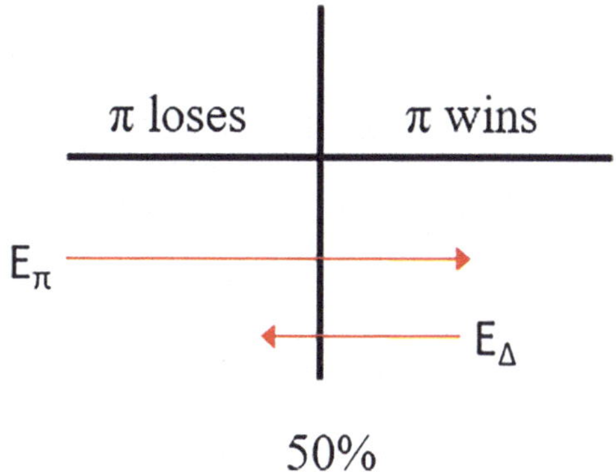

disputed factual issue, denoted by E for plaintiff (π) or defendant (Δ), as the plaintiff's case in chief establishes the fact to be more likely than not and then the case in defense pushes the probability back down.

The academics' turn to probability theory was not surprising. In the late eighteenth century, law and nascent probability theory had begun interacting.[4] That early interaction caused the law to become more open about accepting uncertainty.

Otherwise, however, probabilistic theorizing came only lightly to elaborate Fig. 3.1 until theorists quite recently launched a major assault on evidential proof.[5] The resulting and wonderful "New Evidence" scholarship has made tremendous progress toward a deeper understanding.[6] Those scholars made strides by shifting the focus of evidence theory from rules of admissibility to the nature of evidence and proof, while opening the door to interdisciplinary insights including those from psychology and, albeit less so, from logic.[7] Less successful was their voluminous literature using Bayesian theories of probability to reduce evidential proof to simplistic terms and then to criticize the law for not conforming to their theories. Perhaps the Bayesian turn contributed to the New Evidence's failure to transform the teaching of evidence.

---

year law student knows, the civil preponderance-of-the-evidence standard requires that a plaintiff establish the probability of her claim to greater than 0.5." (footnote omitted)).

[4] See Clermont and Sherwin (2002), pp. 255–258 (discussing this history).

[5] The first effective volleys of that assault on the law arguably were Kaplan (1968) and Finkelstein and Fairley (1970).

[6] See generally Dahlman et al. (2021); Twining (2006), pp. 237–248; Park and Saks (2006).

[7] See Brilmayer (1986), pp. 688–691 (suggesting that the New Evidence tended to neglect the contemporaneous advances in logic); Tillers (2011), p. 171 (presenting a similar argument). Some Bayesians, however, were sympathetic to the new logic. E.g., Schum (1986), pp. 847–853, 865–869.

3.1 Probability Theory

In ancient times, the greats based bivalent logic on an assumption that all propositions are true or false: it allocates all propositions to yes (one) or no (zero), so excluding the middle. Thus, the semantic principle of bivalence holds that a proposition X is either true or false. Not-X is not divided into further sets, but constitutes a single set called false.

Incidentally, classical logic's slightly different, syntactic law of the excluded middle merely holds, as a matter of grammatical structure, that a proposition X is either true or not true.[8] Although bivalence implies the law of the excluded middle, the converse is not true.[9] Thus, bivalent logic is a subset of classical logic. Still, bivalence is the intended (although not necessary) meaning of classical logic, so that classical logic tends to induce bivalent thinking.[10]

With the later development of traditional probability theory, which rests on additional assumptions called axioms, bivalent logic could extend to reflect aleatory uncertainty. By "traditional probability," I am here referring to any system conforming to Kolmogorov's tripartite axiomatization: nonnegativity, normalization, and additivity.[11] Nonnegativity means that probabilities are either positive numbers or zero, so that there are no negative probabilities.[12] Normalization means that the probability of a sure event is 1.0.[13] Additivity needs the additional explanation below.

The other basics of traditional probability theory are common knowledge. Traditional probability includes the probability interpretations that most people think of as probability, that is, the classical, frequentist, and subjective versions of probability.[14] These probabilities run on a scale from 0 to 1 (or 0% to 100%), which indicates how likely it is that randomness will resolve in the affirmative. So, probability is a

---

[8]See Cheng (2018), pp. 63–66 (delineating the law of the excluded middle). "But the excessive simplifications push us into fabricated black and white situations when everything is really in infinite shades of gray and indeed multi-colors." Id. at ix. "In a way the law of the excluded middle is a simplification. . . . [T]here are certain situations we really can't deal with without modifying our logic." Id. at 70.

[9]For example, classical logic could have a third value for propositions not provable now but possibly provable in the future.

[10]See Suber (1997).

[11]See Hájek (2019), § 1 (mapping the whole range of probability theory).

[12]See Anderson et al. (2005), p. 251.

[13]See id.

[14]See Hájek (2019), § 3.1 ("The guiding idea [of classical probability] is that in such circumstances, probability is shared equally among all the possible outcomes, so that the classical probability of an event is simply the fraction of the total number of possibilities in which the event occurs."), § 3.4 ("*[T]he probability of an attribute A in a finite reference class B is the relative frequency of actual occurrences of A within B."*) & § 3.3.2 ("Your degree of [subjective] belief in E is p iff p units of utility is the price at which you would buy or sell a bet that pays 1 unit of utility if E, 0 if not E.").

multivalent metric built on bivalent logic. But a few features of "bivalent probability" theory require the special mention given below.

3.1.1 Additivity

Additivity is for my purposes the most pertinent of the three Kolmogorov axioms. It is implied by the law of the excluded middle. Additivity provides this: "If two events cannot happen jointly, the probability that one or the other occurs is equal to the sum of their separate probabilities."[15] In an additive system, a set and its complementary contradiction add to the universe, or 1.0. That is, the probability that an event will happen and the probability that it will not happen add to one.

Traditional probability is an additive system. It can give the odds of truth, p, with the necessary implication that the odds of falsity are $1-p$.

Consequently, all three of traditional probability's major systems have a suggestive air of frequentism about them. A classical probability of one in four loosely implies that in a hundred trials, the outcome will tend to be 1 twenty-five times and 0 seventy-five times. Although subjective accounts of probability resort to the image of willingness to bet, even they carry the same frequentist implications.

3.1.2 Subjective Probability

Some people unthinkingly assert that probability cannot handle one-time events. But subjective probability theory allows us to speak of the likelihood of a single event, which is the law's usual focus.

A subjective probability measures an individual's personal judgment, grounded on the evidence, about how likely a particular event is to occur or has occurred.[16] The theory is

> based on the notion that it makes sense to ask someone what he would do if offered a reward for guessing correctly whether any proposition, designated *X*, is true or false. If he guesses that *X* is true under these circumstances, we say that *for him* the subjective probability of *X*,

---

[15] Anderson et al. (2005), p. 251; see id. at 254 ("[T]his additivity requirement puts a burden on you that you might not be willing to accept. The conventional system of probability requires that you must always commit all of your probabilistic belief to mutually exclusive and exhaustive events; you cannot hold back any of your belief or leave it uncommitted."); Lindell (2017), p. 154 (calling additive and nonadditive probabilities, respectively, two-sided and one-sided probabilities); Shapira (1998), pp. 1613–1616 (distinguishing additive from nonadditive).

[16] See Hájek (2019), § 3.3.1 (characterizing subjectivism with the slogan of "probability is degree of belief," but that usage differs from mine); Schwitzgebel (2015), § 2.4.

> written P(X), exceeds fifty percent. Symbolically, P(X) > .5. If he would be equally satisfied guessing either way, then we say that, for him, P(X) = .5.[17]

Upon expanding the measure into a complete scale of probabilities from 0 to 1 and accepting the usual logical theorems of bivalent logic, subjective probabilities follow most of the rules of frequentist probabilities.[18] Because of this ability to handle single events in a familiar way, subjective probability provides the usual particularization of probability theory when discussing legal proof.

This subjective probability scheme remains an additive system, so that with all propositions being true or false, the odds of truth and falsity add to one. That is, the probability or chance of truth (p) and of falsity ($1-p$) add to one.

3.1.3 Accounting for Uncertainty

As I have repeatedly said already, traditional probability recognizes only aleatory uncertainty. It does so by expressing the decisionmaker's view of a likelihood that is subject to unavoidable and irreducible random variation. If the situation were to repeat itself a hundred times, the decisionmaker would expect the proposition to turn out true $100p$ times and false $100(1-p)$ times. Given the evidence the decisionmaker got to consider, p is its best first-order guess of the outcome, subject to the inherent randomness of outcome.

As suggested in the earlier urn example,[19] p gives no indication of the information that generated this first-order estimate. It could be an estimate based on airtight evidence, or p could rest on very thin evidence. That is, p hides the epistemic uncertainty. It does not account for epistemic uncertainties that result from the ignorance left by incomplete, inconclusive, ambiguous, dissonant, or unreliable evidence, from the indeterminacy produced by the vagueness of our concepts and expressed perceptions of the real world, and from the limits on our imaginative powers.

Traditional probability's additive nature keeps it from otherwise accounting for the epistemic uncertainty. It cannot account effectively for epistemic uncertainty even by a fudge factor, whereby the decisionmaker would adjust the probability to reflect, say, imperfect evidence. The reason is that any imposed lowering of p would force an offsetting increase in $1-p$ that ignores the evidence.[20] That is, the

---

[17] Tribe (1971), p. 1347 (citing the innovative work of Savage (1954)); see Vick (2002), pp. 1–54; Genin and Huber (2020), § 3.1.

[18] See Tribe (1971), pp. 1347–1348 & n.63 (accepting the product rule because he is assuming bivalence).

[19] See supra Sect. 2.1.1 (drawing a ball when 60 of the 100 balls are black).

[20] See Brilmayer (1986), p. 682 ("If one were to lower the .6 'heads' estimate because it was based upon very little evidence, one would also have to lower the .4 'tails' estimate; it also was based upon very little evidence. After all, both estimates were based upon the same evidence [of an unfair coin].").

decisionmaker could arbitrarily lower p (or equivalently raise the standard of proof against the burdened party) to account for imperfect evidence, but that creates both an inaccurate p and an inaccurate $1-p$ that will introduce errors when further working with probability in deciding the case.

One could strongarm subjective probability into a crude tool here. If one adopts a threshold probability for accepting a proposition, and one attempts arbitrarily to reduce p and increase $1-p$ to reflect imperfect evidence, one could reject propositions that one would otherwise accept. But this tool would then be giving victory to an undeserving opponent. Moreover, this tool preserves all the problems of probability that I turn to below.[21]

Consequently, any traditional probability system will fail the decisionmaker in some tasks, namely, whenever the decisionmaker needs to keep track of epistemic uncertainties in order to achieve accurate decisions later in the proof process. Or as others have put it:

> Human beings have the precious metacognitive ability of being aware of their own uncertainty, with respect to the conjectures they entertain. If we wish to develop models of how individuals make judgments and inferences from uncertain information, we need, first, to characterize their metacognitive representation of uncertainty. We believe this question has been largely ignored, because the answer is all too often assumed right from the start. The temptation is strong to take it for granted that standard probability calculus is the only candidate to constitute a normative psychological model of reasoning with uncertainty.[22]

By contrast, multivalent logic gives a way of accounting for epistemic uncertainty. The multivalent logic that is the subject of this book—nonadditive multivalent logic—rejects as assumptions the postulate of the excluded middle and the axiom of additivity. Thus, degrees of belief and disbelief in a fact, when the factfinder retains some belief as uncommitted between true and false, do not add to one. The uncommitted belief conveys the epistemic uncertainty.

To refine Rumsfeld's division,[23] the world contains (1) known information, (2) unknown but conceivably knowable information, including both known unknowns and possible unknown unknowns, and (3) random variation. Multivalent logic looks to the known information of type #1 in order to create beliefs that are subject in unknowable ways to type #3's random effects. It records type #2's epistemic uncertainty as uncommitted belief.

Meanwhile, traditional probability looks to type #1 in order to create odds that are subject in unknowable ways to type #3. It, however, treats type #2 as randomness. Type #2 is not actually random, however, so traditional probability's simplification is a source of error. The simplification would be tolerable, unless the decisionmaker

---

[21] Nontraditional probability can resolve these problems. See Brilmayer and Kornhauser (1978), pp. 144–145 ("To handle these difficulties, other schools of statistical inference customarily supplement probability statements with higher-order probability statements or nonquantifiable qualifications—statements about the size of the sample, for instance—that bear on the weight of the evidence."); infra Sect. 3.4 (discussing those other schools).

[22] Politzer and Bonnefon (2009), p. 100.

[23] See supra Sect. 2.1.2.

needs to keep track of epistemic uncertainties for accurately combining inferences, evidence, and findings.

3.1.4 Origins of Probability Theory

Most people recount the history here in the terms that I have been using. Probability sprung up, adorned in mathematical phrasing, when Pascal and Fermat got to talking of gambling in 1654. But a great book, *The Science of Conjecture: Evidence and Probability Before Pascal*,[24] has cast a strong new light.

The common account irresistibly raises the question, "Just how dumb were the people in the Middle Ages?" The correct answer is, "Not so dumb." Of course they realized that a world filled with unpredictable disasters was uncertain, as was the proof process. And people had handled it, albeit roughly, from ancient Egypt onward.[25] The Scholastics induced the great flowering of ways to evaluate uncertain evidence in the period from 1050–1200.[26] From there, the common law evolved toward a standard of inner conviction. People came consciously to understand the need to combine evidence and weigh conflicting evidence, in order to determine whether the proof met the required degree of sureness.[27] So, the common law was ready for a great leap. Incidentally, the law began to interplay with probability theory in the late eighteenth century.[28] A feature of this period is the prominent role of lawyers in making theoretical progress. "The law of evidence is the central thread in the history of probability."[29]

This, then, is the history of the slow evolution from subconscious inference about uncertainty to ordinary language reasoning about nonnumerical likelihoods. For my purposes, the principal lesson is this:

> Probability is of two kinds. There is *factual* or *stochastic* or *aleatory* probability, dealing with chance setups such as dice throwing and coin tossing, which produce characteristic random or patternless sequences. Almost always in a long sequence of coin tosses there are about half heads and half tails, but the order of heads and tails does not follow any pattern. On the other hand, there is *logical* or *epistemic* probability, or *nondeductive logic*, concerned with the relation of partial support or confirmation, short of strict entailment, between one

[24] Franklin (2015).

[25] See id. at 1–11.

[26] See id. at 12–39, 344–348.

[27] See id. at 327–330; Leubsdorf (2015), p. 1596 (referring to "a body of late medieval thought considering how one should act when faced with uncertainty as to the facts or as to the correct moral rule, and basing the answer in part on the extent to which certainty was attainable. The idea that there are different levels of conviction thus took root."), pp. 1595–1599 (discussing early formulations of degrees of belief).

[28] See Clermont (2023), pp. 350–351; Clermont and Sherwin (2002), pp. 255–258 (discussing this history).

[29] Franklin (2015), p. 1; see id. at 348–360.

> proposition and another. A concept of logical probability is employed when one says that, on present evidence, the steady-state theory of the universe is less probable than the big bang theory or that an accused's guilt is proved beyond reasonable doubt though it is not absolutely certain. How probable a hypothesis is, on given evidence, determines the degree of belief it is rational to have in that hypothesis, if that is all the evidence one has that is relevant to it.
>
> . . . In the period covered by the present study, logical probability was the main focus of interest, and the word *probability* was reserved solely for this case. The little study of factual probability there was—concerned with dice and insurance—was not seen as connected with logical probability.[30]

Now, that is an insight! Multivalent belief theory has prevailed implicitly for millennia. Pascalian probability was a tangential offshoot, more of a new field than a continuation of the evolution that brought uncertainty into consciousness. Legal factfinding has long dealt in multivalent beliefs, and mathematical probability never shunted them wholly aside.

3.2 Traditional Probability's Problems

Applying the traditional or Pascalian probabilistic model to factfinding introduces puzzles, paradoxes, and other problems aplenty. They derive from the underlying bivalent assumption that all things are either true or false, which implies the excluded middle, which dictates additivity, which leaves no room for unallocated belief to reflect epistemic uncertainty.[31]

This observation about traditional probability's failing does not derive from anti-probabilist prejudice. Traditional probabilities have many a role to play properly in legal proof, as in the handling of statistical evidence.[32] For another example, in calculating the odds of future events for computation of expected costs on a motion for a preliminary injunction, probability's rules would often be appropriate to predict how unknown things will turn out.[33]

In other words, the bivalent assumption sometimes can pay off, in that traditional probability turns out to be very useful in some situations. But as the guru of

---

[30] Id. at xviii (footnote omitted).

[31] See Colyvan (2008) (arguing that probability theory's method of dealing with uncertainty rests on controversial premises and suggesting examples of nonprobabilistic uncertainty); Kosko (1990) (discussing and contrasting fuzziness and probability).

[32] See Ho (2008), pp. 118–121 (discussing appropriate roles for probabilism in evidence).

[33] See Leubsdorf (1978), p. 542 ("The court, in theory, should assess the probable irreparable loss of rights an injunction would cause by multiplying the probability that the defendant will prevail by the amount of the irreparable loss that the defendant would suffer if enjoined from exercising what turns out to be his legal right. It should then make a similar calculation of the probable irreparable loss of rights to the plaintiff from denying the injunction. Whichever course promises the smaller probable loss should be adopted." (footnote omitted)); see also infra Sect. 4.6.2 (discussing the probabilistic standard for reviewing another's decision).

subjective probability, Leonard "Jimmie" Savage, warned early on, traditional probability applies only to "small world" settings.[34] Like Newtonian physics, traditional probability is a very useful oversimplification, but one that gives wrong answers around the extreme edges of its assumptions.[35] By the way, Newtonian physics, based on bivalent logic, breaks down in the face of relativity and especially quantum mechanics, which take down traditional probability's bivalence assumption at the extremes.[36]

Somewhat surprisingly, the law's task of factfinding takes us to the edges of the bivalent assumption. When the theorist proceeds to think more deeply about the nature of evidential proof, traditional probability's failure to account for epistemic uncertainty produces many oddities. Thus, my negative disposition toward traditional probability rests on the modest proposition that its proper roles do not include measuring sureness in finding epistemically uncertain facts that are unverifiable.[37] For this reason, legal academics need to "let go of their love for $p > 0.5$."[38] And they

[34] Savage (1954), p. 16; cf. Binmore (2017), p. 264 (quoting Savage as saying it would be both "preposterous" and "utterly ridiculous" to use his theory except in situations in which the decisionmaker can look before she leaps).

[35] Another fascinating example of such oversimplification derives from the development of non-Euclidean geometry in the nineteenth century. It came about by negating Euclid's questionable fifth (or "parallel") postulate, a move that eventually generated a more general geometry. Euclidean geometry worked well on a human-sized scale. But according to Einstein's general relativity, we in fact live in a non-Euclidean universe. So, for example, moving to non-Euclidean geometry permitted a new explanation of gravity. See Greenberg 2007

[36] See Dummett (1978). As Erwin Schrödinger wrote to Albert Einstein in 1950:

> It seems to me that the concept of probability is terribly mishandled these days. Probability surely has as its substance a statement as to whether something *is* or *is not* the case—an uncertain statement, to be sure. But nevertheless it has meaning only if one is indeed convinced that the something in question quite definitely *is* or *is not* the case. A probabilistic assertion presupposes the full reality of its subject.

Bub (1997), p. 115. Thus, it is often said that quantum mechanics broke classical logic, doing so by rejecting the law of the excluded middle.

By 1950, quantum logic and quantum probability had already emerged in an attempt to overcome the inconsistency of classical logic with quantum mechanics. See generally Wilce (2017) ("Mathematically, quantum mechanics can be regarded as a non-classical probability calculus resting upon a non-classical propositional logic."). Quantum logic constitutes a branch of multivalent logic, but does not speak directly to legal factfinding. It treats metaphysical uncertainty, which is the uncertainty baked into reality and would be a brand of aleatory or epistemic uncertainty depending on whether it is conceivably resolvable. Quantum probability is a nontraditional probability theory. It comprises sets of rules for assigning probabilities to events in quantum mechanics.

[37] See Cohen (1977), pp. 89–91, 265–267 (arguing that the law's interest in provability, given the "inapplicability of betting odds" to "unsettlable issues," means that probability's product rule should not apply).

[38] Cheng (2013), p. 1258.

are doing so. The move is so strong that some say we live in the time of a "paradigm shift" in evidence theory away from probabilism.[39]

Six significant oddities arise from traditional probability's failure to account for epistemic uncertainty. Each plays out in the same manner: theorizing from a probabilistic premise leads to a disturbingly serious clash with the law's rules; the law, in its wisdom, has resolved the clash by simply ignoring the probability-based criticism; and now multivalent logic, as I shall show in the next chapter, arrives to approve the law's wisdom.

3.2.1 Unrealistic Measurement

Take as the first of these oddities the one generated by the usual standards of proof. Probabilistic theorizing induces one to verbalize standards in percentage terms, even as the usual theorist simultaneously admits that a probability percentage is not how people naturally think. Percentages of likelihood are not how people normally think about proof in legal cases.[40]

The standard in civil cases appears to call for a probability of more than 50%. A moment's reflection, however, reveals all sorts of difficulties with such a formulation. To begin, there are the routine objections to speaking of proof in numerical terms, which can only mislead the factfinder.[41] More specifically, it is silly to speak in terms of a razor's edge at 50%. A human factfinder cannot tell 49% from 51%. Equipoise is a fuzzy range in the factfinder's mind.[42]

So, traditional probabilities fail the realism test. They do not capture how humans think of facts. Beliefs are a more natural and accurate way for human factfinders to think than are probabilities. Let factfinders ask themselves whether they adequately believe a party, not what odds they would demand on a feigned bet.

---

[39] Allen and Pardo (2019), p. 5.

[40] See Cheng (2013), pp. 68–75 (explaining why humans perform probabilistic tasks quite weakly).

[41] See id. at 75–78, 113–114 (describing potential problems from quantifying decisionmaking standards, including that "there is no convincing reason to expect that quantification would effectively invoke our nonprecise internal scale of judgment, or otherwise accord with the ingrained way of human thinking").

[42] See United States ex rel. Bilyew v. Franzen, 686 F.2d 1238, 1248 (7th Cir. 1982) (stressing importance of the persuasion burden and observing that "a judge or a jury can experience only a small, finite number of degrees of certainty . . . . Thus cases when the evidence . . . seem[s] in balance are not unique among some infinite variety of evidentiary balances, but instead are among a much smaller number of [ranges of] possibilities that may be perceived by the fact-finder."); Cheng (2013), pp. 18–23 (arguing that equipoise embodies for humans a range of frequently occurring cases, not just the precise point of 50/50).

3.2.2 *Weak Evidence*

Repeating my earlier example[43] can demonstrate a major shortcoming of using traditionally probabilistic odds:

> Assume that the evidence on fact *a*'s existence, say, Dave's identification as the culprit, remains weak after hearing all the available, but very imperfect, evidence. Nonetheless, the affirmative evidence definitely outweighs the evidence that the fact does not exist. Through no one's fault, no other evidence exists. If you were forced to bet on whether accepting the identification is the right course and you wanted to use odds to express the proof, then perhaps you would say Prob(*a*) = 80% and Prob(*not-a*) = 20%. That is, even though your belief one way or the other is fairly weak, if you had to allocate all your belief to either yes or no, you would formulate odds of 80/20.

More generally, imagine that the evidence of the existence or nonexistence of one of several essential facts is very weak, but the factfinder has to decide immediately on the basis of the available evidence. Could 80% and 20% be accurate representations of the factfinder's state of mind? No, I submit again. A weak but reasonably possible belief perceptibly exceeding a very weak disbelief would be a more accurate representation. Therefore, deciding for the defendant would more likely be an error than deciding for the plaintiff.

3.2.2.1 Probability's Illogical Disadvantage for Plaintiffs

Going deeper into this example of weak evidence, one runs into troubles other than inaccurate representation. Not too long ago I confronted a hypo along the following lines, when responding to a survey for a psychology study:

> A company recently identified a security breach concerning some of its proprietary data. The data were downloaded from a server room in the secure wing of one of their office buildings. The secure wing is under 24-hour surveillance and can only be accessed by presenting ID and biometric information (a thumbprint) at the only entrance and exit. Investigators examined the security tapes and found grainy footage showing that only one individual—a white male employee—entered the server room at the time the breach occurred. At the time of the breach, 50 white males were recorded as being in the secure wing of the building. A facial-recognition analysis comparing the person in the video with pictures of all 50 white males who were in the secured area at the time of the breach led investigators to conclude, with 20% certainty, that the person in the video was Mark as compared to anyone else in the office.
>
> [Now the company sues Mark civilly. If you were the factfinder, should the company prevail by a standard of more likely true than not? To put the standard differently, as the survey did, if you were to put the evidence favoring Mark's having stolen the data on one side of a balance scale and the evidence favoring Mark's not having stolen the data on the opposite side, the former evidence has to make the scale tip down somewhat in order to conclude that Mark stole the company's data.]

---

[43] See supra Sect. 1.1.1 (stating that example).

I was puzzled by the 20% figure for facial recognition. It has no technical meaning.[44] So the survey can be read in four different ways.

(1) The allusion might be to probability.[45] The surveyor seemed to mean that the software compared video and pictures and somehow, by some algorithm, spit out that it was 20% probable that it was Mark. So the other 49 candidates had various probabilities totaling 80%, according to the additivity axiom. Assuming no other evidence exists (maybe Mark has since died), the hypo is then an easy one for denying liability.
(2) Alternatively, the hypo could mean that we are 20% certain that Mark is more likely the culprit "as compared to anyone else in the office." In other words, the figure measures how confident we are that the standard of proof was met. More precisely what such a higher-order probability meant is unclear, even as to whether Mark was being compared to each of the others or rather to all of the others together. In any event, the meaning here is different from the preceding interpretation. Still, the result should be no liability.

The lessons so far are several. First, the court cannot choose not to decide, even if it resorts to a "trick" like the burden of production to avoid having to weigh the evidence.[46] Second, probabilities (whereby everything is either true or false) would be almost useless analytically in this legal case, would often constitute at best a wild guess, and would come in at a very low value to reflect the number of suspects. Third, the intriguing general question that emerges from the hypo is how to decide when the evidence on both sides is very weak.

---

[44] Contemporary AI facial recognition for identification came in many varieties. The basic technique was to extract a feature vector of the face to be recognized and then compare it to the vectors of a database of faces. Here the database is the 50 possible suspects.

This so-called 1:N matching can be accurate (i.e., high percent correct when declaring a match) under ideal conditions with lighting and positioning being consistent, facial features of the subject being taken from a clear and unobscured head-on view, and comparison photos showing current ages and similar expressions. Less than ideal conditions cause sharp decreases in accuracy.

The software can also screen results by a percentage-of-confidence threshold, usually set very high in order to avoid false positives. The algorithm can be set to report a match only if it has a certain degree of confidence in the match or, in other words, only if its identification has a statistical significance of x% certain that the null hypothesis (not identified) is not true.

More common than a match and confidence rating is (1) a match (or similarity) score ranging from 0 to 1 and based on how similar the subject's measured features are to those of each face in the database and (2) a match threshold that requires a certain level of similarity to declare a match.

[45] By e-mail to author (June 9, 2020, 16:07 EST) (on file with author), the surveyor wrote: "It is an ambiguous term in part because we leave the interpretation of the value to participants; we then ask participants to provide a probability of their own as a reflection of the likelihood they actually considered when making their yes/no decision."

[46] See Laudan (2007), pp. 304–305 ("The trier of fact cannot say, 'Although plaintiff's case is stronger than defendant's, I will reach no verdict since neither party has a frightfully good story to tell.' Under current rules, if the plaintiff has a better story than the defendant, he must win the suit, even when his theory of the case fails to satisfy the strictures required to qualify his theory as the best explanation.").

Perhaps we headed down the wrong path to answering that last question. The expression "20% certain" sounds more like the language of beliefs. Let us now assume the hypo meant that the proof established a 0.20 belief that it was Mark, and that the analogous belief for each of the other 49 persons was perceptibly lower.

(3) On the one hand, if the 20% figure means something like person #2 was inculpated to a 0.15 belief, person #3 to 0.10, and so on, then the decision must still go for the defendant. The reason then is that the belief it was Mark does not exceed the sum of beliefs it was someone else. This reading seems to remain close to what the surveyor herself probably meant by "20% certain." It resembles the first-order probability interpretation because it does not employ multivalent logic's capacity to leave a good part of the evaluator's full belief uncommitted in order to represent epistemic uncertainty.

(4) On the other hand, if the plaintiff's proof of Mark's culpability established a 0.20 belief that it was Mark and if the proof that it was another person remained perceptibly weaker—so that the belief it was Mark exceeds the belief it was not Mark, while much belief remains uncommitted—then decision should go for the plaintiff. Although this scenario may sound unrealistic, in fact it is not. The video might be very grainy, and the algorithm might be approximate. The video most resembles Mark of the 50 persons. The algorithm reports a weak match for Mark and apparently no match for anyone else. All the other candidates are subject to minuscule or no proof of culpability, even after taking into account any failure to produce evidence and any other relevant features of the evidence. The factfinder has no grounds to embrace a narrative alternative to Mark's committing the theft. So the factfinder thinks it was Mark, but feels uncertain and longs for more evidence. Given massive epistemic uncertainty, the wise opinion might be "I don't know," but this opinion is not open to a court. The court must decide now for either plaintiff or defendant based on the available evidence. The belief that it was Mark is stronger than the belief it was someone else.

When all is said, the last of the four possible readings of the survey is what the survey conveyed to me by "20% certain" that it "was Mark as compared to anyone else in the office": here the factfinder is "certain" in its belief that Mark's identity was 20% proven, and then uncertain in large part before minusculely disbelieving it was Mark.

Speaking expressly in terms of beliefs would have made the hypo clearer and more interesting. But regardless of your agreement on the proper reading, step back now from the four readings. Here come the further lessons.

If the 20% figure were speaking in terms of traditional probabilities, this kind of hypo would result in the plaintiff always losing, as the plaintiff did under the first three readings. A Bayesian might start at a prior probability of 2% for Mark and 2% for each of the 49 others. The Bayesian would never be able to get Mark's posterior probability over 50% when there are 49 other suspects, because, to exceed 50% by Bayes' theorem, the facial-recognition algorithm would have to report, totally unrealistically, that it is virtually certain it was Mark on the grainy video. Indeed, a faithful, but perhaps not too insightful, Bayesian could seldom find liability in any case where there are many suspects.

By contrast, if the hypo were truly speaking in terms of multivalent beliefs, the fact that there are 50 suspects would receive non-Bayesian mathematical treatment. The theorist would see the 2% figure as a so-called classical probability reflecting only the number of possible outcomes, and so not an especially probative probability.[47] The theorist would start at zero for total ignorance. Being one of the suspects would create only a possibility of culpability for Mark, not a belief. If the 2% statistic were viewed additionally as evidence of opportunity for each suspect, it would create a tiny belief that Mark was the culprit and a matching disbelief that it was Mark; the disbelief would represent the belief that the actual thief was some other person who had the opportunity; the disjunction of the beliefs that it was a particular one of the other 49 would, by multivalent logic, be the maximum of those beliefs, not their sum.[48] The uncommitted belief would be huge, reflecting the huge possibility it was not Mark. When the facial-recognition proof comes in and is read to speak only to Mark's culpability, the belief that it was Mark would grow to 0.20, but the actual belief it was not Mark would stay very low.[49] Thus, the plaintiff should win.

The multivalent belief theorist could offer several arguments in support of this outcome in favor of the plaintiff. First, imagine that, instead of facial-recognition software, a sole eyewitness testifies that she thinks, but is unsure, that the culprit was Mark and not someone else. The plaintiff would win. Second, only by focusing on Mark and not-Mark could the system find liability in most cases with multiple suspects. Third, imagine you had to bet on the proper outcome: yes or no. You need to bet now, despite massive epistemic uncertainty. You have a 0.20 belief it was Mark and a very low belief it was not. If you wanted to calculate betting odds in this sea of uncertainty, you would somehow distribute your unallocated belief to yes or no, maybe normalizing to near 60/40 by allocating equal amounts of the unallocated belief to yes and no. You then should be willing to bet that it was Mark. And if you are willing to bet it was Mark, and even if you are a probabilist looking at weak evidence, you would have to admit it was more likely than not Mark!

That bet is the clearest indication of how different the first and fourth readings are as to the meaning of the evidence. The first reads the evidence as a 20% probability it was Mark and an 80% probability it was not, which means 20/80 odds. The fourth

---

[47] As the number of suspects grows, the unlikeliness of the culprit being Mark increases. But normally this is relatively weak proof. The reason is that the classical probability of 98% must be translated into a source of disbelief by connecting that general probability to the particular issue of whether it was Mark, which will lead to a huge swath of uncommitted belief. See supra Sect. 1.1.2 (explaining transformation of probabilities into beliefs). Then it must be aggregated with the individualized facial-recognition evidence on whether it was not Mark, which will lead to a further discount. See infra Sect. 4.5.4.1 (explaining aggregation of evidence).

[48] See infra Sect. 4.2.4.3 (explaining the so-called MAX rule).

[49] See Cohen (1977), p. 270 (saying of proof purely in support of the plaintiff: "Whether on the facts accepted by the jury there is a large, a substantial, or only a moderate [belief] that the winner's contention is true, the loser can have only zero [belief] on his side.").

reads the evidence as beliefs of 0.20 and approximately zero, which might transform into a near 60/40 betting probability.

Obviously, the proper course would be to try to learn what exactly the facial-recognition algorithm was reporting. But picture two different bettors, who have to bet on the unexplained evidence. The Bayesian bettor's odds of 20/80 represent what would be the estimated bivalent outcomes if the scenario played out a hundred times, on the assumption that any variation would be random. Therefore, the Bayesian bets that it was not Mark. By contrast, the multivalent belief theorist is betting on the best factfinding in this one-shot case based on the available evidence. After accounting for epistemic uncertainty, the theorist arrives at a belief it was Mark that is greater than the corresponding disbelief. Therefore, this theorist bets that it was Mark. Who is the better bettor?

3.2.2.2 Law's Resolution

What should judge or jury decide if the evidence, properly interpreted, is weak in showing that it was Mark, but the evidence suggests only the merest indication that it was someone else? Beliefs are the tool for soundly making required decisions when the evidence on both sides is weak. Even if the affirmative belief based on the proof is weak, as long as it is reasonably persuasive and perceptibly stronger than the opposite disbelief, the accurate result is that the plaintiff wins. A decision for such a plaintiff is less likely an error than decision for the defendant, because it was 60/40 more likely Mark than not Mark. A preponderance of the evidence thus supports the claim against Mark, giving important insight into the meaning of "preponderance."

Which logical approach is the more accurate is ordinarily a difficult thing to demonstrate by hypothetical. The reason is that the intuitively correct answer depends on one's underlying assumptions. Say, for example, that element *a* of the plaintiff's claim is measured at 0.60 and element *b* is measured at 0.60. If one is thinking in terms of traditional probabilities, one will intuitively think the plaintiff should lose. But if one were thinking in terms of multivalent beliefs, one would not intuitively go to the product rule in seeking the "right" answer.

Here lies the value of the Mark hypo. It succeeds in actually suggesting which logical approach is more accurate. It presents a situation where one can feel that the plaintiff should win against Mark. If the hypo is indeed inarticulately implying that Mark is the likely culprit, it suggests that the plaintiff's position is stronger than the defendant's position. Dealing in nonadditive degrees of belief yields that interpretation. Thus, one can conclude that this approach produces more accurate findings.

If, as we shall see in the next chapter, the hypo's evidence were solely in terms of additive probabilities, multivalent belief theory could handle that situation too. In this altered Mark hypo, multivalent belief theory would give the proper result that the plaintiff should lose.

To generalize by abandoning the specifics of the Mark hypo, I am saying that in a world of uncertainty, there will be many cases where all the available evidence is such that there is weak evidence on both sides, say, there is nonnegligible but weak evidence that the defendant was at fault, but this evidence is perceptibly stronger than the evidence that he was not. (I find it helpful to say the belief that he was at fault is stronger than the belief that he was not.) Should the plaintiff recover? I say yes, but a devoted probabilist would say no. I contend that I would commit fewer errors in the course of decisions. And the law agrees with me, commanding that decision be made on weak evidence, and be made on the basis of who has the more believable evidence in support.[50]

Why is probability a less accurate way to measure evidence in the generic case? One reason is that probability needs to allocate the unknowns to yes or no, and here it tends inaccurately to allocate most of them to no, as in the 20/80 figure. That tendency could create a sizable disadvantage for plaintiffs.

3.2.2.3 Probability's Illogical Advantage for Plaintiffs

Let me close this discussion of weak evidence with an ironic twist on probability's problem with weak evidence. As shown above, probability theory could be very tough on plaintiffs. Yet, with no awareness of self-contradiction, a devoted probabilist would also treat the civil standard of proof as a ridiculously easy one. In an ordinary case, the factfinder supposedly starts in a state of perfect ignorance, wherein the plaintiff's claim has a 50/50 chance by the indifference principle. So, for the probabilist, introduction of a feather's weight of evidence for the plaintiff should suffice for victory over a silent defendant.

However, we all know that in such a case, the plaintiff would lose. The reality is that the law requires much stronger evidence just to proceed to trial.[51] The rule on judgment as a matter of law requires the plaintiff's evidence, all by itself, to create at least a reasonable possibility.[52] The law accordingly says that a feather's weight does not satisfy the burden of production. That burden guards against irrational error. Thus, the law deems decision by a feather's weight to be irrational.

Belief analysis makes it easier to understand the law's approach. At the end of evidence, only if the plaintiff's weak proof creates at least a reasonable belief and that belief is perceptibly stronger than disbelief of the plaintiff's position, can the

---

[50] See Pardo (2021), p. 283 ("The reason for the misalignment follows from the standard assumption (the complementation axiom) within probability theory that a proposition and its negation sum to 1. Employing this assumption in the context of legal proof and requiring the plaintiff to prove a disputed fact beyond 0.5 gives the defendant the benefit of the unknown probability space, even when the defendant's alternative account is itself less probable than the plaintiff's account. This fails to align with the preponderance standard's generally accepted goals of minimizing errors and allocating the risk of error between the parties roughly equally." (citation omitted)).

[51] See Broun (2013), § 338 ("A 'scintilla' of evidence will not suffice."); infra Sect. 5.2.1.1 (explaining why the burden of production deserves protection).

[52] See, e.g., Fed. R. Civ. P. 50(a)(1) (stating standard of decision as whether "a reasonable jury would not have a legally sufficient evidentiary basis to find for the party on that issue").

plaintiff prevail. Belief analysis thereby obviates not only probability's illogical toughness on plaintiffs but its illogical lenity too.

3.2.3 *Infinite Possibilities*

Simultaneously, a devoted probabilist might see the infinite range of possibilities alternative to the plaintiff's allegations as making the plaintiff's burden nearly impossible to carry. Even if one invokes some viewpoint like plausibility or contextualism to pare down the range of alternatives,[53] one might still argue that few plaintiffs could tell a story more than 50% likely, given the difficulty of proving a likely truth by dissipating all the remaining alternatives:

> If the plaintiff must prove that some fact, *X*, is more probable than its negation, *not-X*, then the plaintiff should have to show not only the probability that the state of the world is such that *X* is true, but also the probability of every other possible state of the world in which *X* is not true. This would mean that in order to prevail, plaintiffs would have to disprove (or demonstrate the low likelihood of) each of the virtually limitless number of ways the world could have been at the relevant time. This would be a virtually impossible task, and thus, absent conclusive proof, plaintiffs would lose.[54]

Accordingly, the probabilist might say in the weak-evidence example of Dave[55] that, because the evidence he was the culprit is weak, the odds are not 80/20 as suggested above, but instead are at most 20/80. The probabilist would view the task from the top down, seeking a first-order probability: it then seems there is at most a 20% chance it was Dave and an 80% chance it was somehow not. So Dave would win.

Likewise, in the example of Mark,[56] the probabilist might say that, because there is a huge list of possible suspects, the odds are at most 20/80, rather than the multivalent belief theorist's near 60/40. There are just too many possibilities other than Mark's culpability. So Mark would win too.

Nevertheless, day in and day out, suits against the Daves and Marks of the world succeed on such evidence. Here the law, and even most theorists, refuses to follow the probabilist's thinking to the bitter end. Imperfect evidence is the norm, after all. If the legal results went for the Daves and Marks, we would have a legal system terribly slanted against plaintiffs, one that could never deliver on its promises of procedural neutrality and economic efficiency. Therefore, the law in practice does not hold the infinite alternatives against the plaintiffs. That is, it does not hold the epistemic

---

[53] See Brown (1983), p. 404 (discussing a plausibility filter); Rysiew (2016), § 3.3 (formulating a contextual response to the skeptical argument).

[54] Pardo (2009), p. 1093 (footnote omitted) (using the "negation, *not-X*," in the sense of *X*'s complement with a probability of 1–*p*); see id. at 1093–1094 (observing this paradox is created by a probabilistic approach to the more-likely-than-not standard, and so proposing the relative plausibility approach explained infra Sect. 4.4.2).

[55] See supra Sect. 3.2.2 (restating that Dave example).

[56] See supra Sect. 3.2.2.1 (explaining that Mark example).

uncertainty against the plaintiffs. It allows recovery upon much less than a 50% showing, when stated in terms of the kind of probability espoused by the devoted probabilist.

The law reaches the desirable result by realizing its task is not to search out perfect knowledge. Instead, it focuses on the evidential showing that it was Dave/Mark and on the evidential showing that it was in fact *not* Dave/Mark, rather than on all the other possible stories. It might get there by reframing the preponderance standard as asking if the plaintiff's case is more than 50% "credible." It so refocuses and reframes because the law has intuitively realized that asking the factfinder either to accept one account or to accept its opposite is the accurate way to proceed.

In other words, the problem of infinite possibilities is merely a theoretical problem generated by the system's assumed adherence to probabilism. Wisely, the law and those who think seriously about the law reject that supposed problem. Multivalent logic's contribution is to defend this wisdom by showing why the disjunction of the infinite possibilities does not augment the disbelief that it was Dave or Mark.

3.2.4 Combining Evidence

Surprisingly, even mathematicians cannot agree on how a factfinder should perform the task of combining evidence and proofs, and so cannot unanimously guide the law on the ideal path to take.[57] This is true not only of combining disparate items of evidence offered to prove a fact, but also of combining established facts necessary to prove a case. Nevertheless, law professors have rallied to Bayes' theorem[58] for accomplishing the first of those two very different mathematical tasks, and to the product rule for the second task.

3.2.4.1 Aggregation by Bayes' Theorem

The legal academics' initial cure for probability theory's unsuitability for legal factfinding was to speak of probability in ever more sophisticated terms. They urged Bayes' theorem in recent decades as the rigorous way to aggregate related evidence that bears on a fact.[59] The theorem links the perceived probability before and after receiving new evidence: by mathematically updating the initial probability with the new evidence, one gets an updated probability.

---

[57] See Tillers (2001) (discussing different mathematical approaches to judicial proof).

[58] See generally Baronett (2019), pp. 646–647 (laying out the basics of Bayes' theorem); McGrayne (2011) (recounting the centuries of controversy generated by Bayes' theorem).

[59] See, e.g., Lempert (1986), pp. 440–450 (championing Bayesianism).

So, Thomas Bayes (or really Pierre Simon Laplace) tells us that for proving fact A we need to start with a prior probability, which the newly admitted evidence will alter into a posterior probability. This starting point is Prob(A), the prior probability of A. Then the posterior probability of A, after accounting for new evidence B, is the conditional probability Prob(A|B), which may be read as the probability that A will occur if B is known certainly to have occurred. Prob(A|B) calculates to be Prob (A) multiplied by the support B provides for A, a support that Bayes equated to Prob (B|A) ÷ Prob(B). The measures Prob(A) and Prob(B) are the probabilities of observing A and B independently of each other. So, here is the theorem:

$$\mathrm{Prob}(A|B) = [\mathrm{Prob}(B|A) \bullet \mathrm{Prob}(A)] \div \mathrm{Prob}(B)$$

The Bayesian "likelihood ratio" is defined as the effect of the new evidence on the odds of A, and it can be derived from the theorem. The odds of A are Prob(A) ÷ Prob (not-A), so that the new evidence's effect on the odds, or the likelihood ratio, is Prob (B|A) ÷ Prob(B|not-A).[60]

Despite its internal mathematical soundness when used within its frequentist or subjectivist realm, and despite the many insights it generates for law, most observers from many disciplines have voiced serious doubts about whether Bayes' theorem should be seen to play a broad role in legal factfinding.[61] Like any probability-based equation dealing with nonstatistical evidence, the problems of Bayes' theorem are numerous.

First, and most fundamental, the theorem leaves no place for epistemic uncertainties, thus painting the world as being black and white even though most of the world appears in shades of gray.[62] That is, it is built on bivalence's additive probabilities, and so does not work with nonadditive multivalent beliefs. Consider again an 80/20 piece of thin evidence. The theorem says that it will affect the posterior probability in the same way as a piece of airtight 80/20 evidence. That result inevitably introduces an error into factfinding. Thus, Bayes' theorem does not handle well the very common situation of incomplete, inconclusive, ambiguous, dissonant, or unreliable information. Now, some probabilists use a fudge factor to make Bayes' theorem account for the state of the evidence. But if they do this by a brute adjustment of the probability, it runs into the problem that for factfinding a lowered p leads to a higher and therefore inaccurate $1-p$ as the measure of falsity.[63]

---

[60] See Broun (2013), § 185 (discussing the likelihood ratio); Lempert (1977), pp. 1022–1025 (deriving the likelihood ratio).

[61] See, e.g., Pennington and Hastie (1981), pp. 262–268 (discussing the theorem's problems); Shafer (1986), pp. 809–816 (same). Compare Bergman and Moore (1991), p. 590 (attacking), with Kaye (1991) (defending).

[62] See Brilmayer (1986), pp. 686–688 (considering second-order evidence that cannot be accommodated by the Bayesian framework).

[63] See supra Sect. 3.1.3 (discussing shortcoming of fudge factor) and infra Sect. 3.4 (discussing how nontraditional probability manages to treat epistemic uncertainty).

Second, and most wonky, traditional probability encounters legendary difficulties with the state of ignorance. The reason again is that traditional probability cannot distinguish among belief, lack of belief, and disbelief. Assume that the factfinder dutifully comes in fresh and sets the initial belief in A at zero. In probabilistic terms, $A = 0$ means that A is impossible. And it means that not-A is certain. Under Bayes' theorem, no amount of evidence could alter an impossibility or a certainty into a possibility. Alternatively, given the proper mindset of initial ignorance in a civil case, a popular starting point is to posit that the plaintiff's claim has a 50/50 chance, on the thought that any fact is either true or false.[64] Indeed, some experimental evidence indicates that lay people, when forced, do tend to start at fifty percent.[65] That starting point unfortunately comports with neither the actual case's probabilities nor the law's instructions on where the factfinder should begin.[66] It also introduces the aforementioned logical problem of making a feather's weight of evidence sufficient to carry the burden of persuasion over a silent defendant,[67] and it produces inconsistencies when there are more than two hypotheses (or suspects) in play.[68] So, zero and 50/50 are out as a starting point. But the theorem fails to give the factfinder any other initial prior probability as a defensible starting point.[69] The starting point must then come out of thin air, as a sort of subjective assertion.

Third, and most obvious, the theorem has no claim to be a realistic representation of how legal factfinders do or could aggregate evidence. It does not conform to the way humans in ordinary life arrive at prior probabilities or the way they combine them with new evidence to produce posterior probabilities.[70] Humans instead use intuitive techniques in a nonquantitative and approximate fashion. Consequently, the law has generally left the assessment of evidence to its factfinders' instinctive treatment—almost never mentioning Bayes' theorem.[71]

3.2.4.2 Conjunction and Disjunction

Switching gears, consider now the different task of conjoining facts. For independent events *a* and *b*, the product rule says that the probability of the conjoined events is

---

[64] Cf. Dahlman and Kolflaath (2021) (discussing criminal cases).

[65] See Martin and Schum (1987), pp. 390–393 (surveying a small sample of students for their odds of guilt used as the prior probability, which turned out to be 1:1 or 50%).

[66] See State v. Spann, 617 A.2d 247, 254 (N.J. 1993) (".5 assumed prior probability clearly is neither neutral nor objective").

[67] See supra Sect. 3.2.2.3 (discussing a feather's worth of evidence).

[68] See Lempert (1986), pp. 462–467 (noting that employing 50/50 as the appropriate odds when ignorant of the true facts can cause many problems).

[69] On problems with choosing any other prior probability, see Jaffee (1985), pp. 980–985.

[70] Compare Kotz and Stroup (1983) (discussing the sophisticated techniques of theory), with Callen (1982) (discussing the simplified practices of law).

[71] See Brilmayer and Kornhauser (1978), pp. 135–148 (laying out other logical problems of a Bayesian approach).

the product of the events' probabilities. For interdependent events, the probability operation for conjunction is Prob(a) multiplied by the conditional Prob($b|a$), so it is still multiplicative. The two rules are called collectively the general product rule, or just the product rule.

As to disjoining events (one or the other, or both, is true), De Morgan's rule provides that the disjunction of two independent statements (say, each 0.25 likely) equals the negation of the product of the negations of those statements ($1 - 0.75^2 = 0.44$). For interdependent statements a and b, the product-rule portion of De Morgan's rule would involve Prob(a) and Prob($b|a$).

Law's Resolution Do these probability rules really apply to legal factfinding? Say you want to sue some partygoer for a battery allegedly committed at last night's party. While you dozed off from boredom, he or she kissed you. To win, says the law, you must prove three elements: (1) the identity of the kisser, (2) the kisser's intention to make contact, and (3) the contact being harmful or offensive.[72] Here is the evidence:

(1) We are not certain who the kisser was, but you have shown by sketchy eyewitnesses that it is 60% probable that the culprit was X.
(2) Intention is always hard to prove, but you have been able to show, given the nature of kissing, an 80% likelihood.
(3) Harmful or offensive is a vague construct, but let us say this unwanted sloppy kiss is at least a 51% member of the set of acts offensive to the ordinary person.

The law requires you to prove that each of your positions is more likely than not. That standard works to minimize error costs, given that the system has no reason to favor either plaintiff or defendant. Would you then win against X? Yes. You need not prove that overall liability is more likely than not. The law is clear on the need to prove only that each element is more likely than not, without attention to whether the whole case is proven to that degree. As long as each element is more likely than not, you win.

Many educated laypersons would now object. They would say, looking only at the first two independent elements of 60% identity and 80% intention, that all you have shown is that their conjunction is 48% true by the product rule. Then there is the third element to consider, bringing the plaintiff's case down to a 25% showing.

Moreover, they would say that, for the fair and efficient allocation of liability, we want to know if X likely committed a tort, rather than whether he or she likely harbored a certain intention and so on. Error-cost minimization would seem to tell us to apply the standard of proof to the plaintiff's whole story. The plaintiff's tale of overall liability should be more likely than all versions of nonliability put together.

---

[72] See Liljegren v. United Rys. Co. of St. Louis, 227 S.W. 925 (St. Louis Ct. App. 1921) (involving kiss by the battery defendant); Mohr v. Williams, 104 N.W. 12 (Minn. 1905) (involving unconsciousness of the battery plaintiff); cf. Van Cleave (2019) (extending consideration to criminal law on kissing). I shall treat identity as a separate element, to be proven to the standard of proof.

The law's result therefore looks like an erroneous outcome, seriously undercutting whatever aim that society is trying to achieve through its law. In this case, traditional probability tells us that you are very likely to fail at simultaneously satisfying all three elements, which are the cumulative conditions for liability—yet X must pay under the law. Why? Because the law tells its factfinder to proceed element-by-element.

Conjunction and Disjunction Paradoxes Troublingly, probability's product rule means that each element's being more probable than not is no guarantee of policy's requirement that the elements' conjunction be more probable than not. Accordingly, the law's refusal to apply its standard of proof to the case's overall factual narrative generates a clash between probability and law. It creates the so-called conjunction paradox, beloved by devoted probabilists.[73] Consider the best-known statement of this infamous paradox:

> We purport to decide civil cases according to a more-probable-than-not standard of proof. We would expect this standard to take into account the rule of conjunction, which states that the probability of two independent events occurring together is the product of the probability of each event occurring separately. The rule of conjunction dictates that in a case comprised of two independent elements the plaintiff must prove each element to a much greater degree than 50%: only then will the plaintiff have shown that the probability that the two elements occurred together exceeds 50%. Suppose, for example, that a plaintiff must prove both causation and fault and that these two elements are independent. If the plaintiff shows that causation is 60% probable and fault is 60% probable, then he apparently would have failed to satisfy the civil standard of proof because the probability that the defendant *both* acted negligently and caused injury is only 36%.
>
> In our legal system, however, jurors do not consider whether it is more probable than not that all elements occurred in conjunction. Judges instruct jurors to decide civil cases element-by-element, with each element decided on a more-probable-than-not basis. Once jurors have decided that an element is probable, they are to consider the element established, repress any remaining doubts about it, and proceed to consider the next element. If the plaintiff proves each element by a preponderance of the evidence, the jury will find in his favor. . . . Thus, jurors may find a defendant liable even if . . . the conjoined probability of the elements is much less than 50%. In such cases, the verdict fails to reflect a probable account of what happened and thus fails to minimize the cost of judicial errors.[74]

---

[73] An early rendition of the paradox lies in the innovative Michael and Adler (1931), pp. 140–143 (also identifying preponderance with the >0.5 standard for the first time, according to Leubsdorf (2015), p. 1579 n.45). More recent scholars reflexively invoke the conjunction paradox as a criticism of current law. E.g., Nance (2016), pp. 74–78; Allen and Jehl (2003); Cheng (2013); Iuliano (2014); Kaye (1979), pp. 38–41; Koehler and Meixner (2015); Pardo (2015).

[74] Nesson (1985), pp. 1385–1388 (footnotes omitted). Professor Nesson saw the paradox as illustrating his broad thesis that the law's process of proof aims at generating acceptable statements about past events and thus at projecting behavioral norms to the public, rather than at reaching probable conclusions in a search for truth:

> Application of the more-probable-than-not test to each element produces the most acceptable conclusion as to that element. The conjunction of these conclusions constitutes a story that is more probable than any other story about the same elements. Suppose, for example, that the elements of a story are A and B, and A (70%) is more probable than not-A (30%), and B

The paradox's implications are profound but boggling. Allowing recovery on a 36% showing of causation *and* fault seems economically inefficient. How embarrassing for the law! Going beyond embarrassment, though, allowing recovery seems to undermine one of civil procedure's most fundamental principles: where possible, the parties should receive equal treatment.[75] Refusing to multiply probabilities would seem to disadvantage defendants.[76]

For another boggle, ponder the apparent criticality of how exactly the ancients (and moderns) divided our causes of action (and defenses) into elements: the more subdivisions, the lower the conjunctive probability that would suffice for victory.[77] And yet: "Anyone who has ever litigated a real case knows the exact opposite of the conjunction paradox is true: the more disputed elements the plaintiff has to prove, the *less* likely the plaintiff is to prevail [because] the jury will find at least one element to be less likely than not."[78]

For a final boggle, the product rule leads to the silliness of the lesser-known disjunction paradoxes. Probability-obsessed theorists would have us convict defendants on the basis of a series of almost-proven crimes:

> Should a court convict a defendant for an unspecified offense if there is no reasonable doubt that he committed an offense, even though the prosecution cannot prove his guilt as to a particular offense beyond a reasonable doubt? Stated otherwise, is committing an offense sufficient for a conviction or must a prosecutor establish what this offense is to justify a conviction? This Article contends that, under certain conditions, a prosecutor should not have to establish the particular offense committed by a defendant—proof that the defendant committed an offense should be sufficient.[79]

These scholars also see a paradox involving multiple independent theories that are alternative routes to the same conclusion, whether that conclusion is a judgment in a case with multiple counts or a decision on a particular claim. These observers lament that the law denies relief to a supposedly deserving plaintiff (or to a defendant with multiple defenses almost proven):

> Consider a case involving three different legal theories and three different factual foundations. Plaintiffs deserve to win if one of the stories embodying one legal theory is true; defendants deserve to win only if all of their competing stories are true (for if this is false, one

---

> (60%) is more probable than not-B (40%). The conjunction (A & B) (42%) may not be more probable than its negation (not-(A & B)) (58%). But the conjunction (A & B) (42%) is more probable than any other version: (A & (not-B)) (28%), ((not-A) & B) (18%), or ((not-A) & (not-B)) (12%). The application of the more-probable-than-not standard of proof on an element-by-element basis will produce the single most probable story.

Id. at 1389–1390 (footnotes omitted).

[75] On the importance of equality to procedural justice, see Redmayne (1999), pp. 171–174; Solum (2004), pp. 286–289.

[76] See infra Sect. 3.2.5 (discussing apparent asymmetries).

[77] See Henderson et al. (1995), pp. 1655–1659, 1667–1675 (discussing "substantive issue separation" and its procedural treatment).

[78] Moran (2003), pp. 946–947, 950.

[79] Harel and Porat (2009), pp. 261–262.

> of the plaintiff's stories is true). For example, assume the plaintiff has alleged defective design, defective manufacture, and failure to warn theories. If the probability of each is 0.25, the "probability" of each not being true is 0.75, but, the probability of at least one being true is $1-0.75^3=0.58$, and perhaps plaintiff should win, even though the individual probabilities of each being false is 0.75.[80]

Some have tried to explain, and thereby to justify as a practical or prudential matter, why the law illogically ignores these disjunction paradoxes.[81] But others overtly attack the law's general refusal to multiply the probabilities of claims and defenses, and then argue for overhauling the law to cure this logical mistake.[82]

As already recounted, many clever legal academics over recent decades have lamented in similar tones that the law illogically ignores the product rule for conjunction.[83] Few of them have questioned their assumption that ignoring the product rule is illogical.

I do.

My impetus is the realization that in performing the legal task of finding facts, the logical and practical problems of applying probabilism's product rule are legion. The most obvious of the problems is that the product rule would start producing nonsensical results for legal cases as the number of conjoined facts starts increasing. Anyone who has to prove a string of elements would be terribly disadvantaged by the product rule. The product will approach 0%, even if all the likelihoods of the numerous elements are substantial. Proof would become nearly impossible. Indeed, we would end up believing almost nothing in the world, as just about any belief rests on connected beliefs. Cumulatively, the product rule seems like an invitation to extreme skepticism.[84]

---

[80] Allen and Jehl (2003), p. 939; see Massachusetts v. U.S. Dep't of Health & Human Servs., 682 F.3d 1 (1st Cir. 2012) (striking down DOMA on both equal protection and federalism grounds), noted in Dorf (2012) for being insufficiently "fuzzy." On similar aggregation in criminal sentencing, see Bennardo (2013).

[81] E.g., Lombardero (1996), p. 289 (observing that the disjunction paradox partially offsets the effect of the conjunction paradox); Schauer and Zeckhauser (1996), pp. 41–47 (conceding the probability argument regarding multiple almost-proven crimes, but arguing that the criminal law still should not convict, for reasons of abundant caution).

[82] E.g., Porat and Posner (2012). For a dismantling of the disjunction paradoxes, see Clermont (2012).

[83] The two most recent forays argue at length that the conjunction paradox is real and that therefore the law should change to conform to the product rule. Schwartz and Sober (2017); Spottswood (2016), p. 290 ("there seems to be no conceptual obstacle to treating the risk of fact-finding errors in probabilistic terms").

[84] See Branion v. Gramly, 855 F.2d 1256, 1264 (7th Cir. 1988) (rejecting multiplication of odds in a legal case by saying: "Every event, if specified in detail, is extremely improbable; indeed, with *enough* detail it is unique in the history of the universe. It is always possible to take some probabilities, small to start with, and multiply them for effect.").

Significance of Paradoxes Some theorists suggest that the practicing lawyer need not worry about these philosophical points and paradoxes.[85] But I disagree again. The conjunction paradox raises major difficulties both practical and theoretical.[86]

Those who downplay the conjunction problem[87] see it as arising only when the factfinder tries to combine the elements of claim or affirmative defense. This restricted perspective on the problem facilitates their downplaying the conjunction paradox as an oddity of little importance, one that intrudes only at the end of a few cases. But those theorists are wrong.

The reality is that conjunction is a necessary act in *every* fact found by a legal factfinder! Conjunction is ubiquitous. Conjoining propositions is a universal and constant task in factfinding because conjunction is the method required for combining inferential steps.[88] Conjunction is necessary for any fact resting on multiple inferences, and every found fact rests on multiple inferences.[89]

---

[85] See Anderson et al. (2005), pp. 102–103 (saying such problems are "not an immediate concern for the practicing lawyer"); Risinger (2013), p. 811 ("[A]rguing either radical skepticism or the primacy of some form of philosophical idealism will not cut any ice in a courtroom.").

[86] See Pardo (2019), pp. 280–282, 288–289 (arguing that paradoxes, such as the conjunction paradox, force one to grapple with fundamental issues).

[87] Many dismiss the conjunction paradox as a mere theoretical wrinkle without practical worry, wishfully arguing for example that most cases involve a single disputed issue and that multiple issues are seldom independent. E.g., Lempert (1986), p. 452 ("One might, for example, argue that the probabilities favoring the existence of the different elements of a plaintiff's case are generally highly dependent, and that successful plaintiffs generally prove the separate elements of their cases by far more than a mere preponderance of the evidence.").

More desperately, others argue that the lamentable distortion caused by ignoring conjunction is offset by other features of the trial process. E.g., Levmore (2001) (invoking the Condorcet jury theorem to argue that supermajority rules offset the failure to require jurors to conjoin probabilities). But see Allen and Jehl (2003), pp. 914–918 (critiquing the supermajority theory of Levmore); Edelman (2002), pp. 343–348 (critiquing the Condorcet theorizing by Levmore); cf. Zamir and Teichman (2018), pp. 120–124, 559–561 (discussing group decisionmaking).

The boldest contend that a bias in favor of plaintiffs is a good thing. E.g., Levmore (2001), p. 733 ("[S]ome observers (and perhaps jurors and judges) will be comfortable with a decision in favor of liability because of the intuition that making negligent parties pay 'too much' is harmless or even healthy."); Stein (2001), pp. 1199–1234 (justifying the suppression of the product rule on deterrence grounds).

Still others contend that because factfinders proceed holistically anyway (or the judge might not clearly state, or the jury might not fully understand, the element-by-element approach to the standard of proof), we can rest content in the thought that the product rule is being applied to the conjunction. E.g., Allen and Pardo (2019), pp. 39, 51–53 (asserting that comparing whole stories somehow avoids the conjunction paradox). But see infra Sect. 4.4.2. Or at least we can be content as long as we do not force the factfinder into a corner by some element-by-element device like a special verdict. See Lombardero (1996), pp. 280–288 (accepting the Bayesian model). But cf. Sood (2021), p. 58 (highlighting "possible perils lurking beneath the preferred use of general verdicts in criminal trials"); Thornburg (1998), pp. 1857–1863 (questioning whether a special verdict actually changes the jury's decisionmaking practice).

[88] See infra Sect. 5.1.1 (describing the process of evidential inference and the essential role of conjoining inferences).

[89] See infra Sect. 5.1.1.1 (establishing this point)

Moreover, the task of conjunction extends well before the end of trial, into pretrial devices and other legal-factfinding settings inside and outside courts, as well as into settlement negotiations and other law-office applications of law that depend on forecast factfinding. Therefore, any proper model of evidential proof must resolve this key conjunction paradox.

The point here is important enough to bear repeating. Conjunction is not an arcane oddity. Any thought worthy of being called a thought in any setting entails reasoning by conjoined inferences. Without them, René Descartes would never have been able to get beyond, or even to reach, "I think, therefore I am."[90] Moreover, the product rule often fails at performing conjunction accurately. No belief worthy of being called a belief would survive the repeated application of the product rule. Descartes would never have been able to infer his way to a belief in God.[91]

Undeniably, the point is huge. In all of daily life, we intuitively find and combine facts in countless settings. In doing so, we reject the product rule constantly. We reject it for the many inputs into "Should I marry X?" Thinkers in many fields follow suit. Imagine ten or more facts from history each believed by a historian to 0.90, which link together as the necessary elements to form a historical account. Should the historian accept that history? Yes, even though the product rule would put the combined probability around 35%. Every story from a historian consists of linked, not multiplied, beliefs.[92]

Law's Wisdom We simply must get conjunction and disjunction right, for the sake of accuracy, fairness, and efficiency. It is our tradition of blind acceptance of bivalence, in preference to employing multivalent logic, that creates the risk of doing them wrong. Bivalence's probability theory gauges the odds of a proposition being completely true rather than completely false. The product rule derives from the givens of bivalent logic and traditional probability, which include the postulate of the excluded middle and the axiom of additivity. By those givens, conjoining probabilistic propositions calls for applying the product rule.[93]

The product rule is inoperative, however, when those givens do not hold. Most tellingly, it is additivity that dictates the proper conjunction operator.[94] The product

[90] See Blackburn (1999), pp. 19–20 (explaining that Descartes's "I think" premise rests on inference from alternative possibilities: either a mind that doubts or a deception by the Evil One).

[91] See id. at 34 (reconstructing the argument as: "I have the idea of a perfect being. This idea must have a cause. A cause must be at least as perfect as its effect. So something at least as perfect as my idea caused it. Therefore such a thing exists. But the thing must be perfect, that is, God.").

[92] See infra Chap. 6 (discussing decisionmaking by historians).

[93] See Stanford Stat30 (2001) (getting from axioms to product rule through the complement rule and conditional probabilities).

[94] See Cohen (1977), pp. 34, 167–169, 220–222, 265–267; Gaines (1978), p. 157 ("both multiplication/addition, and max/min, connectives may be seen to arise from constraints on an underlying probability logic").

rule does not apply in nonadditive systems.[95] I shall show that switching from additive bivalence to nonadditive multivalence replaces the product rule with a more accurate and much less troublesome logical operator.[96]

More generally, traditional probability does not work for factfinding. Its failure to perform conjunction and disjunction accurately, when added to its failure to handle weak evidence accurately and to the failure of Bayes' theorem to aggregate evidence accurately, leads to the conclusion that it fails at every step in factfinding: from building inferences on evidence, to aggregating different evidence as proof, and finally to combining the results in order to reach an accurate decision.

Probabilism fails not only as a realistic description of how humans find facts, but also as an aspiration of how the ideal factfinder should proceed. This conclusion represents more than a fatal practical defect. The inapt concept of traditional probability also leads to the theoreticians' proposed reforms wrongly based on the aforementioned infinite possibilities and on the upcoming misimpression that the parties bear asymmetrical burdens. Law has wisely rejected those reforms and their underlying theory of probabilism.

3.2.5 *Asymmetrical Burdens*

Legal critics contend that more is at stake than producing accurate (and economically efficient) results. Conjunction aside, they attack the law's proof process on the grounds of fundamental fairness as a process and outcome value. They use probability theory again, now to argue that the playing field is not level. Most prominently,[97] they decry that plaintiffs must prove a string of elements, while defendants can succeed by disproving only one, so creating an asymmetry.

Even if criminal cases are supposed to be uneven contests, this asymmetry does look unfair in civil cases. Basically, defendants seem much better positioned than plaintiffs. Some people might argue that this favoritism is how things should be, to lighten the load on put-upon defendants. But approving a pronounced bias should await proving that the bias even exists. Various versions of the bias are asserted.

First among this set of claimed asymmetries, there is the philosopher's version of probability's problem of infinite possibilities. I refer to Hume's problem with

[95] See Gaines (1978), pp. 155–159, 161 (showing that the so-called MIN rule of fuzzy logic reduces to the product rule for independent events in a bivalent world without epistemic uncertainty, but that only the MIN rule applies in a fuzzy world).

[96] See infra Sect. 4.2.4.3 (explaining the MIN rule).

[97] See supra Sects. 3.2.2.3, 3.2.3, and 3.2.4.2 and infra Sect. 5.2 (observing other apparent disadvantages of plaintiffs); see also supra Sects. 3.2.2.3 and 3.2.4.2 (discussing defendants' supposed disadvantages, which are likewise resolved by law's adherence to multivalent logic).

induction.[98] Accumulating observations can fortify a hypothesis, but fortification can never arrive at the point of proven certainty. Meanwhile, a single observation can effectively falsify the hypothesis.[99] This situation seems to create an asymmetry between proof and disproof. The plaintiff faces a Sisyphean task, while the defendant goes for a walk in the park.

Second, the would-be logician's reaction to the conjunction paradox arises from the realization that the plaintiff must prove each of several elements, while the defendant need disprove only one. If the plaintiff fails to show any one element, he loses. If the defendant can succeed on any one element, she wins. Thus, the defendant can push many different possibilities, while the plaintiff is less likely to succeed in backing a consistent story that embraces all the elements.

Third, the lawyer's related idea, developed elegantly in a recent article, holds that any rate of adjudicative error, even if random and unbiased, will hurt plaintiffs and help defendants.[100] "As a result, the plaintiff's chances of losing the case undeservedly are much higher than the defendant's."[101] The authors contend that because a single successful denial will defeat the plaintiff who must proof a string of elements, one unfavorable mistake in factfinding will be fatal to the deserving plaintiff but not to the deserving defendant. The defendant can exploit this asymmetrical risk of error by forcing the plaintiff to settle below true value. The authors propose three shocking reforms to level the playing field: limiting defendants to a single defense for each cause of action; introducing a damage multiplier for plaintiffs who prevail at trial; or fixing all tort and contract damages at a fraction that turns solely on the single issue of the parties' comparative fault.[102]

To me, the extremist nature of these proposed cures suggests error in the diagnosis of disease. I see the triad of asymmetries as another merely theoretical problem raised by the system's assumed adherence to probabilism. Adhering instead to multivalent logic dismantles the asymmetries, as we shall see in the next chapter's reconsideration of all six of probability's problems.[103] The reconsideration will show that the law is correct in deeming the parties' burdens to be symmetrical.

---

[98] See Henderson (2018), § 1 ("The original source of what has become known as the 'problem of induction' is in Book 1, part iii, section 6 of *A Treatise of Human Nature* by David Hume, published in 1739.").

[99] See Einstein (2002), p. 109 ("Thus, a theory can very well be found to be incorrect . . . if a fact is not in consonance with one of its conclusions. But *the truth* of a theory can never be proven."). A related idea here, but one not directly pertinent to standards of proof, is Karl Popper's falsifiability: a statement, hypothesis, or theory has falsifiability (or refutability or testability) only if showing it to be false by observation is conceivable. See Thornton (2016), § 2 (situating falsifiability in Popper's thought).

[100] De Mot and Stein (2015) (arguing that repetitive chance of error by the factfinder on multiple findings unavoidably disadvantages plaintiffs).

[101] Id. at 1261.

[102] See id. at 1276–1285 (sketching proposed reforms).

[103] See infra Sect. 4.5.5 (showing how plaintiff and defendant face equivalent tasks).

3.2.6 Inapt Concept

Most importantly, traditional probability theory departs from the proof standards' purposes. The standards, as developed and deployed by the courts, never embraced the spirit of probability,[104] even though the law's agents often reverted to words of probability.[105] The law is looking more for some sort of internal conviction on the part of its factfinders in an uncertain world.[106]

The best sign of the law's position is its longstanding resistance to employing numerical terms in discussing proof. Probabilists view the law's resistance as a willful, even superstitious, reluctance to speak precisely. But choosing to think or speak in terms of numerical probabilities means abandoning any sense of epistemic uncertainty, without adding anything of interest. Why should the law care that the factfinder would view the odds as 80/20 if forced to bet on very weak evidence? The factfinder should not be called on to deliver a misleading probability for betting on a divined "real" truth. Instead, the factfinder should use the tools that are necessary for accurate factfinding.

---

[104] See Sargent v. Mass. Accident Co., 29 N.E.2d 825, 827 (Mass. 1940) (defining preponderance to require that "it is made to appear more likely or probable in the sense that actual belief in its truth, derived from the evidence, exists in the mind or minds of the tribunal notwithstanding any doubts that may still linger there"); Lampe v. Franklin Am. Trust Co., 96 S.W.2d 710, 723 (Mo. 1936) ("The trouble with [the probability instruction] is that a verdict must be based upon what the jury finds to be facts rather than what they find to be 'more probable.' . . . This means merely that the party, who has the burden of proof, must produce evidence, tending to show the truth of those facts, 'which is more convincing to them as worthy of belief than that which is offered in opposition thereto.'" (quoting Rouchene v. Gamble Constr. Co., 89 S.W.2d 58, 63 (Mo. 1935))); Anderson v. Chi. Brass Co., 106 N.W. 1077, 1080 (Wis. 1906) (saying preponderant evidence "must be such as to satisfy or convince the minds of the jury of the truth of his contention"); Leubsdorf (2015), pp. 1595–1599 (discussing early formulations of degrees of belief); Wright (2018), p. 523 ("the references in the great majority of jury instructions in the United States to persuasion, conviction or belief in the truth of the facts in issue in the particular case, based on evidence specific to that case, are inconsistent with a standard of proof based on mathematical probability").

[105] See Broun (2013), § 339 (citing many cases).

[106] Incidentally, in the absence of Bayesian legal academics, many civilian jurists speak without opposition in terms of the *intime conviction* standard, which requires a peculiarly strong belief. See Clermont (2013), pp. 221–272 (treating the comparative puzzle); Clermont and Sherwin (2002), pp. 245–251, 269–274 (questioning *intime conviction*); Schweizer (2016) (exploring the standard actually applied by civilian jurists); Stadler and Strandberg (2023), ¶ 12.009 (commenting on proposed European code); cf. Tichý (2019) (demonstrating how comparativists can talk past each other, but highlighting the difference between belief and probability).

3.3 Naked Statistical Evidence

Some law professors, as opposed to mathematicians and logicians, fault traditional probability on another ground. They do so by championing the law's seeming aversion to naked statistical evidence. They do not fault the common use of statistical studies coming in as evidence in probabilistic form. They instead make their point through a number of fairly unrealistic hypotheticals in which the probabilistic evidence, if accepted when standing alone, would produce intuitively upsetting results. We are saved seemingly by the law's anti-probabilism.

The best-known hypothetical is the blue bus paradox, based loosely on a real case.[107] The hypo involves an accident where an injured person says she was injured from behind by a bus. The Blue Bus Company with its blue buses operates 80% of the buses on that street, and the Red Bus Company with its red buses operates 20%. There is absolutely no other evidence available on identity. Should the Blue Bus Company be held liable?[108]

The law's answer would be no, although the law's answer would become yes if the sole evidence came instead from an 80%-reliable witness testifying that a blue bus hit the plaintiff. One theoretical camp refutes the seeming illogic of this distinction by imagining that statistical evidence is intrinsically different from ordinary evidence and that we should consequently treat it warily.[109] Another

---

[107] Smith v. Rapid Transit, Inc., 58 N.E.2d 754, 755 (Mass. 1945) ("The direction of a verdict for the defendant was right. The ownership of the bus was a matter of conjecture. While the defendant had the sole franchise for operating a bus line on Main Street, Winthrop, this did not preclude private or chartered buses from using this street; the bus in question could very well have been one operated by someone other than the defendant. . . . The most that can be said of the evidence in the instant case is that perhaps the mathematical chances somewhat favor the proposition that a bus of the defendant caused the accident."). The weak evidence in that case is laid out in Risinger (2022). The *Smith* court quoted Sargent v. Mass. Accident Co., 29 N.E.2d 825, 827 (Mass. 1940) (dictum) ("It has been held not enough that mathematically the chances somewhat favor a proposition to be proved; for example, the fact that colored automobiles made in the current year outnumber black ones would not warrant a finding that an undescribed automobile of the current year is colored and not black . . . ."); see also Guenther v. Armstrong Rubber Co., 406 F.2d 1315, 1318 (3d Cir. 1969) (dictum) (saying, in a case where the plaintiff had been injured by an exploding tire, that a 75-to-80% chance it came from the defendant manufacturer was not enough for the case to go to the jury). See generally Schauer (2003), pp. 79–107.

[108] An alternative is the gatecrasher paradox. It involves a rodeo with 1000 attendees, but only 499 of them paid for a ticket. The rodeo operator sues one attendee for the entry fee, and the only available evidence is that most attendees did not pay. See Cohen (1977), p. 79 (saying of the gatecrasher paradox: "An important part of the trouble seems to be that, if standards of proof are interpreted in accordance with a theory of probability that has a complementational principle for negation, the litigants are construed as seeking to divide a determinate quantity of case-merit, as it were, between them."). The paradox becomes more anguishing as the number of paid tickets decreases.

[109] See, e.g., Enoch (2021); Enoch et al. (2012), p. 199 (invoking "the powerful, uncompromising intuitions of pretty much all of [evidence] scholars" that statistical evidence differs from nonstatistical evidence, and claiming that the law conforms to that intuition).

camp views any different treatment of statistical and nonstatistical evidence as blatantly wrong.[110] Neither camp gets it right. But indeed the law does. And there is no logical problem in the law's solution.

3.3.1 Practical Hazards of Statistical Evidence

The use of mathematics as a tool of decisionmaking has been much discussed in recent years, often triggered by concerns about naked statistical evidence. The large volume of writing in the field reflects, on the one hand, the desire to enhance the objectivity and precision of judicial proof and, on the other hand, the costs of misusing, and perhaps of merely using, mathematical tools.[111]

The hazards of improper use of mathematics are illustrated in *People v. Collins*.[112] There the perpetrators of a robbery in Los Angeles were described as a white woman with her blond hair in a ponytail and a black man with moustache and beard, who were said to flee in a partly yellow automobile. The defendants, who seemed to match these descriptions, were arrested later. At trial the identification evidence was weak. So, the prosecutor tried to bolster it through the testimony of a mathematics instructor designed to show that there was but one chance in twelve million that a couple chosen at random would possess the described characteristics. The prosecutor argued to the jury in effect that there was therefore only one chance in twelve million that the defendants were innocent. The California Supreme Court reversed the conviction, holding that the mathematical testimony was inadmissible and the prosecutor's argument improper.

The hazards become more apparent upon a closer inspection of *Collins*. The mathematician testified to the product rule. Then the prosecutor suggested probabilities for the various characteristics at issue: partly yellow automobile, 1 in 10; man with moustache, 1 in 4; woman with ponytail, 1 in 10; woman with blond hair, 1 in 3; black man with beard, 1 in 10; and interracial couple in car, 1 in 1000. The product rule yielded the one-in-twelve-million figure. The most obvious error in all this was that the prosecutor picked specific probability factors for each of the specified characteristics out of the air and then asked the witness and jury to assume their accuracy without any supporting evidence. The court went on, however, to point out three additional flaws in the mathematical evidence: there was no proof of statistical independence of the six factors; the mathematical approach hid the fact that the characteristics of the true perpetrators might not have been accurately established;

---

[110] See, e.g., Guerra-Pujol (2014) (presenting Bayesian solution).

[111] To get into the widely and hotly divergent literature on this subject, one should read in order Ball (1961), Tribe (1971), Saks and Kidd (1981), Kaye (1982), Nesson (1985), and Koehler and Shaviro (1990). See generally Symposium (1986) (a 600-page symposium); Symposium (1991) (an 800-page symposium).

[112] 438 P.2d 33 (Cal. 1968).

and, all other errors aside, a one-in-twelve-million chance that a random couple would have the specified characteristics can be proven, by complicated mathematics, to mean that there was a better than 40% chance of the existence of a couple in the Los Angeles area other than the Collinses who also had those same characteristics. The court concluded that "under the circumstances the 'trial by mathematics' so distorted the role of the jury and so disadvantaged counsel for the defense, as to constitute in itself a miscarriage of justice."[113]

3.3.2 *Epistemic Nature of Statistical Evidence*

Yet even where the mathematics have not been the subject of misunderstanding, courts seem to frown upon their use in decisionmaking. And this is so even in civil cases.

Why is there this resistance to statistical evidence? Does the resistance to mathematical tools derive from an unreasonable distaste, or do valid reasons justify a preference for nonstatistical proof? To make progress, we should get behind us the matters on which most people agree.

First, we can meaningfully speak in terms of probability even about a past event, although admittedly debate persists about precisely how we should think about those probabilities. Many theorists would speak in terms of subjective probability, which measures how sure a person feels that the event occurred.

Second, resisting something characterized as statistical evidence, in pursuit of some desired benefit, will entail offsetting costs. For example, significantly raising the standard of proof for the civil proponent who necessarily relies on statistical evidence would push toward increasing overall error costs (incidentally, "proponent" here means the party having the burden of proof).

Third, but more contested, is that no real difference exists between statistical evidence and nonstatistical evidence—between evidence that 80% of the buses belong to the Blue Bus Company and eyewitness identification of a blue bus from someone who happens to have an 80% chance of testifying accurately.[114] Evidence may be more or less overtly numerical, rather than qualitative. Moreover, statistical or nonstatistical evidence may be more or less general in relation to the case, rather than particularistic. Evidence may be more or less nonsensitive (high false negatives) or nonspecific (high false positives) to the issue before the court. Any such characteristic of evidence is a matter of degree on a spectrum.[115] One might object on moral

---

[113]Id. at 41.

[114]See Broun (2013), § 210 (observing that "all evidence is statistical," and saying: "In brief, the reluctance to allow testimony or argument about probabilities must be justified, if at all, on the basis of something other than an undifferentiated claim about the logical weakness of relying on probabilities derived from statistics about other persons or things.").

[115]See id.

or policy grounds to, say, convicting someone of a crime solely on proof that he was in a small group where the overwhelming majority of the group actually were involved in committing the crime. But there is no epistemic ground on which to object.[116]

Nevertheless, there is a widely assumed or even admitted resistance among judges to statistical evidence. So, again, why? Writers justifying the resistance operate on a variety of planes ranging from the mystical to the pragmatic, with less or more convincing force. Illustrative arguments include: (1) Statistical evidence moves society away from intuition and ritual, and thus tends to dehumanize justice.[117] (2) Statistical evidence tends to yield decisions that are less acceptable and final in the eyes of the public and the parties.[118] (3) We simply want to encourage the use of nonstatistical proof because it meshes more smoothly and safely with the rest of our legal system and especially with our jury system.[119] Of these, perhaps the more expansive explanations are unnecessary, and indeed prove too much.

Surely courts should worry about and struggle against mishandling of statistical proof, and in fact judges use evidentiary and procedural mechanisms such as Evidence Rule 403[120] and jury instructions to mitigate mishandling. That is not a surprising caution, even though the caution might sometimes become excessive.

Surely, too, courts should want to encourage the introduction of more evidence than mere statistics. So it is that most, if not all, of the mysterious judicial resistance to statistical evidence manifests itself in connection with the burden of production. Usually courts say only that the proponent cannot rely solely on statistical evidence to get judgment as a matter of law and indeed that the proponent cannot rely solely on statistical evidence to get to the jury. To justify this moderate position, less dramatic explanations might suffice, as follows.

The apparent resistance to judgment as a matter of law *for* a proponent relying heavily on statistical evidence seems appropriate in a straightforward way. After all, rationally converting the statistical evidence into a factfinding represents a substantial task, at least in all but the most fanciful cases. The evidence will have to be connected up with the issue in the individualized case by a series of permissible but

---

[116] See Dahlman and Pundik (2021), pp. 334–339 (refuting the latest attempts to develop epistemic objections); Ross (2021), p. 2023 ("As we conjoin together different types of statistical evidence, it becomes increasingly incredible to suppose that a positive verdict would be impermissible.").

[117] See, e.g., Tribe (1971) (writing the classic version of this lament, in which Professor Tribe stressed not only the risk of misuse of mathematical techniques, including inaccurate meshing of numerical proof with soft or unquantifiable variables, but also the undercutting of society's values, including the dehumanization of the legal process); Zuckerman (1986), p. 508 (arguing that probabilistic assessment diminishes "the hope of seeing justice supervene in individual trials," while seeing factfinding as an individualized but value-laden process).

[118] See, e.g., Nesson (1985).

[119] See, e.g., Kaye (1982).

[120] Fed. R. Evid. 403 ("The court may exclude relevant evidence if its probative value is substantially outweighed by a danger of one or more of the following: unfair prejudice, confusing the issues, misleading the jury, undue delay, wasting time, or needlessly presenting cumulative evidence.").

uncertain inferences; also, the evidence may have to be discounted for defects in credibility; the evaluation may have to be adjusted in light of the probative value of the absence of other proof, an effect most often cutting against the proponent; and so on. In short, epistemic uncertainty would have to be accounted for, as the statistic is converted into a belief. This is a job for the jury, within the bounds of rationality. Fixing those bounds of rationality is a daunting task for the judge because it involves consideration of the relevance and reliability of the statistics as well as the party's justifications for relying so heavily thereon. Hence, it should come as no surprise that the judge is reluctant to take the case from the jury by giving judgment for the proponent as a matter of law.

More difficult to explain is the supposed willingness to grant judgment as a matter of law *against* a proponent who has to rely solely on, say, a good 60% showing of identity by statistical evidence. Limited and crude though this rule be, it appears to be the approach that most courts actually employ. Perhaps here the judge is trying to protect the notion of burden of production, which serves to facilitate early termination of weak claims or defenses, to safeguard against irrational error, and to effectuate other process and outcome values.[121] After all, any plaintiff could try to introduce some numerical evidence of a general and nonsensitive and nonspecific nature, such as that 60% of like plaintiffs win, in the hope that the jury might give a verdict for this plaintiff. Perhaps the judge harbors a special fear of the jury's mishandling of statistical evidence when undiluted by other admitted evidence—fear of an unreasoned verdict for the proponent based either on prejudice without regard to the evidence or, less likely, on undue deference to the statistics. To avoid such an outcome, and to ensure that the burden of production means something, the judge would require sufficient evidence of certain kinds, which must be nonnumerical and particularistic and sensitive and specific, at least in the absence of very special circumstances.

Once the proponent clears this production-burden hurdle, the proponent can use statistical evidence to supplement the sufficient nonstatistical evidence, subject to the normal rules of evidence.[122] That is very telling. There is no across-the-board prohibition on the admissibility of statistical evidence. Statistical evidence is not deemed to be special in nature.

The factfinder gives the proponent's statistical evidence its full effect as supplemental evidence. That effect might be considerable or negligible (or even nonexistent), depending on the nature of the statistical evidence. Gauging the effect is a tough job. The evidence should be explained in the clearest and most accurate way possible, after which it is for the factfinder to decide what level of belief it induces.

[121] See infra Sect. 5.2.1.1 (explaining why the burden of production deserves protection).

[122] Cf. Kansas v. Glover, 140 S. Ct. 1183, 1190 (2020) (using statistics to supplement observational evidence that had established a reasonable suspicion). For what turns out to be the doable task of combining statistical and nonstatistical evidence, see infra Sect. 4.6.3.

3.3.3 Legal Treatment of Statistical Evidence

In sum, the courts' only special rule for statistics seems to be that naked statistical evidence normally will not work to carry the proponent's burden of production. The value of that burden's role, coupled with the ease of the proponent's manufacturing a statistic, justifies this special rule. Also, the rule has the incidental advantage of defusing, albeit arbitrarily, most of the discomfiting paradoxes of hypothetical cases built on statistical evidence—including the blue bus paradox.

This approach accords with the treatment of certain other kinds of evidence that do not by themselves suffice to avoid summary judgment against the proponent or to get to the jury. To satisfy the burden of production, the proponent cannot rely on the opponent's failure to testify,[123] on mere disbelief of the opposing testimony,[124] or on demeanor evidence drawn from opposing witnesses.[125] However, any of these kinds of evidence is perfectly proper to introduce as a supplement to positive evidence that satisfies the burden of production.[126]

It turns out, then, that the law's responses to naked statistical evidence do not really pose a logical problem at all.[127] No appeal to multivalent logic is necessary to justify the law.

3.4 Probability's Solutions to Probability's Problems

A voluminous legal literature uses traditional probability theory to raise logical problems with the evidential proof process. This book takes on the significant task of showing that the real problem lies in the invocation of traditional probability, not in the prevailing legal process.

Accordingly, this chapter has surveyed traditional probability's massive problems in analyzing evidential proof. The root cause turns out to be that traditional probability can account only for the uncertainty that comes from random variability. It buries the much more important uncertainty that comes from lack of knowledge.

[123] See Stimpson v. Hunter, 125 N.E. 155, 157 (Mass. 1919) ("The failure of the defendant and of his son to testify although present in court was not equivalent to affirmative proof of facts necessary to maintain the action.").

[124] See Cruzan v. N.Y. Cent. & Hudson River R.R. Co., 116 N.E. 879, 880 (Mass. 1917) ("Mere disbelief of denials of facts which must be proved is not the equivalent of affirmative evidence in support of those facts.").

[125] See Dyer v. MacDougall, 201 F.2d 265, 268–69 (2d Cir. 1952) (holding that although demeanor evidence is probative, it does not suffice to escape a summary judgment).

[126] See, e.g., Baxter v. Palmigiano, 425 U.S. 308, 316–20 (1976) (treating failure to testify as supplemental evidence in a civil case).

[127] See Brook (1985). But cf. Allen (2021), p. 257 (dismissing the problem largely because it involves "weird hypotheticals").

Am I the first to see this shortcoming? Of course not. Many probability theorists have perceived the problem of neglected epistemic uncertainty and so have adjusted their approach.[128] They have brilliantly solved the problem by refining the axioms of probability.

Their work is classified as nontraditional probability. Going down one of three paths, some of the nontraditionalists have created so-called *logical probability*.[129] Here falls the innovative work of Keynes[130] and of Carnap.[131] Their ideas were foreshadowed by the work of the early American logician Charles Sanders Peirce (1839–1914),[132] were significantly elaborated by Gärdenfors and Sahlin[133] among many others, and were recently revitalized by Dale Nance.[134] Their ideas

---

[128] See Hedden and Colyvan (2019), pp. 466–467 ("[T]he legal probabilist has more resources at her disposal than critics appreciate. For example, the legal probabilist need not interpret probabilities as relative frequencies or subjective degrees of confidence, but can instead interpret probabilities as degrees to which the evidence supports a given claim, which will be sensitive to the explanatory considerations emphasised by opponents of legal probabilism. And the legal probabilist can make room for imprecise probabilities and refuse to endorse sharp, precise probability thresholds for the various standards of proof.").

[129] See Hájek (2019), § 3.2.1 ("Indeed, the logical [probability] interpretation, in its various guises, seeks to encapsulate in full generality the degree of support or confirmation that a piece of evidence *e* confers upon a given hypothesis *h* . . . . In doing so, it can be regarded also as generalizing deductive logic and its notion of implication, to a complete theory of inference equipped with the notion of 'degree of implication' that relates *e* to *h*.").

[130] Keynes (1921), p. 71 (adding the nonnumerical notion of the "weight of the evidence" to the traditional probability measure).

[131] Carnap (1950), pp. 554–555.

[132] See Hartshorne and Weiss (1932), p. 421 ("to express the proper state of belief, not *one* number but *two* are requisite, the first depending on the inferred probability, the second on the amount of knowledge on which that probability is based" (quoting from Peirce's collected papers)).

[133] See Gärdenfors and Sahlin (1983) (introducing a decision theory that accounts for second-order uncertainty by a measure of "epistemic reliability"); Gärdenfors and Sahlin (1982) (similar).

[134] See Nance (2016), pp. 1–14 (arguing for adding a measure of Keynesian weight, which turns on the completeness of evidence, to the usual standards of proof that look to the discriminatory power of the evidence). The very insightful Professor Nance has long worked in this area and made major contributions along the way. His book nonetheless speaks in terms of probabilities and accepts the conjunction paradox as a problem. See id. at 74–78. Since then, however, Nance has taken to speaking in terms of belief functions rather than probabilities, like me. See Nance (2019), p. 75 ("It is understandable for legal theorists to attempt to make use of Shafer's theory and its willingness to embrace non-Bayesian belief functions."). And he has lately used multivalent logic's possibility theory to resolve the conjunction paradox. See Nance (2018), p. 1036 ("If one thinks of *A* and *B* as the elements of the claim, *C*, then [possibility theory's MIN rule] provides a potential solution to the so-called conjunction paradox . . . . [W]hether that standard [of proof] has been met as to the claim, *C*, can be determined entirely by assessing whether it has been met as to each of *A* and *B*.").

The minor remaining difference from my theoretical outlook lies in his distaste for my formulation of the higher standards of proof. See infra Sect. 5.2.3.2. My formulation of higher standards is similar, but not equivalent, to Nance's. He would define the higher standards in terms of elevated ratios of *Bel(a)* to *Bel(not-a)*. See Nance (2019), pp. 64–68, 74–75. But see Meester (2020) (refuting Nance). Theorists have long spoken of ratios, but the law has always resisted their vision. So, although Nance's stating the clear-and-convincing standard as, say, $Bel(a) > 2 \bullet Bel(not\text{-}a)$ might

coalesce around the notion of supplementing probability statements with some equivalent of a higher-order probability statement. Yet, without also jettisoning bivalence, these theories require mental gymnastics that go far beyond the capabilities of the law and its factfinders. Only with great effort can any theorist use logical probability to arrive at multivalent logic's conclusions. That is, at least for law, logical probability is a clumsy way to get to the results of multivalent logic.[135]

The most comprehensible elaboration of nontraditional probability is *imprecise probability*.[136] This modern field of mathematics provides a useful extension of probability theory whenever information is conflicting, contradictory, or scarce. Its basic idea is to use interval specifications of probability, with a lower and an upper probability. Bounding the probabilistic estimate with a lower and a higher bound was a major contribution, one that would be picked up by the even more modern logic called possibility theory.[137] Despite its name, imprecise probability is more complete and accurate in the real world than precise traditional probability. In fact, traditional probability appears as a special case in imprecise probability, if additivity is assumed.

Related but quite distinguishable is the *inductive probability* pioneered by the absolutely brilliant but almost impenetrable work of Oxford philosopher L. Jonathan Cohen in 1977, entitled *The Probable and the Provable*.[138] For inspiration, he looked to the law as an exemplar of practical reasoning. He then constructed, on the basis of inductive reasoning, a whole new system of inductive (or Baconian)

---

have some theoretical advantages, the current law does not employ such a standard. That is, speaking in terms of ratios does not accord with accepted legal language and sense. *See* Clermont (2013), pp. 30–31 (explaining ratio approach in criminal context). One reason for the law's approach might be that ratios fail to invoke the factfinder's considerable powers of relative judgment, but rather depend on absolute judgment of likelihood. See infra Sect. 4.3.4.1 (discussing relative and absolute judgment). Also, ratios would lead to quantification of beliefs and maybe to talk of probabilities. Still another reason is that actually speaking of ratios would necessitate a major shift, and a lot more detail, in the current judicial instruction to juries. The required ratio simply could not be communicated to, or understood by, factfinders without a considerable risk of wild mistake on their part.

His call for reform further invents a separate role for the judicial gatekeeper, who should stop a case from going to the factfinder unless, foggily, the completeness of evidence "has been practically optimized by the parties' presentation." Nance (2019), p. 74. I would deal with that concern, as the law does, by the judge's weighing any evidential inadequacies when applying the usual tests for judgment as a matter of law, judicial notice, and like procedures.

[135] See, e.g., Weatherson (2003), p. 112 (arguing that, "where we have little or no evidence for or against p, it should be reasonable to have low degrees of belief in each of p and ¬p").

[136] See generally Walley (1990); Bradley (2019), § 1 ("Among the reasons to question the orthodoxy, it seems that the insistence that states of belief be represented by a single real-valued probability function is quite an unrealistic idealization . . . ."); Genin and Huber (2020), § 3.2.

[137] See infra Sect. 4.2.4.2 (describing multivalent logic's possibility theory).

[138] Cohen (1977), p. 121 (avowedly abandoning probability's axioms, formulating a nonadditive "probability" system, terming his approach "inductive probability," but using imagery that is difficult to grasp). By the way, some versions of logical probability are also confusingly called inductive probability. See Hawthorne (2018).

probability as an alternative to traditional (or Pascalian) probability and its standard axioms. His exercise justified what the law was doing: the law searches for the provable rather than the probable.

Inductive probability measures the strength or informativeness of the evidence in supporting a conclusion.[139] It looks not only at the evidence presented, but also at the evidence not presented, making evidential completeness a significant criterion. The inductive probability of a conclusion can be measured against the strength of the evidence supporting a rival conclusion. For example, a legally found fact could rest on the strength of the evidence supporting the plaintiff's position compared to the strength of the evidence supporting its opposite (not its complement).[140]

Cohen further argued that the alternative of importing traditional probability into the project, including the product rule, produces a whole series of anomalies. To avoid some of the anomalies, his conjunction rule for inductive probability is this: "The conjunction of two or more propositions . . . has the same inductive probability . . . as the least" likely conjunct, because "betting odds" are inapplicable to "unsettlable issues."[141]

All this is simple enough to describe. The obscurities arise when Cohen goes on to systematize a complete logical syntax for his system.[142] His book, I now see after multiple rereadings, constitutes a sophisticated proof of what I had independently formulated in the roughly equivalent but more understandable terms of multivalent logic. I am able to make modest advances on Cohen's work because he was thinking and writing when fuzzy logic was just getting off the ground.[143] Multivalent logic's great leaps forward lay in the future. Multivalent logic would have greatly facilitated his work. But that his conclusions nevertheless accord with mine gives me great reassurance.

These three groups of nontraditional probability are significant. Many readers of this book will find they cannot bring themselves to migrate to multivalent logic, or do not wish to. But they do not have to do so in order to agree with this book's conclusions. They can stick with probability. But they will have to engage probability at a deeper level than traditional probability, which is just too simplistic for the task of understanding evidence and proof.

This book offers an alternative to mastering nontraditional probability theories. Its original contribution is to take a step back from all of probability to show that the problems arise from probability's underlying logic system (bivalent logic), as well as

---

[139] See Cohen (1977), pp. 199–216.

[140] See id. at 252–255. Cohen equates proof beyond a reasonable doubt to elimination of all reasonable inconsistent scenarios. See id. at 249; cf. id. at 255–256 (contemplating the requirement of a high level of inductive probability).

[141] Id. at 89–91, 220–222, 265–267 (concluding that the conjunction of two or more propositions follows the MIN rule: "In sum, the plaintiff proves his over-all case on the balance of probability if, and only if, he thus proves each of his component points.").

[142] See id. at 229–244. A nice, short explanation of inductive probability, along with a sense that the way forward requires abandonment of bivalence, appears in Scolnicov (2000), pp. 287–289.

[143] See infra Sect. 4.2.4.1 (describing multivalent logic's fuzzy logic).

from traditional probability's underlying assumptions (excluded middle and additivity). The cure then lies in retracting those assumptions in order to utilize a more general logic system (multivalent logic).

Multivalent logic is widely accepted and highly developed, but no one has applied it to the relatively mundane tasks of evidence and proof. This book does so. The next chapter will demonstrate that the six much-lamented probabilistic problems of the evidential proof process turn out to reveal the law's wisdom: the law knew to reject probabilism. The chapter after next will show how one should reason from pieces of evidence to the proof of a conclusion, a thought process that incredibly has never been cracked by theory and so has heretofore been left to unguided intuition.

References

Allen RJ (2021) Naturalized epistemology and the law of evidence revisited. Quaestio Facti 2:253–284

Allen RJ, Jehl SA (2003) Burdens of persuasion in civil cases: algorithms v. explanations. Mich St Law Rev 2003:893–944

Allen RJ, Pardo MS (2019) Relative plausibility and its critics. Int J Evid Proof 23:5–59

Anderson T, Schum D, Twining W (2005) Analysis of evidence, 2nd edn. Cambridge University Press, New York

Ball VC (1961) The moment of truth: probability theory and standards of proof. Vand Law Rev 14: 807–830

Baronett S (2019) Logic, 4th edn. Oxford University Press, Oxford

Bennardo K (2013) A quantity-driven solution to aggregate grouping under the U.S. Sentencing Guidelines Manual. Fla St Univ Law Rev 40:791–852

Bergman P, Moore A (1991) Mistrial by likelihood ratio: Bayesian analysis meets the f-word. Cardozo Law Rev 13:589–619

Binmore K (2017) On the foundations of decision theory. Homo Oeconomicus 34:259–273

Blackburn S (1999) Think. Oxford University Press, Oxford

Bradley S (2019) Imprecise probabilities. In: Zalta EN (ed) Stanford encyclopedia of philosophy. https://plato.stanford.edu/entries/imprecise-probabilities/

Brilmayer L (1986) Second-order evidence and Bayesian logic. Boston Univ Law Rev 66:673–691

Brilmayer L, Kornhauser L (1978) Review: quantitative methods and legal decisions. Univ Chicago Law Rev 46:116–153

Brook J (1985) The use of statistical evidence of identification in civil litigation: well-worn hypotheticals, real cases, and controversy. St Louis Univ Law J 29:293–352

Broun KS (gen ed) (2013) McCormick on evidence, vols 1 & 2, 7th edn. Thomson/West, St Paul

Brown WM (1983) The economy of Peirce's abduction. Transact Charles S. Peirce Soc 19:397–411

Bub J (1997) Interpreting the quantum world. Cambridge University Press, Cambridge

Callen CR (1982) Notes on a grand illusion: some limits on the use of Bayesian theory in evidence law. Ind Law J 57:1–44

Carnap R (1950) Logical foundations of probability. University of Chicago Press, Chicago

Cheng Edward K (2013) Reconceptualizing the burden of proof. Yale Law J 122:1254–1279

Cheng E (2018) The art of logic in an illogical world. Basic Books, New York

Clermont KM (2012) Aggregation of probabilities and illogic. Georgia Law Rev 47:165–180

Clermont KM (2013) Standards of decision in law: psychological and logical bases for the standard of proof, here and abroad. Carolina Academic Press, Durham NC

Clermont KM (2023) A theory for evaluating evidence against the standard of proof. Penn St Law Rev 127:345–374

Clermont KM, Sherwin E (2002) A comparative view of standards of proof. Am J Comp Law 50: 243–275

Cohen LJ (1977) The probable and the provable. Clarendon Press, Oxford

Colyvan M (2008) Is probability the only coherent approach to uncertainty? Risk Anal 28:645–652

Dahlman C, Kolflaath E (2021) The problem of the prior in criminal trials. In: Dahlman C et al (eds) Philosophical foundations of evidence law. Oxford University Press, Oxford, pp 287–300

Dahlman C, Pundik A (2021) The problem with naked statistical evidence. In: Dahlman C et al (eds) Philosophical foundations of evidence law. Oxford University Press, Oxford, pp 332–345

Dahlman C et al (eds) (2021) Philosophical foundations of evidence law. Oxford University Press, Oxford

De Mot J, Stein A (2015) Talking points. Univ Ill Law Rev 2015:1259–1286

Dorf M (2012) Is the First Circuit's opinion in the DOMA case insufficiently "fuzzy"? http://www.dorfonlaw.org/2012/06/is-first-circuits-opinion-in-doma-case.html. Accessed 19 Dec 2021

Dummett M (1978) Is logic empirical? In: Truth and other enigmas. Harvard University Press, Cambridge, pp 269–289

Edelman PH (2002) On legal interpretations of the Condorcet jury theorem. J Legal Stud 31:327–349

Eggleston R (1983) Evidence, proof and probability, 2nd edn. Weidenfeld and Nicolson, London

Einstein A (2002) Induction and deduction in physics. In: The collected papers of Albert Einstein (trans: Engel A), vol 7. Princeton University Press, Princeton, pp 108–109

Enoch D (2021) How to theorize about statistical evidence (and really, about everything else): a comment on Allen. Quaestio Facti 2:285–298

Enoch D, Spectre L, Fisher T (2012) Statistical evidence, sensitivity, and the legal value of knowledge. Philosophy Public Affairs 40:197–224

Finkelstein MO, Fairley WB (1970) A Bayesian approach to identification evidence. Harv Law Rev 83:489–517

Franklin J (2015) The science of conjecture: evidence and probability before Pascal, 2nd edn. Johns Hopkins University Press, Baltimore

Gaines BR (1978) Fuzzy and probability uncertainty logics. Info Cont 38:154–169

Gärdenfors P, Sahlin N-E (1982) Unreliable probabilities, risk taking, and decision making. Synthese 53:361–386

Gärdenfors P, Sahlin N-E (1983) Decision making with unreliable probabilities. Br J Math Stat Psychol 36:240–251

Genin K, Huber F (2020) Formal representations of belief. In: Zalta EN (ed) Stanford encyclopedia of philosophy. https://plato.stanford.edu/entries/formal-belief/

Greenberg MJ (2007) Euclidean and non-Euclidean geometries: development and history, 4th edn. WH Freeman, New York

Guerra-Pujol E (2014) Visualizing probabilistic proof. Wash Univ Jurisprud Rev 7:39–75

Hájek A (2019) Interpretations of probability. In: Zalta EN (ed) Stanford encyclopedia of philosophy. https://plato.stanford.edu/entries/probability-interpret/

Harel A, Porat A (2009) Aggregating probabilities across cases: criminal responsibility for unspecified offenses. Minn Law Rev 94:261–310

Hartshorne C, Weiss P (eds) (1932) Collected papers of Charles Sanders Peirce: pragmatism and pragmaticism, vol 2, 3rd edn. Harvard University Press, Cambridge MA

Hawthorne J (2018) Inductive logic. In: Zalta EN (ed) Stanford encyclopedia of philosophy. https://plato.stanford.edu/entries/logic-inductive/

Hedden B, Colyvan M (2019) Legal probabilism: a qualified defence. J Polit Philosophy 27:448–468

Henderson J, Bertram F, Tõke MJ (1995) Optimal issue separation in modern products liability litigation. Tex Law Rev 73:1653–1699

Henderson L (2018) The problem of induction. In: Zalta EN (ed) Stanford encyclopedia of philosophy. https://plato.stanford.edu/entries/induction-problem/
Ho HL (2008) A philosophy of evidence law: justice in the search for truth. Oxford University Press, New York
Iuliano J (2014) Jury voting paradoxes. Mich Law Rev 113:405–427
Jaffee LR (1985) Of probativity and probability: statistics, scientific evidence, and the calculus of chance at trial. Univ Pittsburgh Law Rev 46:925–1082
Kaplan J (1968) Decision theory and the factfinding process. Stan Law Rev 20:1065–1092
Kaye D (1979) The laws of probability and the law of the land. Univ Chicago Law Rev 47:34–56
Kaye D (1982) The limits of the preponderance of the evidence standard: justifiably naked statistical evidence and multiple causation. Am B Found Res J 1982:487–516
Kaye DH (1991) Credal probability. Cardozo Law Rev 13:647–656
Keynes JM (1921) A treatise on probability. Macmillan, London
Koehler JJ, Meixner JB (2015) Decision making and the law: truth barriers. In: Keren G, Wu G (eds) The Wiley-Blackwell handbook of judgment and decision making, vol 2. Wiley-Blackwell, Hoboken, pp 749–774
Koehler JJ, Shaviro DN (1990) Vertical verdicts: increasing verdict accuracy through the use of overtly probabilistic evidence and methods. Cornell Law Rev 75:247–279
Kosko B (1990) Fuzziness vs. probability. Int J Gen Syst 17:211–240
Kotz S, Stroup DF (1983) Educated guessing: how to cope in an uncertain world. Marcel Dekker, New York
Laudan L (2007) Strange bedfellows: inference to the best explanation and the criminal standard of proof. Int J Evid Proof 11:292–306
Lempert R (1986) The new evidence scholarship: analyzing the process of proof. Boston Univ Law Rev 66:439–477
Lempert RO (1977) Modeling relevance. Mich Law Rev 75:1021–1057
Leubsdorf J (1978) The standard for preliminary injunctions. Harv Law Rev 91:525–566
Leubsdorf J (2015) The surprising history of the preponderance standard of civil proof. Fla Law Rev 67:1569–1619
Levmore S (2001) Conjunction and aggregation. Mich Law Rev 99:723–756
Lindell B (2017) Multi-criteria analysis in legal reasoning. Elgar, Cheltenham UK
Lombardero DA (1996) Do special verdicts improve the structure of jury decision-making? Jurimetrics J 36:275–324
Martin AW, Schum DA (1987) Quantifying burdens of proof: a likelihood ratio approach. Jurimetrics J 27:383–402
McGrayne SB (2011) The theory that would not die. Yale University Press, New Haven
Meester R (2020) Classical probabilities and belief functions in legal cases. Law Prob Risk 19:99–107
Miceli TJ (2017) The economic approach to law, 3rd edn. Stanford University Press, Redwood City
Michael J, Adler MJ (1931) The nature of judicial proof. Ad Press, New York
Moran DA (2003) Jury uncertainty, elemental independence and the conjunction paradox: a response to Allen and Jehl. Mich St Law Rev 2003:945–953
Nance DA (1986) A comment on the supposed paradoxes of a mathematical interpretation of the logic of trials. Boston Univ Law Rev 66:947–952
Nance DA (2016) The burdens of proof: discriminatory power, weight of evidence, and tenacity of belief. Cambridge University Press, Cambridge
Nance DA (2018) Formalism and potential surprise: theorizing about standards of proof. Seton Hall Law Rev 48:1017–1038
Nance DA (2019) Belief functions and burdens of proof. Law Prob Risk 18:53–76
Nesson C (1985) The evidence or the event? on judicial proof and the acceptability of verdicts. Harv Law Rev 98:1357–1392
O'Malley KF, Grenig JE, Lee WC (2011) Federal jury practice and instructions: civil, vol 3, 6th edn. Thomson/West, St. Paul MN

Pardo MS (2009) Second-order proof rules. Fla Law Rev 61:1083–1113
Pardo MS (2015) Group agency and legal proof; or, why the jury is an "it.". William & Mary Law Rev 56:1793–1858
Pardo MS (2019) The paradoxes of legal proof: a critical guide. Boston Univ Law Rev 99:233–290
Pardo MS (2021) Grounding legal proof. Philosophical Issues 31:280–298
Park RC, Saks MJ (2006) Evidence scholarship reconsidered: results of the interdisciplinary turn. Boston College Law Rev 47:949–1031
Pennington N, Hastie R (1981) Juror decision-making models: the generalization gap. Psychol Bull 89:246–287
Politzer G, Bonnefon J-F (2009) Let us not put the probabilistic cart before the uncertainty bull. Behav Brain Sci 32:100–101
Porat A, Posner EA (2012) Aggregation and law. Yale Law J 122:2–69
Redmayne M (1999) Standards of proof in civil litigation. Modern Law Rev 62:167–195
Risinger DM (2013) Searching for truth in the American law of evidence and proof. Georgia Law Rev 47:801–835
Risinger DM (2022) Off the rails: the surprising story of Smith v. Rapid Transit, Inc.. https://ssrn.com/abstract=4295311. Accessed 10 Jan 2023
Ross LD (2021) Legal proof and statistical conjunctions. Phil Stud 178:2021–2041
Rowe TD, Sherry S, Tidmarsh J (2020) Civil procedure, 5th edn. Foundation, St. Paul MN
Rysiew P (2016) Epistemic contextualism. In: Zalta EN (ed) Stanford encyclopedia of philosophy. https://plato.stanford.edu/entries/contextualism-epistemology/
Saks MJ, Kidd RF (1981) Human information processing and adjudication: trial by heuristics. Law Soc Rev 15:123–160
Savage LJ (1954) Foundations of statistics. John Wiley, New York
Schauer F (2003) Profiles, probabilities, and stereotypes. Belknap Press, Cambridge MA
Schauer F, Zeckhauser R (1996) On the degree of confidence for adverse decisions. J Legal Stud 25: 27–52
Schum DA (1986) Probability and the processes of discovery, proof, and choice. Boston Univ Law Rev 66:825–876
Schwartz DS, Sober ER (2017) The conjunction problem and the logic of jury findings. William & Mary Law Rev 59:619–692
Schweizer M (2016) The civil standard of proof—what is it, actually? Int J Evid Proof 20:217–234
Schwitzgebel E (2015) Belief. In: Zalta EN (ed) Stanford encyclopedia of philosophy. https://plato.stanford.edu/entries/belief/
Scolnicov A (2000) On the relevance of "relevance" to the theory of legal factfinding. Israel Law Rev 34:260–301
Shafer G (1986) The construction of probability arguments. Boston Univ Law Rev 66:799–816
Shapira RA (1998) Economic analysis of the law of evidence: a caveat. Cardozo Law Rev 19:1607–1634
Solum LB (2004) Procedural justice. Southern California Law Rev 78:181–321
Sood AM (2021) What's so special about general verdicts? questioning the preferred verdict format in American criminal jury trials. Theor Inq Law 22:55–83
Spottswood E (published as Mark) (2016) Unraveling the conjunction paradox. Law Prob Risk 15: 259–296
Stadler A, Strandberg M (2023) General and procedural issues. In: Stadler A et al (eds) European rules of civil procedure: a commentary on the ELI/UNIDROIT model rules. Elgar, Cheltenham UK, pp 252–306
Stanford Stat30 (2001) More probability. https://web.stanford.edu/class/stat30/indep/stark.htm. Accessed 5 Sept 2023
Stein A (2001) Of two wrongs that make a right: two paradoxes of the evidence law and their combined economic justification. Tex Law Rev 79:1199–1234
Suber P (1997) Non-contradiction and excluded middle. https://legacy.earlham.edu/~peters/courses/logsys/pnc-pem.htm. Accessed 18 Dec 2021

Symposium (1986) Probability and inference in the law of evidence. Boston Univ Law Rev 66:377–952
Symposium (1991) Decision and inference in litigation. Cardozo Law Rev 13:253–1079
Thornburg EG (1998) The power and the process: instructions and the civil jury. Fordham Law Rev 66:1837–1893
Thornton S (2016) Karl Popper. In: Zalta EN (ed) Stanford encyclopedia of philosophy. https://plato.stanford.edu/entries/popper/
Tichý L (ed) (2019) Standard of proof in Europe. Mohr Siebeck, Tübingen Germany
Tillers P (2001) Introduction: a personal perspective on "artificial intelligence and judicial proof". Cardozo Law Rev 22:1365–1380
Tillers P (2011) Trial by mathematics—reconsidered. Law Prob Risk 10:167–173
Tribe LH (1971) Trial by mathematics: precision and ritual in the legal process. Harv Law Rev 84:1329–1393
Twining W (2006) Rethinking evidence, 2nd edn. Cambridge University Press, New York
Van Cleave R (2019) Sudden, forced, and unwanted kisses in the #MeToo era: why a kiss is not "just a kiss" under Italian sexual violence law. Univ Detroit Mercy Law Rev 96:627–658
Vick SG (2002) Degrees of belief. American society of civil engineers. ASCE Press, Reston
Walley P (1990) Statistical reasoning with imprecise probabilities. Springer, New York
Weatherson B (2003) From classical to intuitionistic probability. Notre Dame J Formal Logic 44:111–123
Wilce A (2017) Quantum logic and probability theory. In: Zalta EN (ed) Stanford encyclopedia of philosophy. https://plato.stanford.edu/archives/spr2017/entries/qt-quantlog/
Wright RW (2018) Haack on legal proof. Estudios Filosóficos 67:517–528
Zamir E, Teichman D (2018) Behavioral law and economics. Oxford University Press, Oxford
Zuckerman AAS (1986) Law, fact or justice? Boston Univ Law Rev 66:487–508

Chapter 4
Multivalent Beliefs

Nier l'existence des sentiments tièdes parce qu'ils sont tièdes, c'est nier le soleil tant qu'il n'est pas à midi. La vérité est tout autant dans les demi-teintes que dans les tons tranchés.
—Gustave Flaubert (Gustave Flaubert, Correspondance: Première Série (1830–1846), at 417 (1926) (Gustave Flaubert to his mistress Louise Colet, December 11, 1846) ("To deny the existence of lukewarm sentiments because they are lukewarm is to deny the sun when it is not at noon. Truth lies as much in shadings as it does in vivid tones."). This epigraph captures the essence of multivalent logic. See also Helprin (2017), p. 184 ("[A] paradox was more the statement of two contradictory propositions, both of which, nevertheless, were true. That two contending propositions could be correct was for Jules rather easy to accept in that it was an almost ordinary facet of music, and part of what gave music its escape from worldly friction in its ability to embrace even the starkest contradictions.").)

Abstract Classical logic and its supplement of traditional probability fail to account for the epistemic uncertainty that prevails in the real world. The reason is that bivalence allows representation of only two additive measures, truth and falsity. A more general logic system could enable representation of what we do not know. Degrees of belief based on multivalent logic would allow representation of how much we believe a fact, how much we disbelieve it, and how much we are in the dark as to it—while still being a valid logic system. This long chapter concludes that, in the presence of epistemic uncertainty, multivalent beliefs provide an excellent way to understand evidence and proof both in theory and as applied in legal factfinding.

Section 4.1: As a descriptive and normative matter, the legal factfinder concerns itself with degrees of belief based on the evidence presented. The law already conforms to this conception, allowing it to proceed accurately without puzzles or paradoxes in its factfinding and allowing me to avoid calling for radical reform. Section 4.2: The underlying multivalent logic comprises a group of valid logic systems, such as fuzzy logic and possibility theory. They are more general than classical logic, in that they do without the classical assumption that all propositions

K. M. Clermont, *A General Theory of Evidence and Proof*, Law and Philosophy Library 148, https://doi.org/10.1007/978-3-031-66552-3_4

are either true or not true. Section 4.3: Belief function theory delivers a multivalent concept whose imagery best captures and illuminates legal factfinding. A degree of belief can coexist with a degree of disbelief produced by the evidence, that is, a degree of belief in the opposite of the fact. Moreover, the factfinder facing epistemic uncertainty can leave some of its belief uncommitted when forming the degree of belief the fact is true and the degree of belief the fact is false. Combining belief functions' imagery with multivalent logic's operators, a very defensible move, yields "multivalent belief theory," a very expressive system. Section 4.4: Competing theories such as inference to the best explanation, relative plausibility, and ranking theory turn out to act in the same way as multivalent belief theory. But they lack an equivalent fit with legal imagery, an equivalently strong theoretical foundation, and an equivalent ability to dispel the problems of probability. Section 4.5: Multivalent beliefs manage to resolve all of traditional probability's problems that stem from its failure to account for epistemic uncertainty. Multivalent beliefs give a more realistic representation of human factfinding, handle weak evidence on both sides, dissipate the difficulty of infinite possibilities nimbly, provide accurate tools for aggregating uncertain evidence and combining established facts, resolve the apparent asymmetries in the treatment of plaintiffs and defendants, and capture conceptually what we intuitively think of as adequate legal proof. Section 4.6: Multivalent beliefs are the appropriate measure whenever, for the sake of accuracy, the decisionmaker needs to keep track of epistemic uncertainties in addition to any aleatory uncertainty. For example, legal factfinders must hold both kinds of uncertainty in mind when making and combining their findings. Section 4.7: The line of argument in support of multivalent belief theory can be recapitulated as a small series of simple and fairly unassailable steps.

The big drawback of classical logic and its traditional probability is their failure to account for epistemic uncertainty. A major contribution of multivalent logic is to provide a way to represent the epistemic uncertainty that prevails in the real world and, thereby, to instruct on how to handle that uncertainty.

4.1 Degree of Belief Rather Than Probability

Multivalent logic will prompt us to look at beliefs, uncommitted belief, and disbeliefs. But before getting to the details of multivalent logic, we need an understanding of the concept of partial belief.

4.1.1 Truth and Knowledge

On occasion to this point, I have used "belief" to characterize the output of evidence processing. Was that appropriate? Philosophy is of assistance here, even if philosophers like to start upstream. They might pick up my inquiry at the "correspondence theory," which states that what goes on in our heads should correspond to an external reality.[1] The law seemingly buys into this theory as an assumption.[2] This assumption allows me to put aside most of the mountain of articles on the subject of truth and thereby narrow my search for the truth about truth.

What is "truth" then, for my purposes? Truth is the condition where a statement accurately reflects that external world.[3] Thus, a statement is true if and only if it corresponds to the reality it describes.[4]

What is "knowledge"? As Plato classically put it, knowledge is a justified true belief.[5] "Justification" lies in having reasons in evidence and logic for the belief.[6] We know something if and only if we are justified in believing it and also it is true.[7] For Plato, belief, if unadorned by the adjectives "justified and true," is mere opinion.

Is evidential proof aimed at either certain truth or full knowledge? No, they are unattainable in the legal world, even if we frequently say one aim of the legal process

---

[1] See Newman (2002), p. 1 ("The simplest version of the correspondence theory of truth is that a proposition or a sentence is true when it corresponds to an appropriate fact, which is something in the world that makes a proposition or a sentence true."); David (2015).

[2] See Ho (2008), p. 55 ("That primary facts exist as external realities is a basic assumption that renders the purpose of a trial intelligible."); Risinger (2013), p. 811 ("The shared assumptions of the standard rationalist model allowed (and continue to allow) both practitioners and the vast majority of descriptive academics to skip over many issues that might interest professional philosophers, entering the discourse concerning truth at a point where thorny epistemological issues have been resolved by assumption, since such controversies are unimportant to the law as a practical discipline. As a practical matter, we assume the reality of an exterior material world; arguing either radical skepticism or the primacy of some form of philosophical idealism will not cut any ice in a courtroom."); cf. Clermont (2013), p. 136 (discounting the coherence theory as a competitor to the correspondence theory in legal theory).

[3] See Mosteller (2014) (discussing various definitions of truth); David (2015), § 2.3 (similar).

[4] See David (2015), § 3 ("*x* is true iff *x* corresponds to some fact").

[5] See Ichikawa and Steup (2017), § 1 ("There are three components to the traditional ('tripartite') analysis of knowledge."); Steup (2005), § 1 (treating knowledge as the subject of epistemology); cf. Pardo (2015), pp. 1812–1814 (explaining that for knowledge, the justified true belief cannot be accidentally true, following Gettier (1963)). But see Ichikawa and Steup (2017), § 11 (discussing the knowledge-first view of Williamson (2000) that knowledge is a fundamental state not subject to further analysis); Moss (2018) (arguing that probabilistic beliefs can constitute knowledge).

[6] See Steup (2005), § 2 (elaborating justification).

[7] There cannot be knowledge without truth. See Plato (c 369 BCE), 201b–c ("Socrates: Then when judges are justly persuaded about matters which one can know only by having seen them and in no other way, in such a case, judging of them from hearsay, having acquired a true opinion of them, they have judged without knowledge, though they are rightly persuaded, if the judgement they have passed is correct, have they not?"); Pardo (2015), p. 1812 ("an agent's knowledge of *X* requires that *X* be true").

is knowing the truth.[8] Legal proof of past fact, for example, proceeds mainly by inductive logic.[9] Accumulating observations can fortify a hypothesis, but can never verify a fact to the point of proven certainty. Of course, this situation troubled David Hume no end.[10] Yet this situation causes the law no worry because the law does not seek or demand certain truth or full knowledge.[11]

Now, I am not veering off into postmodernism, where objective truth can become irrelevant or cease to exist.[12] The law does value truth in factfinding, but realizes that it will never get completely there. Retaining a veritistic even if not veracious goal, the law must find a way to operate practically in the pursuit of truth, acting upon less than certainty. In sum, although knowledge is not a concern of law, truth still is.[13]

4.1.2 *Belief*

Instead of a justified true belief, the law demands only a justified belief in truth.[14] The law recognizes that a justified belief in truth is the best it can do.

This "belief" has a special meaning. In its modern sense, Plato notwithstanding, belief means the mental acceptance of a statement as true, because it meets some

---

[8]E.g., Fed. R. Evid. 102 ("These rules should be construed so as to administer every proceeding fairly, eliminate unjustifiable expense and delay, and promote the development of evidence law, to the end of ascertaining the truth and securing a just determination."). But this usage is obviously aspirational, rather than philosophically technical. See Risinger (2013), pp. 802–817 (explaining how the law's Rationalist Tradition buys into truth as an aim, while it nevertheless accepts probability as a way of acknowledging uncertainty). Nevertheless, there are rare attempts to argue that criminal and civil standards of proof both call for the factfinder's unqualified or categorical assertion of a belief in truth. E.g., Ho (2008); Whiteley (2021).

[9]See Anderson et al. (2005), p. 100 ("In analyzing the available evidential data and identifying and marshaling the inferences that those data support in preparing for trial, the lawyer relies primarily on inductive reasoning."); Wigmore (1937), § 9 (same).

[10]See supra Sect. 3.2.5 (introducing Hume's problem with induction).

[11]See Cohen (1977), pp. 351–356 (rejecting Hume's skepticism as applied to legal factfinding); Risinger (2013), p. 811 ("In [law], we assume that knowledge (or something counting as knowledge) about past events is possible, even if it is not perfect. Platonic arguments about how perfection is necessary to the concept of true knowledge are beside the point.").

[12]See Allen and Leiter (2001), p. 1492 (lamenting "the unfortunate fascination in some quarters of the legal academy with 'postmodern' conceptions of knowledge and truth, conceptions notable for their superficiality and for the fact that almost no philosophers subscribe to them" (footnote omitted)).

[13]See Enoch et al. (2012), pp. 211–215 (arguing that law's primary interest is accuracy, not knowledge); Sayid (2021) (arguing that in law there is no general norm that facts must be "known").

[14]See Ho (2008), pp. 89–110 (describing justified belief as the epistemic requirement, with truth as the measure of correctness).

standard of strength.[15] It is not firm knowledge. Although such a belief does not require solid truth, it is still not a New Age idea or a subjective sensation. It is not a squishy personal feeling.

Moreover, the law requires its factfinders to "justify" their belief. A belief must rest on the factfinder's attempt to express the state of the real world, as represented in the evidence gathered before it by a reasonable means and processed logically.[16] To justify this manner of justification, the law embraces naturalized epistemology. This branch of epistemology incorporates the social sciences' learning on individuals' mental processing under social influence.[17] Naturalized epistemology justifies beliefs that were produced by a reliable means to seek truth.[18] Does the law employ a reliable means? Yes, somewhat,[19] but legal factfinding's methods have always been a bit peculiar in two regards.[20]

---

[15] See Ichikawa and Steup (2017), § 1.2 (elaborating belief); Moss and Schwab (2019), pp. 2–3 ("[T]here is nowadays a widely accepted notion of belief as the generic attitude of taking something to be the case or taking something to be true. 'Taking' here refers not to a provisional attitude, but to one of endorsement or commitment."). But compare Christensen (2004), pp. 12–13, 69 (saying that some people use "belief" as an unqualified or categorical assertion of truth), with Cohen (1991), p. 479 (using "belief," for his purposes, in the sense of a "passive feeling," and arguing that factfinders should deal instead in acceptance), and Ferrer (2006), p. 294 ("the proof of *p* should be explained in terms of its acceptability (and not simply of its acceptance)").

[16] See Haack (2014b), p. 54 ("[The] standards of proof should be understood, *not* as a simple psychological matter of the degree of jurors' belief, but as primarily an epistemological matter, the degree of belief *warranted by the evidence*."); Jaffee (1985), p. 937 (saying that the preponderance standard "is intended to assure that the factfinder will not believe an assertion of fact without evidence *adequate in logic and experience* to support the belief").

[17] See Goldman (1986), p. 5 ("The multidisciplinary conception of epistemology I like to call *epistemics*, to distinguish it from other, more autonomous, conceptions of the field."); see also Allen and Leiter (2001), pp. 1493–1501 (explaining an empirically based naturalized epistemology in the context of the law of evidence and contending that "naturalized epistemology provides a fruitful way of understanding evidence law"); Pardo (2015), pp. 1810–1816 (extending the theory's reach to group factfinding); Steup (2005), § 6.2 (describing extreme and moderate versions of naturalized epistemology). An alternative route to relaxing the standards for knowledge lies in the recent emergence of contextualism. See Rysiew (2016), § 1.

[18] Classical epistemology treats a belief as justified "when it is reasonable or rational, from *S*'s own point of view, to take *p* to be true. According to evidentialism, what makes a belief justified in this sense is the possession of evidence." Steup (2005), § 1.1. Nonclassical epistemology, like naturalized epistemology, "conceives of the role of justification differently. Its job is to ensure that *S*'s belief has a high objective probability of truth and therefore, if true, is not true merely because of luck. One prominent idea is that this is accomplished if, and only if, a belief originates in reliable cognitive processes or faculties. This view is known as *reliabilism*." Id.; see Allen and Leiter (2001), pp. 1494–1495 (discussing Goldman's reliabilism).

[19] See, e.g., Clermont and Eisenberg (1992), p. 1154 ("Apparently, judge trial and jury trial combine to operate a decisionmaking system that is, at least in [its ability to treat like cases alike], highly reliable."); Metzloff (1991) (showing trial system's usual competence and fairness by an empirical comparison of medical malpractice verdicts and insurers' pretrial evaluations).

[20] See Chappell (2013), § 7.6 ("Plato seems to offer two incompatible explanations of why the jury don't know: first that they have only a limited time to hear the arguments (201b3, 172e1); and second that their judgement is second-hand (201b9).").

First, the law demands a decision now. It cannot leave decision for another day. Other disciplines can leave a question open, or call a result statistically insignificant, and await more evidence and greater certainty to emerge. But legal actors (and all of us in our daily lives) often must form a belief for immediate decision. The belief will be a tentative one, in that it will rest on evidence that is imperfect at the time decision must be made. This quality of tentativeness disqualifies the belief from any strict status of truth.

Second, the law depends on the parties to present the evidence to the factfinder, especially American law. Accordingly, the legal factfinder decides by making a choice based on the two sides' support of belief and disbelief in the proponent's position. While the factfinder's resulting belief in truth is justified within its limited scope, it is merely a relative belief. This quality of relativity also disqualifies the belief from any strict status of truth.

4.1.3 Degree of Belief

A tentative and relative belief may not even be a belief, at least in a categorical sense of mental acceptance of a fact as true. Even if the legal process could yield categorical beliefs, they would not serve the law's purposes adequately. The starkest illustration would be the inability to deal with a party who presents reasonable yet weak evidence and who nevertheless proves a case perceptibly stronger than the opponent's.

There is a way out. A legal factfinder can arrive at "degrees of belief" that measure the strength of acceptance and rejection of the truth of the fact, a degree of truth based on the evidence put before it by a reasonable means and logically and reliably processed.[21] Even when the fact is yes or no, the factfinder's beliefs, given an uncertain world, are a matter of degree of sureness. Belief is divisible.

Perhaps one might be more comfortable characterizing a degree of belief as a measurable inclination to believe. Philosophers sometimes phrase degrees of belief as credences[22] or, better, as partial truths or beliefs.[23] So I want to move from concerns about the notion of belief to exploration of the law's focus on *justified*

---

[21] See Huber (2009), p. 1 (exploring generally the new thinking on degrees of belief, and saying: "Degrees of belief formally represent the strength with which we believe the truth of various propositions. . . . For instance, Sophia's degree of belief that it will be sunny in Vienna tomorrow might be .52, whereas her degree of belief that the train will leave on time might be .23. The precise meaning of these statements depends, of course, on the underlying theory of degrees of belief."); cf. Haack (2014a), p. 13 (describing her epistemology as "gradational," resulting in degrees of "warranted belief").

[22] See Buchak (2014).

[23] See Ho (2008), pp. 124–129 (discussing categorical and partial beliefs); Frankish (2009).

partial beliefs in truth.[24] But, again, this suggested move does not mean that the law is accepting a quasi-belief in lieu of truth. Truth still matters. Moreover, I stay within the range of formal models of belief in truth that are accepted as rational and coherent.[25] "Broadly speaking, these models capture something important about how an ideally rational agent would manage her epistemic life."[26]

Let me be clearer. For my purposes, I am defining a degree of belief (or a multivalent belief) as a measure of the belief in *x* (or *Bel(x)*) that equals the factfinder's estimate of the *degree to which the affirmative of fact* x *has been fully proved by reliable means*, or the "degree of verification."[27] Multivalent logic provides the way to express the degree on a scale running from 0 to 1. The factfinder can then utilize this scale in describing the state of the proof.

As we shall see, a multivalent degree of belief can coexist with the multivalent degree of disbelief, that is, a belief in what I call the opposite of the fact. The complement of *Bel(x)* is the degree to which *x* has not been fully proved (or 1 − *Bel (x)*); it is not the degree to which *not-x* has been fully proved (or Bel(not-x)). Because we are dividing up the full capacity for belief, the degree of disbelief cannot exceed the complement of *Bel(x)*.

Moreover, the factfinder can withhold part of its belief, leaving belief uncommitted to an extent dependent on the quality of the evidence and reflective of unknowns. Any uncommitted belief conveys the epistemic uncertainty, and it causes the degrees of belief and disbelief to add to less than one. Thus, multivalent degrees of belief and disbelief are nonadditive and nonprobabilistic.

This scheme gives a sense of why Professor Cohen's foundational book distinguished "provability" from probability.[28] Unarguably, multivalent beliefs and traditional probabilities both exist. But they are different measures with different uses. A 0.40 degree of belief in a fact's truth represents proof to 40% of full knowledge. It is not a 40% chance of the fact being revealed as true. The latter measure would be the probability of the fact's turning out randomly to be truth, assuming that there were a way to discern the certain truth. Deciding how to proceed in a world of persisting uncertainty (by using multivalent beliefs) differs logically from predicting the outcome into which uncertainty would randomly resolve itself (by using traditional probabilities).

A deeper understanding of the difference can come from thinking about how the factfinder would shift from a multivalent view to a bivalent view. Assume the factfinder has formed degrees of belief and disbelief in an uncertain fact. Even

---

[24] See Shafer (1976), p. 20 (defining the factfinder's belief as an act of judgment "that represents the degree to which he judges that evidence to support a given proposition and, hence, the degree of belief he wishes to accord the proposition"); Shafer (1986), pp. 801–804 (developing a constructive interpretation of probabilistic reasoning that is neither too objective nor too personalistic).

[25] See Genin and Huber (2020), §§ 3.2–.3 (treating belief functions and possibility theory).

[26] Id. at 1.

[27] Dernoncourt (2011).

[28] See supra Sect. 3.4 (discussing his *The Probable and the Provable*).

with very little information in hand, the factfinder could still bet on the outcome.[29] To do so, the factfinder would need to formulate the odds of having uncovered the true outcome if it were to be somehow revealed, formulating the odds by performing one of the variety of transforms out of the credal (from the Latin for belief) stage and into the pignistic (from the Latin for betting) stage.[30] Rather than still leaving some belief uncommitted, the factfinder must allocate all its belief between the two possible outcomes of true and false, thereby committing more belief to p and more belief to $1-p$.[31] This transform process might involve the nature of the particular epistemic uncertainties and might invoke the factfinder's attitudes toward risk and loss, helping to make the proper transform method quite contestable and complicated. In any event, this transform process means retaining no measure of epistemic uncertainty about the allocation and treating all uncertainty as aleatory. Recall that traditional probability buries all epistemic uncertainty and reflects only aleatory uncertainty.

The big point is this: you can bet with very little information in hand, but you must allocate all belief between the two possible outcomes in order to place your bet. Upon the transformation from a belief, the resulting betting odds would normally fall somewhere in that middle range of previously uncommitted belief between belief and disbelief. Accordingly, degrees of belief in a fact and traditional probabilities normally differ in magnitude, with the former being smaller than the latter on a scale running from 0 to 1.

To sum up the difference for factfinding, a degree of belief is the proof-based fractional share of one's full belief that one attributes to a proposition's truth, while traditional probability is a fairly strange construct altogether different. Probability reports the truth in terms of the approximate number of times the proposition would be revealed as true if the scenario were to repeat 100 times—or what odds would make truth and falsity equally attractive to someone betting on revelation. People use "probability" loosely for any sort of uncertainty. They might use it to express a degree of belief, but it is inappropriate for that purpose. Therefore, beliefs and probabilism are not interchangeable concepts, even though people tend to treat them so.

---

[29] See Haenni (2009), p. 129 (discussing betting probabilities); cf. Shafer (1990a), pp. 475–476 (describing betting probability in more complicated settings).

[30] See Cobb and Shenoy (2003) (discussing transform methods); Smets (2005) (discussing difficulties of the transform); cf. Smith (2010), pp. 503–505 (discussing the transform as applied to vague concepts). For a simple example of a transform, proportional normalization will scale up the belief and the disbelief proportionately so that together they add to one; however, it is crude in that it treats all epistemic unknowns as the same. Or, less defensibly, half of the uncommitted belied could go to true and half to false. Either way, if belief exceeds disbelief, the odds of truth exceed 50%.

[31] *See* Huber (2009), p. 11 ("Subjective probabilities require the epistemic agent to divide her knowledge or belief base into two mutually exclusive and jointly exhaustive parts: one that speaks in favor of *A* and one that speaks against *A*. That is, the neutral part has to be distributed among the positive and negative parts. Subjective probabilities can thus be seen as [Dempster-Shafer] belief functions without ignorance.").

4.1.4 Law's Choice

The choice for legal factfinding is whether to deal in probabilities of truth or degrees of belief in truth. The choice is one of wise policy, based on which measure will better handle the task at hand.

What turns on this subtlety between degree of belief and probability of truth? Plenty. First, the two measures invoke different vocabularies and thoughts. Jurists tend to speak in terms of a strong-enough belief on the part of the factfinder, while Bayesian academics invoke traditional probabilist terminology. Second, the two measures differ in magnitude. Because of uncommitted belief, the degree of belief in a fact will normally be smaller than the probability of the fact. Third, multivalent beliefs account for epistemic uncertainty. Traditional probabilities do not. Fourth, as we shall see, the two measures entail different "mathematics." Multivalent degrees of belief registering epistemic uncertainty combine in ways very different from how bivalent predictions of perfect knowledge combine. Fifth, beliefs avoid the many logical and practical problems that probabilities create. Those problems stem from burying epistemic uncertainty.

Admittedly, legal factfinding could choose to deal in probabilities of truth. The factfinder could take an extra step with the case's uncertainty, by allocating the uncommitted belief to either true or false, albeit doing so while largely in the dark. As we have already seen, this extra step would clash with judicial instructions and introduce many problems. Moreover, not only is there no accepted way to allocate uncommitted belief other than by hunch, but also the extra step would not add anything. Transforming into odds would add nothing of value to the factfinder's report on belief of the fact.[32] Instead, that extra step would destroy the sense of those uncertainties that multivalent beliefs carry. The bettor's odds are thus less accurate, posing tangible difficulties when the need arises to combine multiple findings.

Therefore, the legal factfinder should concern itself with degrees of belief based on the evidence presented. The factfinder as a rational agent should act with a keen awareness of how much is unknown. The factfinder should decide by comparing its sureness in the fact to its sureness in the fact's opposite. The degrees of belief and disbelief could be below 0.50, even when added together. The factfinder should accept *a* as a legal truth if it believes *a* more than actively believing *not-a*. The factfinder should close its eyes to the odds for betting on unattainable truth.

Amazingly, the law and its factfinders already conform to this belief-based conception, and they do so expressly. They choose to seek a degree of belief in truth, not a certain truth or the odds of certain truth, as I shall show. They deal with factual beliefs in a world that will remain uncertain, not with the odds of how the facts would turn out if and when they become certain. The law asks only for a comparative sureness measure to be applied to the factfinder's multivalent beliefs. This multivalent approach allows factfinding to proceed accurately.

---

[32] See Kerkvliet and Meester (2016), pp. 138, 149 (saying, compared to traditional probability, "that we lose nothing by working with belief functions, and that belief functions only add flexibility").

The legal approach fits multivalent belief theory so well because the law intuitively knew what it was doing all along. It chose to follow the sound lessons of multivalent logic long before multivalent logic was a thing.[33] Therefore, the law's current approach to evidence and proof needs no drastic reconception or reform.

4.2 Nonclassical Logic

Reassuringly, then, the common law has evolved over the centuries toward the method of factfinding supported by multivalent logic. None of this is to say that one must carry all the logical theory around in one's head. To apply the standards of proof properly, the factfinder need only listen to the law's simple instructions.

As someone aiming to establish the law's factfinding wisdom, however, I must get into the logic. The initial step is to realize that many different systems of logic exist, which vary in effectiveness for any particular setting.[34] The way a logician builds a system is to assume a basic representation of the world, then stipulate a small group of operators that suffices to generate an internally sound and complete logic system, and finally test the system to see if its theorems make sense of our world and hence can be useful. Logic is therefore more of an art, around the edges, than the laity would guess.

There is nothing bizarre about logic's method. Any intellectual construct proceeds by making basic assumptions in the form of postulates, axioms, and operators. The constructs that result will survive if their theorems are useful. Examples of these constructs are probability and geometry.[35] But the resulting theorems are true only hypothetically. The constructs produce truth only if their assumptions hold true.

4.2.1 Logic Systems

More specifically, the logician creates a logic system by assuming a minimal set of "self-evident truths" that provide a basic representation of the world;[36] then stipulating a small but adequate group of "operators," such as conjunction, disjunction, and negation, to generate an internally sound and complete logic system;[37] and

---

[33] For an explanation of law's evolution toward making this choice, see supra Sect. 1.1.2.

[34] This realization is called logical pluralism. See Russell and Blake-Turner (2023).

[35] See supra Sect. 3.2 (discussing geometry).

[36] See Sider (2010), pp. 46–47, 72–73. These truths are often called postulates or axioms. Such statements are considered to be self-evident, or clear, distinct, and undoubtable, and so can be assumed to be true without any proof or demonstration.

[37] See id. at 9–11, 25, 35–37, 67–80 ("Say that a set of [operators] is *adequate* iff all truth functions can be symbolized using sentences containing no connectives not in that set.").

finally testing the new logic system to see if it produces "genuine logical consequences" that make pragmatic sense of our world to us.[38]

At this point, the critical analytic step is to admit that our standard logic is not a brooding omnipresence in the sky, part of the natural order. No, it is a useful tool, built on certain assumptions. The logician must begin with some truths, or basic assumptions about the world. Make other assumptions, and you have a different tool.

For our purposes, the key assumption of classical logic is that every proposition must be either true or not true, an assumption called the law of the excluded middle.[39] The stimulus for rethinking is that this assumption is an odd one to adopt if you want to think about handling evidence in a proof system that regularly produces interim outputs falling between true and false (e.g., element *a* is likely true and element *b* is very likely true). An alternative logic seems in order:

> If we're not careful [classical] logic pushes us to extremes, so if we want to avoid adopting extreme positions all the time we have to do something more human. A human approach is more nuanced than that. It turns out that our brains are able to process gray areas in subtle ways that don't seem entirely logical but do seem to make sense. Rather than use logic to push out the sense, we should find the logic inside the human nuances.[40]

Later, I shall explore how analysis would run if we indeed adopted as a postulate that things can be partly true. The resulting logic system would give different answers than classical logic on very practical problems that the law must confront, such as combining inferences, evidence, and findings. But those new answers, I shall maintain, would be the right answers.

Anyway, back in classical logic, its key assumption of the excluded middle, rather hidden from view, has a huge impact. We are commonly unaware of the assumptions on which our reasoning rests, to say nothing of their effects. So, uncovering the impact of classical logic's encoding facts in binary form, rather than as partial truths, is no easy task. Because the impact derives from an underlying assumption, I cannot merely point out some obviously mistaken logical step in traditional analysis. Understanding the impact will necessarily be the more subtle endeavor of tracing the misleading effects of an implicit assumption.

Whether you finally agree or disagree with my conclusion, acknowledging the subtlety of tracing the impact of an assumption should at least restrain the reader from dismissing my argument out of hand. Conceivable counterarguments, such as saying that common sense obviously dictates multiplying probabilities of uncertain facts, should be put aside for the time being.

---

[38] See id. at 1–2, 4–11, 72–73 ("The question of whether a given formal system represents genuine logical consequence is a philosophical one . . . ."); Gómez-Torrente (2018) ("As it turns out, it is very hard to think of universally accepted ideas about what the generic properties of logical truths are or should be.").

[39] See Sider (2010), pp. 72–73; supra Sect. 3.1 (explaining the law of the excluded middle).

[40] Cheng Eugenia (2018), p. 191.

4.2.2 Logic Operators

The logician constructing any system of logic must stipulate a small but adequate number of logical operators, such as set theory's intersection (or propositional logic's conjunction or $\wedge$ or AND), union (or disjunction or $\vee$ or OR), and negation (or ~ or $\neg$ or NOT).[41]

Classical bivalent logic, which recognizes only the two values of true and false, stipulates the following functions for conjunction and disjunction:

$$\text{truth}(x \text{ AND } y) = 1 \text{ if both } x \text{ and } y \text{ are true, but 0 otherwise}$$

$$\text{truth}(x \text{ OR } y) = 1 \text{ if either } x \text{ or } y \text{ is true, but 0 otherwise}$$

Another way to state these two functions is this:

$$\text{truth}(x \text{ AND } y) = \text{minimum}(\text{truth}(x), \text{truth}(y))$$

$$\text{truth}(x \text{ OR } y) = \text{maximum}(\text{truth}(x), \text{truth}(y))$$

A different format in which to stipulate an operator is by truth table. The one for negation in Fig. 4.1 indicates that the negative of 1 is 0, and vice versa.

Those three operators generate an internally sound system that is complete. All things bivalently logical flow from them.

Fig. 4.1 Negation truth table

~	
1	0
0	1

[41] See Sider (2010), pp. 25, 35–37, 67–80. Set theory provides the mathematical tools to study formal languages and treats collections of objects, so that object *o* can be a member of set *A*. See id. at 12–24. Propositional logic is a formal language that treats variables stated as propositions and studies what can be truthfully inferred from them. See id. at 25–28.

4.2.3 Logic Testing

The logician can employ a logic system by applying its group of operators to its other assumptions and prior theorems. Its output will be internally sound and complete on a formal level, but it will not be useful unless the resulting theorems make sense in our world as we understand it. What "makes sense" translates into the philosophical question of whether the theorems constitute "genuine logical consequences." But philosophers have to punt on this question, saying that the assumptions make sense if their consequences appear to make sense to us.

There are many signs that classical bivalent logic makes a lot of sense. For example, it plays nicely with traditional probability theory. This mathematical tool supplements classical bivalent logic, allowing it to reflect aleatory uncertainty. Traditional probability can express the chance of whether an event has occurred or will occur this particular time, all the while assuming that it occurs, or not, on an all-or-nothing basis. The likelihood of an event implies the complementary likelihood of its nonoccurrence. Betting odds, like 60/40, carry that implication because, under the bivalent assumption, whatever turns out to be not true will be false. Moreover, for combining probabilistic propositions, probability's Bayes' theorem and product rule make sense too.

Classical bivalent logic will break down, nonetheless, when the law of the excluded middle no longer holds—as in the task of factfinding. The evidential proof process investigates a world that is not a two-valued world where disputed facts are either true or false. There is much that we do not know. Humans can accurately represent some things in the world, such as uncertain past fact, only as partial truths. We might never learn whether a disputed fact is certainly true or false, so that any absolute truth remains inaccessible to factfinders' minds.

Moreover, a good portion of the factfinders' task in the real many-valued world, where partial truths exist, is vague and imprecise. Factfinders might properly find that Tom was a 0.60 tortfeasor given what he certainly did, in contrast to finding a 60% chance that he did what would certainly make him a tortfeasor. The nature of tortious behavior is vague. Again, the law must concern itself with partial truths, which comprise the degrees of belief that factfinders construct in a world of varied uncertainty.

In other words, classical bivalent logic fails the testing for factfinding. Versions of nonclassical logic can handle partial truths, however. So they test well in the real world for the task of factfinding.

4.2.4 Multivalent Logic

Nonclassical logic often looks and sounds much like standard logic, but has altered some classical assumptions (and so requires slightly different operators to make sense). At bottom, nonclassical logicians are arguing that their logic makes more sense than classical logic in certain circumstances. "There are many reasons to get interested in nonclassical logic, but one exciting one is the belief that classical logic is *wrong*—that it provides an inadequate model of (genuine) logical truth and logical consequence."[42] Most commonly, the argument is that classical logic, by assuming the excluded middle, assumes one too many truths for use in some practical areas.

Among the nonclassical versions of logic that reject the assumption of an excluded middle, multivalent logic comprises the versions of special interest to lawyers.[43] These multivalent forms of logic boldly decline the simplification offered by two-valued, or bivalent, logic built on a foundation of true/false. They instead recognize partial truths. They are valid logic systems.[44] They are more general than classical logic, as they will yield classical logic as a special case if an excluded middle is re-assumed. This book will use them, for the exemplar of law, to demonstrate that classical logic indeed can be "wrong" and multivalent logic in particular can be "right."

This multivalent logic may be relatively new, but it has an extended history of forerunners. Troubled thinkers have introduced threads of it since before the time when Aristotle embraced bivalence.[45] Multivalent logic has enjoyed a recent flowering, perhaps inspired by the development of quantum mechanics.[46] Indeed, by its central feature of partial truths, so that a fact can be partly true and partly false at the same time, multivalent logic might seem to be the Schrödinger's cat of logic systems. On the one hand, multivalent logic thereby offers a less conflictual and more conciliatory approach to legal problems than classical logic's dichotomia provides. On the other hand, if propositions are not bivalent, so that both x and *not-x* can be true and false to a degree, then one can show that sometimes x equals *not-x*—which seems a rather disquieting contradiction. Fashioning modern multivalent logic thus faced some challenges, which have been overcome during the last half century.

The easiest examples of the effectiveness of multivalent logic come from vague terms like "tall." In a bivalent world, with crisp terminology, a person would be either tall or short. With multivalence, we can describe a person as exhibiting a degree of tallness. But multivalent logic is in no way limited to vagueness.[47] It can

---

[42] Id. at 72.

[43] See generally Priest (2008); Gottwald (2015). The multivalent logic that is the subject of this book—nonadditive multivalent logic—rejects as assumptions the postulate of the excluded middle and the axiom of additivity. Not all multivalent systems, which by definition accept more than two truth values, meet these criteria.

[44] Dissenters exist, of course. Most prominent, perhaps, is Haack (1996). She dismisses multivalent logic as unnecessary (because classical systems can be twisted to the difficult tasks) and unsound (because truth does not come in degrees). See also Haack (2014c), pp. 294, 302 ("*truth itself isn't relative, doesn't come in degrees, and doesn't decompose into parts*," which she infers from her "definition that a belief is true if it is a belief that '*p*' and *p*, but false if it is 'a belief that *p*' and –*p*" (quoting Ramsey (1991), p. 11)). I do not contend that multivalent logic is necessary, but only that it is the best tool for factfinding. Herein I do contend, at length, that partial truths exist as I define them, making multivalent logic a sound alternative to her bivalent logic.

[45] See Brulé (1985) (recounting the history briefly).

[46] See Malinowski (2007); supra Sect. 3.2 (discussing quantum mechanics).

[47] See Bělohlávek et al. (2002), p. 575 (stressing the broad reach of fuzzy logic, which is a type of multivalent logic).

handle any sort of variable, from vague concepts all the way to sureness about the truth of a past fact.

What does tallness have in common with whether the light was red? Both propositions are unknowable with precision. The limits on natural language sometimes impede us in describing, and indeed in thinking about, a person's height. Meanwhile, a past event cannot be retrieved perfectly, because once an event passes into the past it becomes inaccessible.[48] Tallness and redness entail different sources of epistemic uncertainty, but they both evade perfect knowledge in the classical sense. The power of multivalent logic lies in its giving us a measure for expressing all the relevant kinds of uncertainty, that is, giving us a measure of how far we fall short of perfect knowledge. Therefore, even for a past event, one can express a multivalent belief in truth, just as one can vaguely express tallness.[49]

If not for the reach of multivalent logic, past facts would have to be treated as yes/no—even though they actually appear to the investigator not as true or false, but instead as something falling between completely true and completely false. Traditional probability does not suffice. Here is a neat fact pattern, supposedly true, which a logician used to express how multivalent logic fulfills the factfinder's needs:

> Consider Albert Einstein. As the great physicist lay dying, he uttered a sentence just before he passed away. Einstein had dying words. He spoke them in his native tongue, German, the language in which he was by far the most comfortable expressing himself. Unfortunately, he passed away in New Jersey and the only person who heard him was a nurse who spoke no German. So, we will never know what Einstein's last words were. But there is a fact of the matter. There is a sentence which is the last one ever spoken by Einstein. That's a truth of the world; it's just a truth we're unable to know. What was Einstein's final thought on Earth? Any claim that it was some particular sentence is either true or false. But there is a difference between what it is and what we know about it. Three-valued [or multivalent] logic does not seem apt for describing what is, but it does seem appropriate for talking about our knowledge—and our lack thereof.[50]

The factfinder, in practice, can adjudge facts as partly true and partly false. Without sleight of hand and with full allegiance to logic, the law can reject bivalence in favor of multivalence for the purposes of factfinding. Legal factfinding should, can, and does measure a partial belief as established by the evidence, instead of measuring the probability of bivalent truth.

---

[48] See, e.g., United States v. Copeland, 369 F. Supp. 2d 275, 287 (E.D.N.Y. 2005) ("There is no certainty. 'Time is irreversible, events unique, and any reconstitution of the past at best an approximation.'" (quoting Maguire et al. (1973), p. 1), aff'd, 232 F. App'x 72 (2d Cir. 2007); Muller (2016) (developing a theory that time, like space, is expanding and that "now" is the leading edge of the new time); Emery et al. (2020).

[49] See Smith (2010), p. 494 (contending that "uncertainty-based degrees of belief and vagueness-based degrees of belief" must be treated as equivalents).

[50] Gimbel (2016), pp. 530–531.

4.2.4.1 Fuzzy Logic

One multivalent bloom known as fuzzy logic finds its roots in the seminal 1965 article by Berkeley computer scientist Lotfi Zadeh.[51] His critical contribution was to use degrees of membership in a *fuzzy* set, in place of classically strict membership in a *crisp* set classified as no/yes.[52] Yet fuzzy logic is not at all a fuzzy idea. It became a formal system of logic, one that is by now highly refined and hence rather rarefied.

Fuzzy logic measures element x's degree of membership in a particular fuzzy set. The degree may take any value throughout the whole interval [0,1], rather than just the value of 0 or 1. This range allows a more complete and accurate expression of membership, when membership is imprecise.

Take as an example the set A of men from five to seven feet tall. This would be a crisp set. Membership of x in A, represented by $\chi_A(x)$, is not vague. The values of χ_A can be only 0 or 1, at least if we ignore complications at the nanoscale level.

Contrast the set H of men somewhere near six feet tall. It is a fuzzy set. Membership of x in H, represented by $\mu_H(x)$, is imprecise. The values of μ_H may start at 0 for a tiny person, but they soon increase by some function to a value of 1 at precisely six feet, and then start decreasing. The membership function could be linear, although it can take on any shape.

So shortish Tom might be completely in set A but have a degree of membership in set H of 0.30. Figure 4.2 represents these two sets, with graph (a) representing the crisp set of men from five to seven feet tall and graph (b) being one representation of the fuzzy set of men somewhere near six feet tall.

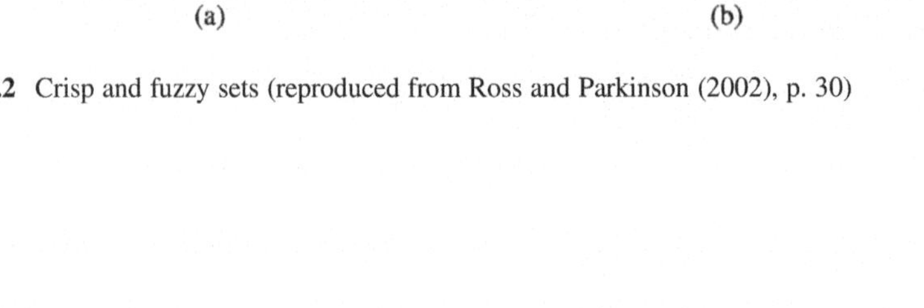

Fig. 4.2 Crisp and fuzzy sets (reproduced from Ross and Parkinson (2002), p. 30)

[51] Zadeh (1965); see Dubois et al. (2007), p. 432.

[52] See Hajek (2010) (discussing the varying versions of fuzzy logic). Fuzzy logic also comes as a version of propositional logic. See Bellman and Giertz (1973), pp. 151–152 (showing the equivalence between fuzzy sets and fuzzy statements); Cintula et al. (2017); Ross and Parkinson (2002) (linking fuzzy propositional logic and fuzzy set theory).

Fuzzy logic better comports with our view of the real world than does bivalent logic. In the real world, boundaries of things often appear indistinct, thus making important or even essential the human ability to process fuzzy information. Better or not, fuzzy logic definitely gives a different measure than probability. Think of a somewhat sloppily drawn circle: Is it more appropriate to say (i) there is a 90% probability that it is a perfect circle or (ii) it has a 0.90 membership in the set of circles?[53]

Fuzzy logic is a very useful tool for some purposes. Of course, it has become so well-known because of its countless practical applications, especially in consumer electronics, control engineering, and artificial intelligence where analysts have to deal with the real world. But its theory is wonderfully broad, extending easily to assessing likelihood of facts.[54]

The way to apply fuzzy logic to legal factfinding is to envisage the set of facts proved as true and ask in regard to x, a particular element of a claim or an affirmative defense, what is its degree of membership in that set. Recall that membership represents how much a variable is in the set. The membership here will be partial. One could express $\mu(x)$ as truth(x). It will tell how much the factfinder believes the element to have been fully proven. Membership thereby creates degrees of truth, or what I have been calling degrees of belief.

Fuzzy set imagery thus allows us to speak of beliefs in terms of a likelihood that a fact is true and a complementary likelihood that it is false.[55] Nevertheless, because it handles epistemic uncertainty by not excluding the middle, fuzzy logic remains a nonadditive system.[56] The epistemically uncertain degree of membership in a fuzzy set finds expression in what is called an ultrafuzzy set (or a type-2 fuzzy set, which operates as an initial step toward type-n fuzzy sets and operates in contrast to the type-1 fuzzy set that is just two-dimensional).[57] Basically, representation of the uncertainty in the degree of membership comes out in a third dimension from the degree of membership represented in two dimensions.[58] The multivalent logical operators must become much more complicated to account for ultrafuzziness.[59]

[53] See Kosko (1993), pp. 44–46 (using this image).

[54] Of course, scholars in other disciplines are finding all kinds of uses for fuzzy logic. See, e.g., Ragin (2017), p. 47 (describing fuzzy-set/qualitative comparative analysis, a new but accepted social-science method developed to combine case-oriented and variable-oriented analysis, in which the coding is done by fuzzy variables rather than crisp ones, and observing: "With fuzzy sets, logical AND is accomplished by taking the minimum membership score of each case in the sets that are intersected.").

[55] See Clermont (2013), p. 187; Ross and Parkinson (2002), p. 33 (showing how complementarity is opposition in fuzzy logic).

[56] See Ross and Parkinson (2002), pp. 33–34. See generally Wygralak (1996).

[57] See, e.g., Jablonowski (2008).

[58] See Mendel (2007), p. 20. The third dimension can be projected back into the two dimensions to create the footprint of uncertainty (or FOU, which I mention just to suggest how cool the terminology in this field gets).

[59] See Karnik and Mendel (2001); see also MacFarlane (2010), p. 453 n.13; Mendel (2009).

However, here there is no reason to explore the sophistication of logical operators for ultrafuzzy sets, because when the law speaks in fuzzy terms it treats beliefs simply as two-dimensional type-1 fuzzy sets.

4.2.4.2 Possibility Theory

Among the powerful progeny of fuzzy logic is possibility theory.[60] This nonadditive set theory is important for my purposes because it builds a bridge between fuzzy logic and the upcoming belief functions.

Possibility theory is a rigorous and complex system.[61] For its image, picture the interval [0,1] with two dividing lines, each of infinitesimal thinness. These lines mark a lower "probability" on the left and an upper "probability" on the right called necessity (or nec) and possibility (or pos), respectively, which fall between 0 and 1. The zone running to the left of the lower bound represents the degree to which the proposition has been proved, and the zone to the left of the upper bound represents the range in which the proposition could possibly be true. Thus, the zone running to the right of the upper bound represents the range in which the proposition cannot be true.

For any proposition U, nec(U) = 1–pos(*not-U*). Consider four cases:

- If nec(U) is 1, then U is certainly true. It implies that pos(U) is 1 also.
- If nec(U) is 0, then U is not necessary, and may or may not be true. It means that pos(U) is unconstrained.
- If pos(U) is 0, then U is impossible, and certainly false. It implies that nec(U) is 0 also.
- If pos(U) is 1, then U is possible, and may or may not be true. It means that nec (U) is unconstrained.

Between necessity and possibility lies epistemic uncertainty. Possibility theory differs from fuzzy logic in its treatment of epistemic uncertainty. Possibility theory treats all epistemic uncertainty front and center in terms of the range between necessity and possibility, while fuzzy set theory moves any epistemic uncertainty into the additional dimensions of ultrafuzziness.[62]

4.2.4.3 Multivalent Assumptions

Recall that this book is focusing on the varieties of multivalent logic that reject as an assumption the postulate of the excluded middle. Systems like fuzzy logic and possibility theory fit here. Under them, the factfinder can retain some belief uncommitted between true and false.

---

[60] See Zadeh (1978) (deriving possibility theory from fuzzy sets).

[61] For an introduction to possibility theory, see Dubois and Prade (2007); Genin and Huber (2020), § 3.3.

[62] See Nance (2018), pp. 1036–1037 (using possibility theory to untangle the conjunction paradox).

Are these systems' assumptions defensible? The postulates of multivalent logic are a subset of the postulates of bivalent logic. So, no problem lies there. The difference to defend lies in the multivalent operators.

The basic operators for multivalent logic are the usual ones used for bivalent logic,[63] except that they now must extend to give results for values between 0 and 1.[64] Thus, the AND and OR operators work in the following way in multivalent logic,[65] when x and y can take any value from 0 to 1:

---

[63] Recall that the bivalent operators for conjunction and disjunction can be stated in MAX and MIN terms. See supra Sect. 4.2.2 (making that point).

[64] See Gaines (1978) (showing that the operators for fuzzy logic and probability theory are the same until the assumption of the excluded middle comes into play).

[65] An accepted demonstration of the operators' suitability went as follows. Reasoning backward from what is necessary for a system to make sense, theorists posited the following:

$$x \wedge x = x \tag{4.1}$$

$$x \vee x = x \tag{4.2}$$

$$x \wedge y \leq x \tag{4.3}$$

$$x \vee y \geq x \tag{4.4}$$

while associativity and distributivity needed to prevail as well,

$$(x \wedge y) \wedge z = x \wedge (y \wedge z) \tag{4.5}$$

$$x \vee (y \wedge z) = (x \vee y) \wedge (y \vee z). \tag{4.6}$$

Then, using (4.2) and (4.3),

$$x \wedge (x \vee y) = (x \vee x) \wedge (x \vee y) \leq x$$

and, using (4.4) and (4.6),

$$x \vee (x \wedge y) = (x \vee x) \wedge (x \vee y) \geq x$$

and their having been shown to be equal, and both $\leq$ and $\geq x$,

$$x \wedge (x \vee y) = x \vee (x \wedge y) = x. \tag{4.7}$$

Now, designate y as the lesser or equal of the two truth values x and y. There should be a z such that $x \wedge z = y$, which allows the final conversions with the use of (4.7) and then of (4.5) and (4.1), respectively:

$$x \vee y = x \vee (x \wedge z) = x = \mathrm{MAX}(x, y)$$

$$x \wedge y = x \wedge (x \wedge z) = (x \wedge x) \wedge z = x \wedge z = y = \mathrm{MIN}(x, y).$$

Bellman and Giertz (1973), pp. 151–155 (proving that the MIN and MAX operators "are not only natural, but under quite reasonable assumptions the only ones possible" for fuzzy sets); see also Aliev (2013), pp. 1, 6; Yager (1991) (giving a technically complete proof). Further support for MIN and MAX appears infra Sects. 4.3.2 and 4.5.4.2.

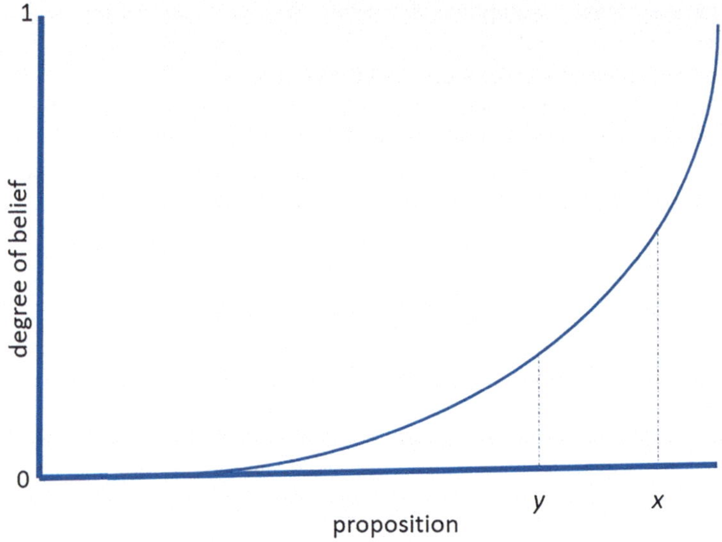

Fig. 4.3 Conjunction in set theory

$$\text{truth}(x \text{ AND } y) = \text{minimum}(\text{truth}(x), \text{truth}(y))$$
$$\text{truth}(x \text{ OR } y) = \text{maximum}(\text{truth}(x), \text{truth}(y))$$

These mathematical formulas can extend from propositional logic's AND and OR to set theory. Designate the membership of element x in set A as truth(x), and the membership of an *independent or interdependent* element y in A as truth(y). Then, the truth of their conjunction equals the smaller of the truth of x and the truth of y, by the so-called MIN operator or MIN rule. (By the way, the truth of a disjunction follows the so-called MAX operator or MAX rule.) Utilizing fuzzy logic's degree of membership in the set of fully proven facts, we can represent truth(x) and truth(y) in Fig. 4.3. The multivalent belief in y might be 0.25. If y is a member of the set to 0.25 and x is believed more, the conjoined membership of x and y in the set should not be moved up or down from 0.25 by the belief in x. The membership of x does not affect the membership of the conjunction. Thus, the membership of the conjunction truth(x) AND truth(y) in the set drops to truth(y): the belief in the conjunction will be the belief in its weakest component.

Indeed, set theory works to show the wisdom of representing factfindings as gradated and nonadditive beliefs and disbeliefs that segregate epistemic uncertainty. Set theory makes clearer that the MIN rule best combines a belief in one element and a belief in another element into a belief in their conjunction. Set theory makes just as clear that the product rule has no role to play. Converting each belief into a probability measure that captures a guess as to randomness, and then multiplying the two probabilities, would tell us nothing relevant to factfinding in an uncertain world.

For a different kind of example, let *A* be one set and *B* be another set in the universe.[66] The two sets might be independent, in the sense that the degree of membership in one set has no effect on the degree of membership in the other set, but they need not be independent. Let *A* be the set of tallness in men and *B* be the set of smartness in men. So, if Tom is a 0.30 member of *A* and a 0.40 member of *B*, then Tom is a 0.30 member of the set of (tallness ∩ smartness). Tom's degree of membership in the intersection of sets does not decrease below the lower of his tallness and smartness levels.

For a last example, consider the controversial principle of conjunctive closure seen in the philosophical literature: if (and only if) a person believes fact *x* and believes fact *y* because each passes a fixed standard of proof for belief, then the person believes *x* and *y* together.[67] That is, if your beliefs are strong enough to prove each of two facts, you have proved both together.

---

[66] See Ross and Parkinson (2002), pp. 31–34 (extending theory to multiple sets).

[67] See Evnine (1999), pp. 201, 214, 222 (stating the principle as "If S is rational, then if S believes *A* and S believes *B*, then S believes *A and B*," and struggling to defend the principle as generally valid while recognizing the remaining difficulties of the preface and lottery paradoxes); Leitgeb (2014) (similar, and stressing the costs to rationality of abandoning conjunctive closure); Schurz (2021). These theorists attempt the near-impossible task of defending the intuitive principle of conjunctive closure while still assuming an excluded middle and while rejecting that something can be both believed and disbelieved. If they were to recognize that beliefs should be treated under the more general system of multivalent logic to account for epistemic uncertainty, then the principle would appear as a logical operator. Moreover, those two paradoxes would become manageable. The paradoxes are worth explaining to show another advantage of differentiating beliefs from probabilities.

The much-debated preface paradox was formulated by Makinson (1965). It imagines that an author's preface asserts that he believes all the propositions in the rest of his book, but acknowledges that experience would suggest some errors remain among those propositions. This is not a flight of imagination, as the paradox would arise implicitly whenever an author writes something like "remaining errors are mine alone." So he believes the conjunction of all the propositions (p_1, p_2 … and p_n), but also seems to believe the opposite of the conjunction ¬(p_1, p_2 … and p_n) because he thinks a nonspecific one or more of the propositions are false. He thus seems irrationally to hold inconsistent beliefs. Seemingly, we therefore would not be justified to believe anything asserted in his book.

The paradox's resolution lies in realizing that the two positions are different in kind, the first being a belief involving epistemic uncertainty and the second being a probability measuring only randomness. First, the author believes that each of his book's propositions is true. By the MIN rule, the conjunction of beliefs is the minimum of those beliefs. If he believes the weakest proposition, then he should believe the conjunction. Second, his position on some error existing is not a disjunction of beliefs in *not-*p_1, *not-*p_2 … or *not-*p_n, which the MAX rule would calculate as being very low. Instead, his position on some error existing is the calculation of the odds of any one of the propositions being wrong. By De Morgan's rule, if there are ten propositions with *probabilities* of 90%, then the probability of one of them being wrong is 65%. This kind of percentage is not a belief. It would be calculated in this instance by converting each belief (p_1, p_2 … and p_n) into a probability, and then disjoining their negations. See infra Sect. 4.6.3 (explaining these processes).

So, given a set of propositions, the author could rationally believe that all his propositions are true and also calculate the odds in a random world to be that at least one is wrong. The two positions are talking about different things and so are not contradictory. The first is a justified belief in truth, the second is an abstract statement about randomness. Thus, the resolution of the paradox all comes

What lies behind this philosophical intuition? Again, it is the realization that beliefs differ from probabilities. On the one hand, beliefs turn on the degree of sureness, the degree to which the fact has been fully proven to exist. If you believe *y* to a certain degree, and you believe *x* to the same or greater extent, your degree of sureness should not slip below *y* when considering their conjunction. On the other hand, traditional probabilities are so-called two-sided characteristics: they represent the additive chances of happening *and* of not happening. The chance of happening obviously goes down for a conjunction of events, because the chances of not happening accumulate. In brief, random happenings (which use the product rule) combine differently from one-sided gradations of belief (which use the MIN rule).

As to the negation operator for multivalent logic, it carries over from bivalent logic, and so equates to the calculation of the complement.[68] However, the multivalent belief and its opposite disbelief do not necessarily add to unity, because multivalent beliefs do not obey the axiom of additivity. There can be an area within the complement where a fact is neither partially true nor partially false, but instead is indeterminate. Multivalent logic thereby picks up the very useful distinction between a lack of belief and a disbelief.[69]

In other words, the complement does not equate to the opposite disbelief. The complement of *Bel(a)* equals 1−*Bel(a)*, but this gives the possibility of *not-a*, not the belief in *not-a*. Indeed, the possibility of *not-a* equals *Bel(not-a)* + uncommitted belief. Hence, there is a big difference between the complement and the opposite disbelief, the difference being the uncommitted belief. A belief in *a* does not imply anything about the active belief in *not-a*, other than that this disbelief cannot be larger than the complement of *Bel(a)*. Given scarce information in support of *a*, one forms a small belief in the proposition, while leaving a lot of belief uncommitted and

down to the fact that beliefs and probabilities are different animals. See Clermont (2023), pp. 283–286.

The lottery paradox is similar to the preface paradox. It was formulated by Kyburg (1961), p. 197. It imagines a fair lottery that sold a thousand tickets and will have one winning ticket. It is reasonable to think that any particular ticket will not win, and so by conjunctive closure it appears reasonable to think that no ticket will win. But again this paradox depends on mixing up beliefs with probabilities. Here no epistemically uncertain beliefs should get involved at all, and hence there will be no call to apply conjunctive closure. Each ticket has .001 chance of winning. By Kolmogorov's additivity axiom, the tickets together have a chance of a thousand .001s added together, or 1.000, that some ticket will win. And by Kolmogorov's normalization axiom, 1 is the probability of a sure event.

[68] Cf. Bellman and Giertz (1973), p. 155 (contending that the negation operator has no unique meaning and that the "borderline between S and 'not S' is no longer sharp"); Sider (2010), pp. 25, 35–37, 67–80 (showing also that in going beyond two-valued logic, one needs to stipulate an implication operator as well).

[69] The difference is recognized in Fed. R. Civ. P. 11(b)(4), which authorizes denials that, "if specifically so identified, are reasonably based on belief or a lack of information." Such a pleading would be appropriate when the pleader has sufficient information to form a substantial lack of belief in the truth of the opponent's position, but does not feel comfortable asserting that it is false. See Boykin v. KeyCorp, 521 F.3d 202, 215 (2d Cir. 2008) (approving such pleading when facts are not within the knowledge of the pleader).

without necessarily forming any belief in the proposition's opposite. One would need an inference of the opposite from the available proof before generating any belief in the opposite. Again, a lack of belief and a disbelief are entirely different states of mind.[70]

4.2.4.4 Multivalent Testing

As for justifying the consequences of multivalence's logical assumptions, there are several signs that multivalent logic makes sense. To begin, multivalent logic is not wildly different from classical logic. It does not require a radical overhaul of worldview.

Furthermore, multivalent logic does not produce nonsensical results. For example, say that we have a partial truth and another partial truth, and we want to express the conjunction as a partial truth. On the one hand, the MIN rule in multivalent logic avoids having the value of a conjunction exceed the value of either component.[71] On the other hand, the MIN rule also avoids having the conjoined value be surprisingly low.[72] More than that, it affirmatively makes sense as the way for conjoining multivalent values: Tom does seem to fall around 0.30 on the scale of tallness combined with smartness, doesn't he?

Finally, the sense of multivalent logic will become more apparent in the next section. The enhancement will come from imaging as belief functions the multivalent logic used for legal factfinding.

Remember that the choice posed here is between (1) bivalent logic with its probability overlay and (2) multivalent logic. In essence, multivalent logic says only that we should account for the undeniable epistemic uncertainty of the world by removing the assumption of an excluded middle and by conformably altering the system's operators. That move seems preferable to relying on the awkward and desperately incomplete afterthought of the probability calculus as the way to bring uncertainty into bivalence.

---

[70] See Haenni (2009), p. 123 (arguing "that the extreme case of total ignorance . . . should never lead to degrees of belief different from zero," so that belief and disbelief are both zero, "which is a particular case of the non-additivity assumption $Bel(h) + Bel(\neg h) \leq 1$").

[71] See Tversky and Kahneman (1983), p. 294 ("If the extension of A includes the extension of B (i.e., $A \supset B$), then $P(A) \geq P(B)$. Because the set of possibilities associated with a conjunction A&B is included in the set of possibilities associated with B, the same principle can also be expressed by the conjunction rule $P(A\&B) \leq P(B)$: A conjunction cannot be more probable than one of its constituents. This rule holds regardless of whether A and B are independent . . . .").

[72] See Dubois and Prade (1985), pp. 89–92 (showing that conjoined membership must be either less than or equal to the minimum membership, but that accepting a value less than that minimum would produce nonsensical results).

4.3 Belief Functions

Of all the available candidates among multivalent systems, belief function theory ("BF") delivers the concept whose imagery best reflects and illuminates legal factfinding. This is not to say that I shall not draw, whenever useful, on other multivalent systems like fuzzy logic and possibility theory.[73] But leading with BF pays the largest dividends.

In the belief function image, a degree of belief *Bel(a)* can coexist with a degree of disbelief *Bel(not-a)* produced by the evidence, that is, a belief in the opposite of the fact. Moreover, when forming the degree of belief that the fact was proven true and the degree of belief that the fact was proven false, the factfinder facing epistemic uncertainty can leave the remainder of its belief uncommitted.

4.3.1 As Mathematics Branch

Like traditional probability, belief function theory began as a branch of mathematics.[74] The theory was formalized and elaborated in 1976 by Princeton statistician Glenn Shafer, in another absolutely brilliant but almost impenetrable book, *A Mathematical Theory of Evidence*.[75] As probability serves bivalent logic by handling a kind of uncertainty for which the underlying logic system does not otherwise account, belief function theory delivers mathematical notions that can extend multivalent logic. While traditional probability treats aleatory uncertainty about the existence of a fact, belief function notions gives a very handy way to treat epistemic uncertainty too.

Shafer's work on belief functions rests on a highly rigorous mathematical base but still nicely conveys a sense of our legal decisionmaking scheme.[76] He used the word "belief" to invoke neither firm knowledge nor some squishy personal feeling, but rather the factfinders' attempts to express their degree of certainty about the state

[73] See Reghiş and Roventa (1998), p. 354 (referencing belief functions and fuzzy logic, and observing: "In order to treat different aspects of the same problems, we must therefore apply various theories related to the imprecision of knowledge."); Schum (1994), pp. 41, 200–201 (disbelieving that it is "possible to capture all of this behavioral richness within the confines of any single formal system of probabilities"); Spohn (2009), p. 187 ("However, there is a multitude of epistemological purposes to serve, and it is entirely implausible that there is one account to serve all.").

[74] See Copi et al. (2011), pp. 539–564.

[75] Shafer (1976) (using "evidence" in a much broader sense than legal evidence, and building on earlier work by Harvard's Arthur P. Dempster); see Shafer (1990b) (summarizing, simplifying, and updating his theory). For an accessible introduction, see Schum (1994), pp. 222–243. For a historical account of the theory, see Haenni (2009), pp. 127–133.

[76] See Shapira (1998), p. 1614 ("In the legally relevant literature, it was Professor Glenn Shafer who introduced fuzzy measures as appropriate formalizations of epistemic functions.").

of the real world as represented by the evidence put before them.[77] His degrees of belief again run on a scale from 0 to 1 and are nonadditive.[78] By allowing for representation of ignorance, indeterminacy of the evidence, and other unknowns, he enabled beliefs to express clearly all relevant kinds of uncertainty.

As Shafer's title admits, however, his book is one treating mathematics only. Moreover, its mathematics are devoted to the problem of how to aggregate multiple pieces of uncertain evidence in proving a single proposition. This important problem is the target of Bayes' theorem in probability theory. Shafer's chosen task was to generalize Bayes in a way that accounts for epistemic uncertainty.

I shall soon turn to this problem of aggregating pieces of evidence, enlisting Shafer's inspiration but ultimately not the new theorem he championed.[79] I pass on his theorem in favor of one of the alternative approaches more recently developed. I do not do this because Shafer was wrong mathematically, but because his theorem's assumptions and also the feasibility of humans' performing the task make his mathematical approach inappropriate for aggregation of legal evidence.

4.3.2 As Logic System

Besides the task of aggregation, law must face the additional problems of how to infer from evidence and how to combine conclusions. For these tasks, my book takes Shafer's logical concept of belief functions rather than his mathematics. I can plug into Shafer's image my similar definition of "degree of belief."[80] I then employ multivalent logic's assumptions and operators. I can thereby develop a general theory on how to infer from a piece of evidence to a conclusion and how to combine separate conclusions.

To justify this brand of multivalent and nonadditive logic systems, I must build a bridge from Shafer's concept to multivalent logic.[81] Multivalent logic teaches that beliefs can be expressed in set theory. A degree of belief becomes a degree of membership in the set of proven facts, which possibility theory terms a "necessity" and which corresponds to the belief function's lower bound of *Bel(a)*. The unallocated zone between *Bel(a)* and the opposite belief of *Bel(not-a)* represents uncommitted belief owing to conceivably knowable unknowns. The belief function's upper bound, which represents the disbelief, also demarks *a*'s maximal "possibility"; it is the extent to which the factfinder thinks *a* is possible or entertainable; that is, it is the sum of the affirmative belief plus the uncommitted

[77] See supra Sect. 4.1.3 (discussing Shafer's view of belief).

[78] See Shafer (1976), p. 11 ("it is the rule of additivity that I reject as a rule for degrees of belief").

[79] See infra Sect. 4.5.4.1 (explaining aggregation of evidence).

[80] See supra Sect. 4.1.3 (defining the term for my purposes).

[81] See, e.g., Godo et al. (2003) (constructing one such bridge).

belief or, equivalently, it equals one minus disbelief.[82] Therefore, a belief function can be, and is, used as an image of possibility theory.[83]

For my purposes, it is critical that belief function theory as a logic system be consistent with fuzzy logic and also with possibility theory. Fortunately, they are indeed consistent.[84] All three approaches are nonadditive and therefore reject the product rule,[85] all three end up equivalent in their essential lessons,[86] and all three stand together in opposition to traditional probability.[87] The multivalent logic systems under consideration are consistent and can be combined.

As we have seen, the three approaches employ the same assumptions and the same operators for conjunction and disjunction. Their multivalent logic brings the MIN and MAX rules into play. In search of an image, shifting from Shafer's mathematical formulas to a compatible set theory such as possibility theory makes the MIN and MAX rules easier to picture. A belief is proven, or necessary, only to the degree that disbelief is not entertainable, or possible—and a disbelief in a conjunction is entertainable all the way to the degree measured by the largest sum of disbelief and uncommitted belief on any component finding.[88] Thus, if $Bel(\mathrm{E})$ expresses a degree of membership in the set of proved facts, $1-Bel(\mathrm{E})$ is the entertainability of not-E given uncertainty. If one then tries to picture $Bel(\mathrm{E} \wedge \mathrm{F})$, it will exist where neither not-E nor not-F is entertainable, which by the MAX rule is the maximum possibility of either not-E or not-F. "The idea is, roughly, that a proposition is at least as possible as all of the possibilities it comprises [disjunctively], and no more possible than the 'most possible' possibility either."[89]

---

[82] See Barnett (2008), pp. 200–201 (providing an effective mental image for these bounds); Dempster (1967) (providing the mathematical proof for upper and lower bounds in belief function theory). In belief function terminology, "possibility" is often phrased as "plausibility." See Schum (1994), p. 236 (using the phrase "plausibility" in place of "possibility").

[83] See Dubois and Prade (2008), pp. 402–403 (discussing the relation of belief functions and possibility theory); Huber (2009), pp. 10–15 (discussing the use of possibility theory for the purpose of extending belief functions); Zadeh (1984), p. 83 (reviewing Shafer's book and treating it as a version of fuzzy logic's possibility theory).

[84] See Dubois and Prade (2008), pp. 402–403 (linking belief functions and fuzzy sets); Zadeh (1978) (deriving possibility theory from fuzzy sets); cf. Schum (1994), pp. 266–69 (observing that one can fuzzify belief functions); Yen (2008), p. 529 (showing how to form beliefs about membership in fuzzy sets).

[85] See Aliev (2013), pp. 106, 108–109 (contrasting additive with nonadditive probability systems, and also showing belief functions to be nonadditive).

[86] There are other multivalent approaches that reject traditional probability and end in similar places. See, e.g., Tversky and Koehler (1994), p. 547 (developing "support theory," and saying: "In contrast to the Bayesian school, which represents degree of belief by an additive probability measure, there are many skeptics who question the possibility and the wisdom of quantifying subjective uncertainty and are reluctant to apply the laws of chance to the analysis of belief."); infra Sect. 4.4.4 (cataloging other similar approaches).

[87] See Anderson et al. (2005), pp. 250–261 (sketching these three approaches in contrast to traditional probability); Schum (1994), pp. 200–266 (same in greater detail).

[88] See Huber (2009), p. 14 (discussing conjunction and disjunction for possibility theory).

[89] Id.

Alternatively put, E and F will be conjoinedly necessary where each of E and F is necessary, which is measurable by the MIN rule. That is, to the extent that not-E or not-F is possibly true, the conjunction of E and F cannot be necessarily true.

4.3.3 Defending Marriage of BF Image with MIN/MAX Rules

This book combines the concept of belief functions with the conjunction and disjunction tools of multivalent logic to create "multivalent belief theory."[90] That is, this marriage's offspring embodies my proposed way for people to express, combine, and assess their views of the evidence. So, I need to defend further the marriage of the belief functions image with the multivalent logic operators.

Admittedly, I am using belief functions and even multivalent logic less for their mathematics than for their logical imagery that so nicely captures legal factfinding.[91] But I have also attended to the technical details where appropriate. I think that my uses of the model and the operators are defensible.

Specifically, then, this book's soundness turns on wedding the conceptual soundness of a nonadditive degrees-of-belief model with the technical soundness of applying the MIN and MAX operators to it.

Using belief functions for an image of nonadditive degrees of belief is a safe step because belief function theory maps right onto the well-established image of possibility theory. My only reliance on Shafer's mathematics is later to establish that there is no unique solution for how to aggregate epistemically uncertain pieces of evidence bearing on one proposition.[92] The choice of aggregation method depends on what kind of evidence the legal factfinder will encounter. I shall survey the various alternative techniques for aggregation that others have developed. I shall then select the method suited for highly conflicting and contradictory items of evidence that is simple enough to be relatively feasible for human factfinders. But this selection is made mainly for illustrative purposes, as a possible representation of humans' intuitive process that they more holistically employ in nonnumerical and approximate terms. Nothing turns on the reader's agreement with my selection.

---

[90] Cf. Saffiotti (1992), pp. 642, 644 n.3 (developing "belief function logic," and saying: "BFL attaches a quantified notion of belief—based on Dempster-Shafer's theory of belief functions—to classical first-order logic.").

[91] For a defense of using a broad view of belief functions and multivalent logic as imagery, see Liu and Yager (2008), pp. 2–12 (formalizing an image of belief functions); cf. Novák (2008) ("Mathematical fuzzy logic has two branches: fuzzy logic *in narrow sense* (FLn) and fuzzy logic *in broader sense* (FLb). FLn is a formal fuzzy logic which is a special many-valued logic generalizing classical mathematical logic .... FLb is an extension of FLn which aims at developing a *formal theory of human reasoning*.").

[92] See infra Sect. 4.5.4.1 (explaining aggregation of evidence).

As to the additional problems of how to infer from evidence and how to combine conclusions, all that I do is to apply the widely accepted MIN and MAX rules to conjoin or disjoin a string of fuzzy measures called degrees of belief. On the one hand, I have already technically justified these operators' use for basic conjunction and disjunction of epistemically uncertain measures of belief, and I further explain these operators in the following pages.[93] On the other hand, I do not contend that the law calls on factfinders to apply multivalent logic in toto.[94] I thus feel no need to get into the advanced manipulations that modern logicians have so impressively elaborated. As the law does not rely on these refinements, this book does not need to take a deep dive into multivalent logic's details.

All this means that there is at most one sticking point for the reader. The point of vulnerability for my approach lies in this pivotal assumption: factfindings should be represented as gradated and nonadditive beliefs and disbeliefs that segregate epistemic uncertainty and that together pose the relevant comparison. If I am permitted to take this step of expressing and comparing factfindings as multivalent beliefs, everything else falls into place. And theory would finally come to conform to what the law already does.

To defend by contrast, bivalent probability assumes instead that everything must be either true or false, subject only to random variation. My point heretofore was that multivalent beliefs better represent factfindings. Immediately below I try to justify using the comparison of gradated and nonadditive beliefs and disbeliefs to each other. Further to defend taking this step of using multivalent beliefs, I have devoted the book's three central chapters to the differences between binary probabilities and multivalent beliefs.

4.3.3.1 Multivalence, Not Bivalence

The impetus for taking this step away from bivalence was the feeling that assuming everything must be either true or false is a very odd assumption to adopt for an evidence-based proof system that regularly produces outputs falling partway between. Much better would be to use a measure that reports where the output actually falls. It thus seems obvious that the more appropriate approach would be to use a system that is designed to encode partial findings along the whole scale of truth.

At first glance, it appears that probability is a way to invoke the whole scale. Probability can modify bivalence by reporting the gradated uncertainty introduced by randomness. But that move would rest on the equally odd assumption that the uncertainty in factfinding is solely aleatory rather than mostly epistemic. Traditional

---

[93] See supra Sect. 4.2.4.3 and infra Sect. 4.5.4.2 (explaining multivalent conjunction and disjunction).

[94] For an example of where the law does not follow multivalent logic to its rarified ends, see supra Sect. 4.2.4.1.

probability is additive, which means that there is no room to capture epistemic uncertainty between p and $1-p$.

4.3.3.2 Beliefs, Not Probabilities

We should instead use a multivalent scheme, like fuzzy logic or possibility theory, that is made nonadditive. The outputs of factfinding could be imaged as beliefs. We would then allow the factfinder to reserve some uncommitted belief, which would convey epistemic uncertainty.

Contrast the different situation where we want to predict an outcome. There probability might provide the proper tools. Recall how probabilities work. For each fact, the predictor buries the epistemic uncertainty in order to announce odds of yes or no as if the only unknowns were random. But note what is being asked: If you had to bet on a resolution of all random uncertainty by some sort of revelation, what would be your odds?

Our historical confusion in choosing between beliefs and probabilities has come from mistakenly thinking that factfinding somehow calls for predicting what a miraculous resolution of randomness, by revelation of reality, would show. But in the absence of any need to predict a revelation, which is the better way to grasp and express the truth: probabilities or beliefs?

For an example, think again of Dave's identification as the culprit.[95] Should we treat that proof as an 80% chance it was Dave or as a 0.20 belief? Odds must deal solely in p and $1-p$, which misrepresents the world and thereby introduces a big source of error.[96] Instead, we should (and the law does) choose to deal in current beliefs about reality, based on the available proof.

For a more anguishing example, think of beliefs of 0.40 and disbeliefs of 0.20 on both independent elements of a plaintiff's civil claim. The belief in the elements' conjunction would be 0.40, with a disjunctive disbelief still at 0.20, which transforms to odds of 67%. But the proportionately normalized odds of each element are 67% too, so that their probabilistic conjunction comes in at 44% by the product rule. For whom would the factfinder most accurately decide, plaintiff or defendant? Beliefs comprise the factfinder's best representation of the world shown by the evidence—it shows everything that was proved and, just as importantly, what was not proved because of epistemic uncertainty. A decision for the plaintiff would conform to the factfinder's belief structure, and so it would feel the more comfortable decision.

---

[95] See supra Sect. 1.1.1 (stating that example).

[96] See supra Sect. 3.2.2.2 (explaining that inaccuracy).

4.3.3.3 MIN/MAX Rules, Not Product Rules

Also, that decision for the plaintiff would be the more accurate, and so would lead to error minimization. Why more accurate? Using odds would require the factfinder to assume that the truth of each element will somehow be sequentially revealed. The factfinder must then transform each belief into a probability, in order to use the product rule in calculating the odds of the elements' conjunction. This process introduces another big source of error, albeit less obviously. The reason is that the transforms involve converting all epistemic uncertainty into randomness. This is a false step. Epistemic uncertainty is an unknown. There is no proof that the epistemically uncertain zone leans one way or the other, toward belief or disbelief. But treating it as somehow randomly allocated to both belief and disbelief magnifies disbelief, which will depress the affirmative probability of the conjunction when the product rule is applied. And that representation is a misrepresentation of the factfinder's actual view of the world. The transforms are necessary to make a prediction of revelation, but such a prediction is an unnecessary step for deciding in accordance with the most accurate view of the facts. In sum, belief and disbelief are more accurate and so would be the right basis for representing the world.

Once we have accepted working with these beliefs rather than additive probabilities, we must apply the associated mathematics. The product rule does not apply in nonadditive systems. Instead, the outputs can be combined with the operators that logicians have shown to be accurate for multivalent logic.

4.3.3.4 Belief Comparison, Not Absolute Testing

Belief functions, a widely accepted and appropriate construct, give us the best way to draw the nonadditive multivalent beliefs, as shown by Fig. 4.4. Given the representation of affirmative belief, uncommitted belief, and negative disbelief, we could demand that the affirmative belief exceed some absolute threshold. After all, we do this under the prevailing probabilistic approach, despite the fact that this move to $p > 50\%$ leads to all sorts of problems. But at least here in legal factfinding, no obvious absolute threshold presents itself.

Or we could demand that belief exceeds its complement, the possibility of its opposite. But, as a general approach, that standard would be very high. Any victory for the plaintiff with limited evidence would be impossible.

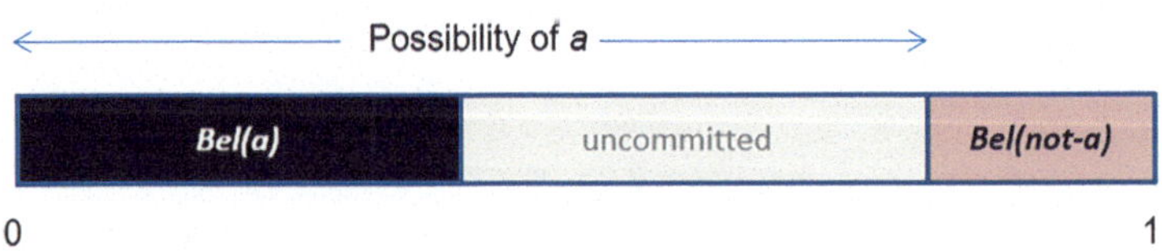

Fig. 4.4 Belief function

Instead, in legal factfinding, we should ask whether the factfinder believes a fact to some degree more than it disbelieves the fact.[97] We might ask in a civil case: Based on the evidence, do you believe the plaintiff's allegation more than you disbelieve it? That focus on proved beliefs against a background of persistent epistemic uncertainty—persistent in the sense that the decisionmaker should keep track of it during the evidence and proof process—will yield the best view of the truth on which to act and with which to live.

Given an adversary system, where the factfinder has to decide immediately on the basis of the presented evidence, we should be comparing belief to disbelief, to see if the factfinder believes the proponent's version to some degree more than the opponent's. It is the combination of the need to decide legal questions now and the commonplace of weak evidence that dictates this standard of decision, this nonabsolute threshold level for belief. In civil cases, we should ask whether the proponent's version is "believable," in the sense that it is more believed than disbelieved, more true than false, more likely than not.

4.3.4 Using Multivalent Beliefs for Legal Evidence and Proof

Multivalent belief theory allows imaging, combining, and evaluating beliefs while also accounting well for uncertainty. The theory's key insights are that, in the face of epistemic uncertainty, (1) a degree of belief can coexist with a degree of disbelief produced by the evidence, that is, a belief in the opposite of the fact, and (2) the factfinder can leave some of its belief uncommitted when forming the degree of belief that the fact is true and the degree of belief that the fact is false.

For example, a thinking religious person or atheist would not calculate odds of the divine, but instead would strive to generate a belief that overcomes disbelief, while retaining a sense of the unknown.[98] This notion of belief is the foundational idea of faith, as contrasted with scientific inquiry. Faith does not require its tenets to be probable, to say nothing of being statistically significant. Important matters will remain unknowable. The beliefs just need to be more believed than disbelieved, while disregarding uncommitted belief. On the one hand, religion has no answer for agnostic nonbelievers, who are those unwilling to disregard the huge range of uncommitted belief. On the other hand, any religion can easily overcome the "argument from inconsistent revelations," which argues that the existence of multiple religions means that none is probably true. That argument would contribute

---

[97] See Model Code of Evidence r. 1(5) (Am. L. Inst. 1942) ("'Finding a fact' means determining that its existence is more probable than its non-existence.").

[98] Pascal's wager is not to the contrary. See Pascal (1670), no. 233. There, rather than determining what to believe, he was in fact contemplating how to place a bet or how to act when the costs of a false negative vastly outweigh the costs of a false positive. See Hájek (2022), § 7. You do not have to believe in God in order to bet or choose an action consistent with God's existence.

slightly to disbelief and heavily to uncertainty, but faith can survive as long as belief exceeds disbelief. The situation resembles having many possible suspects.

For another example, I contend that a civil factfinder—rather than calculating a probability of all-or-nothing—should, can, and does proceed in the following way: the factfinder would form a degree of belief and a degree of disbelief, but retain a sense of uncertainty; the factfinder, required to decide now on the given evidence, would say that it believes one side's position more than or as much as the other side's, although it remains unsure; and the factfinder would proceed to decision, without taking the extra step of saying, "I would wager at such-and-such odds if forced to bet in this sea of uncertainty." Thus:

- First, after the factfinder processes the evidence, the belief in a fact called *a* can range anywhere between 0 and 1. This multivalent degree of belief measures the degree to which the factfinder considers the fact to be proven, measured on the scale running from no-proof-at-all at 0 to a fully proven, and hence fully believed, fact at 1.
- Second, belief in *not-a*, which is disbelief of *a*, falls between 0 and $1-Bel(a)$. This disbelief represents an active belief in *a*'s opposite.[99]
- Third, given incomplete, inconclusive, ambiguous, dissonant, or unreliable evidence, and facing other unknowns, the factfinder retains some belief as uncommitted.[100] In other words, a belief and the belief in its opposite will normally add to less than one.

In sum, the law asks how much the factfinder believes *a* to be a real-world truth based on the evidence, as well as how much it believes *not-a*—while the factfinder remains conscious of ignorance and indeterminacy and the like, and so retains part of its belief as an uncommitted nonbelief.

To fold in some earlier observations,[101] any probabilities with probative value, or tilt, will feed into the construction of the multivalent belief in the fact and the corresponding disbelief. Additionally, there can be higher-order uncertainties about the magnitude of those probabilities. There will also be higher-order uncertainties stemming from the other unknowns about the strengths of belief and disbelief. These two types of uncertainties are what we mean by epistemic uncertainty, which results in the withholding of belief.[102]

---

[99] See Amaya (2021), p. 8 (defining "ambivalence" as the common "attitude consisting in the holding of two conflicting attitudes towards the same object" and, in particular, analyzing ambivalence of factual belief in legal decisionmaking).

[100] See Friedman (2013) (treating uncommitted belief as a genuine attitude, in addition to yes and no); Liu and Yager (2008), pp. 3–4 (describing uncommitted belief); Meester (2020), p. 101 ("[A] portion of the total support provided by the evidence may be 'withheld,' or 'uncommitted' as between the mutually exclusive hypotheses *H* and not-*H*."); Rott (2009), p. 302 (calling uncommitted belief a nonbelief); Srivastava and Shafer (2008), p. 581 ("Belief functions . . . permit uncommitted belief . . . .").

[101] See supra Sects. 1.1.2 and 2.1.2.

[102] See Genin and Huber (2020), § 3.2 (observing that this form of multivalent logic "can also be understood as an attempt to formally distinguish risk from ambiguity")

To illustrate by Fig. 4.4, let *a* be a required finding on a factual proposition, say, that Katie is dead.[103] Any case starts with the whole range of belief standing as uncommitted. The factfinder starts out with everything indeterminate, because the current lack of evidence should make one withhold all of one's belief. The proper representation of lack of proof is zero belief in the plaintiff's position. When *Bel (a)* = 0, it does not mean that *a* is so highly unlikely as to be impossible. It means there is no evidence in support. Although *Bel(a)* = 0, *Bel(not-a)* equals 0 too. In other words, the factfinder does not believe or disbelieve *a*. The uncommitted belief is the entirety or 1, meaning that *a* is completely possible, as is *not-a*.

As the plaintiff introduces proof, some of the factfinder's uncommitted belief should start to convert into a degree of belief in *a*'s existence, and almost inevitably the plaintiff's proof will also have the inadvertent effect of generating an active belief to at least the slightest degree in its nonexistence, namely, that Katie is alive. The zone between *Bel(a)* and *Bel(not-a)* represents the remaining uncommitted belief. If the defendant next introduces effective proof to reduce the belief in *a*, whether the proof comes in the form of negation or as part of an alternative and inconsistent account, the degree of active belief in *a*'s nonexistence would presumably grow. Or the very clash of proofs could diminish the degrees of belief in both *a* and *not-a*. The force of the parties' presentations, including avoidable or otherwise probative absences or defects in evidence, will affect the degree of belief in *a* and in *not-a*. An avoidable or otherwise probative gap in evidence would best be treated as an item of evidence itself, supporting or undermining the finding. But the factfinder should not hold an unavoidable paucity of evidence against the burdened party. In such a situation, the factfinder should instead form beliefs based on the available evidence, while leaving a lot of its belief uncommitted.

When we say after evidence processing that *Bel(a)* = 0.40, we are not saying that *Bel(not-a)* = 0.60. We are saying only that the proof is such that to a degree of 0.60, which could represent uncommitted belief in part or in whole, *a* has not been proven to be true. Imperfect evidence, vague terms, and the possibility of unk-unks (or unknown unknowns) mean that some of the belief will remain uncommitted, after the rest of the belief is divided between *Bel(a)* and *Bel(not-a)*. So, the belief in *a*'s falsity would be smaller than 1−*Bel(a)* = 0.60. In Fig. 4.4, *Bel(not-a)* = 0.20. Hence, there is a big difference between the complement of *a* and the belief in the opposite of *a*, the difference being the uncommitted belief.

In the next chapter, I shall finally get to the standard of proof. But to make the rest of this chapter more comprehensible, it would be good to convey here an idea of where I shall be going. Basically, the standard of proof will involve comparing a belief to its corresponding disbelief, going element-by-element. Thus, for example, I shall argue that the preponderance-of-the-evidence standard is best understood as providing that the burdened party should win on *a* if and only if *Bel(a)* > *Bel(not-a)*.

---

[103] The whole image in Fig. 4.4 is a "belief function," which I shall represent by *BelFunc(a)*. The constituent degrees of belief and disbelief are represented by *Bel(a)* and *Bel(not-a)*. See Shafer (1976), pp. 5–7.

One key difference between the legal factfinder and the religious seeker is that the former must decide immediately on the basis of the available evidence. The factfinder cannot balk at the remaining epistemic uncertainty. The factfinder must decide right away which belief, if either, is perceptibly stronger. But the religious seeker, or the theoretical scientist for that matter, could await further thinking or research. The mere presence of substantial epistemic uncertainty could cause some faith seekers to postpone decision. Similarly, science "must allow for agnosticism."[104] Many kinds of decisions fall into the first kind represented by legal factfinding, and many other decisions allow postponement. But in other respects, all these decisions under epistemic uncertainty are addressed in basically similar ways.

4.3.4.1 Expressing Believability by Multivalent Beliefs

A degree of belief is a measure of the extent to which fact *x* has been fully proven. But how is the factfinder supposed to estimate that degree? It is not an insuperable task.

First, assessing belief is a task we all perform routinely in daily life. We must decide incessantly whether we believe a proposition or person. We do this by assessing how much we believe and disbelieve the proposition or person. It is an intuitive process. This process turns on features such as credibility, comprehensibility, coherence, comprehensiveness, and consistency (both internally and also externally with background information), measured in an approximate and nonquantitative manner.

Second, the decision to believe is a comparative task. Comparing belief and disbelief invokes the factfinder's considerable powers of relative judgment, rather than humans' weak powers of absolute judgment required for placement on some scale of likelihood.[105]

Third, comparative judgment has the added benefit of decreasing the need for a yes/no, or categorical, definition of believability. As long as belief and disbelief are measured by the same intuitive criteria, they can be compared to reach decision.

4.3.4.2 Expressing Strength of Multivalent Beliefs

Parenthetically, amidst all my use of percentages and decimals, bear in mind that one need not quantify degrees of belief in order to work with them, and indeed usually

[104] Lipton (2004), p. 63; see infra Sect. 6.2.1 (comparing science's standards).

[105] Relative judgment concerns the considerable capacity of people to distinguish between two or more different stimuli that they can compare directly. Although not entirely distinct, absolute judgment instead involves reference to a remembered scale. See Dember and Warm (1979), pp. 113, 116–117 (explaining the difference between absolute and relative judgment); see also Clermont (2013), pp. 62–66 (discussing human limitations on absolute judgment).

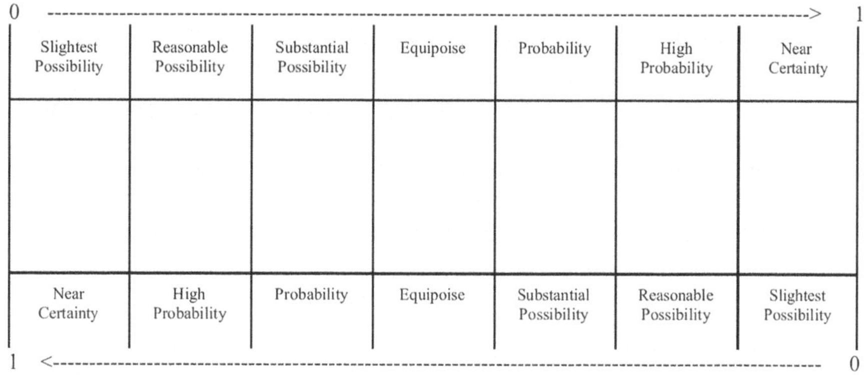

Fig. 4.5 Gradated likelihoods

one should not. Because all that the factfinder usually needs to do is compare the strengths of belief and disbelief, the factfinder need almost never place the fact on a quantified scale of likelihood.

Even if one desired to quantify a particular proposition, one should quantify the belief only in words drawn from a coarsely gradated scale of likelihood, rather than speaking in misrepresentative numerical terms. Figure 4.5 gives an appropriately gradated scale that utilizes natural language and expresses the fuzzy imprecision of probability of a fact, whether the burden of persuasion is on plaintiff (top scale) or on defendant (bottom scale): (1) slightest possibility, (2) reasonable possibility, (3) substantial possibility, (4) equipoise, (5) probability, (6) high probability, and (7) near certainty.[106]

This rough scale works both for traditional probabilities and for degrees of belief, although the degree of belief in a fact will be smaller than the probability (because of uncommitted belief, as I have explained) and although it would prompt a different vocabulary (as depicted in Fig. 5.7).

All importantly, the scale illuminates why, when the factfinder finds that *Bel(a)* exceeds *Bel(not-a)*, it is not drawing a fine line or making a close call, but rather saying that the degree of belief is at least a whole step upward in believability from the corresponding degree of disbelief. That is, *Bel(a)* feels perceptibly stronger than *Bel(not-a)*, creating a feeling of conviction.

The reasons for this coarse gradation partly lie in the cognitive psychology literature. Cognitive limitations leave humans able only weakly to judge likelihood on any sort of scale.[107] Studies of humans' weak absolute judgment, restricted short-term memory, and use of biased heuristics all explain the limited capability of humankind. Those studies suggest that a step-like scale of intervals accords with how humans naturally process such information: judged likelihood customarily finds

---

[106] See Clermont (2013), pp. 35–36, 166–168 (extricating from legal practice this coarsely gradated scale of likelihood); supra Sect. 3.2.1 (discussing equipoise).

[107] See Clermont (2013), pp. 68–75.

expression in terms of a very small set of broad verbal categories.[108] Today, in all the probability and logic theories, there seems to be an emerging sense of the need to confront the limited precision of humans in gradating their beliefs.[109]

It might therefore be more psychologically appropriate to ask people for an approximate degree of belief than for any precise view of probability. Perhaps the law, by an intuitive but wise reconciliation with cognitive limitations, has optimized by conforming to the coarsely gradated scale of likelihood that was already in people's customary use. Accordingly, the law employs three and only three standards of proof to invoke the top three showings of probability, high probability, and near certainty, namely, preponderance of the evidence, clear and convincing evidence, and proof beyond a reasonable doubt.

Thus, Fig. 4.5 constitutes a key component of my theory. But I leave the details of the figure's derivation to my earlier book.[110]

4.4 Alternative Models Similar to Multivalent Beliefs

Most, but not all,[111] people who think seriously about this topic admit that traditional probability conflicts with the logic and law of evidential proof. Accordingly, many have proposed a rethinking of the topic that would allow us to live with the accepted

[108] Important to note is the role of qualifying language as a means of expressing membership in a set. *Evaluative linguistic expressions* are words like small, medium, and big; another example is about, roughly, or near, when used in contrast to not-at-all or really. These words may not be a large part of our natural language. Yet, they are a very important part. They do a lot of work. People use them all the time to evaluate a thing or situation, to communicate their evaluation, and thereafter to perform classification, decisionmaking, and other tasks. Furthermore, people employ *linguistic hedges* to modify their evaluations further. Words such as very or extremely, and fairly or almost, are examples. Obviously, these distinctions are imprecise. But they are supposed to be imprecise, and they work quite well in real life. These words allow people to create and share a gradated scale for their evaluations, as long as the thing or situation is scaled by people in a fairly common and hence objective manner. Research suggests that such verbal categories can work better than numerical translations. See, e.g., Franklin (2015), pp. 325, 327; Zimmer (1983), p. 180.

[109] See Fine (1986), p. 353.

[110] See generally Clermont (2013) (developing in book-length form how the law's pattern in standards of decision conforms to cognitive limitations as well as logical principles).

[111] E.g., Spottswood (2019) (defending probabilism).

puzzles, paradoxes, and other problems that accompany traditional probability.[112] They try to circumvent the difficulties through heightened sophistication. Consequently, their competing models often involve radical reconceptions.

Take the much-condemned conjunction paradox as an example again. Analysis of it has prompted some to abandon truth as an aim of trial and to embrace acceptability of result instead: they argue that it should not matter for acceptability whether the plaintiff's conjoined story is more likely than not, as long as the plaintiff's story is more likely than any other single story.[113] More often, radical reconception calls for even more radical reform. Some argue for changing the standard of proof: they argue that we should raise the standard for the elements to ensure that their conjunction meets the usual standard of proof.[114]

The amazing realization coming from such arguments is that, even at this late date, there is no consensus on what the law of evidential proof requires or should require. It is a theoretical jungle out there, growing in a vibrant, contentious, and extensive literature. There follows discussion of the literature's most promising approaches, which turn out to work much like multivalent beliefs—albeit not as well.

4.4.1 Inference to the Best Explanation

Outside the law, the most invoked of the jungle's various tempting theories is inference to the best explanation ("IBE"). Avoiding traditional probability, this method involves consideration and analysis of alternative conjectures to get the one that *best* explains the evidence.

---

[112]E.g., Ho (2008), pp. 127, 155–156, 171 (arguing that finding a fact in a criminal or civil case requires a categorical belief in the fact, that is, a judging that the fact is true); Stein (2005), pp. 133–140 (arguing for viewing standards of proof in terms of allocation of risk); Engel (2009) (arguing for a standard based on psychological confidence); Meier (2015) (arguing for a standard based on statistical confidence); Risinger (2018) (arguing for a standard based on the degree of the surprise that the factfinder would feel if the found fact hypothetically were revealed to be false); Walker (1996), p. 1136 (arguing that preponderance means "being warranted by the evidence" in the sense that the finding meets "the formal requirements of coherence and consistency" and is "reasonably inferable from that evidence").

[113]E.g., Nesson (1985), pp. 1366–1368 (arguing that the process of proof aims at generating acceptable statements about past events and thus at projecting behavioral norms to the public).

[114]E.g., Dawid (1987), pp. 95–97 (suggesting a cure of raising the standard of proof on each of the elements, so as to satisfy preponderance for the whole claim or defense).

IBE was built on abductive reasoning, a way of thinking first segregated by Charles Sanders Peirce.[115] Abduction is a creative process of potentially fallible insight. It uses data to generate explanatory hypotheses that are possibly true, but which would need to be inductively and deductively tested and then refined. It has many uses in law.[116] A line of argument that captures abduction is this:

A perhaps surprising event, *a*, has occurred.
If a hypothesis, *H*, were true, then *a* would follow.
Thus, reason exists to believe *H* might be true.[117]

Separably, logicians later followed a related thought process to create a new problem-solving method called IBE.[118] It involves generating and testing hypotheses like *H*, then falsifying some and eventually settling on the best one as the explanation.[119] It alters the line of argument thus:

A perhaps surprising event, *a*, has occurred.
If a hypothesis, *H*, were true, then *a* would follow.
No competing hypothesis explains *a* as well.
Thus, reason exists to believe *H* probably is true.[120]

Obviously, a big problem for IBE is the meaning of "best" explanation. The leading expert prefers the "loveliest" to the "likeliest" for defining "best," with loveliness measuring "epistemic value in terms of explanatory virtue."[121] Others attempt to create a checklist of criteria that mark a good explanation.[122] But whatever the metric, it seems that it should involve analysis not wildly different from the kind we intuitively use to generate multivalent degrees of belief.

[115] See Cabrera (2023); Hartshorne and Weiss (1932), p. 106 ("Abduction is the process of forming an explanatory hypothesis." (quoting from Peirce's collected papers)); see also Anderson et al. (2005), pp. 56–58 (discussing abduction in fact investigation); cf. supra Sect. 3.4 (discussing Peirce's work on probability). Very similar representation of thought has gone into creating software for secret intelligence analysis, see, e.g., Keahey and Eick (2004), with the role of abduction therein being discussed by Cluxton et al. (2004).

[116] See Walton (2002), pp. 43–45, 105–108, 233 (legal factfinding); Brewer (2011), p. 178 (legal reasoning).

[117] See Anderson et al. (2005), p. 56 (formulating such a line of argument).

[118] See McAuliffe (2015).

[119] See Harman (1965) (developing the fountainhead of modern IBE); Tuzet (2019) (delineating the relationship of IBE to abduction).

[120] See Amaya (2009), p. 136 (formulating such a line of argument).

[121] Lipton (2004), pp. 59–61 ("Likeliness speaks of truth; loveliness of potential understanding.").

[122] See Laudan (2007), p. 296 & n.13 (listing the variety of tests for "best" that theorists have forwarded); Schum (2001), p. 1659 ("[W]e may not have any settled criterion for saying what is the 'best' explanation."); cf. Amaya (2009), pp. 138–146 (using a coherentist approach to evaluate the explanation); Bex (2009) (judging plausibility by how well the explanation fits a specific description of typical event structures).

IBE also depends on a good-faith and thorough search for a pool of decent explanations. Here arises a strong criticism of IBE, namely, its "argument from a bad lot."[123] All that IBE can deliver is the best explanation from the explanations considered. This best explanation could be merely the best of a bad lot. One could never know if it is true. One could not even know that it is probably true unless one knows that the true explanation was probably included among the explanations considered.

Seemingly more troubling is the problem of infinite alternatives.[124] The infinite range of possibilities would seem to make the problem-solver's task nearly impossible to perform. Almost no one could give an explanation that merits being called the best, given the difficulty of assembling and overcoming all the remaining alternatives.

Nevertheless, IBE dominates the scientific method's production of explanations of generic events,[125] having produced such fruits as Darwin's theories of evolution[126] but also such clunkers as Ptolemaic astronomy.[127] In some fields, IBE goes by the name of the weight of the evidence methodology.[128]

In trying to explain unique events, medical diagnosis obviously employs IBE.[129] There, IBE goes by the name of differential diagnosis.[130] The doctor successively eliminates possible causes of a medical condition to reveal the best explanation among the conceivable possibilities. Here IBE appears to be a proper mode of analysis, correct and useful.

In sum, IBE works well for certain kinds of problems, but can take us only so far. Can it work for legal factfinding, as contrasted with legal reasoning? Medical diagnosis is a different task from legal factfinding. Diagnosis seeks by a process of

---

[123] See Van Fraassen (1989), p. 143 (developing the criticism); Amaya (2009), pp. 152–153 (recounting the criticism).

[124] See supra Sect. 3.2.3 (laying out this problem and mentioning ways to contain this problem).

[125] See Ladyman (2002), pp. 209–210; Okasha (2016), pp. 23–26 ("Scientists frequently use IBE.").

[126] See Amaya (2009), p. 137 (giving examples).

[127] See Laudan (2007), p. 293 (observing that IBE "routinely warrants the acceptance of scientific theories and hypotheses that subsequent empirical research has repeatedly revealed to be false").

[128] See Milward v. Acuity Specialty Prods. Grp., Inc., 639 F.3d 11, 18 (1st Cir. 2011) (admitting expert evidence based on the weight of the evidence approach: "The scientist must (1) identify an association between an exposure and a disease, (2) consider a range of plausible explanations for the association, (3) rank the rival explanations according to their plausibility, (4) seek additional evidence to separate the more plausible from the less plausible explanations, (5) consider all of the relevant available evidence, and (6) integrate the evidence using professional judgment to come to a conclusion about the best explanation.").

[129] See Cohen (1980), pp. 58–59 (developing the benefits of IBE over traditional probability, but likening IBE to the nonadditive logic of inductive (or Baconian) probability).

[130] See Hall v. Conoco Inc., 886 F.3d 1308, 1314 (10th Cir. 2018) (excluding expert evidence based on differential diagnosis, because of an inadequate pool of possible causes, and observing: "An expert need not consider and rule out every *conceivable* cause. But the expert must still consider all plausible causes and rule out the less plausible ones until only the most likely cause remains." (citations omitted)); Westberry v. Gislaved Gummi AB, 178 F.3d 257, 262–63 (4th Cir. 1999) (admitting expert evidence based on differential diagnosis).

elimination the best of all explanations one can imagine, and then uses it to guide tentative steps in treatment. The law is instead asking whether the proponent's version of the facts meets the standard of proof, say, for most civil cases, that it is more likely true than false. Incidentally, medical diagnosis proceeds without any perceptible awareness of multivalence. Although these differences turn out to be superficial, applying IBE to legal factfinding cannot be direct.[131] It requires some work.

4.4.2 *Relative Plausibility*

Still, some have tried to twist IBE to the legal task.[132] These theorists, realizing that IBE does not readily fit, have invented a new approach that merely uses the verbiage of IBE.[133] They call their creation the relative plausibility theory ("RP"), or explanationism in their most recent reworking.[134]

RP posits that the factfinder constructs (1) the overall story (or explanation, in the latest preferred terminology[135]) that the plaintiff is spinning and (2) another story (or stories, in some variants of the theory[136]) that the defendant is or could be

---

[131] Compare Michelon (2019) (justifying the extension of IBE to support legal conclusions), with Laudan (2007), pp. 297–305 (demonstrating that IBE holds little promise of explaining or illuminating the standards of proof, and observing: "IBE cannot function as a standard of proof . . . .").

[132] E.g., Allen and Stein (2013), pp. 567–570 (discussing adjudicative factfinding as IBE); Pardo and Allen (2008) (discussing how IBE explains judicial proof); cf. Amaya (2019), p. 65 (arguing for evidentialist and coherentist versions of "explanationism"); Sullivan (2018), pp. 19–34 (taking important steps toward formalizing the IBE approach as "likelihood theory," which nonetheless remains subject to much of the same rebuttal as relative plausibility).

[133] See Allen and Jehl (2003), pp. 929–943 (explaining the origin of the new approach).

[134] See Allen and Pardo (2019b), p. 6 n.1 (updating name of theory).

[135] See id. at 7 n.7, 17 n.86, 31 (distinguishing "story" from "explanation").

[136] Compare Hastie (2008), pp. 31–32 (expanding the theory to allow for a party's multiple stories), with Pardo (2013), pp. 598–599 (discussing the theory's difficulties in handling multiple stories). In my view, this supposed problem of "story" or "stories" disappears if one takes the plaintiff's story (or the defendant's story on an affirmative defense) to be one that encompasses all parts of the claim that the plaintiff must prove. The defendant's story then includes all versions that negate one or more of those parts. The parties do not have to formulate these stories expressly, as long as the factfinder can construct the stories out of the allegations and evidence. See Allen and Pardo (2019b), pp. 24–26 (accepting this approach to alternative explanations, and repudiating the earlier approach set out in, e.g., Allen (1991), p. 409 ("The defendant could be required to plead and prove an episode that excludes the possibility of instantiating the formal elements of the substantive law, which simply means that if the defendant's claim is accepted, it falsifies at least one formal element.")). Thus, when I refer to a party's "story," I am invoking this broad notion of the party's best explanation, unless otherwise stated.

Note, however, that a broad notion of "story" gives the defendant the benefit of disjunctive proof, while the plaintiff remains saddled with conjunction, given RP's acceptance of probabilism. This asymmetry causes the current formulation of RP to unravel completely, as I shall soon explain.

spinning. The factfinder then compares the two stories and gives victory to the plaintiff if and only if the plaintiff's version is more plausible than the defendant's. This choice between the two competing narratives is largely an ordinal process rather than a cardinal one.[137]

No doubt, RP has some advantages, which explains why it is pushed. It does echo the way lawyers talk about their cases. It embraces the use of humans' strong capacity for relative judgment rather than absolute judgment. It strikes the tone of psychology's holistic models,[138] while echoing the words of abduction and IBE.

Yet, RP aims at the merely descriptive. It has no theoretical underpinning, and so does nothing to explain why RP's path is the right path to follow. RP gives no justificatory reason to think that accepting the better of two stories is an accurate way to proceed. Indeed, RP does not give an analytic reason to think that it is superior to unadorned probability.

There would be impediments if RP were to grasp at any straws of theory. The theories that RP cites do not lend support. Despite claims to the contrary, abduction does not justify RP, as abduction is a way for the investigator creatively to imagine possible explanations for later testing, rather than a way to reason to a conclusion.[139] IBE, which is distinct from abduction, gives a path to a conclusion. However, verbiage aside, RP is not a straightforward version of IBE, so its bow to IBE adds little support. Unlike IBE, RP asks the parties in an adversary system to select the story candidates. It does not consider all possible explanations, or even demand a decent pool of explanations as IBE does. By the RP theorists' fiat it limits consideration to two contesting explanations, being each party's position on the allegations and evidence.[140] This fiat makes life simpler, but sends the "argument from a bad lot" criticism right through the roof. There is no way to justify RP's narrow focus, other than an appeal to adversariness as implying a brutal law of the jungle: "You put up your best story, and you, defendant, do the same. We'll pick the better one."[141]

This lack of theory permeates RP. Another of its fiats dictates that factfinders should handle probability's problems by simply ignoring probabilities. Although RP accepts the relevance of probability, RP does nothing about its puzzles or paradoxes.

---

[137] See Allen and Jehl (2003), p. 938 ("proof is largely comparative or ordinal rather than cardinal").

[138] See infra Chap. 5 (discussing psychology's story model).

[139] See Allen and Pardo (2019b), p. 6 n.1 (claiming that abduction provides the theory's "epistemological foundation"). Those authors simply declare: "Abduction, in other words, is the process by which legal fact-finders arrive at probabilistic—i.e., inductive, non-demonstrative—conclusions." Id. at 20–21. That formulation of abduction has no support in the literature. It seems instead to refer to abductive validation, that is, some technique like IBE to select among the explanations that abduction has yielded. So, RP's reliance on abduction adds nothing to its reliance on IBE.

[140] See Allen and Pardo (2007), pp. 314–317 (defending their conception of IBE in a way that pares it back into a form consistent with bare RP).

[141] See Nance (2001), p. 1575 (criticizing that "the relative plausibility theory is stated in terms of *stories advanced by the parties*").

Consider conjunction yet again. RP accepts traditional probability and the conjunction paradox as facts of life[142] and then sweeps them under the rug.[143] RP theorists claim that they can ignore the paradox because they are simply comparing two whole stories.[144] True, if the factfinder just compares stories, any oddity concerning the necessary likelihood of the elements disappears, but only from view. The paradox is still there. *Given their view of the product rule as a feature of the world*, the plaintiff's elements individually must have satisfied a much higher standard of proof if his conjoined story is to end up being stronger than the defendant's story. Meanwhile, the defendant can combine the probabilities of all her alternative versions of nonliability. That is, the defendant would enjoy the advantage of disjunctive proof, while the plaintiff would remain saddled with conjunction. In brief, applying the RP test only at the end of the case does not avoid the conjunction and disjunction of the elements subject to proof. RP's refusing to ask expressly for element-by-element likelihoods does not make the paradox disappear. That is just sticking one's head in the sand.

Beyond the lack of theory that necessitates resort to fiat, RP presents a host of related practical problems.[145] Most seriously, it contradicts the law in a number of ways. First, by still another fiat, this time in defiance of the law, it repeals the requirement of meeting the standard of proof, at least in any traditional sense. No longer must an element or the case be, say, more likely than not. RP does not try to explain what the law meant when it articulated a standard of proof. RP is preaching that we should ignore what the law says and instead apply an invented test that might give good results. Second, it ignores the law stated in judicial instructions that the plaintiff need only prove "every essential element of plaintiff's claim."[146] RP rests on an assumption that factfinders proceed holistically, even though RP does not

[142] See Allen (2018), pp. 996, 997, 1004 (calling the paradox "a feature of the world"); Allen and Pardo (2019b), pp. 35 n.221, 39, 52 (same); Allen and Pardo (2019a), pp. 212, 213 n.26 (same). The product rule is not a feature of life. It is a feature of calculating traditional probabilities, not of combining beliefs.

[143] See Allen and Pardo (2019b), pp. 17–18 ("Rather than assessing A and B serially and attaching a probability to each, fact-finders evaluate whether the plaintiff's explanation (which will include or entail A & B) is better than the defendant's explanation (which will fail to include A or B, or both).").

[144] See id. at 29 ("Under our account, however, the conjunction problem is avoided because the standard of proof applies to the case as a whole in evaluating explanations and is distributed over both parties."). Lest there be any doubt about its position on conjunction, the current formulation of RP dictates a plaintiff's loss in a civil case with two independent elements whether they are proved to 60% and 60% or to 90% and 40%. See Allen and Pardo (2023), p. 140 & n.49. The authors' generalization in their text is that the plaintiff loses if its probabilistic conjunction (or, a fortiori, its proof on any element) falls to or below 50%. Incredibly, they claim, without citing any authority, that the case law and virtually all commentators agree with their view. But by viewing conjunction as "a feature of the world" and thereby giving the defendant the benefit of probabilistic disjunction, their theory unravels and they give up looking for who has the better story when they reject a 60%-60% case.

[145] See Friedman (2001), pp. 2046–2047 (noting problems with RP).

[146] Supra Chap. 3 (quoting pattern jury instruction); see Allen (2011), p. 14 (acknowledging the inconsistencies between jury instructions and RP).

maintain that holism is normatively sound.[147] RP tells the factfinder to create holistic stories and compare them. It does not even contemplate going element-by-element. It does not formulate a standard of proof that can handle the evidence if the factfinder insists on an atomistic processing method. RP as a method thus comes with a fair amount of baggage.[148] Third, by calling for a head-to-head ordinal comparison of two stories, it has encountered some difficulties with handling standards of proof other than preponderance.[149] On matters like summary judgment and judgment as a matter of law, the attempt to translate the governing standards quickly sinks into incomprehensibility. Fourth, RP might force the defendant to be much more active than the law requires. RP appears to compel the defendant, at least as a practical matter, to formulate a competing version of the truth. The defendant seemingly loses the legal right to stand mute and still possibly prevail.[150]

Finally, even after countless articles, RP is an underdeveloped method. It gives little guidance on how to choose which story is better. IBE at least confronts this problem, albeit with no definite conclusion.[151] RP instead depends on the unfortunate and undemanding word "plausible." It gives victory to the more plausible story. Even accepting "more plausible" as the test, what does it mean? How does it work when, say, the plaintiff's story is strong on all but one element? Resorting to probabilities just for illustration, imagine the plaintiff's story is 54%, 54%, 54%,

---

[147] See Allen and Pardo (2019b), pp. 30–31 (asserting that holism is the prevailing practice); Simon (2019), pp. 86–87 (giving four reasons to beware of holistic factfinding).

[148] See Callen (1991), pp. 432–439 (discussing some problems with RP's baggage).

[149] See Friedman (2001), p. 2047 ("Therefore, Allen has previously recognized that the concept of cardinality must come into play."); cf. Allen (1991), p. 413 (attempting to explain the beyond-a-reasonable-doubt standard as not being satisfied if the factfinder "concludes that there is a plausible scenario consistent with innocence," while admitting that the clear-and-convincing standard is "troublesome" under his theory because it seems cardinal); Allen and Leiter (2001), p. 1528 (saying that the criminal prosecution must "show that there is no plausible account of innocence"); Allen and Pardo (2007), p. 316 ("Jurors ought to convict [only] when there is a plausible explanation consistent with guilt and no plausible explanation consistent with innocence . . . ."); Pardo (2015), p. 1829 (attempting to explain the clear-and-convincing standard as requiring that "the plaintiff's explanation must be clearly and convincingly better than the defendant's explanation"); Pardo (2023), pp. 450–51 ("Under the 'beyond a reasonable doubt' standard, the threshold is met when the prosecution's explanation is the only plausible explanation."). For their latest iteration, see Allen and Pardo (2019b), pp. 16–17, 26–29. But cf. Laudan (2007), p. 303 ("Why IBE will not work as a standard of proof is that it aims to be a universal standard of credibility and not a context-specific measure of degree of proof."); Allen and Pardo (2007), pp. 314–317 (rebuttal).

[150] See Broun (2013), § 339 (explaining that because jurors bring their own viewpoints, it is possible for a verdict to find for a defendant who offers nothing in opposition to the plaintiff's evidence). Admittedly, RP's burden on the defendant could conform to the law if RP allows the defendant's story to come solely from the factfinder's forming its own disbelief of the plaintiff's story. See Allen and Pardo (2019b), pp. 21–24 (arguing, in their latest version, that the defendant's burden is no more burdensome than this).

[151] See supra Sect. 4.4.1 (describing IBE's efforts). Lately, RP theorists have turned toward this inconclusive literature to suggest: "In general, explanations are evaluated based on criteria such as consistency, coverage, simplicity, coherence, consilience, and fit with background knowledge." Allen and Pardo (2019b), p. 7 n.7; see id. at 16, 19 (admitting that there is no general recipe for ranking explanations).

and 40% on four elements, and the defendant's story is 46%, 46%, 46%, and 60%. We cannot easily say which is the more plausible when the factfinder goes to compare those two whole stories.[152]

We cannot even know which stories we should be comparing. Think back to the facial-recognition hypo.[153] We need to decide if Mark did it or someone else did it. The difficulty is that RP gives no way to choose between formulating the defendant's story as an 80% chance that someone else did it or formulating it as a tiny disbelief that Mark did it.

The most sensible meaning of the plaintiff's story being more plausible or better, I posit,[154] is that the degree of belief in each of the elements of the plaintiff's story exceeds the degree of belief in the corresponding denial by the defendant (Mark was not the wrongdoer). Otherwise, the defendant could construct the best story consisting of (1) admissions of all the elements with a weaker denial and (2) denials of the elements where the denial prevails; then, the conjoined elements of the plaintiff's story would not be more believable than the defendant's best story that conjoins those two sets of selected allegations.

4.4.3 *Ranking Theory*

Although RP theorists make no reference to it, an epistemological theory does exist to justify looking only at the defendant's single best version. So-called ranking theory allows ignoring all of the defendant's other versions.[155]

This very complex, nonadditive theory ranks propositions in order of the decisionmaker's disbeliefs in them, with the least disbelieved being top-ranked. Its MAX formula for disjunction of the second to the last of the multiple propositions calculates the disjunction to be the disbelief of the second-ranked proposition. The top-ranked version will therefore outrank all the defendant's alternative propositions combined.[156]

---

[152] See Welch (2020) (faulting RP's failure to define "plausible," and then redefining it in a way that reduces RP to a probabilistic theory). Note that for beyond a reasonable doubt, Professor Allen uses "plausible" as an absolute standard, in that there cannot exist a plausible account of innocence. See Allen (1991), p. 413. Incidentally, the product rule would give victory to this plaintiff for having the stronger story. But Professor Allen gives victory to the defendant because the probability of the plaintiff's conjunction does not exceed 50%. See Allen and Pardo (2023), p. 140 & n.49.

[153] See supra Sect. 3.2.2.1 (setting out this hypo).

[154] See infra Sect. 5.1.3.3 (defending this supposition). The same analysis would apply to the defendant's story on the elements of an affirmative defense.

[155] See Genin and Huber (2020), § 3.4 ("a set of worlds is only as disbelieved as its most plausible member"); Spohn (2009), pp. 187–204 (giving a good general treatment of ranking theory).

[156] See Spohn (2009), pp. 188, 191–192 (giving key definitions as statements numbered 1, 4, and 5, and opening the door to approaching the problem equivalently by ranking in order of decreasing affirmative belief).

The basic idea here is that in the set of all possible worlds there is a world *U* that is ranked as more likely, in some sense, than world *V*. So, *U* has the numerically lower rank. Maybe *U* is the third most likely world, and *V* is no higher than the fourth most likely. By the ranking function, the ranking of the union of *U* and *V* is the minimum of their individual rankings. Thus, the rank of *U* is the ranking of it and all the lesser-ranked worlds put together.[157]

4.4.4 Reconciliation of Alternative Models

Like ranking theory, multivalent belief theory is a way to support RP by curing its major failing, namely, the lack of theoretical justification. Multivalent belief theory would resolve RP's problems of impracticality and impenetrability as well, and do so more clearly and easily than would ranking theory.

Unknowingly, RP theorists have formulated a fuzzy technique for dealing with more likely than not, so that RP ends up as an overly specific statement of the multivalent belief model.[158] I can demonstrate this near equivalence by showing how the multivalent belief model can produce the more dialectical RP model as a special case and by showing conversely how RP can generalize into multivalent beliefs.

First, consider how the multivalent belief model works, using a civil case as the example. If the factfinder goes element-by-element, a plaintiff's win by multivalent beliefs means that each element in the claim is more likely than not, in the sense that the belief in the element exceeds the strongest constructible disbelief of the element. By the MIN rule for conjunction, this means that the plaintiff's best story is more believable than the defendant's best story conjoined out of the allegations and evidence. By the MAX rule for disjunction, the cumulative likelihood of any group of the defendant's possible stories being true is the likelihood of the strongest defendant's story in the group. Accordingly, the plaintiff's conjoined story is more believable than the disjunction of all the contesting stories. And if and only if that is so, the plaintiff's conjoined story is more likely than any story offered by the defendant. Therefore, if the plaintiff prevails (or fails) under the multivalent belief model, it meets the same fate under RP.

Second, consider how RP works. Assume that the best story constructible for the plaintiff is "better" than the best story constructible for the defendant. That

[157] See Halpern (2017), pp. 45–51.

[158] The closest the RP theorists get to acknowledging this reliance is their confusingly, and I think wrongly, noting that, "of course, the most probable explanation supporting each side will be the disjunction of all possible explanations supporting that side (it will be at least as probable as any single disjunct or subset)." Allen and Pardo (2019b), p. 26. In fact, they full-throatedly criticize the multivalent belief model. See Allen (2018), pp. 1003–1014; Allen and Pardo (2019b), pp. 49–58; Pardo (2019), pp. 275–278. But see Clermont (2019) (rebuttal); Clermont (2018), p. 1074 n.43 (same).

should mean, as shown above, the degree of belief in each of the elements of the plaintiff's best story exceeds the degree of belief in the corresponding denial by the defendant. Accordingly, if the plaintiff succeeds (or fails) by RP, then the test of the multivalent belief model gives the same result. Therefore, if and only if the plaintiff prevails under RP, it prevails under the multivalent belief model.

In other words, RP requires the plaintiff to formulate his best explanation, which alleges all elements and is as likely as its weakest link. The defendant can offer her best explanation, but RP theorists provide no justification for so comparing the two stories. Instead, they unknowingly rely on the MIN and MAX rules of multivalent logic for any intuitive hope that if the plaintiff's version is better than the defendant's best position, then the plaintiff's story is superior to all competing accounts. By multivalent logic, one has good reason not to consider all competing accounts, and can justifiably decide that the plaintiff's story is better after focusing on only the defendant's single best constructible position.

The RP approach is cheered by its adherents because of its practical advantages, such as conforming to how adversarial lawyers talk about their cases. But the convergence of RP and the multivalent belief model means that the latter can likewise claim all those practical advantages, as it too can speak in terms of comparing best stories. The difference is that only the multivalent belief model has a firm theoretical foundation for doing so.

The same analysis will work to show that IBE and ranking theory too are largely equivalent to multivalent belief theory for the purposes of factfinding. All these methods are ultimately reconcilable.[159] IBE is similar to, but not the same as, RP, and can be shown to rest on multivalent beliefs. The reason that ranking theory works out consistently is that it, too, rests on degrees of belief. Indeed, ranking theory, alone among the three theories, is self-aware enough to recognize its debt to multivalent logic:

> Epistemology is concerned with the fundamental laws of thought, belief, or judgment. … Often, we talk as if this would be a yes or no affair. From time immemorial, though, we know that judgment is firm or less than firm, that belief is a matter of degree. This insight opens another vast realm of formal epistemology. … [T]here are strong family resemblances among the alternatives. … Ranking theory … belongs to this field as well.[160]

The hidden commonality of the IBE, RP, and ranking theories, if viewed in terms of degrees of belief, is that they all reject additivity and so can invoke the MAX rule for disjunction. The best conceivable position in opposition to an alleged proposition gains nothing from its conceivable alternatives, because the MAX rule makes the disjunction of alternatives no stronger than the best of those positions. The outcome will be the same if one compares the plaintiff's position to the defendant's strongest position or to all the defendant's conceivable positions. If you justifiably believe the plaintiff's position more than you disbelieve it, then you believe it more than all other positions put together, and so you should accept it as the truth.

[159] See supra Sect. 4.3.2 (supporting the compatibility of multivalent versions).

[160] Spohn (2009), pp. 185–186; see Huber (2009), pp. 16–20 (comparing belief function theory and possibility theory to ranking theory); see also id. at 18–19 (relating ranking theory to the degrees of potential surprise developed in Shackle (1949) and Shackle (1969), and recently extended by Risinger (2018)).

Thus, by using the same logical tools for combination of propositions, these competing theories turn out to be largely equivalent to the multivalent belief theory for factfinding. The reconciliation of all these theories is not magic. It reflects the fact that they, along with induction, abduction, inferential reasoning, and even nontraditional probability all employ brands of that big familial classification of logic called non-monotonic logic.[161] This non-monotonic class embraces the methods of potentially defeasible reasoning to reach a conclusion, which would be subject to retraction in light of further information. Various theories tangle with how to conduct that reasoning. At a basic level, however, they are all similar.

4.4.5 Role of Alternative Models

In my view, the best factfinding way to follow in non-monotonia, a way expressively superior to the competing theories, is combining the belief functions image and multivalent logic tools to compose multivalent belief theory. Yet the IBE, RP, and ranking theories are not wrong. So, they can serve as complements to the MIN and MAX rules of multivalent belief theory.

Multivalent beliefs will directly determine whether the factfinder believes a proposition more than it disbelieves the proposition. But determining the best opposing argument, interpretation, or explanation to consider among a group of two or more is a different kind of step in factfinding.

The latter task can be achieved by IBE, RP, or ranking theory. These three models implicitly rely on multivalent logic's MAX rule to do so. Multivalent belief theory, with its MAX rule, could achieve the same. Thus, the three are just unexplained shortcuts for that step in factfinding. For example, an advocate or factfinder could use one of the three alternative models to pick the strongest of all available contrary chains of inference from evidence to either acceptance or rejection of an element. Then the factfinder could return to multivalent belief theory to decide whether that chain should prevail. In short, the alternative models can provide a shortcut in multivalent reasoning.

4.5 Multivalent Beliefs' Solutions to Probability's Problems

Another sign that the law and its factfinders should, and actually do, embrace the multivalent belief model is that this model resolves all those puzzles, paradoxes, and other practical and theoretical problems that plague the probabilistic model. The

---

[161] See Strasser and Antonelli (2019), § 1 (saying for non-monotonic logic that "the truth of the premises does not guarantee or necessitate the truth of the conclusion as in deductive reasoning").

multivalent belief model makes sense. The following discussion describes its resolutions of probability's problems.

4.5.1 Unrealistic Measurement

Probability is an unrealistic tool for factfinding. By contrast, factfinders can feasibly employ multivalent degrees of belief. And they should. Gradated beliefs turn out to be an especially useful way to conceive of likelihood because they can capture all the relevant kinds of uncertainty in the world. Following multivalent logic's rejection of the assumption that all things are either completely true or completely false, belief functions convey the extra information about all those uncertainties.

Moreover, because probabilistic thinking and its usual p>50% formulation of preponderance induce one to speak in quantified terms, multivalent degrees of belief could induce a more realistic expression of factfinding. Comparing belief to its corresponding disbelief is a common task in life, one that avoids the troublesome task of quantification. Additionally, comparing those two beliefs invokes the factfinders' considerable powers of relative judgment, rather than humans' weak powers of absolute judgment required for placement on some scale of likelihood.

4.5.2 Weak Evidence

Using beliefs in lieu of probabilities removes all the mystery from how the law handles evidence that is unavoidably weak on both sides. Say that *Bel(a)* = 0.20 and *Bel(not-a)* = 0.03 after hearing all the available, but very imperfect, evidence. A probabilist might be inclined to decide against the civil plaintiff, saying inaccurately that there is a chance up to 80% that the defendant is not liable. But the belief in favor of the plaintiff is reasonably strong and perceptibly stronger than the corresponding disbelief.

True, the factfinder would feel uncertain and long for more evidence. But the factfinder must decide now for either plaintiff or defendant based on the available evidence. The plaintiff has produced a reasonably believable narrative. There is no reasonably believable narrative contrary to the plaintiff's. On the basis of this evidence, if proportionately normalized, the plaintiff's story is about 87% probably true. A decision for the plaintiff is less likely an error than a decision for the defendant would be. Thus, the plaintiff should win when it presents a case like this.

The plaintiff's good chance of a verdict explains why the civil defendant usually presents a defense to a plaintiff's case that is only reasonably believable. The defendant must make sure that disbelief of the plaintiff's case is at least as strong as belief of the plaintiff's case.

4.5.3 *Infinite Possibilities*

Under the traditional probability model, the infinite range of possibilities alternative to the proponent's allegations appears to make the burden of persuasion very heavy. By contrast, the multivalent belief model does not require the completeness of proof that would be necessary for the burdened party to get belief to some level above 50%, but instead is willing to follow the law by resting decisions on the evidence available.

Furthermore, the multivalent belief model clarifies that the proponent need not dispel all possible alternatives. The burdened party need not fight imaginary fights, trying to disprove every alternative possibility, but instead can focus on elevating *a* and depressing *not-a*. All the possible states of the world that affect neither a belief in *a* nor an active belief in *not-a* fall within the uncommitted belief. Their mere existence does not augment the disbelief in *a* under the MAX rule.

Here is the point at which to recall the Mark hypo.[162] The existence of 50 suspects does not prevent recovery, if the proof is viewed in terms of multivalent beliefs. The beliefs are not 0.02 it was Mark and 0.98 it was not Mark. Instead the facial-recognition proof augments the first belief, while the MAX rule lowers the second belief down to about 0.02. The plaintiff need not disprove that it was one of the other 49 suspects. The defendant, Mark, needs to search out some evidence it was not him.

To generalize, we handle alternative explanations, or alternative suspects, by the MAX rule. It is the disjunction of the alternatives that goes into measuring the disbelief of *a*. The disjunction equals the most believable of the alternative explanations, not some sum of all the alternatives.

This insight about the nature of beliefs could illuminate some substantive problems, by focusing the factfinder's inquiry on the disbelief of an allegation in the specific case. Imagine a medical malpractice action for causing a death by failing to make a timely diagnosis of a brain tumor. The plaintiff's problem is that >50% of patients die from the tumor type. The court cases have consequently tended to say that the plaintiff cannot prove causation.[163] Some judges, however, view that rule as unfair.[164] To me, the rule just seems illogical. The short version is that a >50% chance of a random outcome does not translate into a >0.50 belief in noncausation. In any specific malpractice case, a lot will be unknown about causation. The uncommitted belief will be considerable, and so the belief that the doctor's treatment caused death could exceed the corresponding disbelief. True, a general death rate over 50% will inflate the disbelief. But converting the percentage into a disbelief is a

---

[162] See supra Sect. 3.2.2.1 (explaining the Mark hypo).

[163] See, e.g., Cooper v Sisters of Charity of Cincinnati, Inc., 272 N.E.2d 97, 104 (Ohio 1971) ("[T]he issue of proximate cause can be submitted to a jury only if there is sufficient evidence showing that with proper diagnosis, treatment and surgery the patient probably would have survived."), overruled, Roberts v. Ohio Permanente Med. Grp., Inc., 668 N.E.2d 480, 484 (Ohio 1996).

[164] See, e.g., Herskovits v Grp. Health Coop. of Puget Sound, 664 P.2d 474 (Wash. 1983) (converting the issue into causing a reduction of chance for survival).

difficult task. The percentage must be connected up with causation in the individualized case by a series of permissible but uncertain inferences; the statistical evidence may have to be discounted for defects in credibility; the evaluation may have to be adjusted in light of the probative value of the absence of other proof; and so on. In short, epistemic uncertainty must be accounted for, as the statistic is converted into a belief function with uncommitted belief. Then, other evidence, more specific and perhaps more probative, would come in. In the factfinder's mind, the belief in causation thus might still exceed the disbelief in this malpractice hypo.

4.5.4 Combining Evidence

Traditional probability's fatal defect for factfinding is that, unbeknownst to most of us, it is built on an assumption of bivalence. That is, it assumes that facts must be treated as either true or false, with an excluded middle. In this black-and-white world, *probability of truth*, or p, provides the random chance of the fact being revealed as true. Moreover, the probability of the fact being revealed as false is the complement, $1-p$.

For the purposes of factfinding, a critical theoretical correction is away from bivalence and toward multivalence. The multivalent form of logic declines the simplification offered by bivalent logic and instead recognizes partial truths. Factfinders can believe facts as partly true, ranging in degree from zero to one. It is upon this *belief in truth* that the law should proceed. Both a proposition and its opposite can be believed true to a degree. Furthermore, given imperfect evidence or other sources of unknowns, the factfinder will leave some of its belief uncommitted. The belief and disbelief then will add to less than one. This multivalent logic is nonadditive.

The law's choice comes down to probability of truth versus belief in truth. Legal factfinders can, do, and should focus on the latter. Factfinding should not aim to measure the probability of bivalent truth but rather to gauge partial beliefs established by the evidence. The standards of proof were never meant to deal with the betting odds of having discovered truth, which is all that a bivalent model can deliver. The standards of proof instead operate on multivalent degrees of belief.

Employing degrees of belief brings into play belief functions and multivalent operators. They in turn govern both (1) aggregating evidence and (2) combining inferences, findings, or conclusions. These two are very different mathematical tasks. Once again, I want to stress the difference. Aggregation requires combining the probative force of a piece of evidence with the probative force of another piece in developing a belief in a particular fact being true. Combining found facts to form a belief in their conjunction or disjunction is a totally different mental process, not involving how separate pieces of evidence fit together but rather how one brings separate beliefs together to form a narrative. The accurate solutions for the two tasks are, respectively, (1) an approach that is more intuitive for aggregating evidence than

Bayes' theorem and (2) the highly clarifying MIN/MAX rules for conjunction and disjunction.

4.5.4.1 Aggregation by Dempster-Shafer Theory

Aggregating evidence in support of a single proposition is a mathematical problem whose solution must be derived under the prevailing logic system, be it bivalent or multivalent. The solution is Bayes' theorem under classical logic, but becomes an even more complicated problem under Shafer's belief function theory.

There is no canonical solution for aggregating evidence into a new belief. There are many arguable approaches to this so-called belief update. The main focus of belief function theorists' work indeed involves addressing this problem of how to aggregate items of evidence by combining their belief functions somehow. The theoretical stimulus is the realization that Bayes' theorem is a gross oversimplification for aggregating uncertain evidence, one intentionally built onto traditional probability in order to shear off the epistemic uncertainty and thereby make all the evidence easily commensurable. The result of the belief function theorists' work aimed at generalizing Bayes is an array of sophisticated mathematical tools for aggregating pieces of aleatorially and epistemically uncertain evidence to produce a composite degree of belief.

Shafer and many others relied on the prominent Dempster rule to govern the task.[165] That rule is complicated, because it abstractly addresses the problem in very general terms (Bayes' theorem turns out to be a special case of the Dempster rule, if epistemic uncertainty is assumed away).[166] I could reprint its central formula, but it would be meaningless without many obscure definitions. I do not reprint it here because I shall not be using the Dempster rule. Suffice it to say, the Dempster rule aggregates the belief functions from different pieces of evidence into a new belief function by orthogonal sum, a process beyond the ken of the ordinary factfinder as a practical matter. Significantly, the rule also makes some probabilistic assumptions,

[165] See Shafer (1976), pp. 6, 25, 57–67 ("[W]e construct a belief function to represent the new evidence and combine it with our 'prior' belief function—i.e., with the belief function that represents our prior opinions. This method deals symmetrically with the new evidence and the old evidence on which our prior opinions are based: both bodies of evidence are represented by belief functions, and the result of the combination does not depend on which evidence is the old and which is the new."); Barnett (2008), pp. 198–204 (explaining the Dempster rule).

[166] For a comparison of Bayesian probability judgments with belief functions, see Shafer and Tversky (2008).

which further justifies my using the belief function concept without fully embracing belief function mathematics.[167] Furthermore, the Dempster rule has proved to be theoretically inappropriate for many kinds of evidence.[168]

Accordingly, the Dempster rule is quite contested, generating many competitors.[169] Again, there is no one correct way to aggregate evidence into a new belief function, as each alternative rule makes certain assumptions about the natures of the different pieces of evidence and their uncertainty. In particular, the competing rules differ in how they handle conflicting and contradictory evidence. Almost all are more complicated than the Dempster rule.[170]

Shafer himself suggested one of the simplest alternatives.[171] It is called the discount-and-combine rule. It works when the evidence is highly conflicting and contradictory, as in a legal case. The "discount" step diminishes the belief function derived from an item of evidence in accordance with the belief function's unreliability: the advice is to "discount belief functions at different rates before combining them—discounting at higher rates those belief functions one particularly distrusts and whose influence one wants to reduce."[172] The "combine" step averages the discounted belief functions. To illustrate, let $BelFunc^{d}_{i}(a)$ be the discounted belief function for the element a that is generated from an item of evidence, i, and derived by multiplying $BelFunc_i(a)$ by its discount factor, d_i, where $0 \leq d_i \leq 1$. Then,

---

[167] See, e.g., Dubois and Prade (2008), p. 403 ("If subjective probability theory is acknowledged as being too restrictive to model uncertainty judgments, then Shafer's subjectivist interpretation of upper and lower probabilities can be questioned on the same grounds. From a mathematical point of view, [Shafer's] theory of evidence is nothing but the rules of probability theory applied to imprecise statements, while classical probability theory leaves no room to imprecision. As a consequence the rules of combination of bodies of evidence are given by the rules of probability theory, and what is behind the problem of validating Shafer's theory as a theory of measurement of subjective uncertainty is the validity of the rules of (subjective) probability theory (and especially the rule of additivity).").

[168] See, e.g., Sentz and Ferson (2002), p. 17 ("Suppose that a patient is seen by two physicians regarding the patient's neurological symptoms. The first doctor believes that the patient has either meningitis with a probability of 0.99 or a brain tumor, with a probability of 0.01. The second physician believes the patient actually suffers from a concussion with a probability of 0.99 but admits the possibility of a brain tumor with a probability of 0.01. Using ... Dempster's rule, we find that ... *Bel*(brain tumor) = 1. Clearly, this rule of combination yields a result that implies complete support for a diagnosis that both physicians considered to be very unlikely." (relying on Zadeh (1984), p. 82)).

[169] See id. at 17–27 (describing thirteen alternatives, including the Dempster rule and possibility theory). Exciting new work by mathematicians in the Netherlands has added another complicated alternative that is a close belief function analogue of Bayes' theorem. See Kerkvliet and Meester (2016), pp. 145–151; Meester (2020); Meester and Kerkvliet (2019), p. 288 ("The theory of belief functions is detailed and subtle enough as to allow for various ways of conditioning. Which conditioning (or updating) rules are appropriate in a given context may depend on the interpretation one has in mind.").

[170] See Sentz and Ferson (2002), pp. 8–13 (generalizing).

[171] Shafer (1976), pp. 251–255 (laying out this alternative); see Sentz and Ferson (2002), pp. 17–18 (same).

[172] Shafer (1976), pp. 252–253.

the average discounted belief function based on n items of evidence is $BelFunc^d(a) = [BelFunc^d{}_1(a) + BelFunc^d{}_2(a) + \ldots + BelFunc^d{}_n(a)] \div n$.

A similar alternative for conflicting and contradictory evidence is weighted arithmetic averaging of beliefs.[173] This approach is easier to understand if we speak of combining beliefs and then combining disbeliefs, rather than of combining belief functions.[174] The "weight" step credits the belief from each item of evidence in accordance with its significance. The "arithmetic average" step divides the sum of the weighted beliefs by the total of the weights assigned, which removes the distorting effect of the weighting. Let $Bel^w{}_i(a)$ be the weighted belief in the element a that is generated from an item of evidence, i, and derived by multiplying $Bel_i(a)$ by its weight factor, w_i, where $0 \leq w_i$. Then, the average belief based on n items of weighted evidence is $Bel^w(a) = [Bel^w{}_1(a) + Bel^w{}_2(a) + \ldots + Bel^w{}_n(a)] \div [w_1 + w_2 + \ldots + w_n]$, or:

$$Bel^w(a) = [w_1 . Bel_1(a) + w_2 . Bel_2(a) + \ldots + w_n . Bel_n(a)] \div [w_1 + w_2 + \ldots + w_n]$$

The same would be done for the disbeliefs.

In this weighted arithmetic averaging, what is meant by "significance"? It is not the probative force of the item of evidence, because the inferential reasoning process (described in the next chapter) has already accounted for that factor. It is instead something revealed by the item's belief function itself. If the uncommitted belief is small, the item of evidence is especially powerful.[175] Perhaps w should be inversely proportional to the range of uncommitted belief. Obviously, establishing a w will constitute yet another stab at judgment in the course of the reasoning process, but high accuracy in w is not critical as the effect of the weights is moderated by the formula's denominator.

One insight generated by weighted arithmetic averaging is that a second, separate piece of evidence by itself will have no effect on belief if it generates the same level of belief as the first piece of evidence. This insight about redundant, duplicative, or cumulative evidence might trouble some readers as being counterintuitive. But note that the concern here is not interdependent *corroborating* evidence, which heightens credibility and will come in as ancillary considerations that qualify the generalizations used in some chain of inferences (explained in the next chapter). The concern is

[173] See Ferson and Kreinovich (2001), p. 75 (laying out this alternative); Sentz and Ferson (2002), p. 27 (mentioning this as one of thirteen alternatives).

[174] See Ferson and Kreinovich (2001), p. 75 (showing equivalence).

[175] See id. ("[W]ider intervals [of uncommitted belief] correspond to worse measurements, with larger systematic error. In this case, it makes sense to assign smaller weights to these bad measurements, thus decreasing their impact on the aggregation result.").

converging evidence, that is, separate items of evidence that support one element.[176] If one item leads to a 0.30 belief in an element and another item also induces a 0.30 belief, do we believe the element more than 0.30? No.[177] Still, such converging evidence is relevant and thus admissible, because it will result in counting the repetitive 0.30 belief more heavily when averaged with all the other evidence.

One worry generated by weighted arithmetic averaging is that combining small beliefs generated by weak evidence with powerful beliefs will lower the overall degree of belief, even if the combination involves weighting. Recall, however, it is the comparison of belief and disbelief that ultimately matters, and weak evidence will most often bring down both belief and disbelief.[178] In any event, weighted arithmetic averaging, in this regard of mixing weak and strong evidence, seems superior to probabilistic combination, whereby weak evidence is converted into betting odds and hence rendered indistinguishable from strong evidence for the purpose of Bayes' theorem.

In brief, weighted arithmetic averaging is the belief function method worth further thought. It is appropriate for conflicting and contradictory evidence. It is the alternative that has the greatest claim to feasibility. Remember that all I am trying to do in connection with aggregation is describe, for purpose of illustration, one way to represent approximately what we all do intuitively and constantly in real life.[179]

Weighted arithmetic averaging has several advantages over Bayes' theorem.[180] First, weighted arithmetic averaging allows a place for the indeterminacy of epistemic uncertainties, thus accounting for the world that appears in shades of gray. Accounting for epistemic uncertainty tends to make weighted arithmetic averaging more accurate than Bayes' theorem for aggregating evidence. Second, weighted arithmetic averaging avoids the other problems of Bayes' theorem in the real world. A huge difficulty, for example, is fixing the starting point for factfinding: many a Bayesian is left to assume that when the factfinder knows nothing, the rational starting point is 50%. Under the multivalent belief model, however, the well-behaved factfinder starts not at the midpoint but at zero belief. Then, to get *Bel(a)* to exceed *Bel(not-a)*, the proponent must introduce items of evidence sufficient to

[176] On corroborating and converging evidence, see Anderson et al. (2005), pp. 106–107; Cohen (1977), pp. 94–95, 280–281.

[177] Even under Bayes' theorem, the posterior probability remains the same after introduction of additional evidence of equal probability. For a sophisticated Bayesian discussion of cumulative evidence, see Lempert (1977), pp. 1041–1052.

[178] Under the civil standard of proof, then, the effect of weak evidence will wash out. Under the criminal standard of proof, however, lowered belief and disbelief make it harder for the prosecution to meet the standard. This effect may just make the point that the prosecution's offering weak pieces of evidence is not a good strategy to follow.

[179] Significantly, a weighted-arithmetic-average approach commonly appears in the decisionmaking process of today's fuzzy computer programs. See Kosko (1993), pp. 176–180 (describing its use in fuzzy computer systems).

[180] See supra Sect. 3.2.4.1. Treating factfinding in terms of beliefs and disbeliefs, rather than with Bayes' theorem, avoids the "analytic gap between epistemic relevance and probability" that troubled Pardo (2013), p. 583.

generate reasonable believability, the first degree of belief that is perceptibly above a zero level of disbelief. This requirement conforms to the law's dictate that getting past the gatekeeper-judge to reach the factfinder requires more than a feather's weight of evidence. The multivalent belief standard of proof also conforms to the law by saying that the nonburdened party does not need to develop a competing version of the truth, but can succeed as long as the proponent's case remains very weak. These insights make sense of the notion of a burden of production. That burden is not some additional requirement arbitrarily introduced to supplement belief function theory, but instead flows naturally from the judge's requiring that a reasonable factfinder could find that *Bel(a)* perceptibly exceeds *Bel(not-a)*.[181] Third, weighted arithmetic averaging has some claim, as compared to Bayes' theorem, to be a realistic representation of how legal factfinders could and do aggregate evidence. Factfinders might intuitively use this averaging method already. Indeed, this method happily fits human capabilities and inclinations. Averaging the convincingness of the various pieces of evidence must lie close to the heart of any method instinctively in use.

Interestingly, this method very much resembles the early psychology theory of how factfinders actually find facts: information integration theory.[182] Experiments showed that mock jurors' output conformed with an approach like this: the human decisionmaker making a finding of fact would begin with an initial impression, or predisposition, and then would process additional units of information; each of these units, including the predisposition, would receive a scale value as to evidential strength, **S**, which was seemingly a measure of the probability of the fact's existence if the informational unit were true; each would also receive a weighting factor, **W**, which was seemingly a measure of evidential importance that somehow took into account its credibility and completeness; and the decisionmaker would then combine these into a weighted arithmetic mean that measured the fact's overall likelihood.[183] Of course, the mock jurors may have been viewing evidence more holistically, and they likely were not doing this calculation consciously, but the experiments indicate that their output was consistent with having proceeded by weighted arithmetic averaging. The following thus represents the judged likelihood based on k units of information:

---

[181] See infra Sect. 5.2.1.1 (explaining why the burden of production deserves protection).

[182] See Anderson (1981) (providing a conceptual introduction to this theory that scales stimuli by evaluation, weights them by importance, and algebraically combines them to form an overall judgment); Anderson (1974) (providing experimental support); cf. Lopes (1985), p. 509 ("human judgments often appear to follow an averaging rule"); Shanteau (1975) (providing more experimental support). Professor Anderson updates his theory and experimentally extends it to the legal context in Anderson (2017), p. 85 ("Substantial support for averaging theory has been found in experiments on legal judgment.").

[183] See, e.g., Kaplan (1982), pp. 198–200 ("The process of information evaluation, weighing, and integration is central to understanding the juror's cognition ... ."); Kaplan and Kemmerick (1974), p. 497 ("[T]he information provided to a juror ... possesses both scale value and weight ... .").

$$J = \frac{\Sigma W_k S_k}{\Sigma W_k}$$

This formula's minor differences from multivalent belief theory's weighted arithmetic averaging are that the newer theory treats multivalent beliefs rather than probabilities, moves the predisposition into the proof process more systematically as generalizations and ancillary considerations, redefines **S** as the degree of belief or disbelief, and provides a better definition for **W** in terms of the proportion of committed belief. What the information integration and multivalent belief theories together suggest is that it is both natural and correct for factfinders to look at the probative forces of all evidence bearing on an element and then average them somehow: each item of evidence would have produced a degree of belief and a degree of disbelief, that is, a belief function regarding the element; but obviously the factfinders would not weight all the items of evidence the same, that is, the factfinders would weight each item according to its evidential significance before averaging; so, the factfinders would roughly calculate a weighted arithmetic mean to create a composite belief function for the element.

To sum up, for legal factfinding, I favor weighted arithmetic averaging over its more complex competitors in Dempster-Shafer theory. It is a mathematically acceptable approach to the problem of aggregating pieces of evidence, and it seems suited to the uncertain beliefs and the conflicting and contradictory evidence encountered in real-world legal cases. It is a logical way to proceed in evidence processing, and it is also feasible for human factfinders and may encapsulate what they actually do when aggregating all evidence bearing on an element of the case.

Nevertheless, in this book, my description of weighted arithmetic averaging is mainly for illustrative purposes, as a possible representation of humans' intuitive process that they employ in nonnumerical and approximate terms and likely in a more holistic way. I am not saying that it is the only correct solution to the problem of aggregating evidence. I am not even saying there is a correct solution. I am just saying it is a conceivable and defensible method for aggregating evidence. The rest of this book does not depend on this method. All I need to do in order to proceed is to say that somehow factfinders aggregate evidence to form beliefs in facts.

Moreover, I am of course not suggesting that factfinders be instructed in the terms of weighted arithmetic averaging. The formulas stated above help only to model the logic involved in aggregating pieces of evidence, so that theorists can better understand and further analyze what should (or intuitively does) go on.

4.5.4.2 Conjunction and Disjunction

Consider now the different task of conjoining facts. Speaking in terms of probability brings into play the product rule, which says that the probability of a conjunction is a product of probabilities and thus leads to the conjunction paradox: it would seem that each element's being more likely than not is no guarantee that the elements' conjunction will be more likely than not. The paradox's escape hatch lies in realizing that the mathematical rules of traditional probability are not applicable to combining beliefs in the truth of facts.

In this chapter's Sect. 4.2, I sketched the systems of multivalent logic and their operators. In Sect. 4.3, I combined the image of belief functions with the multivalent MIN/MAX operators to formulate a brand of multivalent logic, the one most useful for my purposes. Now, I want to show how law employs the resultant theory of multivalent beliefs to perform the tasks of conjunction and disjunction in an accurate way that operates without paradox.

MIN and MAX Rules Multivalent logic recognizes that conjunction and disjunction of degrees of belief are mathematical tasks different from conjunction and disjunction of odds.[184] The highly developed and widely accepted mathematics for combining degrees of belief instructs that the conjunction has a degree of belief equal to the weakest of the conjoined beliefs, in accordance with the MIN rule that appears as a basic operator of the multivalent belief logic system.[185] This conjunction operator is a more general replacement for the product rule, which appears as a special case where bivalence and additivity prevail. Turning to the more accurate multivalent logic means that the conjunction paradox vaporizes: if each element is more likely than not, then the elements' conjunction will be more likely than not.

To illustrate, the belief measure for conjunction of beliefs is *Bel(*E AND F*)* = MIN(*Bel(*E*)*, *Bel(*F*))*. In Fig. 4.6, the belief in the conjunction of the beliefs

[184] See Huber (2009), p. 10 (stating "that fair betting ratios should indeed obey the probability calculus, but that degrees of belief, being different from fair betting ratios, need not").

[185] See supra Sect. 4.2.4.3. Philosophers and logicians agree with the mathematics. See Cohen (1977), pp. 89–91, 265–267 (arguing that the conjunction of two or more propositions has the same inductive probability as the weakest conjunct); Russell (1948), pp. 359–361 (arguing comparably that his "degrees of credibility" do not follow the product rule of traditional probability); Dubois and Prade (2008), p. 403 (rejecting the application of "arguments deriving from the study of statistical experiments"); Haack (2012), pp. 217–218 (arguing comparably that her "degrees of warrant" do not follow the product rule of traditional probability); MacFarlane (2010), p. 438 (arguing against the product rule and in favor of the MIN rule); Schiffer (2003), pp. 203–204 (same). MacFarlane's line of argument, id. at 13–14 (footnote omitted), is worth quoting:

1. If classical semantics is correct for vague discourse, then borderline propositions are either true or false; no finer distinctions are made.
2. If borderline propositions are either true or false, then (since we don't know which truth value they have) our attitudes toward them must be attitudes of uncertainty-related partial belief.
3. If our attitudes towards borderline propositions are attitudes of uncertainty-related partial belief, they ought to obey norms of probabilistic coherence.
4. We regard the propositions Jim is tall, Jim is bald, and Jim is smart as independent. That is, we don't think Jim's being bald (or smart, or bald and smart) would make it any more likely that he is tall, and so on.
5. Probabilistic coherence demands that our credence in the conjunction of several propositions we take to be independent be the product of our credences in the conjuncts.
6. But it is not the case that we ought to have much less credence that Jim is bald and tall and smart than we have that he is bald.
7. Therefore, classical semantics is not correct for vague discourse.

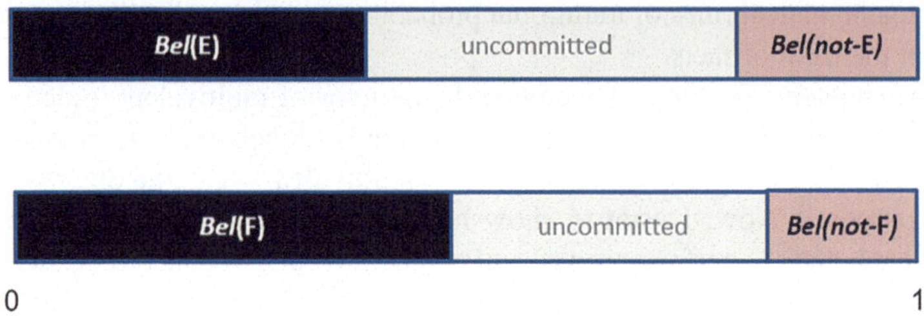

Fig. 4.6 Application of MIN and MAX operators

in propositions E and F is the smaller *Bel(*E*)*. However, the new degree of disbelief will be the maximum of the disjoined disbeliefs, following the MAX rule. The belief measure for disjunction of disbeliefs is *Bel(*not-E OR not-F*)* = MAX(*Bel(*not-E*)*, *Bel (*not-F*)*). In Fig. 4.6, the belief in the disjunction is the larger *Bel(*not-E*)*. Moreover, the same MIN and MAX rules apply whether the beliefs are independent or interdependent, unlike the product rule. Belief and disbelief will range from 0 to 1, and they should add to less than one. The uncommitted belief conveys epistemic uncertainty.

Difference from Odds' Mathematics Why do beliefs combine differently from odds? In one sense, they do not differ. We treat both multivalence and bivalence by MIN and MAX operators.[186] Multivalent logic is the more general system, because it does not assume an excluded middle. Multivalent logic produces bivalent logic and traditional probability as special cases. If we were to assume bivalence and additivity, then multivalence would reduce to the product rule and De Morgan's rule. Thus, combining beliefs only looks different from combining odds. But why do they even look different when probabilities are involved?

As we experience beliefs subject to epistemic uncertainty, they combine into a narrative chain, as strong as its weakest link. No way exists to multiply the beliefs, and if there were a way, it would make no intuitive sense. The degree of belief in *a* just tells you the extent to which *a* was fully proven. It tells you nothing about *not-a*. It tells you nothing about a separate *b*. Instead, if you starkly picture a chain of beliefs as a string of partly proven truths, their conjunction is rather obviously proven to the extent that its weakest link was proven.

Odds, however, are a different measure. They tell you the frequentist likelihood of *a*, after assuming the proof is full and complete. Further, odds of *a* tell you the odds of *not-a*. There is no reservoir of epistemic uncertainty to buffer the effect of conjunction. Conjoin *a* with *b* as probabilities under 100%, and the conjunctive odds have to drop below both *a*'s and *b*'s odds.

Therefore, it makes good sense to stipulate different operators for multivalent beliefs and probabilistic odds. Speaking slightly more technically, probability, built

[186] See supra Sect. 4.2.2 (showing that bivalent operators can be stated in MIN and MAX terms).

on bivalent logic's excluded middle, is an additive system, meaning that *p* as the chance of truth and 1–*p* as the chance of falsity add to one. Multivalent belief and disbelief normally add to less than one, making multivalent belief theory into a nonadditive system. This distinction proves critical, because *the product rule mathematically derives from additivity and so prevails only in additive systems.*[187] The product rule depends on its assumption that if anything is not true, it is false, rather than merely not proven in full. Let me explain again.

On the one hand, the probabilistic odds of *a* dictate under bivalence the odds of *not-a*. The complement of the probabilistic chance of *a*'s being revealed as true is the chance of *a*'s being revealed as false. The chance of *a*'s being revealed as false interacts disjunctively with the chance of *b*'s being revealed as false, so that the chance of *a* or *b* being revealed as false goes up. Conjoining *a* and *b* means increased odds of *not-a* or *not-b*. Accordingly, the chance of *a* and *b* being true goes down, and it goes down by a multiplicative amount in accordance with the product rule.

On the other hand, under multivalent logic, a degree of belief is an evidence-based measure of sureness about the real world. The complement of such a belief is not a disbelief, but it is instead the degree to which the belief was not fully proven. As the factfinder shifts from evidence of *a* to evidence of *b*, the degree of *a*'s not being proven has no effect on or interaction with the degree of *b*'s not being proven. Accordingly, the sureness of *a* and *b* together does not slip below the smaller of the two. So, if my sureness about *a* is adequate to form a belief in *a* as I navigate an uncertain world, the mere fact that I also believe *b* does nothing to lessen my belief in *a*, with the consequence that I believe *a* and *b* to the degree of the lesser of the two beliefs. This explanation underlies the principle of conjunctive closure already stated.[188]

In sum, conjoining nonadditive beliefs looks different from figuring joint odds. The logical fact is that degree of belief and probability of truth are different measures: *extent proven* versus *frequentist likelihood*. If we are not measuring probability, its product rule does not apply. The mathematical fact is that degrees of belief follow the MIN rule, not the product rule.

Some commentators have reacted with the assertion that switching from bivalence to multivalence cannot change reality and therefore cannot change computational results.[189] That view results from a misunderstanding of the role of logic. Multivalence does not try to change reality. It just measures different aspects of it with a different metric. It starts with different assumptions, including that evidence can produce a partially believed fact. Multivalence adopts operators that can accurately handle those measures other than 1 or 0, or yes or no.

These academics dismiss my project out of hand because it appears to them as sleight of hand. But I am not performing a trick. Traditional probability makes the

[187] See supra Sect. 3.2.4.2 (discussing derivation of product rule).

[188] See supra Sect. 4.2.4.3 (stating principle of conjunctive closure).

[189] E.g., Allen and Pardo (2019b), pp. 49–58. But see supra Sect. 1.1.2 and infra Sect. 4.5.5 (refuting a similar assertion).

simplifying assumption that everything is true or false. This efficient assumption will produce real errors when the subject of study appears as partial truths. For factfinding in the real world, unavoidable epistemic uncertainty produces outputs that should not be forced into true or false boxes via randomness. Quite simply, one cannot use the mathematics (traditional probability) based on bivalence to combine partial truths; one must turn to the mathematics (multivalent logic) developed to handle partial truths. This move is just like turning to calculus when the problem requires it. That is all that is going on here. I am applying a mathematical system that can handle the credal output of factfinding.

Thus, one calculates to a different result not by some magical trick of logic, but by utilizing a more appropriate measure. Beliefs can convey the full output of factfinding. Beliefs include a measure of epistemic uncertainty, while probabilities do not. To combine factfindings while still carrying forward all the uncertainties, the factfinder must employ a nonadditive logic system, where belief and disbelief do not necessarily add to one and where some belief can remain uncommitted. By contrast, traditional probability discards epistemic uncertainty before the product rule's multiplication, and thereby gives the wrong answer for conjunction of beliefs. For accuracy's sake, the law should combine beliefs by multivalent logic's rules.

A simple example can demonstrate the accuracy of the MIN rule. Say that *Bel (a)* = 0.90 and *Bel(not-a)* = 0.10 on perfect evidence, and that *Bel(b)* = 0.12 and *Bel (not-b)* = 0.03 on very imperfect evidence. Then, *Bel(a* AND *b)* = 0.12. If instead one were to use probabilities, Prob(*a*) = 90% and Prob(*b*) = 80%.[190] Applying the product rule to these two elements, if independent, yields a 72% probability for the conjunction. Which is the more accurate representation of the strength of the conjunction, a representation on which one might base future actions? Given airtight and thin evidence like this on the two elements, has the proponent made a weak showing of the conjunction, say 0.12, or a fairly strong showing, say 72%? It is easy to see that probability theory introduced an error when it discarded epistemic uncertainties and converted the weak showing on *b* to 80%. An 80% showing on airtight evidence is very different from an 80% showing on thin evidence.

That example is a slam-dunk demonstration of the superior accuracy of the MIN rule. Still, some more light comes from repeating another example that uses vagueness, which is another major kind of epistemic uncertainty captured by multivalent logic and not by traditional probability. Imagine you want to know if Tom is tall and smart. Let *X* be the universe of men, and let *A* be the set of tall men and *B* be the assumedly independent set of smart men. Tom is a 0.30 member of *A* and a 0.40 member of *B*, which means something like "Tom is below average height" and "Tom is not that smart." The MIN rule would yield a 0.30 belief in the intersection of tall and smart traits, or "Because Tom is not tall and Tom is not that smart, Tom is not such a tall, smart man." The probabilistic calculation, however, would yield a 12% chance, or "Because Tom is not tall and Tom is not that smart, Tom is very likely a

[190] Normalizing the beliefs is one means to perform the pignistic transform, as discussed supra Sect. 4.1.3. Proportionately normalizing 0.12 and 0.03 yields 80% and 20%.

short, dumb man." The key insight is that Tom's memberships do not mean that Tom has a 70% chance of being so tiny as to be completely outside the set of tall men and a 60% chance of being truly dumb; instead, they mean a 0.70 and 0.60 degree of the factfinder's not being convinced of tallness or smartness. Multiplication of probabilities gives the chance that Tom is both indubitably tall rather than short and indubitably smart rather than dumb, while what we want to know is the degree to which he belongs to the set of men classifiable as both tall and smart. The inappropriateness of using the product rule becomes even more obvious as one combines more and more elements in the calculation, such as tall, smart, rich, and bald men. The product will approach 0%, even if some of the values are very high, while the MIN rule will go no lower than the minimum belief.

Another way to see the difference between the product rule for odds and the MIN rule for beliefs is to think first of the 1-in-4 odds of flipping two coins as two heads:

The product rule critically utilizes the idea that if a coin is not heads, it is tails. Now imagine that you have eyewitnesses who testify to fairly fleeting views of each of the coins landing as heads. The coins are now gone. The odds of two heads constituted only a classical probability of heads reflecting a nonprobative number of possible outcomes, not a belief.[191] But the eyewitnesses' testimony has generated a belief of 0.60 in heads for the first coin, and the same belief for the second coin, as represented thus:

Now, is your belief 25% in two heads having come up? Or is it 36% or 0.36? The MIN rule of multivalent belief theory says 0.60. Why? The testimony of the eyewitnesses was pretty good, making your beliefs in heads pretty strong. No witness is saying there were tails. A lot of your belief is uncommitted, causing a low belief in a tails. So, when you conjoin the beliefs in heads, you are not working with a 75% chance of a tails; the product rule is inapplicable, and instead the MIN and MAX rules apply. The point is that the 0.60 belief in the coins' having been two heads, expressed as a degree of full knowledge, is different from the odds of two heads in two future flips, the difference deriving from the presence or absence of uncommitted belief that reflects epistemic uncertainty.

Boy-Girl Puzzle Many readers will still be resisting that two beliefs combine differently from two probabilities. To them I offer one of my favorite probability

[191] In possibility theory, for both heads and tails there is a possibility of 1, but a necessity or belief (and disbelief) of 0. See Genin and Huber (2020), § 3.3.

puzzles, the one involving two siblings.[192] A completely unbiased friend has told you that Tom has two children, that she remembers at least one is a boy, and that is all she knows. Her protocol is to tell you all she knows. What are the chances that the other child is a boy? The answer is one-third, because the equally probable possibilities are BB, BG, and GB. But if your companion had said that the elder child is a boy (or the one who plays the violin is a boy), the answer would be one-half! The additional information provided by ordering, seemingly irrelevant, affects the odds dramatically.

In the first situation, you are learning information from your companion about both children, namely, that the GG combination is out. In the second situation, you are learning information about only one of the children. You form a strong belief the elder is a boy. He falls out of consideration, and you consider only the younger child, who is either a boy or a girl with equal probability.

If you resist the result, and persist with two-in-three odds that the other is a girl in the second situation, I propose the following gamble to you. You will bet on whether a hidden flipped coin is heads. But before placing the bets, I flip another coin, and it comes up tails. You then should believe there is a two-thirds chance that the hidden coin is heads, and so should offer me better than even money. Indeed, whenever you face a coin flip, always first flip another coin, as its outcome will tell you what to choose!

The effect of additional information further emerges from this sequence: Flip two coins. What are the odds that they both were heads? One-in-four. If you know at least one of them was heads, what are the odds they both were heads? One-in-three, because knowing the result of a flip tells you something about the other. If instead you know the *first* flip was heads, what are the odds they both were heads? One-in-two.

What is the lesson here? If you find out information about the combination, one outcome affects the odds of the other outcome. But if you learn information about only one outcome (one *specific* child or coin is a boy or heads), the information has no effect on the other outcome. A revised belief on the first child or coin does not carry over to the second. The odds for the second child or coin are the odds of a single trial.

A belief in element a tells you nothing about b. If you believe a, you must approach b afresh. If you come to believe b, then you believe both a and b together. By contrast, the probability of a tells you something about *not-a* and hence something more about the combination of a and b. Although the analogy is not perfect, the boy-girl puzzle indicates that we must calculate the likelihood of the combination differently for beliefs and probabilities.

Law's Choice Uncertain propositions fall mainly into one of two piles: one of bivalent measures for which the product rule suffices (such as frequentist events and betting odds), and another of multivalent measures for which rationality requires

[192] See Rosenhouse (2009), pp. 26, 138–141, 147–148; supra Sect. 2.1.3 (introducing this puzzle).

the more general MIN rule (such as facts resting on imperfect evidence and vague terms). The probability of to-be-revealed truth, with all views committed randomly between true and false, falls into the first pile. The belief in truth, with its accompanying nonbelief and disbelief, goes into the second pile.

I suppose that the theorist could argue for putting legal factfinding in either pile, a decision that then dictates the proper combination rule. However, based on extant doctrine expressed in cases and judicial instructions, there is little doubt that the law has cast legal factfinding into the second pile. By requiring the standard of proof to be applied element-by-element, the law reveals that it has adopted the MIN operator. The pattern instruction does not ask the factfinder any overall question, that is, it does not ask for the bottom line of whether the plaintiff should recover based on the overall likelihood. It does not give separate instructions on how to combine independent and interdependent findings, which would be necessary for calculating overall probability. Instead it tells the factfinder to determine whether an element is likely and, if so, to proceed afresh to the next element. If the factfinder finds each of the elements proven, it is a rule of law—and not the factfinder's practice—that says the plaintiff shall recover. Our lawmakers have chosen multivalent logic, across the board.

I am further contending that the law's choice was a wise one. Although it would be conceivable for the law to ask its factfinders to judge the probability of truth, asking them that question would be very undesirable as a policy matter. The law has been wise to ask its factfinders to adjudge their degrees of belief instead. Choosing that route avoids the many difficulties of dealing in probabilities. Moreover, the law has no cogent interest in the odds for betting on unattainable truth. The second pile fits the image, and so clarifies the theory, of legal factfinding—a process that aims to measure the degrees of belief established by the evidence, while leaving some belief uncommitted to reflect epistemic uncertainty. That, then, is my message: the law has followed good policy in asking factfinders for beliefs rather than for odds.

Actual Practice Finally, whatever the law chooses, it might discover its factfinders are dealing in beliefs anyway. Factfinders are painfully conscious of uncertainty when they pronounce what they believe. They are not about to project the odds of a revelatory event that is difficult even to imagine. Use of the MIN rule for conjoining beliefs, then, could be descriptive of actual legal practice.

Empirically, the safest thing to say about the practice of conjunction is that humans are not perfectly logical.[193] However, one might defensibly go further to

[193] The conjunction fallacy, which is not to be confused with the conjunction paradox supposedly posed by the law's element-by-element application of the standard of proof, emerged from the famous Linda problem: based on a description of Linda (*"Linda is 31 years old, single, outspoken, and very bright. She majored in philosophy. As a student, she was deeply concerned with issues of discrimination and social justice, and also participated in anti-nuclear demonstrations."*), a strong majority of people rank "Linda is a bank teller and is active in the feminist movement" as being more probable than "Linda is a bank teller." That result seems illogical, in that several conditions do

say that, at least in inferential reasoning, nothing in practice suggests that legal factfinders apply the product rule.[194] Avoidance of the product rule is shown by humans' ready willingness to pile inference upon inference in forming inferential beliefs that would never survive the product rule.[195]

More rigorous testing is sketchy, but likewise provides no evidence that humans use the product rule for combining factfindings.[196] In one experiment, subjects had to judge the degree to which objects such as cars and wine barrels were "metallic containers" and, three days later, the degree to which they were "metallic objects" and "containers"; the subjects tended to favor the MIN rule over the product rule.[197] Thus, even if it is not established that humans default to a strict MIN rule, it is quite

---

not combine to be more probable than a single condition. See Kahneman (2011), pp. 156–165 (discussing this conjunction fallacy).

The phrasing of the problem could muddle the results. See Hertwig and Gigerenzer (1999), p. 275 ("We conclude that a failure to recognize the human capacity for semantic and pragmatic inference can lead rational responses to be misclassified as fallacies."). Here is one example: "People do not think of the Linda problem in terms of frequencies, or as an exercise in probabilistic reasoning. They see the description of Linda as a story about a real person, and the biography of Linda which ends only by identifying her as a bank teller is not, without more information, a satisfactory account." Kay and King (2020), p. 91. Indeed, many experiments show that if the Linda problem is phrased in expressly frequentist terms, the subjects are much more inclined to employ the product rule. See, e.g., Tversky and Kahneman (1983), p. 309 (saying that phrasing the problem in terms of frequencies "markedly reduced the incidence of the conjunction fallacy").

[194] The just-described Linda problem demonstrates that humans often neglect the product rule. But it may further indicate the experimenters' neglect of the difference between aleatory uncertainty and epistemic uncertainty. If the categories of bank teller and active feminist are viewed as crisp categories subject only to a random frequency measure, then the product rule is appropriate. But if the requested "probable" categorization is subject to epistemic uncertainties, the measures are beliefs rather than probabilities. Then the product rule does not apply—and the applicable MIN rule implies a much lower level of illogic among the subjects, because the conjunction would be just as believable as her unlikely employment as a bank teller. Indeed, her retention of feminist principles might even make her survival as a bank teller more believable—and, importantly, less disbelievable. Thus, the conjoined characteristics might be more acceptable than her categorization solely as bank teller. See Strasser and Antonelli (2019), § 4 ("In view of the fact that test subjects seem to perform very poorly in various paradigmatic reasoning tests, main streams in the psychology of reasoning have traditionally ascribed to logic at best a subordinate role in human reasoning. In recent years this assessment has been criticized as the result of evaluating performances in tests against the standard of classical logic whereas other standards based on [non-monotonic logic] have been argued to be more appropriate."). In short, the product rule does not apply to the Linda problem, and the persons in the street knew what they were doing when they did not invoke it.

[195] Theorists may wrongly criticize this human practice. See, e.g., Gettys et al. (1973) (lamenting that experimental subjects tended to overstate the likelihood of multiple inferences compared to the "optimal" model based on Bayes' theorem); Saks and Kidd (1981), p. 142 ("In judging the likelihood that an enterprise involving a series of interconnected events will succeed, people will tend to overestimate the probability of success.").

[196] See Zwick et al. (1988) (concluding that people do not naturally use the product rule); cf. id. at 114–116 (finding an averaging method is employed for conjunction).

[197] See Thole et al. (1979). Other experiments give some support to the MAX rule for disjunction. See Zwick et al. (1988), pp. 98, 115 (discussing a previous study and reporting a new one).

conceivable that rough-and-ready factfinding emphasizes the weakest conjoined fact.[198]

Conjunction Summary I thus argue that multivalent logic is the correct way to proceed in evidence processing, and I further argue it is feasible for human factfinders and may encapsulate what they actually do.

The conjoined strength of beliefs theoretically drops to the strength of the weakest belief. The belief in the chain of conjoined elements is as strong as the weakest link. If the evidence supports a disbelief in some elements, the disjoined disbelief is as strong as the greatest disbelief. So, my argument on the conjunction paradox runs this way:

1. Factfinders must deal with degrees of belief or partial truths, that is, propositions that will never be proved beyond a partial degree.
2. Classical logic, by its assumption of the excluded middle, refuses to recognize partial truths.
3. Consequently, classical logic has no tool to conjoin, or otherwise combine, partial truths.
4. By contrast, multivalent logic handles elements that are provable as partial truths.
5. Multivalent logic provides that the partial truth of the conjoined elements equals the minimum of the partial truths of the elements, so that a narrative is as strong as its weakest link.
6. The law has intuitively embraced this multivalent logical operator.
7. If each element in a cause of action is believed, then the truth of the conjunction should be believed.

The conjunction paradox thus implodes under the force of multivalent logic. By following multivalent logic's rules for factfinding, the law appears to have known all along what it was doing.

Aside: "Element" Recall that element means a finding necessary for a claim or an affirmative defense to succeed under the substantive law, a finding that the factfinder must find for the proponent to succeed. On the one hand, within elements the factfinder uses the usual intuitive techniques in a nonquantitative and approximate fashion for aggregating evidence bearing on a fact. On the other hand, even within elements the factfinder uses the multivalent operator for conjunction to conjoin separate and necessary facts, as opposed to the treatment of reinforcing or weakening evidence.

---

[198] See Evnine (1999), p. 214 ("Take any two propositions that are of no special logical or emotional significance to someone, say that grass is green and that snow is white. I contend (this is intended as an empirical observation about our practice) that if we have good grounds for attributing belief in each of these to a person, then, absent any special circumstances, that is all we need to attribute to that person a belief in their conjunction. Or if, for example, we are summing up a position someone has just explained at some length, we can do so by attributing to that person a large conjunctive belief. This conjunctive belief describes in a single proposition a number of different propositions that were expressed severally over a period of time.").

That is, if a grouping that some legal source calls an element actually includes separate and necessary facts, each of those facts should be treated as an element for our purposes. So, if an element is said to entail such facts, the process of combining them is the same as the proof process between elements. The belief in the overall element equals the minimum of the beliefs in the separate and necessary facts. The apparent criticality of the number of elements thus melts away.[199]

4.5.5 Asymmetrical Burdens

The key to meeting the argument that we endure an unfair legal system seriously tilted against plaintiffs (or defendants) is to establish the above-developed conclusion that the multivalent belief model requires that the plaintiff's best story be more believable than the defendant's best story constructible out of the allegations and evidence.[200] From this vantage point, one can see that the plaintiff and the defendant are on a largely level playing field after all.

This refutation of the claimed unfairness should not be surprising. A seriously uneven playing field would result in not only serious bias but also serious economic inefficiency. It is hard to imagine that our legal system could have survived for hundreds of years if it produced skewed inaccuracies with consistency. The law should have evolved, and it did, toward producing optimal results.[201] Likewise astounding, why would commentators and parties have waited centuries to notice such stark injustices?[202] In fact, the commentators today cannot even agree on which party has the advantage.[203] Many stress the load on the proponent to prove a string of elements. But others say the proponent can benefit from how the ancients (and moderns) divided our causes of action (and defenses) into elements: the more subdivisions, the lower the conjunctive probability that suffices for the proponent's victory. Furthermore, although the defendant can choose more than one element to deny, the plaintiff can even things up by choosing more than one theory in formulating the complaint.

---

[199] See Cohen (1977), p. 267 ("So on the inductivist analysis, if the plaintiff gains each of his points on the balance of probability, he can be regarded as gaining his case as a whole on that balance . . . , without any constraint's being thereby imposed on the number of independent points in his case . . . ."); supra Sect. 3.2.4.2 (raising the apparent criticality of the number of elements).

[200] See supra Sect. 4.4.4 (developing that conclusion).

[201] Cf. Miceli (2018), pp. 21–27 (discussing the theory of the common law's efficiency); Posner (2011), § 21.7 (similar). Contrariwise, the law has evolved toward increasing the defendants' options, as it replaced the common law's single-issue rule with alternative and inconsistent pleading. See Field et al. (2023), pp. 1181–1187.

[202] The earliest known observation of the conjunction paradox came in 1931. See supra Sect. 3.2.4.2. The supposed disparate effect of error lay undiscovered until De Mot and Stein (2015), p. 1263 (saying that their article "is the first to identify this bias").

[203] See supra Sect. 3.2.5 (discussing apparent advantages).

Recall the three supposed "asymmetries" already cataloged:[204] (1) accumulating observations can never certainly prove the proponent's hypothesis, but a single observation can effectively falsify the hypothesis; (2) the plaintiff must prove each of several elements, while the defendant need disprove only one; and (3) any rate of adjudicative error, even if random and unbiased, will hurt plaintiffs and help defendants. The three asymmetries stem from quite similar roots. Consequently, one observation—the plaintiff need show only that his theory of the case is better than the defendant's single best theory—can resolve all three. Consider separately the three asymmetries.

First, the civil standard of proof, if not the burdens of production and persuasion, tries to put an equal burden on plaintiff and defendant. The plaintiff need not deliver certain truth, so Hume's problem with induction is no problem for legal trials.[205] The defendant faces a task similar to the plaintiff's. Each has the task of comparatively winning the factfinder's belief.

Second, because the standard of proof is equivalent to comparing the parties' best stories, the criticality of the number of elements disappears. The plaintiff must show that his story is more likely than not, and the defendant depends on the plaintiff's story not being more likely than not. Their tasks are comparable.

Third, there is no disparate risk of error in the battle of best stories. An error in favor of the plaintiff while judging the plaintiff's whole story is as likely as an error in favor of the defendant, so that the error could defeat the defendant as easily as it could defeat the plaintiff. When the parties shift the field of engagement to the elements, the parties will fight over who has the weakest link. The focus will normally shift to the relatively strongest of the defendant's denials. If the plaintiff prevails, the defendant's other denials should fall like dominos. Now, an error could affect the outcome of this fight over the determinant element. The error might weaken the defendant's showing on the element or, just as easily, might weaken the plaintiff's showing. The playing field is essentially level.

I can put my argument simply: once one perceives that the trial process asks whom the factfinder believes more, rather than asking for the multiplicative odds of hypothetical revelations of truth, one can sense that the playing field has largely leveled out. Although asymmetries can affect traditional probabilities, the asymmetries disappear when treating comparative beliefs. Indeed, the whole idea of asymmetrical burdens is largely an illusion, generated by a probability-induced suspicion that proving a string of elements is a tougher task than disproving one. But that suspicion is accurate only if one is betting on a series of random outcomes, that is, only if one imagines that the decision involves the random odds of winning against the relatively strongest denial and then multiplying by the odds of winning against the next denial and so on.[206] If instead one is dealing in partial beliefs, the

[204] See supra Sect. 3.2.5.

[205] See supra Sect. 4.1.1 ("Yet this situation causes the law no worry because the law does not seek or demand certain truth or full knowledge.").

[206] See infra Sect. 4.6.3 (discussing sequential betting).

MAX rule says that the existence of weaker alternative stories favoring the defendant does not increase the cumulative belief in the defendant's stories. The outlook for the defendant is the strength of the defendant's best story, which has to match up against the plaintiff's story. The fight between the parties will tend to reduce to this question: Is the plaintiff's most vulnerable link stronger than the defendant's showing on that link? The field of active engagement will be on that element. The result is a largely level playing field.

The usual comeback to my view is again that adopting a multivalent logic outlook cannot change the world.[207] Because multivalent logic is just another language for talking about likelihood, it assertedly can never change the reality it describes. For example, the argument would be that a compound gamble (where the defendant has multiple grounds on which to win) is riskier for the plaintiff than a single-event gamble (where the defendant has a lone ground on which to win), and switching to multivalent logic will not change those betting odds. So, joining the chorus that choice of logic cannot change the world, Alex Stein has said that

> with everything else being equal, a compound gamble is always riskier than a single-event gamble, and stating those gambles as fuzzy probabilities won't change anything. Looking into current sporting events, I surely have a better chance to be right in predicting that the German soccer team will beat South Korea on Wednesday than in saying this, plus, that Mexico and Sweden will draw. How can any fuzzy or other conceptualization of probability make it different? And if I am right here, then I don't see how the plaintiff's compound gamble in my article differs from this one. You can use the fuzzy sets theory to reason about probabilities, but it can't change the underlying reality . . . .[208]

Of course, I agree as to gambles. The reality is the same, and these betting odds do not change. Within that reality, however, one can focus on different aspects of reality and measure them. The compound gambler is focusing on possible sequences of events—seeking to know the chance of a particular sequence randomly turning up. Each event must be resolved, before considering the next. The only way to conceive of to-be-resolved outcomes is in terms of odds. The only way to combine one such outcome with another is by the product rule.

However, the factfinder does not confront compound gambles in the course of the parties' fighting over belief and disbelief. The law is looking at a different aspect of reality than is the bettor. It is looking at the extent to which an overall position is

---

[207] See Allen and Pardo (2019b), p. 51 ("There are four major problems with Clermont's application of fuzzy set theory to juridical proof. The first is that changing one's theory of probability does not change the world or one's knowledge of the world."). But see supra Sects. 1.1.2 and 4.5.4.2 (refuting their assertion as to the roles of probability and logic); cf. The Affair: 406 (Showtime television broadcast July 22, 2018) (Helen explaining "manifesting" to Alison, whereby Californians believe that "you can manifest your reality," the idea being that "if there's something in your life you want to change, you just need to think differently and it will change").

[208] E-mail from Alex Stein, Professor of Law, Brooklyn Law School, to author (June 23, 2018, 17: 49 EST) (on file with author and reprinted with permission). Now a Justice of the Supreme Court of Israel, he is another who has made many very intelligent contributions to this field over the years—including in the Israeli case of *Israel v. Bezalel* (2019) (Stein, J.) (treating the prisoners-in-the-yard paradox), http://legal1.cit.cornell.edu/private/Bezalel.pdf.

proven—seeking to determine the most believable of all possible versions of that reality. The law is asking the factfinder which side's overall position is more believable, rather than for the cumulated betting odds on a string of guesses about future events. It is looking at beliefs, not probabilities.

So, I would say in response to Justice Stein that he should think of two athletic contests in the ancient past for which almost all records have been lost. Do we think that Sparta won both? If you believe on balance that the Sparta Spartans won the first against the Athenian Thinkers and also that the Spartans won the second against the Ithaca Islanders, you should not multiply the likelihoods to decide whether the Spartans won both. I am saying that the mental task of unearthing the truth here differs from the task of placing a bet on upcoming soccer games, that the difference lies in the presence or absence of a measure for persistent epistemic uncertainty, and that the difference calls for different mathematical operations.

Compound gambles differ from the historical inquiry much as the two versions of the boy-girl puzzle differ.[209] The odds of having had a sequence of two boys is one-in-four. But the odds of having had two boys when you know that the older is a boy is one-in-two. The outcome of one Spartan game does not greatly affect the historical view of the outcome of the other game. The views of the outcomes combine as beliefs.

Therefore, probability of truth and degree of belief really do differ. If what we want is a prediction of whether an unknown will randomly reveal itself to be true or false, we want to use traditional probability. It nicely represents the chance of one of two outcomes, subject only to randomness of outcome. But it requires the bettor to act as if he or she knows all there is to know, short of the effects of randomness. Instead, if we want a complete representation of the state of an unknown, we want to use belief functions. They nicely incorporate what we do and do not know. Probabilities and beliefs represent different quantities, and combining them requires different mathematical tools. To recapitulate:

- As to the mere existence of differences between probabilities and beliefs, based on their differing treatment of uncertainty, there can be little logical dispute by now.
- There is no mathematical doubt that if the factfinder is thinking in terms of degrees of belief, then the MIN and MAX rules should govern how to combine beliefs.
- Thinking in those credal terms and applying those rules clarify how evidential proof should operate.

Embracing these three propositions will yield many practical benefits, such as avoiding the logical difficulties of probabilities and quashing misguided "reforms" to cure nonexistent asymmetry.

[209] See supra Sect. 4.5.4.2 (laying out the puzzle).

4.5.6 Inapt Concept

Most importantly, traditional probability does not deliver the message that standards of proof should convey. The law is looking for some sort of conviction on the part of its factfinders, not a probability. Moreover, humans naturally hope for a sense of conviction expressed in terms of belief.

While multivalent beliefs provide a good way to think about inner conviction, they also seem to represent how a legal factfinder actually thinks. The factfinder encounters a proponent who alleges all the elements necessary for success under the substantive law. The opponent can deny any of those allegations. The factfinder then pertinently and naturally asks itself whether it believes each element more (or much more) than it disbelieves the element. This way of thinking tracks multivalent belief theory.

Moreover, the multivalent belief model does not differ revolutionarily from the law's traditional concepts of proof. It is not telling the factfinder to think a new way. The major contribution of multivalent beliefs is to provide a formal way to represent the evidential uncertainty that prevails in the real world and, thereby, to understand the handling of that uncertainty.

The multivalent belief model not only better communicates the standards' message, but also better serves the law's other purposes.[210] For the most salient example, the reformulated preponderance standard achieves the goal of minimizing error costs when there is no reason to favor plaintiffs or defendants differentially.

The mathematics of beliefs instruct in civil cases that if each belief is stronger than its disbelief, the conjunction of the beliefs will be strong enough. That is, the conjoined story will be as likely as its weakest element, which has already satisfied the standard of proof because each element is more true than false. Moreover, the disjunction of the falsities, which combines all possible negations, is only as likely as the strongest of the falsities, which has already failed the standard of proof. The affirmative story will be stronger than all other possible stories combined. That is, if each element of a cause of action passes the standard of proof, the story of liability will be the most believable story, more believable than all the stories of nonliability combined.

To minimize error in these circumstances, the law should decide in conformity with the strongest chain. Refusing to accept the MIN and MAX rules' version of the overall truth will always involve choosing a lesser truth at some step in telling the story. If the law were to refuse to accept the result because of some residual attraction to bivalent probability theory, the law would be falling into error. Therefore, deciding on the basis of betting odds would increase the error rate.

[210] See Cheng and Pardo (2015) (considering various purposes of standards, but prioritizing accuracy).

4.6 Where to Use Multivalent Beliefs

Probabilities and beliefs represent different quantities. And combining probabilities and beliefs requires different mathematical tools. Therefore, a lot turns on which measure to use for a particular task. So, at last, let me generalize about the kinds of decisions for which multivalent beliefs are the appropriate measure.

The distinction is certainly not legal versus nonlegal decisionmaking. In daily life, some decisions about future events turn mainly on traditional probabilities (should I carry an umbrella today?) and some should instead employ beliefs (should I buy a gun for self-protection?—a decision that involves combining contestable evidence with imprecise values and so prevents the conscientious decisionmaker from allocating all belief on each factor to either true or false, unlike the umbrella decision that is dominated by probabilities).

Nor is the distinction drawn between factfinding and other decisions. In law outside factfinding sensu stricto, some decisions even about past events rest on probabilities (should an appellate court reverse a judgment for serious error?) and some involve beliefs (should we give a remedy that depends on whether a violation of some procedural rule occurred and whether it affected outcome?).

Other distinctions—such as unsettlable facts in contrast to facts that will be eventually revealed, or explanatory versus betting tasks, or past versus future facts, or vague versus crisp facts—are suggestive but remain under- or over-inclusive.

4.6.1 When Multivalent Beliefs Must Be Used

A better sense of the distinction will come from contemplating whether, for the sake of accuracy, the decisionmaker needs to keep track of epistemic uncertainties in addition to any aleatory uncertainty. The appropriate metric will vary with the nature of the assigned decisionmaking task.[211]

Traditional probability hides epistemic ignorance and indeterminacy resulting from imperfect evidence, vagueness, and unknown unknowns. But multivalent beliefs use uncommitted belief as a measure of these epistemic uncertainties. Does the assigner of the task want the decisionmaker to account for the weakness or absence of evidence and to measure any vague elements or other epistemic uncertainties?

Such is the case for legal factfinding. Any asserted fact that the law decides to subject to a proof process is not susceptible to being viewed as certainly, or even near certainly, true or false. The system otherwise would just take the fact as a given. When factfinders must resolve questions on weak evidence or face infinite possibilities, it helps to remain attuned to epistemic uncertainties. Indeed, merely assessing

[211] See generally Meyer et al. (2002) (treating other factors that sometimes make a fuzzy measure, rather than traditional probability, the appropriate measure for the agent's response).

imperfect evidence when comparing a belief and its disbelief requires attention to epistemic uncertainties. When factfinders draw inferences, aggregate evidence, and conjoin or disjoin findings, factfinders must estimate the epistemic uncertainties that lie behind the beliefs. Legal factfinding based on evidence always requires continuing attention to epistemic uncertainties in connection with the ubiquitous tasks of linking inferences from a piece of evidence in order to reach a conclusion, aggregating the probative force of several pieces of evidence that bear on a single conclusion, and combining separate conclusions. These tasks are omnipresent and unavoidable in factfinding. In every proof process, the factfinder will perform them multiple times. Multivalent beliefs, and their rules for combination, are therefore the way to go for legal factfinding.

If instead what the assigner wants is a prediction of whether a random unknown will reveal itself to be true or false, the factfinder should assume bivalence and use traditional probability. Probability better represents the chance of one of two outcomes, subject only to randomness of outcome. Probability's product rule better calculates the expected sequence of two random true/false events. By contrast, if we want a complete representation of the state of unknowns, we want to use multivalent beliefs as the measure of how fully proven each fact is. These beliefs nicely represent what we do and do not know.

Although multivalent belief theory will reduce to bivalent probability theory if we assume bivalence and assume away epistemic uncertainty by means of additivity, multivalent logic's unreduced MIN rule is inaccurate for combining pure probabilities.[212] The reason is that the product rule and MIN rule are telling us different things. The former is calculating the expected sequence of random true/false events. The latter is measuring how fully proven is their coexistence. The two approaches give different answers, appropriate in different circumstances. Therefore, there is a dividing line for appropriate use, a line cutting across the realm of decisionmaking tasks.

We should use multivalent beliefs when necessary for accuracy in performing an assigned decisionmaking task. But when is that? The answer is whenever traditional probability is inaccurate, which sounds but is not circular. Probability rests on certain restrictive assumptions: all things are either true or false, and all predictions of truth or falsity are adequately expressible as being subject only to aleatory uncertainty. We can use probability accurately when the questions of interest permit those simplifying assumptions.

However, these key assumptions will go unsatisfied whenever epistemic uncertainty has a persistent role to play, as in combining inferences or factfindings. When those key assumptions go unsatisfied, the decisionmaker should shift to an appropriate measure. An appropriate measure is one that treats the thing as partially true

[212]Bivalence implies additivity for probability, which in turn implies for any probability of truth a complementary probability of falsity. Conjoining probabilities thus requires disjoining falsities, which depresses the conjunction's probability. The result is that the MIN rule yields to the product rule when there is no epistemic uncertainty measured. See supra Sect. 4.5.4.2.

and partially false and allows tracking of persistent epistemic uncertainty. Multivalent beliefs provide such a measure. Therefore, whenever you encounter unresolvable epistemic uncertainty and have to keep track of it, traditional probability ceases to work, and multivalent beliefs operate as the accurate measure. When must you keep track of epistemic uncertainty? Whenever you need to take an action before the epistemic uncertainty is resolved, unless the action is merely to predict the ultimate resolution of randomness. If you want to act accurately in the face of persistent epistemic uncertainty, you should act in accordance with the facts that you accept as true. If you must act upon the evidence at hand, you should accept the facts you believe more than you disbelieve.

More generally, use of nonadditive multivalent logic is proper when the decisionmaker must measure a nonadditive variable with multiple values, as when, for example, the variable expresses a one-sided share of the whole rather than a pignistic position on a yes-or-no outcome. Those shares of the whole combine by the MIN and MAX rules. Here in factfinding, it is epistemic uncertainty that makes the degree of being fully proved into the appropriate focus and also makes those beliefs nonadditive. Thus, multivalent logic is the route to error minimization.

4.6.2 When Traditional Probability Must Be Used

If and only if you want to describe something about the state of the bivalent world after an unknown or a sequence of unknowns is randomly revealed as true or false, then traditional probability is the way to go. Given the assumptions of a bivalent world subject only to randomness, this is the route to error minimization.

When the assigner wants the decisionmaker to keep track of epistemic uncertainty, the decisionmaker must turn to multivalent logic. But there might be only aleatory uncertainty in the situation. An example would be large-sample data analysis. Or the assigner of a decisionmaking task might want the decisionmaker to hide epistemic uncertainty and act as if there is only aleatory uncertainty. An example would be where one assigns the boy-girl puzzle and begins by assuming away epistemic uncertainty. Another example might be where a decisionmaker decides for her own purposes to make a quick, rough-and-ready fact determination.

Still another example would be where the person is asked to predict an event or a sequence of events in the absence of epistemic uncertainty. If the person has to predict a sequence, she would use traditional probability and its rules for combination of separate measures. In operating on additive measures like these, as in combining a set of odds, the product rule gives the right answers.

In placing a bet or making a prediction of an outcome to be revealed, you are estimating, top-down, a simple first-order probability to represent randomness. I describe the process as "top-down" in the sense that when you state the probability you are acting as if you know all that there is to know, leaving as uncertain only the effects of randomness in fixing the yes-or-no outcome. This is the essence of additive probability: it is premised on your knowing all there is to know that is nonrandom.

Perceiving this essence explains why traditional probability treats an 80% chance on airtight evidence the same as an 80% chance on thin evidence. If you assume you know all that there is to know, you are assuming that all the persisting uncertainty is random. Therefore, the predicted outcome should eventuate 80 out of 100 times, whether the odds rest on thick or thin evidence. If you encounter beliefs in the course of predicting the outcome, you will need to convert the separate and necessary beliefs into probabilities.[213]

Therefore, in some situations, probability will be the only accurate measure. Think back to the urn with 60 of 100 balls being black. You know all there is to know about the odds of unbiasedly picking a black ball. No epistemic uncertainty exists. Likewise, if you are combining pure probabilities (e.g., drawing two black balls), you use the product rule to calculate the aleatory uncertainty of any combinations.

Here is a legal example. Inside the law but outside the act of factfinding, the law employs the probabilistic approach in many of law's standards of decision. Consider when a court is reviewing (or restraining in advance by judgment as a matter of law) a jury's factfinding for reasonableness. There we do not expect the reviewer to retain uncommitted belief in applying the standard of review. Instead, the reviewer should disregard epistemic uncertainties. The "evidence" for applying the standard of review is complete, in that the question is whether the jury impermissibly erred in deciding the case *on the given proof.* We expect the reviewer roughly but directly to estimate probability of error and measure the estimate against the given standard of review. We want from the reviewer a yes/no answer based on the odds of the jury's having unreasonably weighed its beliefs and disbeliefs when it found for its winner, with the odds' complement being the probability of the jury's having had the authority to find for its winner. We do not want the reviewer's "belief."

The reference to a reasonable jury reflects the fact that on such a motion the judge is reviewing the jury's hypothesized application of the standard of proof.[214] The judge's standard of decision turns on whether a jury could not reasonably, or rationally, find for the nonmovant. That is, a civil defendant on motion must show that a verdict for the plaintiff, given the standard of proof, was not reasonably possible. We can state this standard of review in terms of Fig. 4.5's coarsely gradated scale of possibilities and probabilities, without the complications of epistemic uncertainty. The judge must ask whether it is more likely than not that the jury could not rationally find for the plaintiff, that is, more likely than not that there is no reasonable possibility of the plaintiff's being in the right. We want from the judge the likelihood of jury irrationality in finding for its winner, with the complement being the likelihood that the jury had authority to find for its winner.

More generally, application of such standards of review will be a two-step process that involves (1) retracing decisions based on beliefs and then (2) calculating the probability of incorrectness.[215] So, on appeal, we want from the judges the likelihood of error in the lower decisionmaker's deciding a case for the winner, with

---

[213] See supra Sect. 2.1.3 (analyzing Obama's bet).

[214] See Fed. R. Civ. P. 50(a)(1) (stating standard of review as whether "a reasonable jury would not have a legally sufficient evidentiary basis to find for the party on that issue").

[215] See supra Sect. 1.1 (discussing iterated epistemological operators).

the complement being the likelihood of the lower decisionmaker's legal authority to decide for the winner.[216]

4.6.3 When Beliefs and Probability Both May Be Used

Hence, there are limits, inside and outside the law, on the propriety of beliefs and of probabilism. When you are the original decisionmaker and you encounter any epistemic uncertainty, you usually need to back away from traditional probability. Admittedly, nothing is lost by transforming to probability terminology at the end in order to state the outcome in terms of probability. Indeed, this last-minute transform has allowed us to live with all the probabilistic notions that have seeped into legal factfinding. We can talk of a case having to be 51% proven without hopelessly misleading everyone. But to the extent the decisionmaker needs to keep track of epistemic uncertainty in performing multiple steps before the end, using probabilism sacrifices the accuracy that multivalent beliefs would deliver.

So, there is a realm for probabilism and a realm for beliefs. Are there situations where both have a good use? I shall start with the decisionmaker's having to answer different questions about the same situation.

Different Questions for Different Purposes Consider a situation where either measure could be rationally used, although beliefs and probabilities will tell you different things. Imagine a long sequence of yes-or-no events subject to epistemic uncertainty. You could construct a belief function for each event based on the evidence. If your belief in each event exceeded your corresponding disbelief, you would believe the conjunction of events took place. Instead, imagine that the outcome of each event was going to be revealed somehow, and you had to bet on the resulting sequence of yes-or-no outcomes. Each of the events would have been resolved, so that epistemic uncertainty would be gone. Common sense suggests that a sequence of all yes outcomes is very unlikely. You in fact could calculate the odds by transforming each event's belief function into a probability that states randomness, and then applying the product rule to get the tiny probability of all the "cards" turning up yes. This comparison of the two approaches shows once again the difference between beliefs and probabilities. In factfinding we want to act on our best representation of the world based on the evidence, so we should use beliefs to get the most believable story. The factfinder will want to work with beliefs to construct the most accurate view of the uncertain world, rather than making preliminary and unnecessary conversions to probabilities that sacrifice accuracy by discarding measures of epistemic uncertainty. However, when betting we want to predict the most likely of all possible revelations of a random sequence, so we use

---

[216] See Clermont (2013), pp. 141–144 (generalizing use of probabilities for legal standards of decision other than the standard of proof).

probabilities. Therefore, although either approach is usable, selecting an approach will turn on what you want to know.

This situation—the contrast between transforming to a probability at each step versus looking only at the belief function for each event—is very instructive. On the one hand, each transform to a probability converts epistemic uncertainty to aleatory uncertainty and hence augments the negative results that would occur over 100 trials. The product rule then yields a tiny probability of uniformly affirmative results. It tells you the odds of turning over the "cards" sequentially and getting all affirmative results. On the other hand, that probability is an erroneous depiction of a world that has not been revealed, because the transforms treated epistemic unknowns as known percentages. If you want an accurate proof-based depiction of whether you believe the all-affirmative sequence more than you disbelieve it, you must account for the persistent epistemic uncertainty by using belief analysis.

The factfinder should decide by putting all the proof together to decide if it believes the all-affirmative sequence more than it disbelieves that sequence. The bettor, however, should compute the overall probability of one or more to-be-revealed negatives in accordance with De Morgan's rule. The bettor's interest in sequential revelation thus fundamentally differs from the factfinder's interest in evidential proof. The bettor is actually picturing the sequence probabilistically produced through a process whereby the uncertainty surrounding card number one is resolved into certainty with no nonrandom unknowns, and the same for card number two, and so on. The bettor seeks to know the chance of a particular sequence turning up. The factfinder is instead reasoning to the overall reality established by the proof. The factfinder seeks to determine the most believable of all possible versions of that reality.

Why I say that this situation is especially instructive is that it finally exposes the real inappropriateness of probabilism for factfinding. For factfinding, we want to know reality, not how reality came to be. The odds of any single feature of current reality coming to be are effectively 0%. If it took a hundred steps to get to reality, the odds of any one feature of reality becoming true would be near 0%. But our view of reality should instead be determined by belief and disbelief. We can form sizable beliefs about the way reality turned out. When legal theorists think about factfinding, they naively jump to say that we want to know the odds of this or that element being true. No! Right there is their mistake, which derived from their unknowing reliance on assumed bivalence and additivity. We actually want to know the most believable account of reality's content. *We arrive at that account by looking at the state of things, not their chances of getting there.*[217]

[217]I found it difficult to phrase this point, until I ran across the comic legal novel by Cecil (1957). The plot turned on a criminal case for insurance fraud, where the bald and lame defendant told a preposterous story of coincidences, the most amazing being that he had happened to use the same typewriter employed in three previous insurance frauds that were committed by one or more men describable only as bald and lame. The defendant explained that he had only recently bought the typewriter from a barrow boy.

This point is so important but nonintuitive that I shall take another stab at stating it. If you want to predict how things will turn out randomly, in a condition of considerable ignorance, then use traditional probabilities. If instead you want to determine how unknown things most believably have turned out, then use multivalent beliefs. The appropriate metric turns on whether the process is a series of revelations or a series of proofs: *how unknown things will turn out versus how unknown things are*. Legal factfinding falls into the second camp.

Say, we are in the semifinals of a match-play golf tournament. The odds of Lydia Ko winning the tournament are roughly the odds of her winning her semifinal match multiplied by the odds of her winning the final. If, however, the tournament is long over and eyewitnesses testify that she won the final, would you consider those odds? No. You would use the evidence to formulate a belief and disbelief that Lydia won.

Other complex decisions may sometimes call for using both multivalent beliefs and traditional probabilities for different parts of the decisional process. These decisions may involve multiple factual elements or may involve a single fact resting on aspects both pignistic and credal in nature.

Multiple Elements or Successive Inferences If the desire should arise for a factfinder to conjoin elements where there are both purely probabilistic elements and also elements with persistent epistemic uncertainty, the way to proceed is, first, to treat the outcome of all the probabilistic elements as a single belief function and, second, to combine it with the epistemically uncertain belief functions. Thus, the transformable compatibility of probabilities and beliefs is essential for accurate factfinding. It allows combination of a randomly uncertain set with an imprecise set, in accordance with multivalent logical operators. Consider the two steps.

First, the product rules for interdependent and independent probabilities are the accurate way to proceed when dealing with the rare matters treatable as purely additive probabilities. Ideally, gather all those probabilities and perform the probability calculus to produce a single composite probability. Multivalent logic can then effortlessly express even the purest probability as membership in a set, that is, treat the probability as the degree to which the imagined universe of all tests would be believed to belong to the set of positive results.[218] The probability would

---

The judge and the prosecutor were very skeptical. But during the trial both encountered incredible coincidences in their own lives. So, in closing the prosecutor argued that he had earlier been wrong to compare the defense to a million typing monkeys' producing *Hamlet*. "Well, members of the jury, . . . I think it is right that I should now put the case differently to you. I suggest that you should consider whether the Crown has satisfied you that the defendant is lying when he says he bought the typewriter from the barrow boy, and that the barrow boy was lying too. If you are satisfied as to these matters, then I invite you on behalf of the prosecution to find the accused guilty." Id. at 155–156. Then the judge in charging the jury said: "Is it not better then to judge this case on the evidence you heard, on the demeanour of the witnesses, rather than on the probability or improbability of their story? Of course you may take any probability or improbability into consideration, but I suggest to you that, in doing so, you should not weight the scales too heavily against the accused merely because at first blush the chances of his story being true seemed small." Id. at 159.

[218] See Kosko (1993), pp. 55–64 (calling this set "the whole in the part").

equal the belief for, say, the chance of selecting one of 60 black balls from an urn holding 100 balls. But any epistemic uncertainty for the probability estimate would create some uncommitted belief. The composite probability can thereby be stated in the form of a single nonadditive belief function, where p equals or exceeds the belief and $1-p$ equals or exceeds the disbelief. The belief function is then ready to combine with the epistemically uncertain belief functions.

Second, the combinatory steps for beliefs—when considering and combining inferences, evidence, and conclusions—should employ the degrees of belief and disbelief as they appear in belief functions and the rules of multivalent logic. This is the accurate way to combine nonadditive beliefs. Probabilities were already converted into the common currency of beliefs, allowing application of multivalence's combination rules to all beliefs.

In other words, a decision may rest on a number of factual elements, some of which involve purely aleatory uncertainty, while others show some vagueness or other epistemic uncertainty as well. The need in decisionmaking to combine these factfindings with a common currency counsels the conversion to an inclusive logic system, because "we cannot coherently countenance two different kinds of degree of belief."[219] Convert the probabilistic elements into a belief, and then integrate it with the other beliefs.

Using both systems thereby demonstrates another advantage of multivalent logic. It is the more inclusive system. It includes two-valued logic. Multivalent logic neither requires nor forbids that anything have an on-or-off nature, be only true or false, or rest completely inside a set or outside that set. By contrast, the bivalent logic of probability demands the existence of sets exclusively with strict membership classifications, an in-or-out characteristic symbolized respectively by values of either 1 or 0. Yet those crisp sets really are just one kind among fuzzy sets. Bivalence is a special case of multivalent logic. The world of black or white is a special, extreme case of the world shaded in grays. Thus, multivalent logic can handle crisp sets.

Multiple Aspects of an Element Purely additive probabilities will usually not appear in factfinding. Even when factfinding entails a single yes-or-no issue that seems to involve only aleatory uncertainty, the reality is normally more nuanced. Most often, epistemic uncertainty is present, diluting the accuracy of the probabilities. Indeed, even statistical evidence will entail epistemic uncertainty. Statistical evidence will have to be connected up with the disputed issue in the individualized case by a series of permissible but uncertain inferences; the evidence may have to be discounted for defects in credibility; also, the evaluation may have to be adjusted in light of the probative value of the absence of other proof, an effect most often cutting against the proponent; and so on. In short, epistemic uncertainty would have to be accounted for, by a belief function with uncommitted belief.

[219] Smith (2010), p. 491 (cataloging the difficulties that would come from entertaining both probabilities and degrees of belief, when the two underlying logic systems employ different operators).

In some situations, though, a fact can be both fuzzy and crisp. For an example of "normative" uncertainty,[220] it might be that there was a .70 blameworthy act. By contrast, it might be that while the act would be completely blameworthy, there was statistically a 70% chance that it occurred, creating "factual" uncertainty. So, what about a 70% chance of a .70 degree of fault? The act is arguably subject both to epistemic uncertainty and to some purely aleatory uncertainty.[221]

Sometimes, the two kinds of uncertainty can appear in items of evidence that need to aggregated in evaluating a single fact. Although probability theory can say little on how to reason about things that are not completely true or false or not solely random, multivalent belief theory can handle these more mixed and complex situations. It can handle all kinds of facts, and can do so much better than probability for most of them. The inclusiveness of multivalent belief theory suggests its use for each fact as well as for combining evaluations of different evidence. Multivalent belief theory provides the needed common currency. It should smooth the usual intuitive, nonquantitative, and approximate techniques for aggregating evidence bearing on one fact.

Consequently, the reader cannot dodge my argument by concluding that multivalent belief theory reaches, if any, only some kinds of facts. Instead, multivalent belief theory handles a fact embodying both factual uncertainty and normative uncertainty, as well as combinations of evidence items exhibiting random uncertainty with others showing epistemic uncertainty.

Law's Choice Because of multivalent beliefs' general inclusiveness, and because of the prevalence of epistemic uncertainty, law should choose beliefs as its predominant mode of measurement in factfinding. Relying instead on the mathematical supplement of the probability calculus would almost always prove to be so awkward or incomplete as to be nonsensical. If there are any matters in play to be treated as purely additive probabilities, they should be transformed into beliefs, as described above.

On the descriptive question, law has indeed chosen multivalent beliefs as its sole mode of output. In its instructions to factfinders, the law does not explicitly distinguish between probabilism and multivalence. It instead speaks in terms of a common currency, mixing the questions of whether and how much an event occurred. Regardless of whether the issue is occurrence or blameworthiness of an act, the instructions deal only in degrees of belief. Mandating a single currency makes sense

[220] See Porat and Posner (2012), pp. 5–6 (coining the alternative terms "normative aggregation" and "factual aggregation" with similar senses). Philosophers had already plowed this ground, distinguishing a "vagueness-related partial belief" from a "standard uncertainty-related partial belief" or, better, distinguishing taking-to-be-partially-true from partially-taking-to-be-true. See MacFarlane (2010), pp. 445–447. Of course, normative uncertainty is a term widely used with dissimilar meanings. See, e.g., Cox (2023), p. 751.

[221] For this particular example, the two findings should be combined as separate and necessary facts. See supra Sect. 4.5.4.2 (explicating the definition of "element").

only if dealing in multivalent logic, because only it can handle the various kinds of facts and mixes of pignistic and credal inputs.

Multivalent logic will give us degrees of belief in truth for use in legal factfinding. Envisage the set of true facts and ask as to x, a particular element of a claim or an affirmative defense: What is its degree of proven membership in that set, $\mu(x)$? Recall that membership represents how much a variable is in the set. The membership here will be partial. It will tell how true the factfinder finds the element to be on the proof given. Membership thereby creates degrees of belief in truth. We could express $\mu(x)$ as truth(x).

While this membership will turn on likelihood of truth in a sense, the sense is different from the classical understanding of the probability that the element is true. Such probability crisply deals with the probability of x having in actuality a value of 1, while multivalent belief theory more imprecisely deals with gradated degrees of belief. A multivalent belief's complement represents not opposition but instead the degree to which the belief is not proved. Proof of the opposite may have also come in, generating a contrary belief. The uncommitted zone between a belief and any active belief in its opposite represents uncommitted belief. Looking at the law in action, I submit that the law employs multivalent beliefs as the measure of truth in factfinding.

Therefore, a clearer approach to theory is doable. But I need not lobby for reform of practice. The instructions to the jury should stay pretty much the same: keep the instructions simple, and avoid reference to probabilities.

4.7 Logical Summary

I am proposing a new way to look at legal factfinding: multivalent belief theory. My argument in its favor ran along these lines:

1. Whenever a decisionmaking task entails persistent epistemic uncertainty, the outputs are best treated as partial beliefs or partial truths, which represent how far the proposition has been fully proved and which avoid the problems created by classical logic and its probability theory's ignoring epistemic uncertainty.
2. Partial beliefs are best imaged by mathematics' scheme of belief functions, which express in one shot an affirmative belief, uncommitted belief, and the corresponding disbelief.
3. The belief and the disbelief are best analyzed under a nonadditive multivalent logic system without an excluded middle, which system allows a full accounting for uncertainty.
4. For combining beliefs or disbeliefs, nonadditive multivalent logic's operators come into play.
5. Those operators include the MIN and MAX rules, which succeed in dispelling puzzles such as the conjunction and disjunction paradoxes.

6. Factfinding decisions, under the standard of proof, follow from a comparison of the belief function's belief and disbelief, thus resolving problems such as weak evidence.
7. This combination of belief functions' image with multivalent logic's operators explains factfinding's process of evidential proof from beginning to end, as shown in the next chapter.

To locate my proposal in the world of logic, I am proposing substituting multivalent belief theory for the prevailing theoretical role shared by bivalent logic and traditional probability in the operation of legal factfinding. My move lies in the bottom line of this chart of logic:

System	Assumptions	Types	Notes
I. Classical logic	Identity Noncontradiction Excluded middle	First-order logic Higher-order logic	Aristotelian in distant origin
A. Bivalent logic	Only two truth values	Cross-cutting principle	Big subset of classical logic
B. Probability	Built on bivalent conception	Traditional Nontraditional	Mathematical supplement to bivalent logic
Traditional	Nonnegativity Normalization Additivity	Classical Frequentist Subjective	Treats all uncertainty as aleatory
Nontraditional	Eliminates traditional assumption, like additivity	Logical Imprecise Inductive	Treats aleatory and epistemic uncertainty
II. Nonclassical logic	Eliminates classical assumption, like excluded middle	Notably, multivalent logic	More appropriate for certain tasks
Multivalent logic	More than two truth values	Notably, nonadditive multivalent logic	Big subset of nonclassical logic
Nonadditive multivalent logic	Eliminates excluded middle and additivity assumptions	Fuzzy logic Possibility theory Multivalent belief theory	Big subset of multivalent logic; treats aleatory and epistemic uncertainty

To justify my shift from familiar logic to a type of nonclassical logic, the argument runs along these lines:

1. The example of an 80% showing on airtight evidence differing from an 80% showing on weak evidence suffices to demonstrate that bivalent logic with traditional probability is deficient. Another variable—epistemic uncertainty—needs to be measured, even when the proposition being proved has a yes-or-no nature.
2. Traditional probability does not cure the deficiency because it remains additive. Thus, it treats all uncertainty as aleatory.
3. One solution for these problems, which arise when encountering epistemic uncertainty, is to reject both bivalence and additivity in favor of nonadditive

multivalent logic. The reasons for choosing this solution are that it is readily comprehensible (as compared to nontraditional probability) and it is the solution apparently chosen by the law (as compared to, say, relative plausibility theory with its embedded conjunction paradox).

References

Aliev RA (2013) Fundamentals of the fuzzy logic-based generalized theory of decisions. Springer Science+Business, Heidelberg

Allen RJ (1991) The nature of juridical proof. Cardozo Law Rev 13:373–422

Allen RJ (2011) Standards of proof and the limits of legal analysis. https://ssrn.com/abstract=1830344. Accessed 28 Dec 2021

Allen RJ (2018) The declining utility of analyzing burdens of persuasion. Seton Hall Law Rev 48: 995–1015

Allen RJ, Jehl SA (2003) Burdens of persuasion in civil cases: algorithms v. explanations. Mich St Law Rev 2003:893–944

Allen RJ, Leiter B (2001) Naturalized epistemology and the law of evidence. Va Law Rev 87:1491–1550

Allen RJ, Pardo MS (2007) Probability, explanation and inference: a reply. Int J Evidence Proof 11: 307–317

Allen RJ, Pardo MS (2019a) Clarifying relative plausibility: a rejoinder. Int J Evidence Proof 23: 205–217

Allen RJ, Pardo MS (2019b) Relative plausibility and its critics. Int J Evidence Proof 23:5–59

Allen RJ, Pardo MS (2023) Evidence, probability, and relative plausibility: a response to Aitken, Taroni, and Bozza. Int J Evidence Proof 27:126–142

Allen RJ, Stein A (2013) Evidence, probability, and the burden of proof. Ariz Law Rev 55:557–602

Amaya A (2009) Inference to the best legal explanation. In: Kaptein H et al (eds) Legal evidence and proof: statistics, stories, logic. Ashgate, Farnham UK, pp 135–159

Amaya A (2019) The explanationist revolution in evidence law. Int J Evidence Proof 23:60–67

Amaya A (2021) Epistemic ambivalence in law. Phil Issues 31:7–23

Anderson NH (1974) Cognitive algebra: integration theory applied to social attribution. Adv Exp Soc Psychol 7:1–101

Anderson NH (1981) Foundations of information integration theory. Academic Press, New York

Anderson NH (2017) Moral science. https://psychology.ucsd.edu/_files/norman-anderson-book/Chapter%204.pdf. Accessed 28 Dec 2021

Anderson T, Schum D, Twining W (2005) Analysis of evidence, 2nd edn. Cambridge University Press, New York

Barnett JA (2008) Computational methods for *A Mathematical Theory of Evidence*. In: Yager RR, Liu L (eds) Classic works of the Dempster-Shafer theory of belief functions. Springer Science +Business, Heidelberg, pp 197–216

Bellman R, Giertz M (1973) On the analytic formalism of the theory of fuzzy sets. Info Sci 5:149–156

Bělohlávek R, Klir GJ, Lewis HW III, Way E (2002) On the capability of fuzzy set theory to represent concepts. Int J Gen Sys 31:569–585

Bex F (2009) Analysing stories using schemes. In: Kaptein H et al (eds) Legal evidence and proof: statistics, stories, logic. Ashgate, Farnham, pp 93–116

Brewer S (2011) Logocratic method and the analysis of arguments in evidence. Law Prob Risk 10: 175–202

Broun KS (gen ed) (2013) McCormick on evidence, vol 2, 7th edn. Thomson/West, St Paul

Brulé JF (1985) Fuzzy systems—a tutorial. http://www.austinlinks.com/Fuzzy/tutorial.html. Accessed 27 Dec 2021
Buchak L (2014) Belief, credence, and norms. Phil Stud 169:285–311
Cabrera F (2023) Inference to the best explanation: an overview. In: Magnani L (ed) Handbook of abductive cognition. Springer Science+Business, Heidelberg, pp 1863–1896
Callen CR (1991) Kicking rocks with Dr. Johnson: a comment on Professor Allen's theory. Cardozo Law Rev 13:423–444
Cecil H (1957) Much in evidence. Michael Joseph Ltd, London
Chappell SG (2013) Plato on knowledge in the *Theaetetus*. In: Zalta EN (ed) Stanford encyclopedia of philosophy. https://plato.stanford.edu/entries/plato-theaetetus/
Cheng Eugenia (2018) The art of logic in an illogical world. Basic Books, New York
Cheng Edward K, Pardo MS (2015) Accuracy, optimality and the preponderance standard. Law Prob Risk 14:193–212
Christensen D (2004) Putting logic in its place. Oxford University Press, Oxford
Cintula P, Fermüller CG, Noguera C (2017) Fuzzy logic. In: Zalta EN (ed) Stanford encyclopedia of philosophy. https://plato.stanford.edu/archives/fall2017/entries/logic-fuzzy/
Clermont KM (2013) Standards of decision in law: psychological and logical bases for the standard of proof, here and abroad. Carolina Academic Press, Durham
Clermont KM (2018) Common sense on standards of proof. Seton Hall Law Rev 48:1057–1080
Clermont KM (2019) The silliness of magical realism. Int J Evidence Proof 23:147–153
Clermont KM (2023) Beliefs and probabilities: the errors that remain are mine alone. Wash Univ Juris Rev 15:273–289
Clermont KM, Eisenberg T (1992) Trial by jury or judge: transcending empiricism. Cornell Law Rev 77:1124–1177
Cluxton D, Eick SG, Jie Y (2004) Hypothesis visualization. In: IEEE symposium on information visualization, Austin TX 2004. https://ieeexplore.ieee.org/document/1382915. Accessed 28 Dec 2021
Cobb BR, Shenoy PP (2003) A comparison of methods for transforming belief function models to probability models. In: Nielsen TD, Zhang NL (eds) Symbolic and quantitative approaches to reasoning with uncertainty. Proceedings of the seventh European conference, Aalborg Denmark 2003. Springer Science+Business, Heidelberg, pp 255–266
Cohen LJ (1977) The probable and the provable. Clarendon Press, Oxford
Cohen LJ (1980) Bayesianism versus Baconianism in the evaluation of medical diagnoses. Br J Phil Sci 31:45–62
Cohen LJ (1991) Should a jury say what it believes or what it accepts? Cardozo Law Rev 13:465–483
Copi IM, Cohen C, McMahon K (2011) Introduction to logic, 14th edn. Routledge, New York
Cox CM (2023) The uncertain judge. Univ Chic Law Rev 90:739–811
David M (2015) The correspondence theory of truth. In: Zalta EN (ed) Stanford encyclopedia of philosophy. https://plato.stanford.edu/entries/truth-correspondence/
Dawid AP (1987) The difficulty about conjunction. Statistician 36:91–97
De Mot J, Stein A (2015) Talking points. Univ Ill Law Rev 2015:1259–1286
Dember WN, Warm JS (1979) Psychology of perception, 2nd edn. Holt, Rinehart and Winston, New York
Dempster AP (1967) Upper and lower probabilities induced by a multivalued mapping. Ann Math Stat 38:325–339
Dernoncourt F (2011) Fuzzy logic: between human reasoning and artificial intelligence. https://www.researchgate.net/publication/235333084_Fuzzy_logic_between_human_reasoning_and_artificial_intelligence. Accessed 18 Aug 2023
Dubois D, Prade H (1985) A review of fuzzy set aggregation connectives. Info Sci 36:85–121
Dubois D, Prade H (2007) Possibility theory. In: Scholarpedia. http://www.scholarpedia.org/article/Possibility_theory

Dubois D, Prade H (2008) A set-theoretic view of belief functions: logical operations and approximations by fuzzy sets. In: Yager RR, Liu L (eds) Classic works of the Dempster-Shafer theory of belief functions. Springer Science+Business, Heidelberg, pp 375–410

Dubois D, Esteva F, Godo L, Prade H (2007) Fuzzy-set based logics—an history-oriented presentation of their main developments. In: Gabbay DM, Woods J (eds) Handbook of the history of logic, vol 8. Elsevier, Amsterdam, pp 325–449

Emery N, Markosian N, Sullivan M (2020) Time. In: Zalta EN (ed) Stanford encyclopedia of philosophy. https://plato.stanford.edu/entries/time/

Engel C (2009) Preponderance of the evidence versus *intime conviction*: a behavioral perspective on a conflict between American and Continental European law. Vt Law Rev 33:435–467

Enoch D, Spectre L, Fisher T (2012) Statistical evidence, sensitivity, and the legal value of knowledge. Phil Pub Affairs 40:197–224

Evnine SJ (1999) Believing conjunctions. Synthese 118:201–227

Ferrer BJ (2006) Legal proof and fact finders' beliefs. Legal Theory 12:293–314

Ferson S, Kreinovich V (2001) Representation, elicitation, and aggregation of uncertainty in risk analysis—from traditional probabilistic techniques to more general, more realistic approaches: a survey. https://scholarworks.utep.edu/cgi/viewcontent.cgi?article=1420&context=cs_techrep. Accessed 28 Dec 2021

Field RH, Kaplan B, Clermont KM, Clopton ZD (2023) Materials for a basic course in civil procedure, 14th edn. Foundation, St Paul

Fine TL (1986) [The axioms of subjective probability:] comment. Stat Sci 1:352–354

Frankish K (2009) Partial belief and flat-out belief. In: Huber F, Schmidt-Petri C (eds) Degrees of belief. Springer Science+Business, Heidelberg, pp 75–93

Franklin J (2015) The science of conjecture: evidence and probability before Pascal, 2nd edn. Johns Hopkins University Press, Baltimore

Friedman RD (2001) "E" is for eclectic: multiple perspectives on evidence. Va Law Rev 87:2029–2054

Friedman J (2013) Suspended judgment. Phil Stud 162:165–181

Gaines BR (1978) Fuzzy and probability uncertainty logics. Info Control 38:154–169

Genin K, Huber F (2020) Formal representations of belief. In: Zalta EN (ed) Stanford encyclopedia of philosophy. https://plato.stanford.edu/entries/formal-belief/

Gettier EL (1963) Is justified true belief knowledge? Analysis 23:121–123

Gettys CF, Kelly C, Peterson CR (1973) The best guess hypothesis in multistage inference. Organ Behav Hum Perform 10:364–373

Gimbel S (2016) An introduction to formal logic. Great Courses, Chantilly

Godo L, Hájek P, Esteva F (2003) A fuzzy modal logic for belief functions. Fundamenta Informaticae 57:127–146

Goldman AI (1986) Epistemology *and* cognition. Harvard University Press, Cambridge

Gómez-Torrente M (2018) Logical truth. In: Zalta EN (ed) Stanford encyclopedia of philosophy. https://plato.stanford.edu/entries/logical-truth/

Gottwald S (2015) Many-valued logic. In: Zalta EN (ed) Stanford encyclopedia of philosophy. https://plato.stanford.edu/entries/logic-manyvalued/

Haack S (1996) Deviant logic, fuzzy logic. University of Chicago Press, Chicago

Haack S (2012) The embedded epistemologist: dispatches from the legal front. Ratio Juris 25:206–235

Haack S (2014a) Epistemology and the law of evidence: problems and projects. In: Evidence matters: science, proof, and truth in the law. Cambridge University Press, New York, pp 1–26

Haack S (2014b) Legal probabilism: an epistemological dissent. In: Evidence matters: science, proof, and truth in the law. Cambridge University Press, New York, pp 47–77

Haack S (2014c) Nothing fancy: some simple truths about truth in the law. In: Evidence matters: science, proof, and truth in the law. Cambridge University Press, New York, pp 294–323

Haenni R (2009) Non-additive degrees of belief. In: Huber F, Schmidt-Petri C (eds) Degrees of belief. Springer Science+Business, Heidelberg, pp 121–159

Hajek P (2010) Fuzzy logic. In: Zalta EN (ed) Stanford encyclopedia of philosophy. http://plato.stanford.edu/archives/fall2010/entries/logic-fuzzy/ (archives)
Hájek A (2022) Pascal's wager. In: Zalta EN (ed) Stanford encyclopedia of philosophy. https://plato.stanford.edu/entries/pascal-wager/
Halpern JY (2017) Reasoning about uncertainty, 2nd edn. MIT Press, Cambridge
Harman G (1965) The inference to the best explanation. Phil Rev 74:88–95
Hartshorne C, Weiss P (eds) (1932) Collected papers of Charles Sanders Peirce: pragmatism and pragmaticism, vol 5, 3rd edn. Harvard University Press, Cambridge
Hastie R (2008) What's the story? Explanations and narratives in civil jury decisions. In: Bornstein BH et al (eds) Civil juries and civil justice. Springer Science+Business, New York, pp 23–34
Helprin M (2017) Paris *in the* present tense. Harry N. Abrams, New York
Hertwig R, Gigerenzer G (1999) The "conjunction fallacy" revisited: how intelligent inferences look like reasoning errors. J Behav Decis Mak 12:275–305
Ho HL (2008) A philosophy of evidence law: justice in the search for truth. Oxford University Press, New York
Huber F (2009) Belief and degrees of belief. In: Huber F, Schmidt-Petri C (eds) Degrees of belief. Springer Science+Business, Heidelberg, pp 1–33
Ichikawa JJ, Steup M (2017) The analysis of knowledge. In: Zalta EN (ed) Stanford encyclopedia of philosophy. https://plato.stanford.edu/entries/knowledge-analysis/
Jablonowski M (2008) An ultra-fuzzy model of aggregate growth in catastrophic risk potentials. In: Annual meeting of the North American Fuzzy Information Processing Society, New York NY 2008. http://ieeexplore.ieee.org/xpl/freeabs_all.jsp?arnumber=4531214. Accessed 27 Dec 2021
Jaffee LR (1985) Of probativity and probability: statistics, scientific evidence, and the calculus of chance at trial. Univ Pitt Law Rev 46:925–1082
Kahneman D (2011) Thinking, fast and slow. Farrar Straus, New York
Kaplan MF (1982) Cognitive processes in the individual juror. In: Kerr NL, Bray RM (eds) The psychology of the courtroom. Academic Press, New York, pp 197–220
Kaplan MF, Kemmerick GD (1974) Juror judgment as information integration: combining evidential and nonevidential information. J Pers Soc Psychol 30:493–499
Karnik NN, Mendel JM (2001) Operations on type-2 fuzzy sets. Fuzzy Sets Sys 122:327–348
Kay J, King M (2020) Radical uncertainty: decision-making beyond the numbers. Norton, New York
Keahey TA, Eick SG (2004) A visualization architecture for intelligence analysis. In: Proceedings electronic imaging, San Jose CA 2004. https://doi.org/10.1117/12.539241. Accessed 28 Dec 2021
Kerkvliet T, Meester RWJ (2016) Assessing forensic evidence by computing belief functions. Law Prob Risk 15:127–153
Kosko B (1993) Fuzzy thinking: the new science of fuzzy logic. Hyperion Books, New York
Kyburg HE Jr (1961) Probability and the logic of rational belief. Wesleyan University Press, Middletown
Ladyman J (2002) Understanding philosophy of science. Routledge, London
Laudan L (2007) Strange bedfellows: inference to the best explanation and the criminal standard of proof. Int J Evidence Proof 11:292–306
Leitgeb H (2014) The review paradox: on the diachronic costs of not closing rational belief under conjunction. Noûs 48:781–793
Lempert RO (1977) Modeling relevance. Mich Law Rev 75:1021–1057
Lipton P (2004) Inference to the best explanation, 2nd edn. Routledge, London
Liu L, Yager RR (2008) Classic works of the Dempster-Shafer theory of belief functions: an introduction. In: Yager RR, Liu L (eds) Classic works of the Dempster-Shafer theory of belief functions. Springer Science+Business, Heidelberg, pp 1–34
Lopes LL (1985) Averaging rules and adjustment processes in Bayesian inference. Bull Psychon Soc 23:509–512

MacFarlane J (2010) Fuzzy epistemicism. In: Dietz R, Moruzzi S (eds) Cuts and clouds: vagueness, its nature, and its logic. Oxford University Press, Oxford, pp 438–463

Maguire J et al (1973) Cases and materials on evidence, 6th edn. Foundation, Mineola

Makinson DC (1965) The paradox of the preface. Analysis 25:205–207

Malinowski G (2007) Many-valued logic and its philosophy. In: Gabbay DM, Woods J (eds) Handbook of the history of logic, vol 8. Elsevier, Amsterdam, pp 13–94

McAuliffe WHB (2015) How did abduction get confused with inference to the best explanation? Trans Charles S. Peirce Soc 51:300–319

Meester R (2020) Classical probabilities and belief functions in legal cases. Law Prob Risk 19:99–107

Meester R, Kerkvliet T (2019) A new look at conditional probability with belief functions. Statistica Neerlandica 73:274–291

Meier L (2015) Probability, confidence, and the "reasonable jury" standard. Miss Law J 84:747–816

Mendel JM (2007) Type-2 fuzzy sets and systems: an overview. IEEE Comput Intell Mag 2(1): 20–29. http://sipi.usc.edu/~mendel/publications/MENDEL%20CI%20Magazine%202007.pdf

Mendel JM (2009) Type-2 fuzzy sets and systems: how to learn about them. IEEE SMC eNewsl # 27 (June 2009). https://ieeesmc.org/newsletters/back/2009_06/SMC-Mendel.html. Accessed 27 Dec 2021

Metzloff TB (1991) Resolving malpractice disputes: imaging the jury's shadow. Law Contemp Probs 54(1):43–129

Meyer MA, Butterfield KB, Murray WS, Smith RE, Booker JM (2002) Guidelines for eliciting expert judgment as probabilities or fuzzy logic. In: Ross TJ et al (eds) Fuzzy logic and probability applications: bridging the gap. Society for Industrial and Applied Mathematics, Philadelphia, pp 105–123

Miceli TJ (2018) Contemporary issues in law and economics. Routledge, London

Michelon C (2019) The inference to the best legal explanation. Oxford J Leg Stud 39:878–900

Moss S (2018) Probabilistic knowledge. Oxford University Press, Oxford

Moss J, Schwab W (2019) The birth of belief. J Hist Phil 57:1–32

Mosteller TM (2014) Theories of truth: an introduction. Bloomsbury, London

Muller RA (2016) Now: the physics of time. Norton, New York

Nance DA (2001) Naturalized epistemology and the critique of evidence theory. Va Law Rev 87: 1551–1618

Nance DA (2018) Formalism and potential surprise: theorizing about standards of proof. Seton Hall Law Rev 48:1017–1038

Nesson C (1985) The evidence or the event? On judicial proof and the acceptability of verdicts. Harv Law Rev 98:1357–1392

Newman A (2002) The correspondence theory of truth: an essay on the metaphysics of predication. Cambridge University Press, Cambridge

Novák V (2008) Modeling with words. In: Scholarpedia. http://www.scholarpedia.org/article/Modeling_with_words

Okasha S (2016) Philosophy of science: a very short introduction, 2nd edn. Oxford University Press, Oxford

Pardo MS (2013) The nature and purpose of evidence theory. Vand Law Rev 66:547–613

Pardo MS (2015) Group agency and legal proof; or, why the jury is an "it". Wm Mary Law Rev 56: 1793–1858

Pardo MS (2019) The paradoxes of legal proof: a critical guide. BU Law Rev 99:233–290

Pardo MS (2023) What makes evidence sufficient?. Ariz Law Rev 65:431–478

Pardo MS, Allen RJ (2008) Juridical proof and the best explanation. Law Phil 27:223–268

Pascal B (1670) Pascal's pensées. Dutton, New York (1958)

Plato (c 369 BCE) Theaetetus. http://www.perseus.tufts.edu/hopper/text?doc=Perseus%3Atext%3A1999.01.0172%3Atext%3DTheaet.%3Asection%3D201b. Accessed 26 Dec 2021

Porat A, Posner EA (2012) Aggregation and law. Yale Law J 122:2–69

Posner RA (2011) Economic analysis of law, 8th edn. Aspen, New York
Priest G (2008) An introduction to non-classical logic: from if to is, 2nd edn. Cambridge University Press, Cambridge
Ragin CC (2017) User's guide to fuzzy-set/qualitative comparative analysis. http://www.socsci.uci.edu/~cragin/fsQCA/download/fsQCAManual.pdf. Accessed 27 Dec 2021
Ramsey FP (1991) In: Rescher N, Majer U (eds) On truth: original manuscripts (1927–29) from the Ramsey Collection at the University of Pittsburgh. University of Pittsburgh Press, Pittsburgh
Reghiş M, Roventa E (1998) Classical and fuzzy concepts in mathematical logic and applications. CRC Press, Boca Raton
Risinger DM (2013) Searching for truth in the American law of evidence and proof. Ga Law Rev 47:801–835
Risinger DM (2018) Leveraging surprise: what standards of proof imply that we want from jurors, and what we should say to them to get it. Seton Hall Law Rev 48:965–994
Rosenhouse J (2009) The Monty Hall problem. Oxford University Press, Oxford
Ross TJ, Parkinson WJ (2002) Fuzzy set theory, fuzzy logic, and fuzzy systems. In: Ross TJ et al (eds) Fuzzy logic and probability applications: bridging the gap. Society for Industrial and Applied Mathematics, Philadelphia, pp 29–53
Rott H (2009) Degrees all the way down: beliefs, non-beliefs and disbeliefs. In: Huber F, Schmidt-Petri C (eds) Degrees of belief. Springer Science+Business, Heidelberg, pp 301–339
Russell B (1948) Human knowledge: its scope and limits. Allen and Unwin, London
Russell G, Blake-Turner C (2023) Logical pluralism. In: Zalta EN (ed) Stanford encyclopedia of philosophy. https://plato.stanford.edu/entries/logical-pluralism/
Rysiew P (2016) Epistemic contextualism. In: Zalta EN (ed) Stanford encyclopedia of philosophy. https://plato.stanford.edu/entries/contextualism-epistemology/
Saffiotti A (1992) A belief-function logic. In: AAAI proceedings of the tenth national conference on artificial intelligence, San Jose CA 1992. AAAI Press, Menlo Park, pp 642–647. https://www.aaai.org/Papers/AAAI/1992/AAAI92-099.pdf
Saks MJ, Kidd RF (1981) Human information processing and adjudication: trial by heuristics. Law Soc Rev 15:123–160
Sayid C (2021) Knowledge—norms in a common-law crucible. Ratio 34:261–276
Schiffer S (2003) The things we mean. Oxford University Press, Oxford
Schum DA (1994) The evidential foundations of probabilistic reasoning. Northwestern University Press, Evanston
Schum DA (2001) Species of abductive reasoning in fact investigation in law. Cardozo Law Rev 22:1645–1681
Schurz G (2021) Rational belief in lottery- and preface-situations: impossibility results and possible solutions. In: Douven I (ed) Lotteries, knowledge, and rational belief: essays on the lottery paradox. Cambridge University Press, Cambridge, pp 128–146
Sentz K, Ferson S (2002) Combination of evidence in Dempster-Shafer theory. Sandia National Laboratories, Albuquerque. https://www.osti.gov/servlets/purl/800792. Accessed 28 Dec 2021
Shackle GLS (1949) Expectation in economics. Cambridge University Press, Cambridge
Shackle GLS (1969) Decision, order, and time in human affairs, 2nd edn. Cambridge University Press, Cambridge
Shafer G (1976) A mathematical theory of evidence. Princeton University Press, Princeton
Shafer G (1986) The construction of probability arguments. BU Law Rev 66:799–816
Shafer G (1990a) Belief functions: introduction. In: Shafer G, Pearl J (eds) Readings in uncertain reasoning. Morgan Kaufmann, San Mateo, pp 473–481
Shafer G (1990b) Perspectives on the theory and practice of belief functions. Int J Approx Reason 4: 323–362
Shafer G, Tversky A (2008) Languages and designs for probability judgment. In: Yager RR, Liu L (eds) Classic works of the Dempster-Shafer theory of belief functions. Springer Science+Business, Heidelberg, pp 345–373
Shanteau J (1975) Averaging versus multiplying combination rules of inference judgment. Acta Psychologia 39:83–89

Shapira RA (1998) Economic analysis of the law of evidence: a caveat. Cardozo Law Rev 19:1607–1634

Sider T (2010) Logic for philosophy. Oxford University Press, Oxford

Simon D (2019) Thin empirics. Int J Evidence Proof 23:82–89

Smets P (2005) Decision making in the TBM: the necessity of the pignistic transformation. Int J Approx Reason 38:133–147

Smith NJJ (2010) Degree of belief is expected truth value. In: Dietz R, Moruzzi S (eds) Cuts and clouds: vagueness, its nature, and its logic. Oxford University Press, Oxford, pp 491–506

Spohn W (2009) A survey of ranking theory. In: Huber F, Schmidt-Petri C (eds) Degrees of belief. Springer Science+Business, Heidelberg, pp 185–228

Spottswood E (published as Mark) (2019) On the limitations of a unitary model of the proof process. Int J Evidence Proof 23:75–81

Srivastava RP, Shafer GR (2008) Belief-function formulas for audit risk. In: Yager RR, Liu L (eds) Classic works of the Dempster-Shafer theory of belief functions. Springer Science+Business, Heidelberg, pp 577–618

Stein A (2005) Foundations of evidence law. Oxford University Press, Oxford

Steup M (2005) Epistemology. In: Zalta EN (ed) Stanford encyclopedia of philosophy. https://plato.stanford.edu/entries/epistemology/

Strasser C, Antonelli GA (2019) Non-monotonic logic. In: Zalta EN (ed) Stanford encyclopedia of philosophy. https://plato.stanford.edu/entries/logic-nonmonotonic/

Sullivan SP (2018) A likelihood story: the theory of legal fact-finding. Univ Colo Law Rev 90:1–66

Thole U, Zimmermann H-J, Zysno P (1979) On the suitability of minimum and product operators for the intersection of fuzzy sets. Fuzzy Sets Syst 2:167–180

Tuzet G (2019) Abduction, IBE and standards of proof. Int J Evidence Proof 23:114–120

Tversky A, Kahneman D (1983) Extensional versus intuitive reasoning: the conjunction fallacy in probability judgment. Psychol Rev 90:293–315

Tversky A, Koehler DJ (1994) Support theory: a nonextensional representation of subjective probability. Psychol Rev 101:547–567

Van Fraassen BC (1989) Laws and symmetry. Clarendon Press, Oxford

Walker VR (1996) Preponderance, probability and warranted factfinding. Brook Law Rev 62: 1075–1136

Walton D (2002) Legal argumentation and evidence. Pennsylvania State University Press, University Park

Welch JR (2020) Rebooting the new evidence scholarship. Int J Evidence Proof 24:351–373

Whiteley JHL (2021) How jurors' beliefs count. Miss Law J 90:383–439

Wigmore JH (1937) The science of judicial proof as given by logic, psychology, and general experience, and illustrated in judicial trials, 3rd edn. Little Brown, Boston

Williamson T (2000) Knowledge and its limits. Oxford University Press, Oxford

Wygralak M (1996) Vaguely defined objects. Springer Science+Business, Heidelberg

Yager RR (1991) Connectives and quantifiers in fuzzy sets. Fuzzy Sets Syst 40:39–75

Yen J (2008) Generalizing the Dempster-Shafer theory to fuzzy sets. In: Yager RR, Liu L (eds) Classic works of the Dempster-Shafer theory of belief functions. Springer Science+Business, Heidelberg, pp 529–554

Zadeh LA (1965) Fuzzy sets. Info Control 8:338–353

Zadeh LA (1978) Fuzzy sets as a basis for a theory of possibility. Fuzzy Sets Syst 1:3–28

Zadeh LA (1984) Book review. AI Mag 5(3):81–83. www.aaai.org/ojs/index.php/aimagazine/article/download/452/388

Zimmer AC (1983) Verbal vs. numerical processing of subjective probabilities. In: Scholz RW (ed) Decision making under uncertainty. North-Holland, Amsterdam, pp 159–182

Zwick R, Budescu DV, Wallsten TS (1988) An empirical study of the interpretation of linguistic probabilities. In: Zétényi T (ed) Fuzzy sets in psychology. North-Holland, Amsterdam, pp 91–125

Chapter 5
Factfinding Deconstructed Logically

Sherlock Holmes closed his eyes and placed his elbows upon the arms of his chair, with his finger-tips together. "The ideal reasoner," he remarked, "would, when he had once been shown a single fact in all its bearings, deduce from it not only all the chain of events which led up to it but also all the results which would follow from it."
—Arthur Conan Doyle (Arthur Conan Doyle, The Five Orange Pips, in The Adventures of Sherlock Holmes 128, 143 (London, Electric Book Co. 2001) (1892). Sherlock Holmes, championed for his (allegedly) deductive logic, was actually using (very lucky) abductive reasoning—which is not so surprising considering that his stories were written by Arthur Conan Doyle and inspired by Joseph Bell, both medical doctors. See Fox (2018), pp. xix–xx, 42, 70–77 (documenting Bell's influence). "When Holmes says, as he does in his debut appearance, 'In solving a problem of this sort, the grand thing is to be able to reason backward,' he is singing the praises of abduction." Id. at 81; see id. at 79 n.* ("Conan Doyle, per common parlance, tended to use 'deduction' as a general rubric denoting any type of logical inference."); cf. Blutman (2021) (squeezing Holmes's thinking into the category of induction).)

Abstract Multivalent beliefs can be best understood if seen in action, as the factfinder processes evidence and evaluates proof. Before viewing them in action, though, one must dissect the stage of factfinding into two distinct phases: (1) processing each item of evidence by connecting it to a necessary fact before aggregating those connections to form a belief in the fact, and then (2) evaluating the beliefs in each of those necessary facts against the standard of proof. This fairly long chapter's study of examples manages to lay bare our intuitive ways both of linking an evidential item to a belief through a chain of inferences and of somehow averaging the various items of evidence to produce overall beliefs in each of the elemental facts. Likewise, multivalent belief theory works well for analyzing our intuitive way of evaluating the resultant beliefs against the standard of proof.

K. M. Clermont, *A General Theory of Evidence and Proof*, Law and Philosophy Library 148, https://doi.org/10.1007/978-3-031-66552-3_5

Section 5.1: The initial phase of factfinding entails the processing of the evidence. First, the factfinder should connect each item of evidence to a fact to be proved, or element, by constructing a chain of inferences. Second, the factfinder must aggregate the probative force of all the items of evidence that bear on any one element. Third, the factfinder may choose to combine the elements of claim or affirmative defense, but the better approach is to proceed directly to applying the appropriate standard of proof to each element. In sum, the factfinder should abductively construct a chain of inferences to produce a belief function for each item of evidence bearing on an element, and then weight and average them to produce for each element a composite belief function ready for applying the element-by-element standard of proof. Section 5.2: The final phase of factfinding entails evaluating the evidence as proof against some standard of proof. The preliminary topics of the burdens of proof translate readily and advantageously into the terms of belief functions, as does the standard of proof itself. First, the burden of production, which effectuates multiple process and outcome values, means that the decisionmaker or reviewer must patrol the sufficiency of the evidence to ensure that there is rationally enough of a belief to warrant the factfinder's applying the burden of persuasion. Second, any view of the burden of persuasion that rests on probabilities should yield to a reformulation along the lines of belief functions. Third, on the key topic of the standards of proof, belief functions make indispensable contributions to understanding. For example, preponderance of the evidence is best understood as providing that the burdened party should win if and only if $Bel(a) > Bel(not\text{-}a)$. The higher standards of proof demand a greater predominance of belief in relation to disbelief.

Multivalent beliefs can be best understood if seen in action, as the factfinder processes evidence and evaluates proof. Factfinding is foundational for law. The great minds of Locke,[1] Bentham,[2] and Wigmore[3] laid the modern foundation.[4] Of late, factfinding has become the subject of theoretical innovation[5] and even

---

[1] See Wright (2018), p. 520 (quoting Locke's treatment of varying degrees of belief).

[2] See Anderson et al. (2005), p. 80 n.4 (crediting Bentham as the source of the so-called Rationalist Tradition); see also Twining (2006), pp. 75–80 (describing the common-law system's Rationalist Tradition).

[3] See Anderson et al. (2005), pp. 87–88 (crediting Wigmore as the inspiration of the so-called New Evidence movement).

[4] The modern law of evidence rests on the free evaluation of the evidence: the relevant evidence comes in, subject to some exceptions, and the factfinder rationally processes it without legal restraints. This approach prevails in common-law countries as well as in civil-law countries, even if the latter countries sometimes lob claims of heresy against the former. See Damaška (1995), pp. 343–348. Free evaluation supplanted the medieval formal theory of evidence, or *la preuve légale*: supposedly medieval legal proof had assigned weights to specified classes of evidence, such as admissions and oaths, and prescribed exactly when a set of evidence amounted to full proof. See Damaška (2019), pp. 2–3, 5 (arguing that the differences between free evaluation and medieval proof are not as pronounced as conventional wisdom would have it); Franklin (2015), pp. 12–37 (describing medieval proof); Schauer (2021) (defending rule-based exceptions to free evaluation).

[5] See Lempert (1986), pp. 440–450 (describing the developing field called New Evidence).

comparative study.[6] As already said, the New Evidence scholarship has made tremendous progress toward a deeper understanding of factfinding.[7] Still, here in the United States, we cannot even agree on how to spell it: should it be one word, hyphenated, or two words?[8]

Facts As the very first move in understanding factfinding at a level deeper than the orthographic, I need to locate the subject. Recall about "fact" that I mean it loosely to suggest anything out in the real world that a court, other institution, or person subjects to a proof process in order to establish whether to treat it as truth.[9] Nonetheless, discussion will be easiest if we focus on the legal task for judge or jury of reaching a dichotomous finding on a past fact material to a claim or affirmative defense.

Stages Next, I need to deconstruct the legal factfinding process. The "finding" of facts breaks down into three stages: "the fact-gathering stage, the evidence stage and the decision-making stage."[10] The first is the search for and the sharing of relevant information.[11] The second is the presentation of evidence to the decisionmaker.[12] In the third or "decision stage, the decision maker will mentally assess and weigh the evidence and render a decision on matters of fact."[13] The law extensively treats the first two stages by the provisions of procedural and evidence law. But the law treads very lightly in the third stage.

Phases This book addresses only the third stage. In Fig. 5.1, I divide that mental stage, in turn, into an evidence-processing phase and a proof-evaluating phase.[14]

---

[6] See Verkerk (2010).

[7] See supra Chap. 3 (introducing New Evidence scholarship). Although "new," this work represented the necessary return to abandoned insights by past greats such as Wigmore. See, e.g., Anderson et al. (2005) (building explicitly on Wigmore (1937)).

[8] Writing "fact finding" as two words is now considered archaic. "Fact-finding" is most common. "Factfinding" is considered the trend, albeit an incipient trend. See Garner (1987), p. 237. Yet the US Government Printing Office (1973), p. 94, which was long treated as authoritative on such matters by the *Bluebook*, says to write "factfinding." See Columbia Law Review Ass'n et al. (2000), r. I.2 (referring "punctuation, capitalization, compounding, and other matters of style" to the GPO); cf. Columbia Law Review Ass'n et al. (2020), r. 8(c) (now mentioning capitalization only).

[9] See supra Sect. 1.1 (defining "fact").

[10] Verkerk (2010), p. 1.

[11] See generally Zwierl and Bocchino (2015).

[12] See generally Broun (2013). "Evidence rules" determine what the factfinder considers. They include the "principles of proof," which are logically anterior to "exclusionary rules." The principles are materiality, which is determined by substantive law, and probative force, which is determined by logic and general experience but which is only loosely cabined by various legal prescriptions. The exclusionary rules, such as hearsay, privilege, and incompetency, are a mixed group of historically based exceptions to the general rule of free evaluation. See Anderson et al. (2005), pp. 289–94 (mapping the evidence rules).

[13] Verkerk (2010), p. 2.

[14] See Tillers and Gottfried (2006), p. 142 (observing the difference between processing evidence and applying standards of proof); Tuzet (2021), p. 90 (observing that "the evidentiary inferences

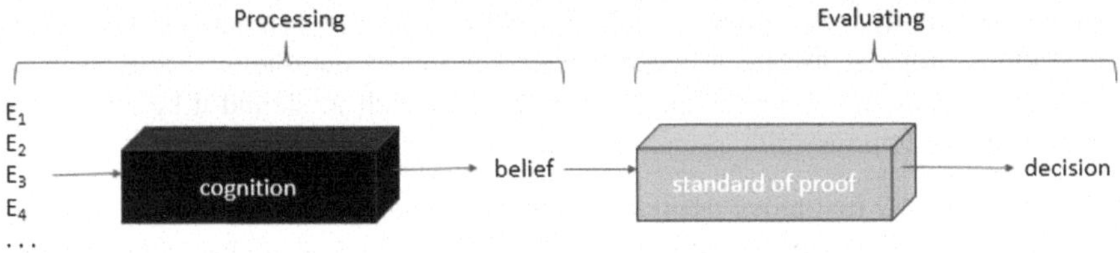

Fig. 5.1 Decision stage

First, the law imposes virtually no enforceable restraints on factfinders' methods during the initial phase's processing of pieces of evidence (E_1, E_2, etc.),[15] other than any review of an output for irrationality, clear error, or the like.[16] The factfinders just do it. Psychologists have made some limited progress in figuring out how they do it, progress on which I shall draw. The actual process may be explicitly rational[17] or merely intuitive,[18] although it should always involve so-called critical common sense as the minimum standard.[19] It may proceed atomistically[20] or holistically.[21]

---

and arguments at stake must be assessed to determine the evidentiary support, or warrant, or justification provided by the premises to the conclusions," as distinguished from the phase in which "fact-finders need to consider whether the evidence meets the relevant standard of proof").

[15] See Anderson et al. (2005), p. 226 (noting that "there is an almost total absence of formal regulation in respect of evaluating evidence or, to put it differently, the Anglo-American law of evidence has almost no rules of weight").

[16] See, e.g., Fed R. Civ P. 50(b) (reasonability test), 52(a)(6) (clearly erroneous test). One might add to standards of review the overturning or impeachment of a verdict for certain misbehaviors, such as jurors' expressing racial bias. See Peña-Rodriguez v. Colorado, 580 U.S. 206 (2017).

[17] See, e.g., Morgan (1950), pp. 943–945 (surmising the logical method that jurors use to process evidence). "Rational" here means logical. See Anderson et al. (2005), p. 56 (saying that "a conclusion based upon the evidence can only be justified as rational through the use of [deductive, inductive, or abductive] logic").

[18] See, e.g., Spottswood (2013) (applying the dual-process psychological framework to legal factfinding). "Intuition" is analyzed in Lindell (2017), pp. 80–97.

[19] See Risinger (2013), p. 813 (discussing "the notion of critical common sense and its attendant implication that participation in rational factfinding about legal issues is possible for most humans of normal intelligence").

[20] American law seems to envisage an atomistic approach. See Malsch and Freckelton (2009), pp. 130–131 (linking the adversary system to atomism). Judicial instructions impose on the jury the duty to proceed element-by-element. See supra Chap. 3 (quoting pattern instruction). Theorizing on the fit between law and logic should therefore depart from an atomistic approach.

[21] American practice seems to follow a holistic approach. See Simon (2004), pp. 559–569 (arguing that factfinders consider evidence holistically rather than atomistically); Simon (2019), pp. 86–87 (giving four reasons to beware of holistic factfinding). Holistic methodologies are typified by the well-known story model, which posits that the factfinder measures the likelihood of the proponent's whole story rather than judging its parts separately. See Anderson et al. (2005), p. 280 ("Empirical research . . . suggests that American juries determine 'the truth' about alleged past events mainly by constructing . . . stories rather than critically evaluating arguments from evidence. These findings have been confirmed in other disciplines (e.g., medical diagnosis and history) and extended to fact determination by legal professionals and the police . . . . Simply put, the widely accepted thesis is that human beings need stories in order to make certain kinds of decisions and, more generally, to

The factfinders need to combine into a single measure all sorts of evidence on each of the necessary facts, which range from likelihood of a contested occurrence to a vague and partly normative characterization of blameworthiness. My view, based on psychology and introspection, posits that factfinders process the credibility and weight of the evidence largely by intuition and in an approximate and nonquantified way, perhaps while looking simultaneously at the whole case. They then take a stab at forming beliefs as to the truth. Although the stabs seem to be generally reliable, this kind of cognition remains a black box, both in the study of law as a logical matter and in the study of practice from a psychological perspective.

Second, in the evaluation phase, whereby beliefs lead to decision, the law gets involved. Here the standards of proof reign. Psychologists have thus far had very little to contribute to our understanding of the standards of proof. Philosophical logic takes over here, providing a theoretical basis for standards. Given that basis, the law specifies a standard of proof as the measure of sureness required in an uncertain world for decision about each necessary fact, fixing the requirement's level to achieve policy goals.

Deconstruction of Evidence and Proof The huge subject of the theory of evidence and proof—those two phases of the mental stage—remains largely unexplored. Just as for many foundational ideas, we tend to invoke the idea of factfinding all the time without pursuing the idea all the way down. For example, we readily state the test for granting judgment as a matter of law against a party in terms of whether "a reasonable jury would not have a legally sufficient evidentiary basis to find for the party on that issue."[22] The judge therefore needs to determine the limit of reasonable, or rational, factfinding. In this context, and in many others, it would undeniably be appropriate for judges and lawyers to think deeply about how a jury ought to find a fact. But we do not, remaining willing to represent factfinding, and especially its evidential processing phase, as opaque as a black box.

This chapter's impetus stems from an unwillingness to leave factfinding as a black box. In particular, the chapter will focus on the logical ideal for factfinders to process evidence and evaluate proof. The result is an original account of how facts should be found, that is, a systematic logic for factfinding.

Because my interest thus falls mainly on the normative side, I shall leave it to psychologists to conduct further research on how factfinding is actually done and, in

make sense of the world."); cf. Simon (2019) (clarifying the distinction between holism and the story model). See generally Frederick (1987), pp. 296–299 (providing a brief overview of the story model of evidence processing); Hastie and Pennington (1983), pp. 22–23 (providing a brief summary of empirical studies supporting the story model); Hannaford et al. (2000), pp. 629–633 (discussing three predominant models of jury decisionmaking); Hastie (2008), pp. 31–32 (expanding the story model to allow for a party's multiple stories); Huntley and Costanzo (2003), p. 29 (presenting research that "extends the story model to civil litigation and tests a story-mediated model against an unmediated model of jury decision-making"); Pennington and Hastie (1993) (detailing the story model and summarizing empirical studies testing it).

[22] Fed. R. Civ. P. 50(a)(1).

particular, how the practice departs from the logical. I shall therefore not focus heavily on the undoubted role of bounded rationality and of heuristics, emotions, and biases in factfinding.[23] Still, I do observe that my multivalent belief model, in lieu of probabilities, may make more comprehensible any future discussion of the role of bounded rationality, heuristics, emotions, and biases.

Nevertheless, I am not engaged in pure theory. I am trying to formulate an ideal, remaining conscious of the greater legal system's purposes and constraints while still keeping at least one eye open to human limitations. The normative logic for factfinding will turn out to be legally acceptable and rather feasible practically to perform. I make no call for change to law or practice, as none proves necessary. I describe how I think good factfinders should, could, and largely do proceed.

In sum, human factfinding—especially as it involves reasoning inferentially from a piece of evidence to beliefs regarding an element and also aggregating different pieces of evidence that bear on the same element—is and will remain largely intuitive, approximate, and nonnumerical. For eons, humans have less or more competently formed beliefs by juggling evidential features such as credibility, comprehensibility, coherence, comprehensiveness, and consistency (both internally and also externally with background information). Yet, any decent effort to excavate factfinding's systematic logic promises the huge practical benefits of understanding.

Aside: Group Decisionmaking I shall be focusing on logic for a single factfinder.[24] But I do not think that having a group of factfinders complicates the logical picture. The idea would be that each factfinder in the group mentally does his or her own thing to process the evidence. Then each of them should apply the proper standard of proof to produce their own tentative decision.[25] Thus, the logic developed for the single factfinder carries over.

All of the factfinders must next deliberate in order to convince a certain number of them, a number sufficient to satisfy the governing unanimity or nonunanimity rule, to agree on one outcome.[26] Deliberations make decisionmaking into a social process,

---

[23] See, e.g., Kahneman (2011); Kahneman et al. (2021); Phalen et al. (2021); Thornburg (2019), p. 1571 (arguing that factfinders are "influenced in their thinking by factors such as heuristics, implicit biases, and cultural cognition").

[24] See Pardo (2015); see also Larsen (2011), p. 1608 (discussing utilization of standards of proof by a group of factfinders).

[25] See Johnson v. Louisiana, 406 U.S. 356, 362 (1972) ("The remaining question under the Due Process Clause is whether the vote of three jurors for acquittal can be said to impeach the verdict of the other nine and to demonstrate that guilt was not in fact proved beyond [reasonable] doubt. We hold that it cannot. Of course, the State's proof could perhaps be regarded as more certain if it had convinced all 12 jurors instead of only nine . . . . In our view disagreement of three jurors does not alone establish reasonable doubt . . . . That rational men disagree is not in itself equivalent to a failure of proof by the State, nor does it indicate infidelity to the reasonable-doubt standard."), overruled on other grounds by Ramos v. Louisiana, 140 S. Ct. 1390 (2020). Remember that for *either* side to win, it must achieve the required supermajority or unanimity of the multiple factfinders.

[26] On the mathematics of group decisionmaking, see Dietrich and Spiekermann (2023).

as well as an epistemic one.[27] By law, the requisite percentage of factfinders must agree on each element, where element means a fact necessary for a claim or defense to succeed under the substantive law, but they need not agree on the evidence, grounds, or theories underlying each element.[28] The acceptability of a verdict resting on different evidence, grounds, and theories for a necessary finding lies in the recognition that the requisite number of factfinders are agreeing at least that one or another sufficient evidence, ground, and theory supports each element.[29] The key distinction for whether the group's agreement is required or unrequired lies between necessary findings and sufficient findings.[30]

In the situation of a nondichotomous decision, such as awarding damages, group deliberation might involve some sort of averaging process, as well as entail its own effects of emotions and biases.[31]

5.1 Processing Evidence

Steps This section will further deconstruct the factfinder's evidence-processing phase into three logical steps: (1) reasoning inferentially from a piece of evidence to a degree of belief and a degree of disbelief in the element; (2) aggregating pieces of evidence that all bear to some extent on one element in order to form a composite

---

[27] See Diamond (2006), pp. 758–761 (discussing the effect of jury deliberations on juror decisionmaking); Hannaford et al. (2000), p. 640 fig. 3 (graphing the percentage of jurors who made up their mind at different stages of a trial and thereby showing that half the jurors formed their decision in the deliberations stage); MacCoun (2022), p. 11 ("standards of proof operate, at least in part, as social standards rather than epistemic ones").

[28] See Richardson v. United States, 526 U.S. 813 (1999); Schad v. Arizona, 501 U.S. 624, 630–45 (1991) (plurality opinion); Jazzabi v. Allstate Ins. Co., 278 F.3d 979, 984 (9th Cir. 2002) ("Liability cannot be established until after the jurors unanimously agree that [each and every one of] the elements are satisfied and they unanimously reject [each of] the affirmative defenses."); Ark. Midland Ry. v. Canman, 13 S.W. 280 (Ark. 1890).

[29] See Ginsburg (1965) (arguing that unanimity is required on "ultimate issues"); Trubitt (1983), p. 511 ("Patchwork verdicts are not acceptable . . . where the 'patched' grounds are not part of a sole transaction, do not have a common focus of injury, or do not call for exactly the same remedy.").

[30] See Roth (2011) (making the required distinction between alternative elements and alternative routes to proof of a single element). On a distinguishable matter, courts are now tending to hold that under a nonunanimous decision rule, different jurors can provide the support for different elements. See, e.g., Harris v. State ex rel. Dep't of Transp. & Dev., 997 So.2d 849, 869–71 (La. Ct. App. 2008); Williams v. James, 552 A.2d 153 (N.J. 1989); Spottswood (2021), pp. 327–329 (discussing this "discursive dilemma" for group decisionmaking); cf. Nash (2003) (treating appellate court analogy). This different-jurors holding is correct because, by analogy to the disjunction paradox, see supra Sect. 3.2.4.2, the substantive law requires element-by-element proof, rather than an overall finding.

[31] See infra Chap. 6 (treating nonbinary decisions).

degree of belief and of disbelief in the element; and (3) considering the series of elemental beliefs and disbeliefs to prepare for decision.

Now, before the reader rebuts that these distinctions are ridiculously naïve and no human would conform to my prescriptions, I repeat that I am still dealing in the normative here. I think that establishing the logical normative is a necessary passage in the analysis. I shall later consider briefly whether humans realistically could and do act in rough conformity with the ideal.

5.1.1 Inference from Piece of Evidence to Element

The place for anyone to begin understanding the logical processing of evidence by the factfinder is the marvelous book *Analysis of Evidence*.[32] In it, Professors Anderson, Schum, and Twining break down the mental process in finding facts.[33] They explain that "inferences" are the mental strides in connecting a piece of evidence to the fact to be proved, that is, the element or their so-called probandum. Each inference progresses toward proof of the element by invoking an inductively derived "generalization" that deductively implies the next inference in a chain. "Ancillary considerations" are the evidence and understandings that refine each generalization.

The authors then inject these concepts into Wigmore's celebrated charts for evidential analysis.[34] But they run into two problems. First, their expanded charts soon become incredibly complicated, way too complicated to represent the factfinder's actual reasoning.[35] The authors, however, were trying to represent, through argument-visualization, the theoretical analysis required of a lawyer in

[32] Anderson et al. (2005); see Twining (2019), pp. 175–189, 214–216, 265–266 (discussing *Analysis of Evidence*). But see Head (2021–2022) (challenging *Analysis of Evidence* as being unrealistic, while urging a dialectical method).

[33] See Anderson et al. (2005), pp. 78–122 (treating "principles of proof" and "methods of analysis").

[34] See, e.g., Wigmore (1937), § 178.

[35] See, e.g., Anderson et al. (2005), p. 139 (using a palette of symbols to signify all sorts of different evidential influences, while showing just a tiny fragment of a case's proof involving proof of opportunity (6) on the identity element (4) in a case of murder (1)):

preparing a case, a lawyerly task that benefits from almost any increase in rigor. Second, by adhering to traditional probability theory,[36] the authors make their analysis much more complicated and opaque than need be. Shifting from their

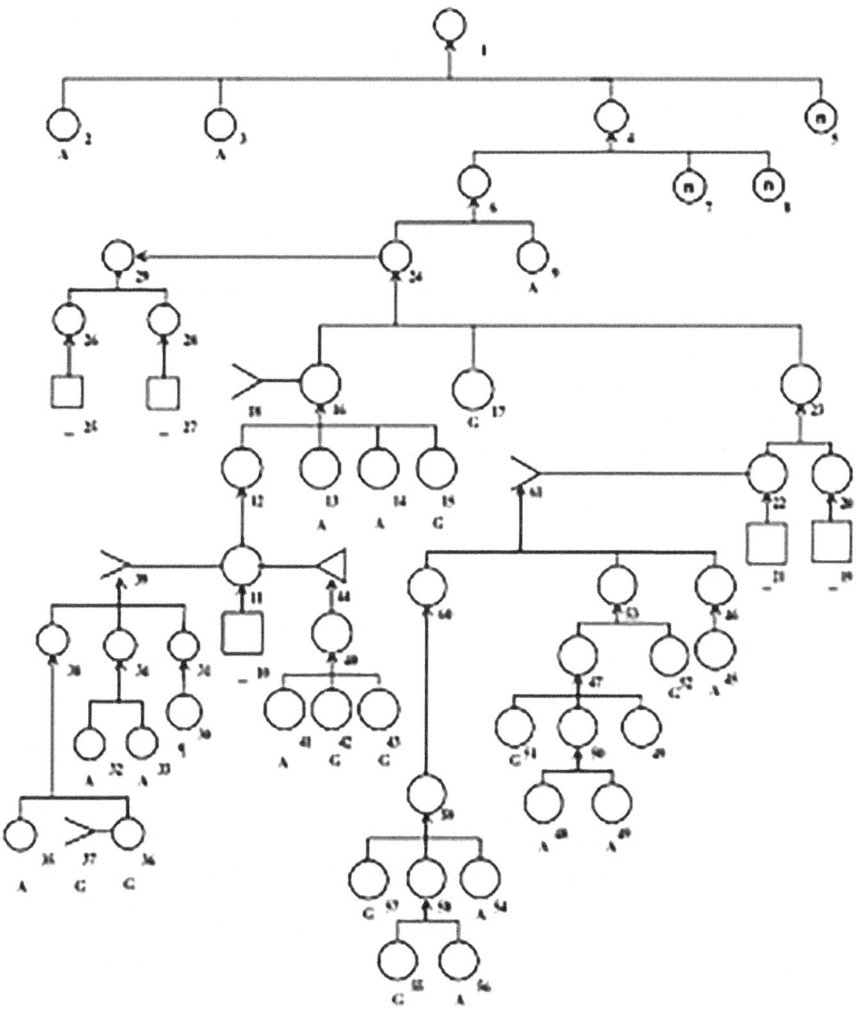

[36] See, e.g., id. at 107 & n.38 (accepting that compound propositions must be believed as less certain than the weakest component), 251, 256–257 (seeming to accept Bayes' theorem for combining evidence), 103–04, 381 (leaving the conjunction paradox unresolved). Although the authors by their second edition claimed to be agnostic as to the appropriate logic system, see id. at 250–261, they never abandoned traditional probability. See also id. at xx–xxi (discussing the book's appendix on probability theory).

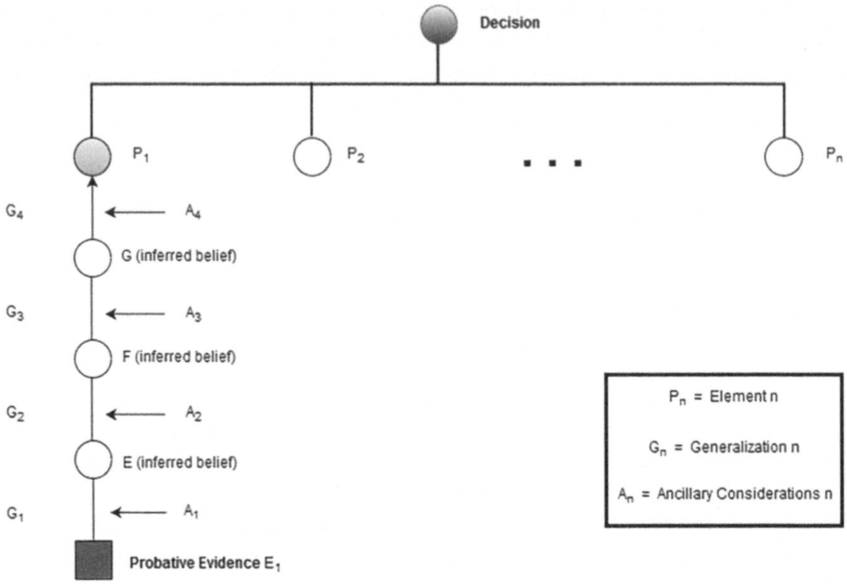

Fig. 5.2 Representation of inferential reasoning

inapt focus on odds to the insight of multivalent beliefs would have made everything simpler and clearer.[37]

5.1.1.1 Mental Process

So, I can simplify their Wigmorean charts by representing the processing of evidence only from the factfinder's perspective and by analyzing in terms of multivalent belief theory. I diagram how the factfinder should logically link, in an accurate but feasible way, each piece of evidence to the particular element through a series of inferred multivalent beliefs. I do so in Fig. 5.2. A real-life example will come in Fig. 5.3.

Figure 5.2 starts at the bottom with a piece of "probative evidence," so called because it tends to prove or disprove an element in the claim or affirmative defense with some credibility and weight. It could represent part or all of any introduced evidence, testimonial or real. The piece of probative evidence, E_1, connects up to the element or probandum, P_1, through a chain of inferences of varying force. The same evidence, if it bears on more than one element, will produce multiple chains.

[37] The authors' allegiance to traditional probability prevents them from ever resolving the logically correct way to combine chained inferences, pieces of evidence, or separate elements—leaving these within the cognitive black box. See, e.g., id. at 106 ("Again putting aside questions concerning the degree of additional strength provided when two propositions converge . . . ."). Compare id. at 103 ("These are questions that Wigmore did not address in any detail."), with id. at 260 (suggesting that Wigmore foresaw fuzzy logic).

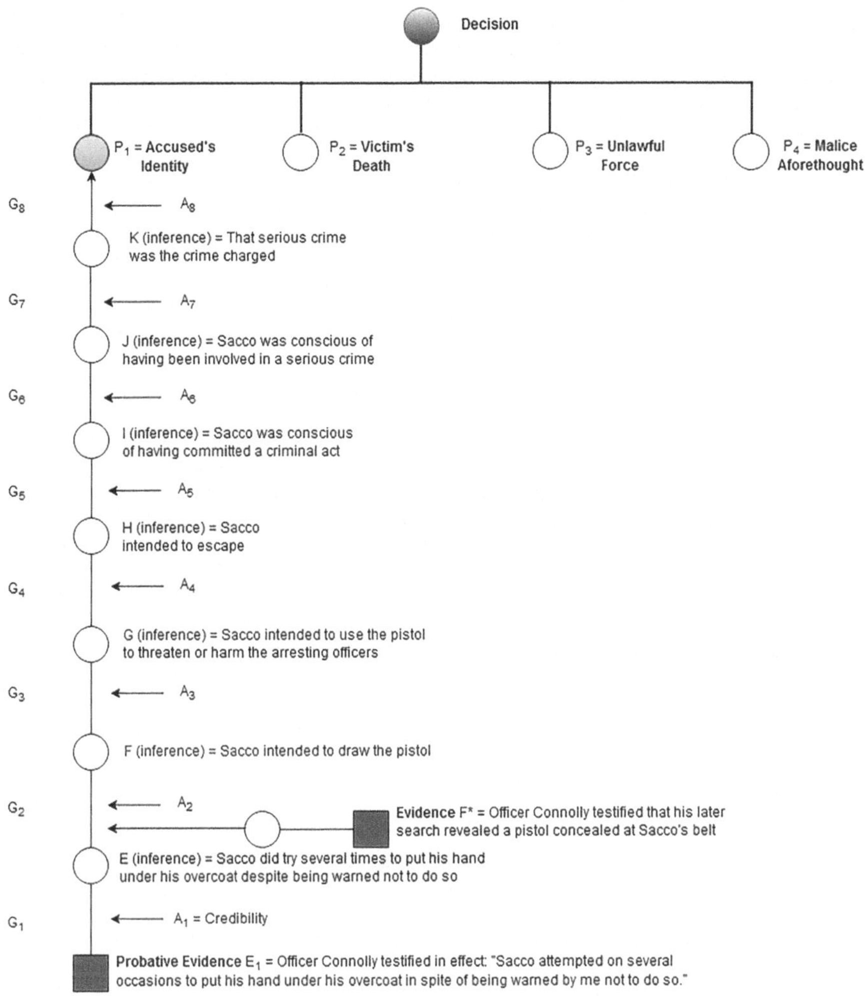

Fig. 5.3 Inferential reasoning in Sacco & Vanzetti

Instead of probative evidence, those authors call E_1 "directly relevant evidence,"[38] but I think "relevant" adds nothing because irrelevant evidence is inadmissible, while "direct" gets us unnecessarily into the thicket of direct/circumstantial evidence.[39] The accepted distinction of direct/circumstantial is this: "Direct evidence is evidence which, if believed, resolves a matter in issue," while for circumstantial evidence, even if "accepted as true, additional reasoning is required to reach the

[38] See id. at 62–63 (inventing that term).

[39] See id. at 76–77 (acknowledging that thicket).

desired conclusion."[40] But others have observed: "*Rule No. 1*. All evidence is either direct or circumstantial. *Rule No. 2*. There is no such thing as direct evidence."[41] The thinking behind *Rule No. 2* is that any argument can be further broken down, so that "in reality all evidence is subject to the frailties of circumstantial evidence."[42] Thus, it is best to use direct and circumstantial only as loose terms suggestive of few or many levels of inference, respectively.

The piece of probative evidence can be positive or negative, building to belief or disbelief, respectively, in the element. Or usually one piece of evidence would affect both the belief and the disbelief. The goal of evidential processing is to use E_1 in producing degrees of conviction, ranging from 0 to 1, in both a belief and a disbelief of P_1. Beliefs and disbeliefs will undergo comparison at the eventual standard-of-proof phase.

The opponent's *contradictory* evidence will come in as an ancillary consideration on the proponent's chain of inferences. By contrast, if a piece of *conflicting* evidence (that is, one of two items of evidence that could both be true, but that lead to different conclusions by way of rival explanation) is offered by the opponent, then a new chain of inferences builds from the new conflicting evidence to a belief in not-P_1; the opponent must support each inference in the new chain, while the other party tries to defeat some of those inferences to create a disbelief in not-P_1 (that is, a belief in P_1).[43]

In other regards, the end-point concepts of the probative evidence, E_1, and the element, P_1, are apparent. But the middle part in the chain of inferences requires more explanation, which follows.

Inferences In Fig. 5.2, evidence E_1 is linked to the element by a reasoning chain indicated by inferred propositions E, F, G, and P_1. The factfinder would plot the chain's route by the logical process of abduction,[44] with the lawyers working hard to prod the factfinder into following the route that seems most convincing and favorable to their side by use of ranking theory.[45]

The logical stride from proposition to proposition is inference.[46] The chain of reasoning can be long, that is, many inferences may lie between evidence and

---

[40] Broun (2013), § 185.

[41] Binder and Bergman (1984), p. 77.

[42] Id. at 79; see Tuzet (2022), p. 151 ("By itself, evidence proves nothing. Nor does it yield verdicts. It must be 'inferentialised.'").

[43] On contradictory and conflicting evidence, see Anderson et al. (2005), pp. 69–70.

[44] See supra Sect. 4.4.1 (explaining abductive reasoning).

[45] On the lawyer's processing of facts, see Binder and Bergman (1984); Faruki (2019).

[46] See O'Malley et al. (2011), § 12:05 (instructing the jury that "inferences are simply deductions or conclusions which reason and common sense lead the jury to draw from the evidence received in the case").

element.[47] Although chains can be more complex than the one drawn, they are all subject to the same analysis.[48]

Each of the inferences may be to some degree false and thus create doubt interposed between the evidence E_1 and the element P_1.[49] The doubt could arise because the inference rests on a wobbly generalization, which has been further undermined by ancillary considerations that question the generalization's quality.[50] Accordingly, the factfinder must proceed by formulating for each inference a belief function that reflects these doubts, as explained below.

Generalizations Generalizations supply justification for each reasoning stride upward, so that every inference is founded upon a generalization. Generalizations are inductive if-then statements that are assertions about the world. Base rates are a nice example. They often rest on a probabilistic assertion, but they always are subject to some question as to their quality. The factfinder uses the generalization to infer from the prior proposition in the chain of reasoning to a posterior proposition. The generalization acts as a major premise for deductive reasoning along these syllogistic lines (the minor premise is the prior proposition, taken as true, and the conclusion is the posterior proposition):[51]

Most [many, some, etc.] *a*'s are *b*'s

X is an *a*

X is likely [might well be, could be, etc.] a *b*.

These generalizations might have been entered into evidence, or been judicially noticed, to the limits of the rules of evidence. Most are implicit, however, with their induction often occurring intuitively; the factfinder is permitted to bring to bear common knowledge, although not personal knowledge, in formulating generalizations.[52]

---

[47] See Morgan (1950), pp. 943–945 (giving an example). On combining these so-called catenate inferences, see Anderson et al. (2005), pp. 107–108.

[48] Alternative generalizations supporting one inference seem complex. See Schum (1994), p. 85 ("These additional linkages involving the elements of argument are extremely important in our attempts to capture a wide array of important and interesting subtleties in evidence."). If freed from the misleading implications of traditional probability, however, we can collapse the alternative routes into a single chain by the MAX rule. The resultant single chain will be the strongest route from evidence to element. Likewise, alternative (or disjunctive) elements are subject to the same collapsing treatment.

[49] Anderson et al. (2005), p. 61 (making precisely this point).

[50] See Schum (1994), p. xiii ("In any inference task our evidence is always incomplete, rarely conclusive, and often imprecise or vague; it comes from sources having any gradation of credibility.").

[51] See Kyburg (1996), pp. 366–367 (showing how uncertainty of major premise carries forward to the conclusion).

[52] See Tanford (1986), p. 700 (distinguishing common experience from personal experience).

The inference is only as sound as the generalization's strength and accuracy.[53] It is critical to identify expressly the generalization upon which an inference depends in order to determine the force of the inference and thereby identify the weak points in the reasoning. Obviously, generalizations can be dangerous, especially if implicit and unexpressed.[54] They might be speculative in origin or vague in phrasing. They are apt to be value-laden stereotypes drawing on myths and prejudices. Nevertheless, use of generalizations is endemic to inferential reasoning.[55]

In Fig. 5.2, generalizations (labeled G_1 through G_4) are associated with each of the four links in the chain of reasoning from evidence E_1 to element P_1, running through propositions E, F, and G. Thus, generalization G_2 justifies the inference of proposition F from proposition E. This generalization might say: "If an event like E occurs, then usually [frequently, often, etc.] a result of F will follow."[56] That is, if E were true, the factfinder would believe F to a degree x that reflects the quality of the generalization. The belief in F would thus measure the certainty of inferring from E to F. It is a conditional belief, which assumes E to be true. In other words, $x = Bel(F|E)$, which may be read as the degree of belief in F if E is fully believed.

Ancillary Considerations Ancillary evidence and understandings comprise reactions to a generalization. Like a generalization, an ancillary consideration can derive from evidence actually introduced by any party, or it can spring from an interjection of judicial notice or of the factfinder's critical common sense. The ancillary consideration can undermine or support the generalization as a major premise.[57] It will entail its own chain of questionable inferences when linking up to that premise. The various ancillary considerations bearing on the generalization must be combined with the original data underlying the generalization, perhaps by the

[53] See Anderson et al. (2005), pp. 264–265 (distinguishing between strength and accuracy of a generalization). A qualified or amorphous generalization might give only weak support to the inference. Indeed, the more cautious and precise and hence accurate the generalization, the weaker the support for the inference is likely to be.

[54] See id. at 276 (using "Generalizations are dangerous" as section heading). Although jurors' generalizations are part of the reason that the Constitution requires jury trial, they are also part of the reason that we fear the jury. Beyond imposing a limit on irrational factfinding, judges normally do not check the jurors' generalizations. But see Peña-Rodriguez v. Colorado, 580 U.S. 206 (2017) (inquiring into racial prejudice).

[55] See Binder and Bergman (1984), pp. 82–89 (discussing inferential reasoning); Stein (2005), p. 96 ("The generalization factor is not intrinsically problematic . . . . Weight of generalizations that factfinders use derives from the empirical instances systematically exhibiting the factual pattern that purports to be a generalization. The word 'systematically' embraces two criteria: that of number and that of variety. A recurrent factual pattern acquires the generalization status when both the number of its individual instances and their variety increase . . . .").

[56] Anderson et al. (2005), p. 62 (making precisely this point).

[57] See id. at 62–63, 380 (using the terms "ancillary evidence" or "indirectly relevant evidence").

weighted-arithmetic-averaging method described above,[58] to produce degrees of belief and disbelief of the next proposition up the inferential chain.[59]

In Fig. 5.2, ancillary considerations A_1 lie between E_1 and E. Just because evidence E_1 says that event E occurred does not establish that E did occur. The generalization G_1 could be that such evidence is usually trustworthy. But obviously, there is here a matter of "credibility." Credibility means the extent to which we believe what the probative evidence says. Credible *testimonial* evidence should be on personal knowledge and have (1) veracity (testimony in accordance with the witness's beliefs), (2) objectivity (testimony not based on expectations or desires), and (3) sensitivity and specificity (testimony resting on good sensory evidence); credible *real* evidence should be (1) authentic (in that it is what it purports to be), (2) accurate (and based on a sufficiently sensitive and specific sensing device), and (3) reliable (or repeatable).[60] Ancillary considerations would raise any of these features of credibility to undermine or support the generalization G_1.

Ancillary considerations can affect the higher-level inferences too. These considerations would attack or reinforce the corresponding generalization. In a sense, they thereby address the credibility of the generalization. Thus, although A_1 determines what might be called the primary credibility of E_1, A_2 through A_4 can also bear on the credibility of G_2 through G_4. They do so by addressing the accuracy of their corresponding generalization.

In sum, getting from evidence to probandum always involves inference. In fact, because all evidence is circumstantial and because the initial inference involves primary credibility, there will always be multiple inferences. Each of the inferences E, F, G, and P_1 may be to some degree false and thus create doubt interposed between the evidence E_1 and the probandum P_1. Given the nature of the inferences fraught with epistemic uncertainties, the resulting interim propositions can best be represented as multivalent degrees of belief and disbelief.

Example A well-known legal example of inferential reasoning comes from the infamous case of Sacco and Vanzetti.[61] These Italian immigrants and anarchists were convicted of and executed for the robbery and fatal shooting on April 15, 1920, of two payroll guards in South Braintree, Massachusetts. A few weeks after the shooting, they were arrested on unrelated suspicions. Sacco was then carrying a pistol. Much later they were charged with the murders.

[58] See supra Sect. 4.5.4.1 (stating the formula).

[59] See Schum (1994), pp. 83–85 (discussing complex combinations of evidence).

[60] See Anderson et al. (2005), pp. 63–70 (discussing credibility generally); Simon-Kerr (2023).

[61] On this case, see Anderson et al. (2005), pp. 21–23, 124–125, 160, 251–252, 285–286, 335–336; see also Ehrmann (1969); Fraenkel (1931); Frankfurter (1927); Joughin and Morgan (1948); Kadane and Schum (1996); Montgomery (1960); Russell (1962); Transcript (1928); Young and Kaiser (1985).

The big issue at the murder trial was identity. One of the arresting officers, Connolly, testified about Sacco's behavior upon arrest.[62] The factfinder had to connect that testimony to the identity element. The path of reasoning proceeded through Sacco's supposed consciousness of guilt, on which the prosecution had to rely heavily in order to prove his identity as one of the murderers.[63] But that path revealed many sources of uncertainty.[64]

Figure 5.3 is admittedly complicated. And it is the tip of the iceberg, because a chain or chains had to be constructed for every piece of probative evidence on every issue in the long trial. But it is not unrealistic. The diagrammed chain is a necessary minimum of reasoning, even if it usually is achieved by an intuitive leap. The factfinder could not properly avoid the task of inferring from each piece of evidence to the element or elements that the evidence tended to prove or disprove.

To begin somewhere, the generalizations involved in Fig. 5.3 would run something like this:

G_1 = Any events to which an officer testified under oath usually had occurred
G_2 = Arrestees with a concealed weapon sometimes attempt to draw it
G_3 = Arrestees who draw a weapon usually intend to use it
G_4 = Arrestees who use a weapon often intend to escape
G_5 = Arrestees who intend to escape usually are conscious of having committed a criminal act
G_6 = Arrestees who act with consciousness of having committed a criminal act frequently will be conscious of having committed a serious crime, like a robbery and shooting
G_7 = Arrestees who are conscious of having committed a serious crime often will be conscious of having committed the charged crime
G_8 = Arrestees with consciousness of guilt as to the charged crime usually committed it

As to each generalization, ancillary considerations are relevant. For a prime example, A_1 bears on the primary credibility of Connolly's testimony.[65] Ancillary chains of inferences as to his veracity, objectivity, sensitivity, and specificity would feed into the G_1 generalization. Also, ancillary evidence, such as the facts that Connolly had never mentioned Sacco's hand movements incident to arrest until Connolly testified on the stand[66] and that pressures existed for him to testify a certain way, would undercut G_1. Similarly, A_2 considerations contain multiple strains,

[62] See 1 Transcript (1928), p. 753 (reprinting transcript of this evidence's introduction).

[63] See id. at 2257 (charging the jury: "Therefore, the mind, being conscious of every bodily act theretofore committed, it knows whether or not such act is one of innocence or guilt. If it indicates guilt, that is evidence of consciousness of a guilty act, and evidence of a consciousness of a guilty act is evidence tending to prove commission of such guilty act, and evidence of the commission of a criminal act tends to prove the identity of the author of such criminal act.").

[64] See Schum (1994), pp. 75–92 (composing an inferential chain adapted here).

[65] See id. at 109–112 (discussing the testimony's credibility).

[66] See Young and Kaiser (1985), pp. 67–70, 162–163 (making this observation).

including evidence F* that appears in Fig. 5.3. For other examples, the A_6 pieces of evidence that Sacco was illegally carrying a pistol at arrest and that Sacco was a despised radical who had been involved in distributing anarchist literature were alternative explanations of his behavior that seriously undercut generalization G_6 that he was likely conscious of committing a serious offense like a robbery and shooting, while the A_7 ancillary consideration that the prosecutors' evidence had suggested no other serious crime committed by Sacco would support generalization G_7 that the serious crime in consciousness was the charged crime.

Other pieces of evidence E_2, etc., such as lies Sacco told police officers, would also show Sacco's consciousness of guilt (K). And, independently of his consciousness of guilt, still other evidence E_{n+1}, etc., such as bullet forensics or the carrying of a pistol itself, would help support or undercut identity (P_1).

5.1.1.2 Probative Force

The "probative force" of evidence means how powerful the piece of evidence is in favoring or disfavoring some element in the case at hand.[67] In Fig. 5.2, G_1, G_2, G_3, and G_4 and A_1, A_2, A_3, and A_4 all contribute to determining the probative force of E_1 on P_1. The force will depend on (i) the weight and credibility of the relevant evidence, which turns on analysis of (ii) the force of each necessary inference from E_1, through E, F, and G, to P_1, as determined by the strength of its generalization and as ancillarily affected by its generalization's accuracy, and (iii) the force of the whole chain of inferences taken together. Yet, in trying to measure probative force, one will encounter great disagreement among legal theorists about how grading of probative force should be done. Here I move into contested territory.

First, to begin with definitions for (i), evidence is relevant if, taken as true, it allows us to revise our belief or disbelief in some element.[68] For one way to determine relevance, we can return to the likelihood ratio.[69] It expresses the relative likelihood of the existence of the given item of evidence upon the alternative assumptions that the fact to be proved exists and that the fact does not exist, which reduces to $\text{Prob}(E_1|P_1) \div \text{Prob}(E_1|\text{not-}P_1)$. The likelihood ratio thus conveys relevance by showing whether the evidence allows the factfinder to revise a prior zero belief or disbelief in the element to form a different posterior belief or disbelief.

To get at weight of the evidence, we need to determine the extent of that revision of belief or disbelief. If we want to separate weight from credibility, we should keep

[67] See Anderson et al. (2005), pp. 71, 226–229, 384–385 (defining "probative force").

[68] Cf. Fed. R. Evid. 401(a) (defining as "relevant" evidence having "any tendency to make a fact more or less probable than it would be without the evidence"); Cohen (1994), p. 181 ("Anything that can sanction a reason, even if an incomplete or inconclusive reason, for accepting a particular type of proposition as a correct answer, or for rejecting it as an incorrect answer, to an askable type of question can count as a criterion of relevance.").

[69] See supra Sect. 3.2.4.1 (discussing "likelihood ratio").

matters of primary credibility to the side.[70] Fixing the weight of the evidence will inevitably be a bit of a stab at judgment. But it will involve determining the convincingness of the chain of inferences. I submit that multivalent beliefs is the accurate way to determine that convincingness, as I shall elaborate below. Once done, and after we re-inject the primary credibility, we have the raw materials for estimating probative force, that is, the weight and credibility of the relevant evidence.

Second, moving to (ii), assessment of belief in a specific inference presents another challenge. As already explained, the factfinder will conditionally believe the move in going, say, from E to F to a degree x, which depends on the strength of the generalization G_2 as adjusted for its accuracy by ancillary considerations A_2. The probative forces of the multiple ancillary considerations bearing on any generalization need to be combined, with each other and with the generalization's underlying data, by something like the weighted-arithmetic-averaging method. So, measuring the conditional belief x in that move will likely be an approximate process.

Third, the biggest source of disagreement concerns (iii): how to combine the inferential strides into an overall belief function for the element generated by the piece of evidence. Conditional beliefs in the strides to E, F, G, and P_1 have to be accepted in order to support the element. The process is conjunction, because each link in the chain must be accepted. The evidence's affirmative probative force so presents a problem of conjoining a string of degrees of belief.

Should the factfinding process treat the inferences E, F, G, and P_1 as bivalence's probabilities or as multivalence's beliefs? The proper approach is to view them not as the probability of events that must all happen together to produce a result, but as degrees of belief.[71] Classical logic would not even hesitate at the conjunction problem.[72] The probability operation for a AND b is multiplicative on the probabilities of the constitutive propositions. But multivalent logic recognizes that combining beliefs is a mathematical task different from combining odds. The mathematics for combining degrees of belief instruct that the conjunction has a degree of belief equal to the weakest of the conjoined beliefs.

Think of the MIN rule in action. Think first of separate beliefs. A typical legal test asks whether a violation of some procedural law occurred and whether it affected outcome. No one would ever think of applying the product rule, and so nobody would require an exaggerated showing on the two issues. We look instead at the minimum of the two beliefs.

Next, the beliefs in inferences E and F are not totally separate beliefs, in that the belief in F is a conditional belief dependent on E. But they conjoin the same way.

[70] On credibility, see supra Sect. 5.1.1.1.

[71] See supra Sect. 4.5.4.2 (justifying the use of multivalent logic).

[72] See Morgan (1950), p. 944 ("Now it must be obvious that the value of item A as probative of F varies inversely with the number of inferences between A and F.").

Let ⇒ mean "implies." Theorists have derived an inference rule that says if α and ($\alpha \Rightarrow \beta$) are proved as beliefs to degree λ and μ, respectively, then we can assert β at degree MIN(λ, μ).[73] So, if one views E as a belief and views the inference (E ⇒ F) as a conditional belief, then the belief in F will be the minimum of those two beliefs.

As one goes up the chain of inferences, one will believe the latest inference to the degree of the minimum of all the preceding beliefs in the chain. That is, one will believe P_1 to the extent of the weakest link in the chain. If one believes each link more than one disbelieves it, then one believes the whole chain, as I shall explain below.[74]

Thus, if one accepts that the legal factfinding process involves conjoining multivalent beliefs, then multivalent mathematics will give the answer. And the answer will be correct. Inferences form a chain, whose strength does not disappear from the ravages of the product rule. That is, the MIN rule is the correct approach because it gives the accurate calculation of probative force. Multivalent belief theory is the correct way to proceed in this first step of evidence processing, and I further argue it is feasible for human factfinders to perform and may encapsulate what they actually do when inferring from an item of evidence to an element of the case. Indeed, I maintain it is what we all do intuitively in the inferential reasoning we perform countless times every day of our lives.

5.1.2 Aggregating Pieces of Evidence Bearing on an Element

The combined probative force of the pieces of evidence on an element can decrease (as by conflict or contradiction) or increase (as by convergence or corroboration)[75] with a new piece of evidence.[76] In the Sacco & Vanzetti example of evidence of consciousness of guilt, we have seen how other evidence E_{n+1}, etc., such as eyewitness testimony and bullet forensics, would help undercut or support the same element of identity, P_1.

[73] See Gerla (2001), pp. 113–116 (describing so-called necessity logic, which is an offspring of possibility theory); cf. Dubois and Prade (1980), pp. 167–168 (arguing, outside the context of necessity logic, that the multivalent belief in β is not less than MIN(λ, μ)).

[74] See infra Sect. 5.1.3.3.

[75] On these types of evidence, see supra Sects. 4.5.4.1 and 5.1.1.1.

[76] See Al-Adahi v. Obama, 613 F.3d 1102, 1105 (D.C. Cir. 2010) ("Those who do not take into account conditional probability are prone to making mistakes in judging evidence. They may think that if a particular fact does not itself prove the ultimate proposition (e.g., whether the detainee was part of al-Qaida), the fact may be tossed aside and the next fact may be evaluated as if the first did not exist."). That court's reasoning has been much criticized in habeas scholarship. E.g., Ahuja and Tutt (2012), pp. 204–213 (criticizing the D.C. Circuit's emphasis on aggregating evidence). But I interpret their criticism as an inarticulate but valid complaint that Bayes' theorem ignores epistemic uncertainties. See supra Sect. 3.2.4.1.

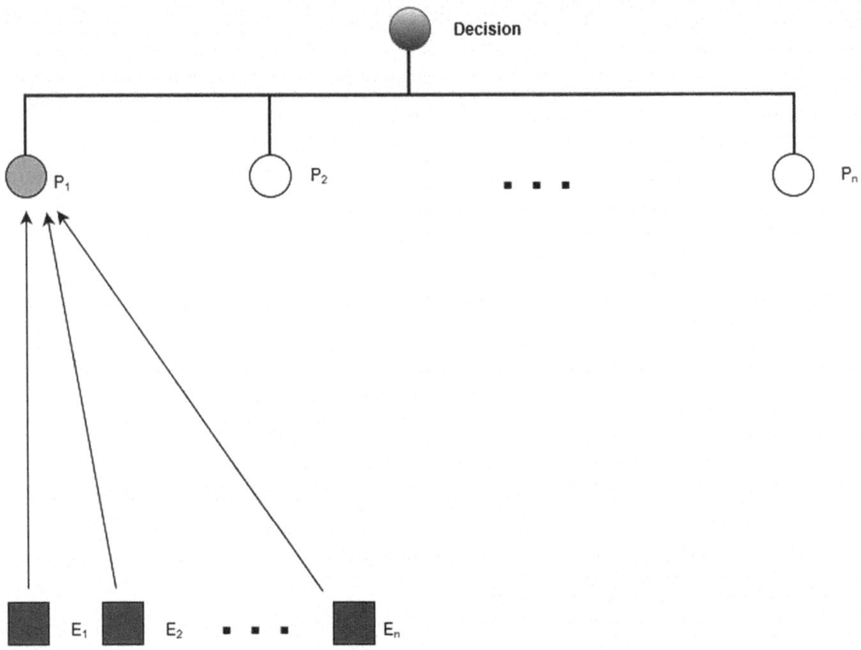

Fig. 5.4 Representation of aggregating evidence

5.1.2.1 Mental Process

Aggregation of evidence takes place even when inferring from a single piece of evidence to an element, as when one combines a generalization with ancillary considerations. But now our focus expands to aggregating separate pieces of evidence that bear on a single element. As a normative matter, then, how should the factfinder aggregate evidence to calculate the new composite belief function for the element based on the evidence taken together? Figure 5.4 represents the aggregation of all evidence on P_1.

This mental process of aggregating evidence is completely distinguishable from the above-treated process of conjoining beliefs. Aggregating evidence does not centrally involve conjunction, wherein each belief must be accepted, but instead it calculates how items of reinforcing or undercutting evidence, E_1, E_2, etc., add to or subtract from one another to form a composite belief (and a composite disbelief) in P_1.[77]

[77] See Haack (2014b), pp. 216–228 (discussing the aggregation task generally as an epistemological matter).

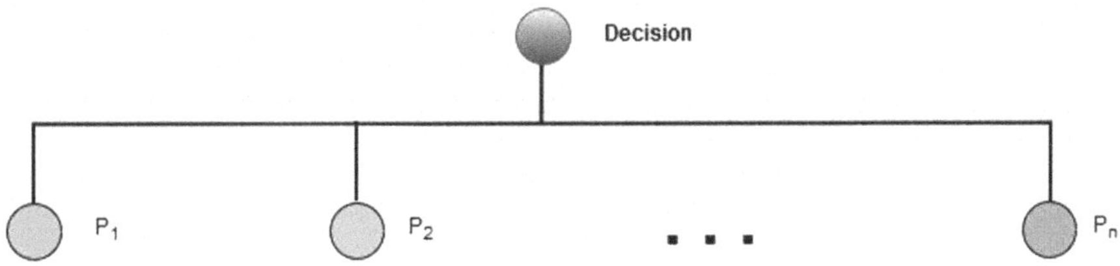

Fig. 5.5 Representation of combining elements

5.1.2.2 Mathematical Method

Aggregating evidence is perhaps easier to picture than conjoining beliefs, as it seems simpler and more intuitive, but it is much harder to formalize. Both problems' solutions turn on the applicable logic system, be it bivalent or multivalent. On the one hand, conjoining (and disjoining) beliefs follows directly from the basic operators and axioms of the logic system. The product rule governs in bivalent additive systems. For multivalent beliefs the operator would be the MIN (or MAX) rule, because this multivalent logic system is nonadditive. On the other hand, aggregating evidence is a complex mathematical problem. Its solution is Bayes' theorem under classical logic. Some extension of Dempster-Shafer theory governs under multivalent logic.

For factfinding, we should aggregate the pieces' probative force in a manner consistent with multivalent belief theory. Something like weighted arithmetic averaging serves that function, and serves it well by being able to handle conflicting or contradictory evidence and being comprehensible enough for humans to employ.[78]

So, the various pieces of evidence bearing on an element each produce a degree of belief and of disbelief. Then, logic and policy say to take the belief function produced by each piece of evidence and aggregate all those beliefs, as by weighting their significance and by averaging. Do the same for disbeliefs, and we have created a new composite belief function for P_1.

5.1.3 Combining Elements to Construct a Conclusion

A legal case will often involve more than one element (a finding necessary for a claim or defense to succeed under the substantive law), as shown in Fig. 5.5. In the Sacco & Vanzetti example, we focused on the element of identity (P_1). But the prosecution also had to prove beyond a reasonable doubt the other elements: the victim's death (P_2) by unlawful force (P_3) with malice aforethought (P_4).

The step of combining elements would proceed by the conjunction/disjunction methods rather than by anything like the weighted-arithmetic-averaging method,

[78] See supra Sect. 4.5.4.1 (discussing aggregation of evidence under multivalent belief theory).

because the elements are all necessary. If the elements were to be combined, they would be joined by the MIN and MAX rules. But does it matter if the factfinder performs any such combination before, rather than after, the application of the standard of proof?

5.1.3.1 Atomistic Processing

Once the factfinder has developed a composite belief function for each element, the factfinder could move from the processing phase to the evaluation phase. There the factfinder would apply the standard of proof to reach a decision on the element. And there this section on evidential processing meets up with my next section on evaluating proof.

The law finally intrudes here, specifying a course of decision rather than leaving factfinding to the factfinder's common sense. The law tells the factfinder to proceed element-by-element. To put simply the law's dictate, apply the standard of proof to each element; do not apply it to the whole claim or affirmative defense; if each element passes the standard of proof, then the whole claim or defense succeeds legally. So, if the *factfinder* believes P_1, believes P_2, believes P_3, and believes P_4, then the *law* believes the conjunction of those elements.

According to the law, then, the factfinder need not, and should not, combine the elements at all. The factfinder compares belief and disbelief for each element. If belief prevails over disbelief on each element, the burdened party wins.

5.1.3.2 Holistic Processing

By contrast, holistic theorists contend that the typical human factfinder ignores the law's instructions and evaluates the case as a whole, as by using the story model. If these theorists are correct, and they very well may be, then the factfinder dissolves the elements to get a sense of the whole case.

To the extent the holistic factfinder proceeds with any accuracy, it would in effect have determined the beliefs in all the elements before applying the standard of proof to the whole case. As long as the factfinder believed each element more than the factfinder disbelieved it, then the plaintiff's overall story will prevail as the strongest version. (Otherwise, the defendant could construct a better story consisting of (1) admissions of all the elements with a weaker denial and (2) denials of the elements where the denial is equal or stronger; then, the conjoined elements of the plaintiff's best story would not be more believable than the defendant's story consisting of those selected allegations when conjoined.) If each element passes the standard of proof, then the elements' conjunction will pass the standard of proof. Or, conversely, if the elements' conjunction is more likely than not, then each element must be more likely than not.

So, it should make no difference whether the factfinder proceeds atomistically or holistically, whether the factfinder applies the standard of proof element-by-element or the factfinder applies the standard to the parties' overall stories. The two approaches should work out to the same outcome. This happy consequence of dealing in beliefs means that we can stop worrying about any differential effect of procedures that preclude the jurors from taking a holistic approach, such as when the judge requires a special verdict that asks the jury only to find each element by a preponderance.[79] We can also stop worrying about the jurors' not fully understanding the pattern instruction and thereby falling into holistic ways.

The holistic approach, however, does require some understanding care by the factfinder. Think of a case where the denial of element P_1 is stronger (0.40) than the plaintiff's position thereon (0.30), but another element P_2 has a weaker belief (0.20) and still weaker denial (0.10). The MIN rule would report that the conjunction of the plaintiff's story (0.20) beats the conjunction of the defendant's story (0.10). But in fact the defendant should win, if only the defendant were viewed as admitting P_2. Element-by-element, rather than comparing conjunctions, is the safer way to go.

Even though it would make little or no difference to outcome if a factfinder were to apply the standard of proof correctly to the whole claim or defense, the pattern instruction's more systematic element-by-element approach has practical advantages. Telling factfinders to proceed element-by-element makes them more comprehending, careful, and diligent.[80] It also makes instructing them on how to proceed a simpler and more comprehensible process. Finally, the element-by-element instruction avoids the need to instruct on using the MIN rule and not using the product rule. Therefore, the judges' practice of stressing the element-by-element instruction is a commendable procedure.[81]

5.1.3.3 Correct Approach

I thus argue that, in the main, element-by-element application of the standard of proof is a logical and feasible way to proceed. The factfinder need never combine the elements. Indeed, the path to decision will be more comprehensible to the factfinder and, once understood, more apt to encourage careful and diligent following. The result is that there will be no step #3 for combining elements. The factfinder can

[79] See supra Sect. 3.2.4.2 (discussing special verdicts, while making the point that commentators cannot agree on whether the holistic approach generally helps or hurts defendants).

[80] A more controlled element-by-element processing could have a potential effect on outcome that might push, say, criminal defendants to favor an element-by-element instruction.

[81] Particular attention, or institutional change, is necessary where a legal rule requires an affirmative decision before proceeding to another legal rule. See Clermont (2020), pp. 797–799 (describing this kind of decision). An example would be negating intellectual disability before reaching the issue of the death penalty. See Blume et al. (2014), pp. 409–412, which found that juries are more apt to find no-disability than judges. One explanation might be that judges are trained to go issue-by-issue while juries, following the story model, answer the overall question of death-worthiness rather than first focusing on intellectual disability alone. See also Nunn (2022) (showing interplay of the merits with jurisdictional elements of crimes); Rachlinski et al. (2011) (providing another illustration involving probable cause); supra Sect. 1.1 (discussing iterated epistemological operators).

proceed directly from completing the create-belief-function-for-each-element task of step #2 to the standard-of-proof phase.

There is, however, at least one hiccup in analyzing an element-by-element approach.[82] The MIN/MAX analysis, which is a little more complicated than described so far, produces a difficulty when a fairly strong disbelief, which is nonetheless insufficient under the standard of proof to overcome the belief in the same element, is bigger than a sufficiently big belief on another element. For example, in a hypothesized civil case, if *Bel(a)* = 0.40 and *Bel(not-a)* = 0.25, and if *Bel(b)* = 0.20 and *Bel(not-b)* = 0.00, then *Bel(a* AND *b)* = 0.20 and *Bel(not-a* OR *not-b)* = 0.25. Thus, the element-by-element approach would produce a result (proponent wins) different from the seemingly logical overall approach (proponent loses). The law rejects this "logical" outcome by insisting on element-by-element application of standard of proof. Still, there are a number of reasons to think the law's approach might be correct.

First, the "logical" outcome seems intuitively wrong or at least overcautious. The instinct of most observers is that the proponent should win after convincingly prevailing on each element. The law would otherwise be giving a lot of play to the 0.25 disbelief of element *a*, on which element the proponent won after all. If the plaintiff wins on an element-by-element testing, the plaintiff's story is more believable than each and every one of the defendant's stories. It thus makes limited sense to let a relatively strong denial, which failed to convince on its element, carry over to defeat the plaintiff's whole story. The plaintiff might very well win in real life, whether the jury took an atomistic or holistic approach to beliefs or to probabilities. Maybe the law should be wary of going against such strong intuition.

Second, the law would not want to, and does not, charge its factfinders to perform the difficult mental task of comparing belief and disbelief of different elements. Combining a series of elements is already difficult even to verbalize. Add the difficulty of comparing a belief in one element to the disbelief of a different element, and you have a process that is apt to stymie most factfinders. The law's element-by-element method is more comprehensible (and corralling) than any "cross-elements" comparison of belief with disbelief.

Third, even if a cross-elements argument were available and understood, the defendant is unlikely to make it. On the one hand, if the parties and the factfinder choose to go the best-story-overall approach, the focus is on which side's story conjoins as more likely, without attention to disjunction. This approach would mask the subtle cross-elements argument. On the other hand, if the parties and the factfinder choose to go element-by-element, this approach would obscure the subtle cross-elements argument even better.[83]

Fourth, I note that the step of evaluating elements coincides with a switch in commonly employed legal images: law and lawyers tend to shift unconsciously from

---

[82] See Rott (2009), p. 310 (describing the "tension between degrees for beliefs and degrees for disbeliefs").

[83] See supra Sect. 4.5.5 (dispelling the illusion of asymmetrical burdens).

a style of thinking that conforms with multivalent beliefs (used by factfinders when processing evidence, with acute awareness of uncommitted belief) to a form of speech that conforms with fuzzy logic (used by lawyers when discussing the output of evidence processing as "more probable than not" or whatever, having set aside the uncommitted belief).[84] Fortunately, multivalent beliefs and fuzzy logic are compatible, being alternative versions of multivalent logic and each applying the MIN and MAX rules.[85] Multivalent beliefs differ from fuzzy logic in their treatment of uncertainty. Multivalent beliefs treat epistemic uncertainty front and center in terms of uncommitted belief, while fuzzy set theory moves any higher-order uncertainty, that is, uncertainty about the estimate of degree of membership, into the additional dimensions of ultrafuzzy sets.[86] It is fuzzy logic's separation of first-order uncertainty from higher-order uncertainty that makes the operation of its MIN and MAX rules simpler in appearance. This switch in multivalent logical frameworks is not necessary, but the switch both conforms to lawyers' imagery and makes it easier to picture and discuss what is going on in applying the standard of proof. So, by normalizing the degrees of belief at the end of evidential processing, we can speak of fuzzy beliefs being the likelihood that a fact is true and a complementary measure of being false, even though we remain in a nonadditive system. In terms of those fuzzy beliefs, we at least can feel more comfortable with the notion that if the belief in each element is stronger than its corresponding disbelief, the conjunction of all the elements' beliefs is always stronger than the disjunction of all the disbeliefs.

Fifth, the trump card on this hiccup is to realize that the "logical" outcome is actually wrong. Using the MIN and MAX rules together to choose a decision based on belief functions relies on either an assumption that the sets of beliefs and disbeliefs are well-behaved, in the sense that if *b* is less believable than *a*, then *not-a* should be less believable than *not-b*,[87] or an assumption that each constituent belief has passed an absolute standard for belief.[88] If, however, the parties are

---

[84] See Haack (2014a), p. 57 (illustrating the legal system's verbal usages). It is worth re-emphasizing that switching at the end of evidential processing phase to odds-like language and image is perfectly okay. The output is going to be binary: liable or not, guilty or not. And so language and image consistent with bivalence become natural, and they can be used without risk of misleading. It is the processing of evidence before the final output that requires belief functions.

[85] See supra Sect. 4.3 (supporting the compatibility of these multivalent versions). For a mathematical defense of a complete switch from belief function theory to fuzzy logic and its fairly straightforward MIN and MAX rules, and for the simplifying assumptions on which the switch rests, see Dubois and Prade (1990), pp. 419, 421 ("Viewing a fuzzy set as a consonant random set, it is shown how to construct fuzzy sets that may act as approximations of belief functions."). See also Rudolph et al. (2008); Yager (1991), pp. 1017–1024 (explaining approximate reasoning).

[86] See supra Sect. 4.2.4.1 (explaining this difference).

[87] See Rott (2009), pp. 310–311 (assuming contraposition when combining belief functions, so that if *b* is less believable than *a*, then *not-a* should be less believable than *not-b*); cf. Cohen (1977), pp. 114, 221, 256, 267 (assuming contraposition for his inductive probability). This assumption is required only for combination of belief functions, not for other types of multivalent logic.

[88] This complication is no concern when an absolute standard for belief is applicable. There, if and only if you believe *a* and believe *b*, you believe *a* and *b* together. Thus, the principle of conjunctive

building stories on the same elements and if the factfinder tests only for each belief exceeding the corresponding disbelief, neither assumption is necessary. In this situation, the disjunction of the defendant's denials becomes inapposite, and one looks more at the conjunctions of the two parties' positions. Take the numerical example above where the plaintiff is contending *a* and *b*. The defendant could deny both or could deny *a* but admit *b*, as both of these stories would be 0.25 believable. But the defendant could improve these stories by admitting *a* as well as *b*, which would be adopting the plaintiff's story. So, the plaintiff's story is better than the defendant's best stories to the contrary. Accordingly, the defendant's conjoined story should overcome the plaintiff's conjunction only when the big disbelief equals or exceeds the corresponding belief in the same element.

More generally, if each belief exceeds its disbelief, you know the plaintiff wins because you could improve the defendant's story by substituting the corresponding belief for any denial (and so embrace the plaintiff's story). Any move from the plaintiff's story to any defendant's story would require substituting a less believable denial for a stronger belief. Conversely, if any belief fails to exceed its denial, then you could improve the plaintiff's story by substituting a denial for that belief (and so create the defendant's better story). That is to say, the principle of conjunctive closure reasserts itself: if and only if you believe *a* and believe *b*, you believe *a* and *b* together.

This line of thinking thus reveals a subtle but significant point: when comparing the competitors to the most believable account, you do not disjoin a competing account's negations of the elements. Instead, you compare the elements of each competing account's propositions, and only then do you contemplate the disjunction of all the competing accounts.

In sum, this hiccup constitutes another reason to prefer element-by-element to holistic processing. We do not want factfinders to compare a belief in one element to a disbelief of a different element. This is a big insight. The holistic approach risks giving the wrong result, unless the factfinder remembers to apply the atomistic approach by going element-by-element at least implicitly.

5.1.4 Overview

Abandoning probabilistic images—by going from bivalent logic to multivalent logic—is mentally and emotionally challenging, so the proper reasoning has long remained hidden. Theorists have accepted a cognitive black box. But once one recognizes that degrees of belief capture the output of factfinding, and that traditional probability does not, the way to represent the logic of factfinding becomes fairly

closure is usually stated without qualification, because philosophers are not thinking of the law's comparative standard of proof. See supra Sect. 4.2.4.3. It is only when beliefs and disbeliefs are compared that the hiccup starts to concern.

obvious. This book thus employs degrees of belief to pioneer a transparent account of how to reason logically from evidence to a factual decision.

First, the factfinder should connect each item of evidence to one or more factual elements to be proved by constructing one or more chains of inferences. Each inference rests on a generalization, which ancillary considerations can support or undercut. By multivalent logic's usual rule for conjunction, the factfinder's degree of overall belief in the fact to be proved will be as strong as the belief in the weakest inference in the chain. The overall degree of disbelief is constructed the same way. There is a chain of inferences building to the disbelief. It will be as strong as the weakest inference in the chain. A belief function amalgamates the belief and the disbelief, along with uncommitted belief that conveys epistemic uncertainty. It can give a sense of the probative force of the item of evidence on the fact to be proved.

Second, the factfinder must aggregate the probative force of all the items of evidence that bear on any one element. To do so, the factfinder could compute, albeit intuitively, a weighted arithmetic mean of the belief functions for all the items: get the belief function for each item; weight beliefs and disbeliefs in accordance with evidential significance; and divide the separate sums of the weighted beliefs and disbeliefs by the sum of the weights. The result is a composite belief function for the element.

Third, the factfinder may choose to combine the elements of claim or affirmative defense. But the better approach is to apply the appropriate standard of proof to each element. This means that the factfinder would proceed directly to the evaluation phase, which will involve a standard of proof that compares the degree of belief that appears in the element's composite belief function with the degree of disbelief. Evaluation does not require a combining of the elements.

To put it more compactly, the factfinder should construct a chain of inferences to produce a belief function for each item of evidence bearing on an element, and then weight-and-average them to produce for each element a composite belief function ready for applying the element-by-element standard of proof.

Mapping this simple normative method for processing legal evidence has been a worthy undertaking. More significantly, the mapping provides further demonstration of how embedded the multivalent belief model is in our law. The law appears so consistent with this logic that it must have been built on that logic. Traditional probability has a tight hold on modern legal minds, but not on the law itself. Acceptance of multivalent belief theory by modern legal minds, in lieu of bivalence's probabilism, would solve so many theoretical problems, disarm so many criticisms of the law, and just explain so much for us that one must wonder why it meets academic resistance.

5.2 Evaluating Proof

My conceptualization has thus far led me to think that the law and its factfinders should not and do not employ the prevailing academic view of the evidence and proof process that rests on a bivalent logical approach. Factfinders instead determine their beliefs as degrees of real-world truth based on the evidence, just as the law expects of them. Eventually they end up with *Bel(a)* and *Bel(not-a)*, both falling between zero and one, and normally adding to less than one, with *a* being either an element or a whole claim or affirmative defense. What then should and do they do?

At last, I come to the matter of applying a standard of decision. The law dictates that factfinders decide by subjecting their beliefs to a standard of proof in order to come to an unambiguous output. That is, at this point the law forces factfinders back into what looks like a two-valued logic, by making them decide for one party or the other.[89]

Here the determined probability theorist could pursue the bivalent image. The ultimate task of applying a standard of proof would appear to require unavoidably the placement of the fact on a scale of likelihood running from 0% to 100%.[90] But I contend that so speaking in terms of bivalent logic tends to mislead on standards of proof.

A better understanding of standards of proof would result from continuing to think in terms of multivalent logic and belief functions. Even though decisionmaking later requires converting from multivalent beliefs to an output that sounds two-valued, the factfinder need not do it before applying the standard. All the factfinder has to do is compare the strengths of belief and disbelief. The path to decision would involve comparing *Bel(a)* and *Bel(not-a)*, after setting aside the uncommitted belief. By requiring only a comparison, multivalent beliefs would never require placement on a scale of likelihood or believability.

Before getting to the standard of proof, however, a few words on the burden of proof are in order. Let me start with some background on how the law has long viewed the burden of proof, say, in a jury trial.[91] The burden of proof dictates who must produce evidence and who must ultimately persuade the jury on which elements of the case.[92] Burden of proof thus encompasses two concepts: burden of

---

[89] See Strat (1990), pp. 391–392 (recognizing the need for some type of method to proceed from beliefs to decisions).

[90] See, e.g., Brown v. Bowen, 847 F.2d 342, 345 (7th Cir. 1988) ("[T]he trier of fact rules for the plaintiff if it thinks the chance greater than 0.5 that the plaintiff is in the right.").

[91] The burden of proof works much the same in a nonjury case. Even the burden of production initially works the same, through the mechanism of summary judgment under Fed. R. Civ. P. 56(a). However, once the nonjury trial starts, the burden of production reduces under Fed. R. Civ. P. 52(c)'s judgment on partial findings to whether the nonmovant's burden of persuasion is currently carried.

[92] On the allocation of the burdens, see Field et al. (2023), pp. 1480–1481. The plaintiff normally bears the burdens, on the thought that he is launching a claim we have no reason to suppose is meritorious. But a burden could instead fall on the defendant if one or more of four factors is big enough to shift the balance of costs and benefits: (1) the plaintiff's relative expense of presenting

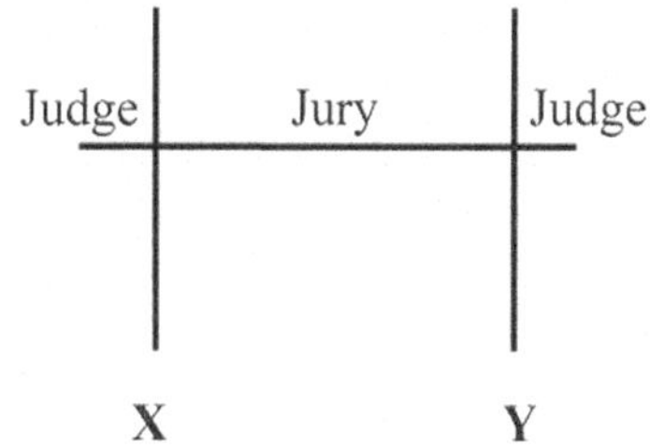

Fig. 5.6 Burden of production

production and burden of persuasion. The burden of production might require a party at a given time during trial to produce evidence on an element or suffer the judge's adverse determination on that element; one party has the initial burden of production on any particular element, but that burden may shift during the trial if the burdened party produces certain kinds and strengths of evidence. By contrast, the burden of persuasion requires a certain party ultimately to persuade the jury of the truth of an element or suffer the jury's adverse determination on that element; except in connection with certain presumptions, the burden of persuasion does not shift.

5.2.1 Burden of Production

This subsection will use multivalent belief theory to explain why the traditional view of the law's burden of production tends slightly to mislead. Then, it will provide a better perspective for viewing that burden.

5.2.1.1 Traditional View

In discussing the academic view of the burden of production, I need to use a new diagram.[93] Figure 5.6 represents the role of the judge in patrolling the extreme outer limits of rationality on the jury's task of applying the burden of persuasion.

Imagine a single disputed issue of typical fact, *a*, on which the plaintiff bears the initial burden of production and the burden of persuasion. Then imagine a scale

---

evidence to support his position on the issue, (2) the plaintiff's likelihood of being correct on such an issue, (3) the relative amount at stake for the plaintiff, and (4) the relative social cost of an erroneous decision against the plaintiff. See Hay (1997), p. 677. Allocation matters. See infra Sect. 5.2.2.1. Professor Thomas Main has suggested to me that even if the trial burdens are not so burdensome, they project backwards to impose significant pretrial burdens on the plaintiff. The party with the laboring oar must plead a plausible case to survive motions to dismiss and then assemble enough evidence to survive summary judgment. Indeed, procedural changes of late have intensified the pretrial gantlet for that burdened party, rather than trying to spread the pretrial burdens more equally.

[93] See Wigmore (1981), § 2487 (providing this diagram to represent the interactions between judicial rulings and evidentiary burdens); cf. McNaughton (1955) (offering alternative diagrams).

representing the judge's disagreement with a potential verdict for the plaintiff, or equivalently the judge's view of likelihood of error in such a verdict, with disagreement decreasing from one on the left to zero on the right. It is important to realize that this diagram represents the likelihood of jury error in finding that the disputed fact exists, not the judge's view of the evidential likelihood that the disputed fact exists. In other words, this diagram represents *the judge's thought process in externally overseeing the jury that acts as factfinder*, not the judge's thought process as if the judge were finding facts. Alternatively stated, this diagram represents the burden of production, not the burden of persuasion.

The plaintiff in the imagined case starts at the left of the diagram. If he presents no evidence, the judge will ordinarily grant the defendant's motion for judgment as a matter of law against him. The plaintiff is consequently bound to go forward with his evidence until the judge is satisfied that a reasonable jury would be warranted in finding for him.[94] That is, he must get to line X by presenting enough evidence to make a jury question of the imagined single issue of fact. The plaintiff's getting to or beyond line X means that although the judge might still disagree with a verdict for the plaintiff, the judge thinks a reasonable jury viewing the same evidence could find that the plaintiff sustained his persuasion-burden, and therefore the judge will hold that the plaintiff sustained his production-burden. If the plaintiff does not get to line X, the judge would so vehemently disagree with a verdict for the plaintiff as to consider the jury irrational, and therefore the judge can grant the motion for judgment as a matter of law. Line X, again, represents the judge's view on the limit of rationality in the jury's finding for the plaintiff, rather than the judge's view of the evidential likelihood that the disputed fact exists. For example, if the judge disbelieved all of the plaintiff's abundant evidence, but still acknowledged that a reasonable jury could believe it, then the judge should rule that the plaintiff has carried his production-burden, because a reasonable jury could disagree with the judge about the evidence and conclude that the plaintiff sustained his persuasion-burden.

If the plaintiff produces enough evidence to get beyond line Y, he should later succeed on a motion for judgment as a matter of law in his favor unless the defendant comes forward with enough evidence to push the case leftward back to line Y or beyond. If the defendant so succeeds in carrying her burden of production, it is again a case for the jury. She may, however, be so successful that her evidence carries the case beyond line X. If so, the defendant should later get judgment as a matter of law unless the plaintiff in his turn comes forward with more evidence. If, at the close of all the evidence, the case lies between lines X and Y, it goes to the jury and the plaintiff has the persuasion-burden. He will then lose if the jury is not persuaded.

As a theoretical matter, the production-burden may thus shift several times with the pull and haul of the evidence. As a practical matter, however, such multiple shifting on a single issue of fact is very unlikely. The reason is that conflicting and contradictory evidence on a single issue would, in most realistic settings, remain in

---

[94] See supra Sect. 4.6.2 (explaining the standard for judgment as a matter of law).

the zone between lines X and Y where decision is properly for the jury: a reasonable jury could find either way, and so the judge cannot grant judgment as a matter of law. Thus the pull and haul of the evidence will usually result only in oscillation within the jury's realm.

So far, this diagrammatic scheme works pretty well to represent the law's approach. Moreover, the diagram helps in understanding other concepts and special rules. A *permissive inference* (and res ipsa loquitur is one in the view of most courts[95]) describes an inference that a jury is authorized but not required to draw from certain evidence; in other words, the inference satisfies the plaintiff's production-burden by getting the case to line X, although not beyond line Y. A true *presumption* (such as the presumption against suicide as the cause of death) shifts the burden of production to the opponent after the introduction of the evidential premise; in other words, the presumption puts the case to the right of line Y and so requires the jury to find the presumed fact, unless the opponent introduces enough evidence to carry her production-burden and so push the case at least back into the jury zone between Y and X.[96]

Most significant among the other special rules, certain kinds of evidence will not satisfy a burden of production. To satisfy that burden, the burdened party cannot rely on the opponent's failure to testify, on mere disbelief of the opposing testimony, on demeanor evidence drawn from the opponent's testimony, or on naked statistical evidence.[97] However, any of these kinds of evidence is perfectly proper to introduce as a supplement to positive evidence that satisfies the burden of production. The idea behind these special rules is that they are necessary to protect the notion of a burden of production.

Why protect the burden of production? The reason is that it serves important functions. It facilitates early termination of weak claims or defenses, safeguards against irrational error, and effectuates other process and outcome values.[98] In the absence of this special rule, any burdened party could produce enough evidence to reach the factfinder, this evidence possibly being merely in the form of silence, disbelief, demeanor, or general statistics (such as that the defendant manufactured 55% of the supply of the injury-causing device of unknown provenance). Perhaps we harbor a special fear of the factfinder's mishandling of such weak evidence when undiluted by other admitted evidence, and of the factfinder's consequent rendering of an unreasoned decision for the proponent based either on prejudice without regard to the evidence or on undue deference to such bewildering evidence. To avoid such an outcome, and to ensure that the burden of production means something, the judge

---

[95] See Thorne (1980) (justifying res ipsa loquitur by use of fuzzy logic).

[96] See Fed. R. Evid. 301 ("In a civil case, unless a federal statute or these rules provide otherwise, the party against whom a presumption is directed has the burden of producing evidence to rebut the presumption. But this rule does not shift the burden of persuasion, which remains on the party who had it originally."). On presumptions, see Field et al. (2023), pp. 1487–1492.

[97] See supra Sect. 3.3.3 (discussing this special rule).

[98] See Summers (1974) (discussing generally the importance of process values).

should require evidence of other kinds sufficient to satisfy the burden. Once the proponent clears that hurdle, the tribunal should allow the feared evidence its probative effect.

5.2.1.2 Revised View

Thus, the law and practice seem fairly compatible with the traditional view of the burden of production. The only diagrammatic qualification would be that representing the judge's view of jury error as a series of fuzzy intervals rather than crisp lines would better capture reality. The leftmost judge zone would correspond to Fig. 4.5's slightest possibility and the rightmost to near certainty. The jury zone would run from reasonable possibility all the way through high probability, although of course juries' most questionable decisions in the jury zone could still be subject to a motion for a new trial.

A deeper challenge for the traditional view is fixing the starting point for factfinding. The probabilist might assume that when you know nothing, the rational starting point for the initial burden of production is fifty percent.[99] Then, if the plaintiff offers a feather's weight of evidence, he in theory would thereby carry not only his burden of production but also his burden of persuasion. The real-life judge, however, hands only defeat to the plaintiff with nothing more than a feather's weight of evidence, and does so by summary means.[100]

How to accommodate that reality? The revised view of the burden of production should specify that the factfinder starts not at fifty percent but at the far left, so that to get to X requires more than a feather's weight. The proper representation of lack of proof is zero belief in the plaintiff's position—but also zero belief in the defendant's position. The full range of belief is properly uncommitted.[101] That insight makes sense of the notion of the burden of production, rescuing the traditional diagram's usefulness. But the insight also suggests that in practice, by starting at zero belief, the law is proceeding by multivalent belief theory.

Concomitantly, the paradoxical difficulties in traditionally applying the burden of production to weak proof dissipate. For an example, imagine a motion for judgment as a matter of law made by a civil defendant in a single-issue case. The motion requires the judge to ask if no reasonable jury could find for the burdened plaintiff with the view that $Bel(a) > Bel(not\text{-}a)$. At the end of the plaintiff's case, if the maximally reasonable $Bel(not\text{-}a)$ is effectively zero (a slightest possibility), then the inequality requires the minimally reasonable $Bel(a)$ to exceed zero (a reasonable possibility). That the plaintiff must have established a reasonable possibility is the embodiment of the civil burden of production. It is what keeps the plaintiff from

---

[99] See supra Sect. 3.2.4.1 (discussing starting point under Bayes' theorem).

[100] See supra Section 3.2.2.3 (explaining that a scintilla of evidence will not suffice).

[101] See supra Sect. 4.3.4 (introducing this idea); cf. Laudan (2006), pp. 104–106 (parsing the presumption of innocence to mean an epistemic blank slate).

surviving with a mere feather's weight of evidence. An illustrative situation would be where the plaintiff has produced only a little evidence, but it is "pure" evidence that gives the defendant no support.[102] If a reasonable jury could find for the plaintiff on such proof, the judge should deny the motion. If the defendant then produces no effective evidence during the rest of the trial, but moves again at the end of all the evidence, the judge still should deny the motion and the case should go to the jury. The jury, if it were to take the same view of the evidence as the judge hypothesized, should find for the plaintiff—even on such thin evidence—as long as the jury found that $Bel(a) > Bel(not\text{-}a)$.

Furthermore, once one recognizes that the burden of persuasion is a comparative operation on sometimes thin evidence, the notion of a burden of production becomes not only sensible but almost necessary. The judge should patrol the sufficiency of the evidence to ensure that there is rationally enough to warrant the factfinder's applying the burden of persuasion. Otherwise the factfinder might irrationally begin at fifty percent or rely on overly slim evidence.

5.2.2 *Burden of Persuasion*

This subsection will use multivalent belief theory to explain why the traditional view of the law's burden of persuasion misrepresents the standards of proof. Then, the next subsection will demonstrate how the law actually conceives of its three standards of proof as different tests for comparing belief and disbelief.

5.2.2.1 Traditional View

To convey the traditional view of the burden of persuasion, I return to Fig. 3.1 showing the pull and haul of the evidence. Unlike Fig. 5.6, Fig. 3.1 goes *inside the factfinder's head*, trying to represent the internal thought process of the factfinder in ultimately weighing the evidence. The scale measures the factfinder's view in a civil case of the evidential likelihood that the disputed fact exists, with likelihood increasing from 0% on the left to 100% on the right.

The plaintiff in the imagined civil trial starts at the left of Fig. 3.1. By presenting evidence on the issue, he must get beyond the midpoint. That is, he must show that it is more likely than not that the disputed fact exists. If, after the plaintiff has given his best shot, the factfinder thinks that he is not past the 50% line, then the factfinder should decide for the defendant.

Even overlooking the unrealism and difficulties of a probabilistic theory, such as in dealing with weak evidence on both sides, Fig. 3.1's diagram of the burden of

[102] See Liu and Yager (2008), pp. 18–19 (discussing Leibniz's notions of pure and mixed evidence).

persuasion serves mainly as an impetus to thinking about these matters rather than as a source of definitive statements thereon.

The diagram can confuse. For example, the law handles a finding of equipoise in a civil case by means of the burden of persuasion. If the evidence ends up as evenly matched, the burden-bearer loses. That observation usually generates the reaction that the burden of persuasion does not matter much. After all, in probability theory, the burden should work only as a tiebreaker in the highly unusual case of a precise tie.

The Supreme Court has recently bought into this misconception yet again, saying that the "burden of persuasion will have bite only when the court finds the evidence in equipoise—a situation that should rarely arise."[103] Yet, in practice, lawyers and judges fight and suffer over the burden of persuasion at trial. Why?

First, the diagram in Fig. 3.1 does not mean that a 50% line exists in reality. The psychological truth is that equipoise is more of a zone, or range of probabilities, than a line. As already suggested in Fig. 4.5, a useful way to envisage the whole scale of likelihood is as a set of fuzzy categories, or intervals, of likelihood. Each category, such as more likely than not, embodies some range of approximate likelihoods. Equipoise is not different from the other categories. A range of evidential states may strike the factfinder as evenly balanced. Equipoise being a zone means that the burden of persuasion will affect many more cases than those few in which all the conflicting and contradictory evidence results precisely in a dead heat.[104]

Second, given the selection effect, close cases are common.[105] Uneven cases falling far from the standard of proof tend to settle, while the cases where the parties can reasonably disagree on the prediction of outcome tend disproportionately to go to trial. The burden of persuasion decides many of these close cases.

Third, still other reasons for caring about the persuasion-burden lie in psychology. How the law frames a question—whether the plaintiff or the defendant bears the risk of nonpersuasion of a fact, that is, whether the plaintiff or the defendant appears to be starting from "zero"—really matters.[106] One reason is that an anchoring heuristic lowers the willingness of the factfinder to determine that the burdened party has prevailed, because factfinders fail to adjust fully from a given starting point, even if the starting point was arbitrarily set.[107] Another reason is that loss aversion, status quo bias, and omission bias make it difficult for a burdened plaintiff to carry the burden of persuasion. The idea is that the disutility generated by the defendant's loss of something by verdict seems to exceed the utility reaped from the

---

[103] Goldman Sachs Grp., Inc. v. Ark. Teacher Ret. Sys., 594 U.S. 113, 127 (2021).

[104] See supra Sect. 4.5.1 (discussing equipoise).

[105] See Priest and Klein 1984) (presenting a nonrandom model of the relationship between disputes settled and disputes litigated, focusing on solely economic determinants and the parties' rational estimates of the outcome).

[106] See Zamir and Ritov (2012), p. 197 n.23 (describing the challenge that placing the burden of proof on a party adds, even with no heightened degree of persuasion).

[107] See Tversky and Kahneman (1974), p. 1128 (describing the anchoring phenomenon that happens when people, starting from an initial value, make an estimate).

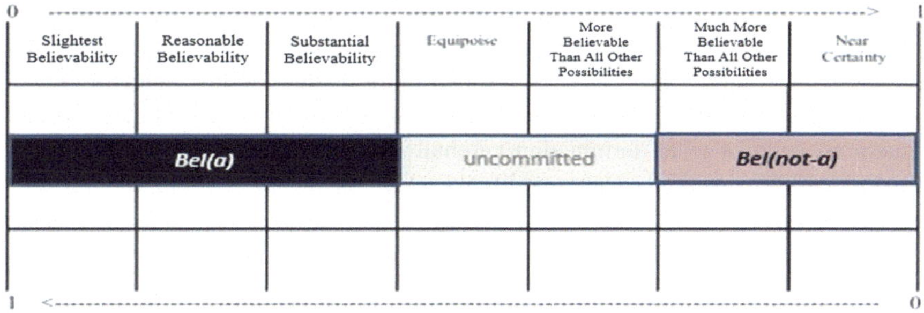

Fig. 5.7 Burden of persuasion

plaintiff's equal gain; that the burdened plaintiff appears undesirably intent on disrupting the status quo; and that the factfinder's harmful commission by making an erroneous award would inflict more cost psychologically than would a harmful omission. Also, such a judgment for the plaintiff requires the system to elevate action over inaction and so risk incurring regret costs. Accordingly, people perceive the cost of a judgment for the burdened plaintiff as larger than the cost of a judgment for the defendant.[108]

5.2.2.2 Revised View

Thus, factfinders rely on the burden of persuasion more often than one might imagine. We therefore need a clear understanding of the prevailing approach. The law does not and should not conform to the traditional academic view, which rests on probabilities. The traditional diagram for the burden of persuasion is fundamentally misleading, in need of a redrawing rather than the mere refinement of a fat 50% line. Understanding the redrawing, in Fig. 5.7, must follow a reformulation of the standards of proof into the terms of belief functions.

5.2.3 *Standards of Proof*

American law has settled on three, and only three, standards of proof for purposes of trial.[109] They apply in different circumstances: (1) The standard of preponderance of the evidence translates into a more-likely-than-not standard. It is the usual standard

[108] See Schweizer (2015), pp. 134–138 (explaining how these cognitive psychological factors heighten the effective standard of proof).

[109] See Clermont (2013), pp. 15–16, 41–42, 61–82 (using cognitive psychology to explain the limited number of standards of proof); McBaine (1944) (arguing that, for standards of proof, only three levels of strength of proof exist); McCauliff (1982). For treatment of the many standards of decision, other than standards of proof, that employ the limited set of standards less demanding than

in civil litigation, but it appears throughout law.[110] (2) Next comes the intermediate standard or standards, often grouped under the banner of clear and convincing evidence and roughly translated as a much-more-likely-than-not standard. These variously phrased but similarly applied standards govern on certain issues in special situations, such as when terminating parental rights.[111] (3) The standard of proof beyond a reasonable doubt means a virtual-certainty standard. It very rarely prevails outside criminal law.[112]

Among academics, the traditional doctrine reeks of probability theory. Sometimes the three standards are even stated as 51%, 75%, and 90% or the like.[113] Moreover, the traditional view does not do a good job of framing the proof question for the factfinders, in view of the usual states of evidence. It poses odd questions to the factfinders instead: for example, despite any evidential imperfections and other sources of epistemic uncertainty, what is the chance the plaintiff is right in an absolute sense, and how does that chance compare to the applicable standard of proof?

Belief functions better reflect the factfinder's actual frame of mind when applying a standard. Instead of betting that Dave's identity as the culprit is or is not probable, the factfinder should think and speak in terms of degrees of belief.[114]

As to the standards' formulation, the law could conceivably require, say, that the evidence have some specified completeness or that a belief meet some absolute threshold. For a specific but important example, the law could require that $Bel(a)$ exceed half-believability. But never has such a formulation accorded with the import of real cases. Given the law's need for immediate decision, it does not require the completeness of proof that would be necessary to get a belief above 0.50. The law is willing to rest decisions on the evidence presented. Nor has the law ever embraced probabilism. Accordingly, any talk of requiring elements to exceed fifty percent is misleading.

Partly in recognition of the law's adversarial presentation of evidence, the cases' standards are more comparative than absolute. However, the cases do not inquire simply which side has the comparatively greater evidence. They instead compare the resulting belief and disbelief in the burdened party's position. I agree with that approach. To apply the standard of proof, the factfinder should compare belief to disbelief. However, a variety of comparisons of beliefs and disbeliefs is conceivable,

---

preponderance of the evidence, see, e.g., Clermont (2013), pp. 38–40 (police actions); Clermont (2006), pp. 978–980 ("prima facie" proof).

[110] See Clermont (2013), pp. 16–18 (outlining the debate over the meaning of the preponderance-of-the-evidence standard).

[111] See id. at 23–25 (describing the clear-and-convincing-evidence standard).

[112] See id. at 26–31 (describing the proof-beyond-a-reasonable-doubt standard).

[113] See id. at 103–116; Seltzer et al. (2016).

[114] See McBaine (1944), pp. 248–249 (examining what level of belief a factfinder needs to accept the burdened party's position).

involving either sizes or ratios.[115] How best to formulate the standards of proof in a comparative way?

5.2.3.1 Preponderance of the Evidence

What should preponderance of the evidence, or its translation as more likely than not, mean in a comparative sense? One should directly compare *Bel(a)* to *Bel(not-a)*. In comparing them, *Bel(not-a)* is the opposite belief in the contradiction of *a*, not the complement of *Bel(a)*. It represents how much the factfinder actively disbelieves *a*, the fact in dispute. The comparison should look at actual belief in *a* and actual disbelief of *a*. If the factfinder were to work with only those two beliefs in *a* and *not-a*, and set aside the uncommitted belief, the most obvious course in civil cases would be to say that the burdened party should win if and only if *Bel(a)* > *Bel(not-a)*. Once the burden of production is met, the factfinder would decide for the plaintiff if *Bel(a)* exceeds *Bel(not-a)*, but decide for the defendant if *Bel(a)* does not exceed *Bel (not-a)*.[116] This standard not only is readily comprehensible but also avoids any need to quantify the beliefs.

Although belief functions thus do not require placement on a scale, the factfinder in effect might end in believing the burdened plaintiff's position on a disputed fact to be only "substantially believable" on Fig. 5.7's coarse scale of seven gradations. That situation does not mean that the plaintiff should lose, however. The factfinder, if forced to express a measure of believability, might believe the falsity of the plaintiff's position merely as "reasonably believable." The plaintiff should then win. All the factfinder need do is to compare belief and disbelief; and all that preponderance of the evidence requires is that the strength of the factfinder's belief that the plaintiff is right must exceed its belief that the plaintiff is wrong. Although some of the factfinder's belief remains uncommitted, the plaintiff's position is then a winning one in the sense of being more likely true than false in the factfinder's mind.

Sometimes, then, we would be talking of whether a smallish belief exceeds its smallish disbelief. Figure 5.7 adds the idea that the factfinder in such a case, working with only seven gradations, must have a belief in the element's truth perceptibly stronger than the belief in its falsity. The comparison of belief and disbelief does not call for drawing a fine line or making a close call, but rather determining whether the degree of belief is at least a whole step upward in believability from the corresponding degree of disbelief. Here lies another reason that the burden of persuasion matters.

---

[115] See Nance (2019), pp. 57–58, 64–65, 72–73 (sketching various comparison possibilities); see supra Section 3.4 (rejecting Professor Nance's preference for requiring specified ratios of belief and disbelief).

[116] See Cohen (1977), p. 255 ("The cardinal question to be settled by the trier of fact may always be construed as this: on the facts before the court, is the conclusion to be proved by the plaintiff more inductively probable than its [opposite]?").

If *Bel(a)* > *Bel(not-a)*, the factfinder would say it believes *a*. A preponderance of the evidence therefore means that *Bel(a)* > *Bel(not-a)*, not that *Bel(a)* > 0.50. If the plaintiff's position is perceptibly stronger than the defendant's position after taking into account any failure to produce evidence and any other relevant features of the evidence, decision must go for the plaintiff. The court cannot choose not to decide, and a decision for the plaintiff is less likely an error than decision for the defendant would be.

The comparative approach to the civil standard of proof means as well that the nonburdened party does not need to develop a competing version of the truth, but can rely on negation of one or more elements. A belief in the falsity of the burdened party's version of the truth may develop naturally in the course of trial. A disbelief could arise even upon hearing only the burdened party's evidence. Thus, the nonburdened party can, even by silence, prevail if the factfinder disbelieves any element as much as or more than it believes the element. Any evidence from the nonburdened party should contribute to raising *Bel(not-a)* further.

Relatedly, the burdened party need not fight imaginary fights. Some scholars worry that the opponent's denial puts the burdened party in the impossible situation of disproving every alternative possibility. But that worry comes from confusing lack of belief with disbelief. Disbelieving *a* entails the degree to which the factfinder thinks *a* is false. The mere possibility of other states of the world in which *a* is not proven or disproven goes into the uncommitted belief, and not into *Bel(not-a)*; recall that the possibility of *not-a* equals *Bel(not-a)* plus the uncommitted belief; again, the degree of believing that Dave is not the perpetrator is quite different from envisaging the chance that he is possibly not the perpetrator. The proposed comparison involves the belief in *not-a*, and does not involve the possibility of *not-a*.

More clarifications and advantages flow from the belief functions' standard of proof. Not only does its comparative approach comport with the natural cognitive method that follows from telling the factfinders they must look to their beliefs and then decide for one side or the other, but also it invokes the factfinders' considerable powers of relative judgment rather than their absolute judgment of believability.

Moreover, the belief functions' standard does nothing to interfere with the current procedural and substantive functioning of the standard of proof. Picture, as a final step, a normalization process of disregarding the uncommitted belief and scaling *Bel(a)* and *Bel(not-a)* up proportionately so that they add to 1. Call the recalculations *bel(a)* and *bel(not-a)*. If *Bel(a)* = 0.50 and *Bel(not-a)* = 0.20, then *bel(a)* = 0.71 and *bel(not-a)* = 0.29. These new *bel* numbers need to travel less mental distance to get to the traditional view of standards of proof, because *bel(a)* > *bel(not-a)* if and only if *bel(a)* > 0.50. Preponderance then retains a connotation of likelihood exceeding fifty percent. Hence, this normalization renders my reformulation much less jarring, and it also demonstrates that I did not pull the reformulation out of thin air.

Admittedly, something about the traditional formulation of the preponderance standard as a showing of a probability greater than fifty percent for civil cases just seems appealing. Among competing fixed standards,[117] it minimizes the expected number of erroneous decisions and also the expected sum of wrongful amounts of damages. It also treats plaintiffs and defendants equally, which is another goal that the law has chosen to pursue by its civil standard. But these are not arguments against the belief functions' reformulated comparative standard. It too has the properties of error-cost minimizing and equal-treatment maximizing, but achieves them in the real world where the assumption of bivalence does not hold and where considerable epistemic uncertainty prevails.

For an idea of an economic proof adapted from the usual probabilists' proof,[118] let *bel(a)* = *p* be the apparent probability that the defendant is liable (for *D* dollars). If *Bel(a)* > *Bel(not-a)*, then $p > ½$; in that case, call *p* by the name p_1. If *Bel(a)* ≤ *Bel (not-a)*, call it p_2. On the one hand, under the preponderance standard, the expected sum of false positives and false negatives over the run of cases is $\sum[(1-p_1)D + p_2D]$. On the other hand, under a very high standard of proof that eliminates false positives, the analogous sum is $\sum[p_1D + p_2D]$. Therefore, given that $(1-p_1)$ is less than p_1, a heightened preponderance standard increases expected error costs over the performance of *Bel(a)* > *Bel(not-a)*.

Likewise, one of civil procedure's most fundamental principles is that, where possible, the parties should ordinarily receive equal treatment and bear equal risk.[119] The common law has long championed the traditional view of the preponderance rule as an inarticulate manifestation of that principle. By comparing belief to disbelief, the reformulated standard preserves the level playing field while more clearly articulating equality.

To summarize, the preponderance standard for civil cases asks the natural question that the law seems to pose by "more likely than not?": Is the fact shown to be more true than false, that is, do you believe the burdened party's allegation more than you believe the opponent's denial? This believed-more-than-disbelieved standard calls for constructing separate beliefs for *a* and *not-a* while leaving some belief uncommitted, and then just comparing the sizes of the beliefs in *a*'s truth and falsity. The uncommitted belief can then be ignored, because it has finished playing its role in constructing an accurate belief and disbelief.

To look farther back over this book, the basic idea has been that multivalent beliefs should be used because they will deliver the most accurate representation of the factfinder's state of mind, including its view of epistemic uncertainty. The belief function embodies the factfinder's view of reality, given the available evidence. At the end, the factfinder should compare the belief and the disbelief. Given the need to decide, adopting the more believable of the two conceivable views of reality will

[117] See Clermont (2013), pp. 15–16, 73–82 (recounting the law's rejection of variable or sliding-scale standards of proof, which could be theoretically desirable); cf. Ho (2015) (questioning that desirability).

[118] See Kaye (2002); cf. Schweizer (2015), pp. 128–132 (offering more formal proof).

[119] See supra Sect. 3.2.4.2 (discussing preference for level playing field).

maximize accuracy, efficiency, and fairness for ordinary civil cases. Therefore, this method is the logical way to go.

5.2.3.2 Clear and Convincing Evidence

Besides preponderance, American law employs the two standards of clear and convincing evidence and beyond a reasonable doubt. When the cost of a false positive in factfinding considerably exceeds the cost of a false negative, the law tries to minimize error costs by raising the standard of proof. In doing so, it considers not just the costs of erroneous decisions ex post but also the benefits of correct decisions in setting ex ante incentives.[120] Here is not the place to reconsider the law's complicated and contentious calculations in setting policy through standards of proof. On these higher standards, I shall therefore shift from a normative approach to trying just to explain in terms of beliefs what the law has decided to do.

Clear and convincing evidence means *Bel(a)* >> *Bel(not-a)*, which is what the current law appears to say.[121] This standard requires "a firm belief or conviction."[122] It means that fairly close calls go against the proponent. This standard would not be that difficult to apply. We are quite used to such a requirement of being clearly convinced of something, in life and in law. That standard of decision means that it is not enough to lean toward a decision, but instead one must think that the opposite decision would be a serious error.

If one wanted a more explicit formulation, one could say that the factfinder needs to be more convinced than merely believing *a* more than *not-a* on Fig. 5.7's scale of seven gross categories of believability, and instead the factfinder needs to believe that it is at least two categories higher. Or one could partially capture the standard by explicating clear and convincing to the factfinder as the standard that lies between preponderance and beyond a reasonable doubt.

I admit that the cases do not make perfectly evident what clear and convincing means. Alternatively, or perhaps additionally, this standard could impose a requirement about the completeness of evidence. It could require admission of enough evidence to reduce uncommitted belief to the point that *Bel(a)* exceeds the so-called maximal possibility of *not-a*, or $Bel(a) > 1 - Bel(a)$. I am open to those viewpoints, but I nondogmatically doubt the law demands this extra. Although the clear-and-

[120] See Cameron (2018) (applying the factors carefully in the particular context of refugee law); Clermont (2013), pp. 5, 13, 25–31 (treating the setting of standards as policy judgments).

[121] See McBaine (1944), p. 263 (proposing an instruction to the effect that "the probability that they are true or exist is substantially greater than the probability that they are false or do not exist"); Morgan (1933), p. 67 ("its truth is much more probable than its falsity").

[122] Manual of Model Civil Jury Instructions for the Ninth Circuit 1.7 (2019) ("When a party has the burden of proving any claim or defense by clear and convincing evidence, it means that the party must present evidence that leaves you with a firm belief or conviction that it is highly probable that the factual contentions of the claim or defense are true. This is a higher standard of proof than proof by a preponderance of the evidence, but it does not require proof beyond a reasonable doubt.").

convincing cases are not explicit, they do seem to speak in terms of the necessary degree of belief being stronger than what preponderance requires, and not in terms of a standard of proof that differs in kind, as by demanding more complete evidence.[123]

5.2.3.3 Beyond a Reasonable Doubt

Proof beyond a reasonable doubt, however, does seem different in kind as to demandingness under current law.

At the least, it obviously must require more than clear-and-convincing's *Bel(a)* >> *Bel(not-a)*. It might merely require *Bel(a)* >>> *Bel(not-a)*, as the probabilists would have it.[124] But more realistically and effectively, current law appears to place separate demands on *Bel(a)* and *Bel(not-a)*, demanding that proof of guilt be strong and that no real belief in innocence persists. Those separate demands of a sizable *Bel(a)* and a tiny *Bel(not-a)* will ensure that *Bel(a)* >>> *Bel(not-a)*, but they require more.

Although there are many conceivable approaches to the extra requirements, my conjectured formulation of the current law would require both (1) that the belief in guilt (*Bel(a)*) be strong enough to exceed the maximal possibility of innocence (1 − *Bel(a)*) and (2) that no reasonable belief in innocence exist, that is, that the factfinder could not reasonably hold that *Bel(not-a)* exceeds the lowest category of slightest believability on the scale of seven gross categories. Another way to look at this double requirement is to see the first of the two as more of a subjective test of belief in guilt, while viewing the second as a more objective test of whether a rational person could accept any "alternative hypothesis" to guilt.

The first requirement of strong proof of guilt ensures that the belief in guilt outweighs any belief in alternative possibilities. Thus *Bel(a)* must exceed the maximal possibility of innocence. This part of the standard remains comparative. Asking for a belief that guilt is stronger than all alternative possibilities is fairly

---

[123] See Tauese v. State, Dep't of Labor & Indus. Relations, 147 P.3d 785, 819–820 (Haw. 2006) ("Under Hawai'i law, 'clear and convincing' evidence is 'defined as an intermediate standard of proof greater than a preponderance of the evidence, but less than proof beyond a reasonable doubt required in criminal cases.' This standard requires 'that degree of proof which will produce in the mind of the trier of fact a firm belief or conviction as to the allegations sought to be established, and requires the existence of a fact be highly probable.'" (citations omitted) (quoting Masaki v. Gen. Motors Corp., 780 P.2d 566, 574–575 (Haw. 1989) (observing: "The law has evolved three standards of levels of proof for different types of cases."))); Molyneux v. Twin Falls Canal Co., 35 P.2d 651 (Idaho 1934) (saying that "clear, positive, and unequivocal" overstates the clear-and-convincing standard); Broun (2013), § 340 (citing cases on the clear-and-convincing standard). But see Walsh (2018), p. 602 (arguing for a fourth standard of "clear, unequivocal, and convincing" evidence applicable in immigration cases, which would be higher than clear and convincing).

[124] Cf. McBaine (1944), p. 266 (proposing an instruction to the effect that a reasonable doubt exists when "you cannot honestly say that it is almost certain that the defendant did the acts which he is charged to have done"); Morgan (1933), p. 67 ("the preponderance of probability must be so great as to banish all reasonable doubts").

communicable to and understandable by the factfinder. The point is that the proof of guilt must be solid. The factfinder cannot be swimming in uncommitted belief. We do not want to convict when, although there is some evidence of guilt, we really do not know what happened. The first requirement thus requires a completeness of evidence not required on the civil side. The *belief* in guilt must exceed the logical *possibility* of innocence.[125]

The second requirement expresses the accepted idea implicit in the criminal standard that the factfinder cannot recognize a reasonable belief in innocence or, equivalently, a reasonable doubt as to guilt.[126] The second requirement works to satisfy those who contend that the criminal standard "is intended to make even the juror who thinks that the defendant 'did it,' in everyday terms, think twice."[127] The second requirement explains why some infamous celebrity defendants who were "obviously guilty" were nevertheless properly acquitted. So, having "no reasonable doubt" means that the factfinder does not find *Bel(not-a)* perceptibly to exceed zero. On the view that anything is possible, zero as a coarsely gradated degree of belief equates to slightest believability. *Bel(not-a)* in excess of zero thus refers to a step up from slightest believability. Consequently, that the factfinder does not find *Bel (not-a)* > 0 actually means that the factfinder does not perceive innocence as reasonably believable. For a conviction, the prosecutor must show that *no reasonable doubt* of guilt exists.

Of course, I offer this conjecture only to clarify the elevated standard of proof for theoretical discussion. The conjecture's terms should not be conveyed explicitly to the jurors. How to elaborate the criminal standard is hotly debated. Some authorities argue that "reasonable doubt" should not be defined at all.[128] Yet, some pattern instructions do make an attempt to aid the jurors. I do not think those attempts

---

[125] Also, the first requirement might mollify those who treat the criminal standard as a unitary but very high probability standard and then argue that the standard is much too demanding to be optimal. E.g., Allen and Laudan (2008), p. 68 ("While the prospect of convicting or executing a truly innocent person is horrifying, this type of mistake occurs within a highly complicated matrix of relationships where other equally horrifying mistakes go unnoticed in the conventional discourse."); cf. Picinali (2018) (reconciling deontologists' and consequentialists' views). Still, given the usual limits on available evidence, achieving such a high degree of belief that *Bel(a)* > 1−*Bel(a)* constitutes a demanding standard. Bear in mind that requiring *Bel(a)* to exceed 1−*Bel(a)*, along with requiring a tiny *Bel(not-a)*, would usually convert by pignistic transform into requiring a very high probability of around 85%, not far from the probabilities often mentioned in association with beyond a reasonable doubt. See Clermont (2013), pp. 108–111 (surveying empirical studies suggesting an 80–90% threshold); cf. White and Cicchini (2019) (describing a study that suggested a 65% threshold).

[126] See Clermont (2013), pp. 36–38 (delineating what equivalent standards are when the burden shifts sides).

[127] Ashford and Risinger (1969), p. 199; see Pardo (2015), p. 1829 & n.142 (seeing the beyond-a-reasonable-doubt standard as imposing a double requirement).

[128] See, e.g., Pattern Criminal Federal Jury Instructions for the Seventh Circuit ¶ 2.04 (1998) ("The Committee recommends that no instruction be given defining 'reasonable doubt.'"); Note (1995). But cf. Newman (1993), p. 984 ("I find it rather unsettling that we are using a formulation that we believe will become less clear the more we explain it.").

require much amendment. For example, the Tenth Circuit's pattern instruction runs this way:

> Proof beyond a reasonable doubt is proof that leaves you firmly convinced of the defendant's guilt. There are few things in this world that we know with absolute certainty, and in criminal cases the law does not require proof that overcomes every possible doubt. It is only required that the government's proof exclude any "reasonable doubt" concerning the defendant's guilt. A reasonable doubt is a doubt based on reason and common sense after careful and impartial consideration of all the evidence in the case. If, based on your consideration of the evidence, you are ~~firmly~~ convinced that the defendant is guilty of the crime charged, [*as against all alternative possibilities,*] you ~~must~~ [*may*] find him guilty. If on the other hand, you think there is a real possibility that he is not guilty, you must give him the benefit of the doubt and find him not guilty.[129]

I would add only the words in italics. My use of "may" might water down the jury's duty to convict, but it conveys that there are multiple requirements to convict without being too pedantic. I would eliminate the repetition of "firmly" because the subsequently stated two requirements spell out what "firmly" should convey, and because including the redundant word might be taken to exaggerate the standard into something like being firmly convinced of being firmly convinced.

5.2.4 Overview

My views on evaluating proof, then, are not at all subversive. Overall I merely contend, in accordance with multivalent beliefs' teaching, that the law charges factfinders to form coarsely gradated degrees of belief and disbelief in the burdened party's position, while leaving some belief uncommitted in the face of epistemic uncertainty, and then to apply the standard of proof by comparing the belief to their disbelief. Many observers of the legal system would find that contention, putting its slightly new vocabulary to the side, unobjectionable.

Nonetheless, a reader always feels the temptation, upon seeing what looks like a plea for reconceptualization, to dismiss it as a pie-in-the-sky academic musing. When the reconceptualization involves the standards of proof, the specialists have the added temptation of dismissing it as another of the common anti-probabilist rants or pro-probabilist paeans. After all, if my reformulation were a sound one, someone would have come up with it before. So I hasten to undercut my contribution further by stressing that my ideas are not new at all. I am trying little more than to explain what the law has been doing all along.

The easiest way to convey the lack of newness would be to refer back to the normalization process that converts beliefs into probabilistic outputs. That process allows expression consistent with traditional probability theory. Yet, I resist taking that normalization route for ordinary use. First, converting to seemingly additive

[129] Criminal Pattern Jury Instructions, United States Court of Appeals for the Tenth Circuit ¶ 1.05 (2021).

beliefs loses information and would reintroduce the probabilistic imaging that led to the problems and paradoxes of the traditional view. Second, normalization requires quantification of *Bel(a)* and *Bel(not-a)*, a complicated conversion otherwise unnecessary, and a conversion that is much more difficult for humans to perform than simply comparing beliefs. Third, I contend that directly comparing *Bel(a)* and *Bel (not-a)* conforms better to the law's actual instructions than normalization does.

Instead of normalizing, I urge taking a new look at actual practice. Courts express sometimes divergent views of the standard of proof. Thus, some writers have concluded that various courts interpret preponderance in one of three ways: (1) "more convincing," which requires the burdened party to tell a better tale than the opponent tells; (2) "more likely than not," which requires a showing of the fact's existence stronger than the showing of its nonexistence; or (3) "really happened," which requires a showing by evidence of what probably transpired outside in the real world.[130]

My reformulated standard would conform to the middle option #2, rather than either the comparison #1 suggested by relative plausibility theory or the absolute measure #3 required by probability theory. The evidence at trial will support *a* to an extent while supporting *not-a* to another extent, and the reformulated standard says that the factfinder need only compare those two beliefs. To see how this middle option has worked in courts, consider a couple of classic cases.

In *Livanovitch v. Livanovitch*,[131] the trial court gave the following charge: "If . . . you are more inclined to believe from the evidence that he did so deliver the bonds to the defendant, even though your belief is only *the slightest degree* greater than that he did not, your verdict should be for the plaintiff."[132] The appellate court said:

> The instruction was not erroneous. It was but another way of saying that the slightest preponderance of the evidence in his favor entitled the plaintiff to a verdict . . . . All that is required in a civil case of one who has the burden of proof is that he establish his claim by a preponderance of the evidence . . . . When the equilibrium of proof is destroyed, and the beam inclines toward him who has the burden, however slightly, he has satisfied the requirement of the law, and is entitled to the verdict. "A bare preponderance is sufficient, though the scales drop but a feather's weight." This rule accords with the practice in this state as remembered by the justices of this court, and is well supported by the authorities.[133]

In *Lampe v. Franklin American Trust Co.*,[134] one of the defendant's affirmative defenses was that the promissory note in suit had been altered after it had been signed by the defendant's decedent. The trial court refused the defendant's request for an instruction that the jury should find that the instrument was not the decedent's note "if you find and believe that it is *more probable* that such changes or alterations have

[130] See, e.g., Covington (2006), pp. 99–100 (describing the three explanations that courts have given of the term "preponderance of evidence").

[131] 131 A. 799 (Vt. 1926).

[132] Id. at 800.

[133] Id. (apparently quoting Leggett v. Illinois Cent. R.R., 72 Ill. App. 577, 579 (1897)).

[134] 96 S.W.2d 710 (Mo. 1936).

been made in the instrument after it was signed by the deceased and without his knowledge and consent, than it is that such alterations and changes were made at or about the time that the deceased signed the instrument and under his direction and with his knowledge and consent."[135] Holding the denial of that instruction to have been proper, the appellate court said:

> The trouble with this statement is that a verdict must be based upon what the jury finds to be facts rather than what they find to be "more probable." . . . This means merely that the party, who has the burden of proof, must produce evidence, tending to show the truth of those facts, "which is more convincing to them as worthy of belief than that which is offered in opposition thereto."[136]

These two cases' formulations sound contradictory. But if one interprets the quotations as speaking in terms of the coarsely gradated belief in the fact compared with the coarsely gradated belief in the fact's opposite, based on the evidence presented, the apparent contradiction evaporates. They both seem to be saying that the burdened party should win if and only if *Bel(a)* > *Bel(not-a)*. Avoiding speaking of probabilities, *Livanovitch* says the plaintiff must destroy the equilibrium of proof.[137] Admittedly, though, the court's opinion slips unfortunately into the image of a feather's weight. More clearly, *Lampe* rejects probabilities. It speaks instead of convincing beliefs in truth.

Indeed, careful readings will convince that the majority of cases in fact conform to option #2's "more likely than not." Authorities say that preponderance means the evidence "produces in your minds belief that what is sought to be proved is more likely true than not true"[138] or "more probably true than false."[139] In the end, I submit that comparison of coarsely gradated beliefs is the most accurate representation of what the law already tells a factfinder to do with a standard of proof. Adjudicators should stay away from just weighing the quantity of evidence. They should also avoid thinking in terms of numerical probabilities. Professor Morgan had this suggestion:

> If the trial judge tells the jury that the burden is upon a party to prove a specified fact by a preponderance of the evidence, he should explain that this means only that they must find

[135] Id. at 723.

[136] Id. (quoting Rouchene v. Gamble Constr. Co., 89 S.W.2d 58, 63 (Mo. 1935)).

[137] Cf. Model Civil Jury Instructions for the District Courts of the Third Circuit ¶ 1.10 (2015) ("To say it differently: if you were to put the evidence favorable to plaintiff and the evidence favorable to defendant on opposite sides of the scales, plaintiff would have to make the scales tip somewhat on his side. If plaintiff fails to meet this burden, the verdict must be for defendant.").

[138] O'Malley et al. (2011), § 104.01 (redefining "more probable than not" as "such evidence as, when considered and compared with the evidence opposed to it, has more convincing force, and produces in your minds belief that what is sought to be proved is more likely true than not true"); see Sand et al. (2015), ¶ 73–2 ("To establish a fact by a preponderance of evidence means to prove that the fact is more likely true than not true.").

[139] Nissho-Iwai Co. v. M/T Stolt Lion, 719 F.2d 34, 38 (2d Cir. 1983) ("The term 'preponderance' means that 'upon all the evidence . . . the facts asserted by the plaintiff are more probably true than false.'" (quoting Porter v. Am. Exp. Lines, Inc., 387 F.2d 409, 411 (3d Cir. 1968))).

> that the fact does not exist unless the evidence convinces them that its existence is more probable than its non-existence. Indeed, there is no need for him to talk of burden of proof or of preponderance of evidence. He may well confine his instruction on this matter to a specification of the disputed propositions of fact and a direction as to which party must fail on each proposition unless the jury is convinced by the evidence that the truth of that proposition is more probable than its falsity.[140]

Professor McBaine actually composed an instruction:

> The court instructs you that by the law of this state burdens of proving facts are imposed upon parties to lawsuits, and other types of legal proceedings, for the purpose of reaching wise and just decisions.
>
> The court instructs the jury, wherever you have been instructed in other instructions in this case, that a party to this action has the burden of proving a fact or facts by the preponderance or greater weight of the evidence, that the burden of proof imposed upon that party is the following:
>
> The burden is not a burden of merely producing a greater number of witnesses or a greater quantity of evidence. The burden therefore is not necessarily carried by the introduction of the greater number of witnesses or the greater quantity of evidence. A greater number of witnesses or a greater quantity of evidence are factors which you may take into account in determining whether the burden of proof has been carried. Neither the greater nor the lesser number of witnesses or quantity of the evidence is the sole test to be applied in determining whether the burden of proof, imposed by law, has been carried because the burden so imposed is one of convincing your minds. Belief in the truth of assertions, therefore, is not to be reached by merely calculating the numbers of witnesses or by estimating the quantities of evidence.
>
> The burden is not a burden of convincing you that the facts which are asserted are certainly true or that they are true to a high degree of probability.
>
> The burden imposed is to convince you upon all the evidence before you that the facts asserted are more probably true than false.
>
> If then upon consideration and comparison of all the evidence in the case you believe that it is more probable that the facts are true than it is that they are false you must find that the facts have been proved.
>
> If, on the other hand, you believe that it is more probable that the facts asserted are false than it is that they are true, you will find that the party upon whom this burden of proof has been placed has not proved the facts.
>
> Also, if you find that the probabilities of truth and falsity are evenly balanced; that it is just as probable that the facts are true as it is that they are not true, you will find that the burden of proof imposed upon him has not been carried, because he has not proved that the facts are more probably true than not true.[141]

In sum, under current conceptions or under my modest reconception, when the judge explains preponderance of the evidence in civil cases, the explanation should convey the idea that the factfinder has to find that *Bel(a)* is "more likely than *not*,"

[140] Morgan (1933), pp. 66–67.

[141] McBaine (1944), pp. 261–262.

which means *Bel(a)* > *Bel(not-a)*. If any change were made, the instruction should avoid using the word "probable." It might go like this:

> "Establish by a preponderance of the evidence" means evidence that, as a whole, shows the fact sought to be proved is more true than false. You should determine the level of your belief that the fact actually exists and also determine the level of your belief that the fact actually does not exist. If the former belief is stronger than the latter belief, then the burdened party has established the fact.

By literally instructing factfinders to decide between truth and falsity, the law would urge them more effectively to focus on belief and disbelief and then to compare them.

References

Ahuja JK, Tutt A (2012) Evidentiary rules governing Guantanamo habeas petitions: their effects and consequences. Yale Law Policy Rev 31:185–226

Allen RJ, Laudan L (2008) Deadly dilemmas. Tex Tech Law Rev 41:65–92

Anderson T, Schum D, Twining W (2005) Analysis of evidence, 2nd edn. Cambridge University Press, New York

Ashford HA, Risinger DM (1969) Presumptions, assumptions, and due process in criminal cases: a theoretical overview. Yale Law J 79:165–208

Binder DA, Bergman P (1984) Fact investigation: from hypothesis to proof. West Academic, St Paul MN

Blume JH, Johnson SL, Marcus P, Paavola E (2014) A tale of two (and possibly three) *Atkins*: intellectual disability and capital punishment twelve years after the Supreme Court's creation of a categorical bar. William & Mary Bill Rights J 23:393–414

Blutman L (2021) The language and logic of inquiry: some basic problems. FORVM: Acta Juridica et Politica 11(1):5–21

Broun KS (gen ed) (2013) McCormick on evidence, vols 1 and 2, 7th edn. Thomson/West, St Paul MN

Cameron HE (2018) Refugee law's fact-finding crisis: truth, risk, and the wrong mistake. Cambridge University Press, Cambridge

Clermont KM (2006) Jurisdictional fact. Cornell Law Rev 91:973–1020

Clermont KM (2013) Standards of decision in law: psychological and logical bases for the standard of proof, here and abroad. Carolina Academic Press, Durham NC

Clermont KM (2020) Rules, standards, and such. Buff Law Rev 68:751–804

Cohen LJ (1977) The probable and the provable. Clarendon Press, Oxford

Cohen LJ (1994) Some steps towards a general theory of relevance. Synthese 101:171–185

Columbia Law Review Ass'n et al (2000) The Bluebook: a uniform system of citation, 17th edn. Harvard Law Review, Cambridge

Columbia Law Review Ass'n et al (2020) The Bluebook: a uniform system of citation, 21st edn. Harvard Law Review, Cambridge

Covington JS (2006) The structure of legal argument and proof, 2nd edn. Rothman, Buffalo NY

Damaška M (1995) Free proof and its detractors. Am J Comput Law 43:343–357

Damaška M (2019) Evaluation of evidence: premodern and modern approaches. Cambridge University Press, Cambridge

Diamond SS (2006) Beyond fantasy and nightmare: a portrait of the jury. Buff Law Rev 54:717–763

Dietrich F, Spiekermann K (2023) Jury theorems. In: Zalta Edward N (ed) Stanford encyclopedia of philosophy. https://plato.stanford.edu/entries/jury-theorems/
Dubois D, Prade H (1980) Fuzzy sets and systems: theory and applications. Academic Press, New York
Dubois D, Prade H (1990) Consonant approximations of belief functions. Int J Approx Reason 4: 419–449
Ehrmann HB (1969) The case that will not die: Commonwealth vs. Sacco and Vanzetti. Little Brown, Boston
Faruki CJ (2019) Using critical thinking to analyze facts. Litigation 45(4):52–58
Field RH, Kaplan B, Clermont KM, Clopton ZD (2023) Materials for a basic course in civil procedure, 14th edn. Foundation, St Paul MN
Fox M (2018) Conan Doyle for the defense. Random House, New York
Fraenkel OK (1931) The Sacco-Vanzetti case. Knopf, New York
Frankfurter F (1927) The case of Sacco and Vanzetti. Little Brown, Boston
Franklin J (2015) The science of conjecture: evidence and probability before Pascal, 2nd edn. Johns Hopkins University Press, Baltimore
Frederick JT (1987) The psychology of the American jury. Michie, Charlottesville VA
Garner BA (1987) A dictionary of modern legal usage. Oxford University Press, New York
Gerla G (2001) Fuzzy logic: mathematical tools for approximate reasoning. Kluwer Academic, Dordrecht, Netherlands
Ginsburg RB (1965) Special findings and jury unanimity in the federal courts. Colum Law Rev 65: 256–271
Haack S (2014a) Legal probabilism: an epistemological dissent. In: Evidence matters: science, proof, and truth in the law. Cambridge University Press, New York, pp 47–77
Haack S (2014b) Proving causation: the weight of combined evidence. In: Evidence matters: science, proof, and truth in the law. Cambridge University Press, New York, pp 208–238
Hannaford PL, Hans VP, Mott NL, Munsterman GT (2000) The timing of opinion formation by jurors in civil cases: an empirical examination. Tenn Law Rev 67:627–652
Hastie R (2008) What's the story? explanations and narratives in civil jury decisions. In: Bornstein BH et al (eds) Civil juries and civil justice. Springer Science+Business, New York, pp 23–34
Hastie R, Pennington N (1983) The psychology of juror and jury decision making. In: Reid H et al (eds) Inside the jury. Harvard University Press, Cambridge MA, pp 15–36
Hay BL (1997) Allocating the burden of proof. Indiana Law J 72:651–679
Head M (2021–2022) The fact-finders' dialectic: beyond rationalist optimism and realist pessimism. Kentucky Law Rev 110:511–565
Ho HL (2015) The legal concept of evidence. In: Zalta Edward N (ed) Stanford encyclopedia of philosophy. https://plato.stanford.edu/entries/evidence-legal/
Huntley JE, Costanzo M (2003) Sexual harassment stories: testing a story-mediated model of juror decision-making in civil litigation. Law Human Behav 27:29–51
Joughin GL, Morgan EM (1948) The legacy of Sacco and Vanzetti. Harcourt Brace, New York
Kadane JB, Schum DA (1996) A probabilistic analysis of the Sacco and Vanzetti evidence. John Wiley, New York
Kahneman D (2011) Thinking, fast and slow. Farrar Straus, New York
Kahneman D, Sibony O, Sunstein CR (2021) Noise: a flaw in human judgment. Little Brown Spark, New York
Kaye DH (2002) The error of equal error rates. Law Probabil Risk 1:3–8
Kyburg HE (1996) Uncertain inferences and uncertain conclusions. In: Eric H, Finn J (eds) Proceedings of the twelfth conference on uncertainty in artificial intelligence, Portland OR 1996. Morgan Kaufmann, San Francisco, pp 365–372
Larsen AO (2011) Bargaining inside the black box. Georgetown Law J 99:1567–1612
Laudan L (2006) Truth, error, and criminal law. Cambridge University Press, Cambridge
Lempert R (1986) The new evidence scholarship: analyzing the process of proof. Boston Univ Law Rev 66:439–477

Lindell B (2017) Multi-criteria analysis in legal reasoning. Elgar, Cheltenham UK

Liu L, Yager RR (2008) Classic works of the Dempster-Shafer theory of belief functions: an introduction. In: Yager Ronald R, Liu L (eds) Classic works of the Dempster-Shafer theory of belief functions. Springer Science+Business, Heidelberg, pp 1–34

MacCoun RJ (2022) Standards of proof: theories and evidence. https://ssrn.com/abstract=4029030. Accessed 8 May 2022

Malsch M, Freckelton I (2009) The evaluation of evidence: differences between legal systems. In: Hendrik K et al (eds) Legal evidence and proof: statistics, stories, logic. Ashgate, Farnham UK, pp 117–134

McBaine JP (1944) Burden of proof: degrees of belief. Calif Law Rev 32:242–268

McCauliff CMA (1982) Burdens of proof: degrees of belief, quanta of evidence, or constitutional guarantees? Vand Law Rev 35:1293–1335

McNaughton JT (1955) Burden of production of evidence: a function of a burden of persuasion. Harv Law Rev 68:1382–1391

Montgomery RH (1960) Sacco-Vanzetti: the murder and the myth. Devin-Adair, New York

Morgan EM (1933) Instructing the jury upon presumptions and burden of proof. Harv Law Rev 47: 59–83

Morgan EM (1950) Introduction to evidence. In: Scott Austin W, Simpson Sidney P (eds) Cases and other materials on civil procedure. Little Brown, Boston, pp 941–1031

Nance DA (2019) Belief functions and burdens of proof. Law Probabil Risk 18:53–76

Nash JR (2003) A context-sensitive voting protocol paradigm for multimember courts. Stan Law Rev 56:75–159

Newman JO (1993) Beyond "reasonable doubt." New York Univ Law Rev 68:979–1002

Note (1995) Reasonable doubt: an argument against definition. Harv Law Rev 108:1955–1972

Nunn GA (2022) Jurisdictional elements and the jury. Cornell Law Rev 107:515–566

O'Malley KF, Grenig JE, Lee WC (2011) Federal jury practice and instructions: civil, vol 1A & 3, 6th edn. Thomson/West, St. Paul MN

Pardo MS (2015) Group agency and legal proof; or, why the jury is an "it". William & Mary Law Rev 56:1793–1858

Pennington N, Hastie R (1993) The story model for juror decision making. In: Reid H (ed) Inside the juror: the psychology of juror decision making. Cambridge University Press, Cambridge, pp 192–222

Phalen H, Salerno JM, Nadler J (2021) Emotional evidence in court. In: Bandes Susan A et al (eds) Research handbook on law and emotion. Elgar, Cheltenham UK, pp 288–311

Picinali F (2018) Can the reasonable doubt standard be justified? a reconstructed dialogue. Canadian J Law Jurisprud 31:365–402

Priest GL, Klein B (1984) The selection of disputes for litigation. J Legal Stud 13:1–55

Rachlinski JJ, Guthrie C, Wistrich AJ (2011) Probable cause, probability, and hindsight. J Empirical Legal Stud 8(Spec Iss):72–98

Risinger DM (2013) Searching for truth in the American law of evidence and proof. Georgia Law Rev 47:801–835

Roth JA (2011) Alternative elements. UCLA Law Rev 59:170–216

Rott H (2009) Degrees all the way down: beliefs, non-beliefs and disbeliefs. In: Franz H, Christoph S-P (eds) Degrees of belief. Springer Science+Business, Heidelberg, pp 301–339

Rudolph S, Tserendorj T, Hitzler P (2008) What is approximate reasoning? In: Diego C, Georg L (eds) Web reasoning and rule systems, 2008 edn. Springer Science+Business, Heidelberg, pp 150–164

Russell F (1962) Tragedy in Dedham: the story of the Sacco-Vanzetti case. McGraw-Hill, New York

Sand LB et al (2015) Modern federal jury instructions: civil, vol 4. Matthew Bender, New York

Schauer F (2021) The role of rules in the law of evidence. In: Christian D et al (eds) Philosophical foundations of evidence law. Oxford University Press, Oxford, pp 69–82

Schum DA (1994) The evidential foundations of probabilistic reasoning. Northwestern University Press, Evanston IL
Schweizer M (2015) Loss aversion, omission bias and the civil standard of proof. In: Klaus M (ed) European perspectives on behavioural law and economics. Springer Science+Business, Heidelberg, pp 125–146
Seltzer R, Canan Russell F, Cannon M, Hansberry H (2016) Legal standards by the numbers: quantifying burdens of proof or a search for fool's gold? Judicature 100(1):56–66
Simon D (2004) A third view of the black box: cognitive coherence in legal decision making. Univ Chicago Law Rev 71:511–586
Simon D (2019) Thin empirics. Int J Evid Proof 23:82–89
Simon-Kerr J (2023) Law's credibility problem. Wash Law Rev 98:179–214
Spottswood E (published as Mark) (2013) The hidden structure of fact-finding. Case Western Res Law Rev 64:131–200
Spottswood E (published as Mark) (2021) Paradoxes of proof. In: Dahlman Christian et al (eds) Philosophical foundations of evidence law. Oxford University Press, Oxford, pp 317–331
Stein A (2005) Foundations of evidence law. Oxford University Press, Oxford
Strat TM (1990) Decision analysis using belief functions. Int J Approx Reason 4:391–417
Summers RS (1974) Evaluating and improving legal processes—a plea for "process values." Cornell Law Rev 60:1–52
Tanford JA (1986) An introduction to trial law. Missouri Law Rev 51:623–713
Thornburg E (2019) (Un)conscious judging. Washington Lee Law Rev 76:1567–1665
Thorne JF (1980) Mathematics, fuzzy negligence, and the logic of res Ipsa loquitur. Northwest Univ Law Rev 75:147–174
Tillers P, Gottfried J (2006) Case comment—*United States v. Copeland*, 369 F. Supp. 2d 275 (E.D.N.Y. 2005): a collateral attack on the legal maxim that proof beyond a reasonable doubt is unquantifiable? Law Probabil Risk 5:135–157
Transcript (1928) The Sacco-Vanzetti case: transcript of the record of the trial of Nicola Sacco and Bartolomeo Vanzetti in the courts of Massachusetts and subsequent proceedings 1920–7, vols 1 & 2. Holt, New York
Trubitt HJ (1983) Patchwork verdicts, different-jurors verdicts, and American jury theory: whether verdicts are invalidated by juror disagreement on issues. Okla Law Rev 36:473–559
Tuzet G (2021) Evidence assessment and standards of proof: a messy issue. Quaestio Facti 2:87–113
Tuzet G (2022) On probatory ostension and inference. In: Ferrer Beltrán J, Vázquez C (eds) Evidential legal reasoning: crossing civil law and common law traditions. Cambridge University Press, Cambridge, pp 138–158
Tversky A, Kahneman D (1974) Judgment under uncertainty: heuristics and biases. Science (n.s.) 185:1124–1131
Twining W (2006) Rethinking evidence, 2nd edn. Cambridge University Press, New York
Twining W (2019) Jurist in context: a memoir. Cambridge University Press, Cambridge
US Government Printing Office (1973) Style manual, Rev edn. GPO, Washington DC
Verkerk RR (2010) Fact-finding in civil litigation: a comparative perspective. Intersentia, Antwerp
Walsh HG (2018) Unequivocally different: the third civil standard of proof. Univ Kansas Law Rev 66:565–602
White LT, Cicchini MD (2019) Is reasonable doubt self-defining? Villanova Law Rev 64:1–24
Wigmore JH (1937) The science of judicial proof as given by logic, psychology, and general experience, and illustrated in judicial trials, 3rd edn. Little Brown, Boston
Wigmore JH (1981) In: Chadbourn James H (ed) Evidence in trials at common law, vol 9. Little Brown, Boston
Wright RW (2018) Haack on legal proof. Estudios Filosóficos 67:517–528
Yager RR (1991) New paradigms for reasoning with uncertain information. Cardozo Law Rev 13: 1005–1024

Young W, Kaiser DE (1985) Postmortem: new evidence in the case of Sacco and Vanzetti. University of Massachusetts Press, Amherst MA

Zamir E, Ritov I (2012) Loss aversion, omission bias, and the burden of proof in civil litigation. J Legal Stud 41:165–207

Zwier PJ, Bocchino AJ (2015) Fact investigation: a practical guide to interviewing, counseling, and case theory development, 2nd edn. NITA, Boulder CO

Chapter 6
Generalizing Beyond Factfinding

As I see it, for all the "ballyhoo" about the supposed method of science, there really is no such thing; there is no distinctive "logic of scientific inference," nor are there modes or procedures of inquiry used by all scientists and only by scientists. Scientists go about figuring out how things are in much the way we all proceed in the most mundane of everyday inquiry . . . .
—Susan Haack (Susan Haack, The Art of Scientific Metaphors, 75 Revista Portuguesa de Filosofia 2049, 2054 (2019) (footnote omitted).)

Abstract This book's theory extends far beyond factfinding. Section 6.1: Deciding questions of pure law is no different in nature from legal factfinding. Section 6.2: Science, in its pursuit of truth, proceeds not so differently. Multivalent degrees of belief, rather than traditional probability theory, underlie and justify how scientists most often should reason and theorize about the universe(s) in the face of epistemic uncertainty. Section 6.3: This book's theory reaches all decisionmaking under persistent epistemic uncertainty.

To this point, I have mainly focused on factfinding. Indeed, I have discussed in detail only legal factfinding, and further only those factual decisions of a binary nature. For example, my concern was that either the defendant will be found negligent or not, which might turn in part on whether the defendant breached the reasonable-person standard of care or not. Although the decision may be binary, the level of sureness is not. So, the standard of proof specifies how sure the factfinder must be to find a violation of the applicable substantive criterion for the required level of care.

Do not mistake my focus on legal binary factfinding for narrowness of concept, however.

First, this book has expressed no limitation to *legal* factfinding. Everything in this book carries over to any sort of factfinding that involves persistent epistemic uncertainty. Moreover, I used a broad definition of "fact" so as to include any matter

K. M. Clermont, *A General Theory of Evidence and Proof*, Law and Philosophy Library 148, https://doi.org/10.1007/978-3-031-66552-3_6

out in the real world that a court, other institution, or person subjects to some sort of proof process in order to establish whether to accept it as true.

I have pointed out that thinkers in many disciplines follow suit. I referred to the humanities. I imagined ten or more facts from history each believed by a historian to 0.90, which link together as the necessary elements to form a historical account. The historian should accept that history, even though the product rule would put the combined probability around 35%. Every story from a historian consists of linked, not multiplied, beliefs. Rejecting that path to decisionmaking, and instead applying the product rule, would lead to such idiocies as Holocaust denial: the denier would wonder how anyone could think that so many events conjoined to produce the Holocaust.[1]

Second, the methods of this book can be extended to nonbinary decisions. Outputs can be yes/no or can be selected among multiple choices, that is, dichotomous or nondichotomous outputs.[2] A nondichotomous output is not only possible but indeed common in fixing terms of injunctions, criminal sentences, or money damages. For a nondichotomous output, the factfinder could consider the decisional factors sequentially with respect to each available outcome and choose the optimizing one. For example, a cost-minimization balancing technique would guide the court in selecting the terms of any injunction. Alternatively, the factfinder could formulate its best judgment for the factors' satisfaction by placing its estimate for each outcome on some commensurable scale. With the latter sort of method, the law can be especially comfortable with a range of outputs. Each possible output would correspond to a point on or a portion of the scale. Sometimes the law would correlate decisional categories, like the degrees of the crime, to the scale's metric. Sometimes the scale's metric would directly produce the output, as is done with money damages.[3] Thus, nondichotomous outputs will involve extra steps supplemental to the logic laid out in this book for the underlying factual findings.

As decisions become more complex in terms of multiple factors to consider simultaneously, and especially as the options among possible decisions begin to multiply, we need to turn to more general decisionmaking theory.[4] For example, simple additive weighting, or SAW, requires the decisionmaker to specify the n criteria that guide decision and then to weight them, $w_{1\to n}$.[5] The decisionmaker

---

[1] See Salter (2017), p. 22; cf. Baade (2021) (discussing "historical truth"); Resta and Zeno-Zencovich (2013) (presenting another historical case study). See generally Twining and Hampsher-Monk (2003), pp. 2–62; Twining (2006), pp. 352–353.

[2] See Kolber (2014), pp. 666–668 (calling dichotomous outputs bumpy, and nondichotomous outputs smoother).

[3] See, e.g., Hans (2014), pp. 941–950 (describing a "gist model" positing that factfinders first make a categorical gist judgment of money damages' being warranted, then make an ordinal gist judgment ranking the damages deserved as low, medium, or high, and finally construct numbers to fit that magnitude).

[4] See supra Sect. 1.3 (referencing general literature on decisionmaking under uncertainty).

[5] See Lindell (2017), pp. 72–77.

then scores each of the i options with respect to each specified criterion, $s_{1 \rightarrow n}$. That will produce an overall score, $S_{1 \rightarrow i}$, for each option, x, equal to:

$$S_x = w_1 s_1 + w_2 s_2 + \ldots + w_n s_n$$

The decisionmaker finally chooses, from the i choices, the option with the highest overall score. Thus, SAW can serve as a tool for solving many optimization problems. But even here, scores that involve persistent epistemic uncertainty would be more accurate if multivalent belief methodology were employed.

Third, this book has much to say about decisionmaking that does not remotely resemble factfinding. In everyday life, one can speak of decisions on whether to go out to the movies tonight. Or whether to marry this particular person.[6] The same methods are employed across human endeavors whenever decisions need to be made in a way that accounts for epistemic uncertainty.[7]

I already referenced social scientists, beginning with the economists' suggestion that we should shrug in the face of epistemic uncertainty and just ask "What is going on here?" I argued instead that after recognizing the distinction between aleatory and epistemic uncertainty, we must think more about the optimal methodology for deciding. In general, probabilities work for the puzzles of aleatory uncertainty, but any encounters with epistemic uncertainty would counsel decisionmakers' switching to multivalent beliefs. Let me expand further by discussing decisions on pure law and then decisions in the natural sciences.

6.1 Pure Law

Proving domestic law, as opposed to making law,[8] is another example of where the lessons of epistemic uncertainty carry over. Questions of law are epistemically equivalent to questions of fact.[9] "If one makes any propositional claims about what the law *is*, regardless of what one has in mind by 'law,' one is making claims of fact."[10]

---

[6] See Fedel (2010), p. 219 ("In practical reasoning, whether it is aimed at drawing inferences or making decisions, we need to give appropriate weight both to our uncertainty, about facts or events or consequences of our actions, and to the indeterminacy that arises from our ignorance about [these] matters.").

[7] Thus, multivalent belief theory works to unravel many "everyday" problems spawned by probability theory, such as the preface and lottery paradoxes and Linda's conjunction fallacy. See supra Sects. 4.2.4.3 and 4.5.4.2.

[8] Cf. Clermont (2020), pp. 785–786 (using multivalent ideas as a guide in making law). A useful analogy here is the recent explosion of interest in moral uncertainty. See supra Sect. 1.1.

[9] See Lawson (2017), pp. 28–44.

[10] Lawson (1992), p. 865; see id. ("a proposition by definition is the sort of statement that can be either true or false"); id. at 863 ("Whatever one's metaphysical theory of law may be, any positive

Thus, the analysis of finding fact extends to proving law.[11] However, this point does not imply that the rules for pronouncing law need be exactly the same as for finding fact. The legal system does draw a law/fact line.[12] On the law side of the line, adversary principles do not apply.[13] The effort is instead a collective one to determine the "true" law.

Also, the burden of proof has no role to play in proving law. Given our system of stare decisis, we need to get the right answer. We would not want the law to turn on which party is named the proponent or on how good a job the parties did in arguing the law. Consequently, there is no burden of proof, especially in the sense of the risk of nonpersuasion.[14]

The standard of proof as it applies to issues of law requires more thought. It is a profound but neglected question. Perhaps because the process of determining law comprises a usually internal and fairly intuitive or automatized chain of cognition, we tend not to speak of standards of decision for law. "By and large, the law says nothing to initial decisionmakers who wonder what standard of proof they should apply to propositions of law. Fact finders are always given a standard; law finders are generally on their own."[15] Judges just have to find the law and make conclusions of law—doing so by a process that goes largely unexamined.

Nevertheless, one simply cannot talk about accepting a proposition without, at least implicitly, invoking a standard of proof. "The need for standards of proof and the effect of standards of proof on interpretative outcomes are independent of the admissibility and significance rules of one's theory of interpretation."[16] The necessity of a standard of proof is therefore just as real for law as for fact.

Superficially, this question turns out to have a relatively straightforward answer. The standard of proof for law normally seems to be "more likely than not."[17] The judge would start with the seemingly most likely of the alternative views of the law occurring to him or her, one in which the judge believes each inference more than the judge disbelieves it. By the MIN rule, the chain leading to this selected interpretation is as likely as its weakest link. The parties could offer alternative views. The judge

---

propositions derived from that theory are, from an epistemological standpoint, claims of fact."). But cf. Friedman (1992), p. 942 ("My overall conclusion is that the matter is very complex, perhaps far more than Lawson recognized . . . .").

[11] See Brewer (2011). But see Stein (2022) (sticking determinedly with probabilism for proving law).

[12] See Louis (1986) (comparing the law/fact boundary for appellate review and for the jury right). But cf. Allen and Pardo (2003), p. 1770 ("Thus, the quest to find 'the' essential difference between the two that can control subsequent classifications of questions as legal or factual is doomed from the start, as there is no essential difference."); Nunn (2021) (arguing that the line turns on the proper allocation of decisionmaking authority).

[13] See Field et al. (2023), pp. 1786–1790 (discussing lawyers' ethical duty to reveal adverse law).

[14] See Fenoll (2023).

[15] Lawson (1992), p. 888.

[16] Id. at 875.

[17] Accord Stein (2022), pp. 1401–1404; see Alexander (1992). But see Lawson (1992), p. 893.

would then test all alternatives to see if any is better. Dead-heat ties would be resolved by some canon of construction aimed at believability. In multivalent logic, as already shown, the MAX rule means that the final, most believable interpretation is more believable than all competing interpretations put together.[18] Therefore, the judge believes that final interpretation more than he or she disbelieves it, and believes it more than any competing interpretation.

Sometimes, however, the standard of proof differs from this neutral one, in order to avoid the special costs of error in one particular direction. The most prominent example is where a clear-statement rule, such as the rule of lenity in criminal law, raises the bar for finding a change in the law. When a clear-statement rule prevails, the evidence must convincingly compel the new interpretation being urged.[19]

Finally, Professor Gary Lawson beautifully makes the point that thinking about the epistemology of law lays the groundwork for generalization to the realm of pure law and beyond:

> As it happens, law is an especially fruitful avenue for exploring these ideas precisely because, at least with respect to proof of facts, the law sometimes thinks self-consciously about some of the abstract features of proof and how they bear on decision making. But I believe that the structure of proof that I discuss here is universalizable to any cognitive endeavor.[20]

6.2 Science

My contention here is a simple albeit controversial one: law and science, in their pursuit of truth, proceed not so differently. However, the law seems to have worried more publicly about how to conduct the pursuit. Of course, there is the fabulously rich work on the philosophy of science, which treats such basic questions as what is science (it is something at least tied to observation and theorizing) and what is its purpose (here the realists debate the instrumentalists), thus getting into science's relation to truth.[21] But there seems to be little general work on the logic of science,

---

[18] See supra Sect. 4.4.4 (explaining this result for IBE, RP, and ranking theories).

[19] See Lawson (1992), pp. 888–890. For another specific example, finding a statutory exception to full faith and credit requires an "affirmative showing" of a "clear and manifest" congressional purpose. Kremer v. Chem. Constr. Corp., 456 U.S. 461, 485 (1982). Presumptions used in legal interpretation, such as the presumption of territoriality used within the realm of legislative jurisdiction, can play a similar role. See EEOC v. Arabian Am. Oil Co., 499 U.S. 244 (1991). But see Stein (2022), p. 1402 ("In the domain of statutory and constitutional interpretation, however, things are different because the risks of error on both ends are stable and symmetrical.").

[20] Lawson (2017), p. 2.

[21] See Okasha (2016), pp. 2, 54 ("Another important feature of science is the construction of theories. Scientists do not simply record the results of experiment and observation in a log book—they usually want to explain those results in terms of a general theory. . . . Realists hold that the aim of science is to provide a literally true description of the world. Instrumentalists hold that the aim is rather to provide a convenient way of predicting the results of observation and experiment."). See generally Curd et al. (2012) (providing an anthology of articles organized by

leaving scientists monogamously wedded to traditional probability.[22] Thus, the law may have some lessons to teach scientists.[23]

Scientists must constantly perform the mental processes of drawing inferences and forming hypotheses. A specific example could come from a field like plate tectonics, where geologists had to observe real systems, rather than manipulate experiments, to spin the new theory.[24]

What are these mental processes I am talking about? First, I am talking about inferring a factual conclusion from an observation, where each inferential step must be valid. Second, I am talking about combining elemental conclusions into an explanatory theory, where the scientist has to conjoin the theory's established but still uncertain conclusions to create a picture of reality and then to fill in the gaps by abductive conjecture. These two processes have two things in common: they involve various kinds of uncertainty, and critics can disprove a conclusion or a theory by disproving any inference, element, or conjecture.

In science, traditional probability and its product rule have all kinds of proper uses, such as when we want to perform tests to check whether a drug is safe and effective. But for many tasks, probability fails.[25] First, in the countless situations where scientists are trying in a realistically uncertain world to build understandings from their hard observations, they need to process inferential beliefs rather than traditional probabilities. Second, when scientists try to conjoin epistemically uncertain conclusions and conjectures to construct an explanation, multivalent logic's MIN rule would seem to provide a proper tool.

In science, law, and all the rest of life, when facing epistemic uncertainty, if a person believes *a* and believes *b*, then the person believes *a* and *b* together. This

---

cross-cutting topics in philosophy of science); Ladyman (2002), pp. 5–8 (emphasizing the topics of epistemology and metaphysics).

[22] See Jaynes (2003) (giving the classic treatment of the subject and capturing the book's range in its title—*Probability Theory: The Logic of Science*).

[23] See Univ. of Cal. Museum of Paleontology (2021) ("Taken together, the expectations generated by a scientific idea and the actual observations relevant to those expectations form what we'll call a scientific *argument*. This is a bit like an argument in a court case—a logical description of what we think and why we think it. A scientific argument uses evidence to make a case for whether a scientific idea is accurate or inaccurate. For example, the idea that illness in new mothers can be caused by doctors' dirty hands generates the expectation that illness rates should go down when doctors are required to wash their hands before attending births. When this test was actually performed in the 1800s, the results matched the expectations, forming a strong scientific argument in support of the idea—and hand-washing!"). A precedent exists in the centuries-long interaction of legal theorists with probability theorists during the development of the mathematical rules of probability. In the eighteenth century, legal theorists and their examples made many contributions to the rapid advances in the science and philosophy of probability. See supra Sect. 3.1.4 (discussing this history).

[24] See Ben-Ari (2005), pp. 189–199. Geology is a beautiful example, because so much of earth science is unsettlable. But other hard sciences also have many features that are not "hard" and so entail much epistemic uncertainty. And of course the social sciences, like economics, rest heavily on inferential reasoning and constructive theorizing.

[25] See Franklin (2015), pp. 369–370.

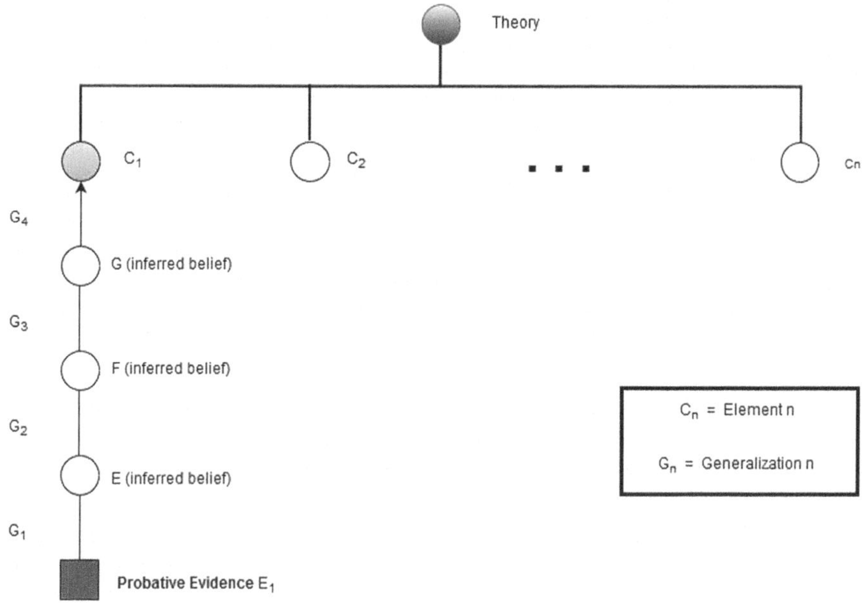

Fig. 6.1 Scientific reasoning

credal logic, which employs multivalent degrees of belief rather than traditional probability theory, underlies and justifies how scientists most often reason and theorize about the universe(s), as well as how legal decisionmakers find fact and law. This brand of logic applies because of its felicity in handling the epistemic uncertainty so prevalent in the world.

In explaining science's logic, I shall be dealing in the normative. But multivalent thinking in these scientific tasks turns out to be feasible to perform, and seemingly conforms to how scientists often do think.

"We are forever inferring and explaining, forming new beliefs about the way things are and explaining why things are as we have found them to be."[26] I shall separately discuss these two cognitive processes of science, inferring and theorizing, in the next two subsections. In Fig. 6.1, the vertical left side represents the former process and the horizontal top represents the latter. My point will be that multivalent belief theory helps to understand and justify both processes.[27]

[26] Lipton (2004), p. 1.

[27] Multivalent logic also has a big impact on what I have been calling step #2: how scientists should combine disparate pieces of evidence to support a conclusion. Basically, Bayes' theorem prevails in science today. It combines evidence but assumes bivalence with its excluded middle. For a remarkably even-handed discussion of the pros and cons of Bayesianism for use in confirming scientific hypotheses and theories, see Earman (1992). In my view, scientists should instead use some variant of belief function theory's more general Dempster-Shafer theorem for combining evidence from the uncertain world we inhabit.

6.2.1 Inferential Reasoning

Inferential reasoning, or inductive inference, is science's bread-and-butter.[28] How is it done? Diagramming it starts at the bottom with an empirical observation, which can be called a piece of "probative evidence" because it tends to prove with some weight and credibility a "conclusion," which may in turn serve as an element in a bigger theory or explanation. This piece of evidence E_1 is linked to the conclusion C_1 by a reasoning chain indicated by propositions E, F, G, and C_1. The logical step from proposition to proposition is inference. The chain of reasoning can be long, that is, many inferences may lie between evidence and conclusion. The reasoner would construct the chain by the process of abduction.

Getting from evidence to conclusion always involves multiple inferences. The steps to E, F, G, and C_1 all have to be accepted in order to establish the conclusion. The process of linking inferences is conjunction, because each step in the chain must be accepted. So the process reduces to a problem of conjoining a chain of inferences. How to do that?

Use of the product rule would be a big worry, because its application would render inferential reasoning a dead end. Repeated applications of the product rule up the chain of reasoning "cumulatively seem like an invitation to extreme skepticism. It regularly provides strong ammunition for attacking an opponent's argument and for questioning one's own. So many generalizations seem so vulnerable in so many respects that one may be led to the conclusion that all arguments about evidence are built on shifting sands."[29]

This worry would seem even more intense for scientists than for lawyers. First, science's standard of proof is higher than the standard for civil cases, which requires only that $Bel(a) > Bel(not\text{-}a)$. Beyond its level being elevated, science's standard is not explicitly stated. It appears to be a high absolute standard. Second, a scientist might also resist believing a conclusion until the uncommitted belief is brought down to an acceptable level, as suggested by science's sometimes applicable test for statistical significance. Third, it is fashionable to accentuate, or exaggerate, other undeniable differences between law and science, such as that science proceeds nonadversarially and without a deadline.[30] At the least, one must admit that science's standard of proof communicates a special devotion to reaching for truth.

There is nothing peculiar about applying different standards of proof to different questions. We have seen this in civil and criminal law cases. As already suggested, we could see this in questions of hard and social sciences and in matters of religious

---

[28] See Okasha (2016), p. 16.

[29] Anderson et al. (2005), p. 102.

[30] See, e.g., Haack (2014), p. 90 ("[T]he core business of science *is* inquiry. . . . [T]he legal system could hardly be more different: adversarial, focused on the specific case, formally-procedurally-anchored, valuing promptness and finality, relying on precedent, and not only relevant, but also highly sensitive, to policy.").

faith. And in everyday life, we would see different standards, one would hope, in deciding whether to go to the movies and whether to marry a particular person.

Nevertheless, regardless of the standard of proof and differences in the procedures for deciding, there is no sign that inferential reasoning in science differs from the approach prevailing in other cognitive fields. The basic theory of evidence and proof is the same for science and law. And so conjunction in scientific reasoning works just as it does in legal factfinding. Given the nature of the inferences fraught with epistemic uncertainties, the resulting propositions can best be represented as multivalent degrees of belief. If one views E as a belief and views the inference ($E \Rightarrow F$) as producing a conditional belief, then the strength of belief in F will be the minimum of the belief in E and the conditional belief in F. As one goes up the chain of inferences, one will believe the latest inference to the minimum of all the preceding beliefs. That is, one will believe the conclusion C_1 to the extent of the weakest link in the chain.

Thus, scientists implicitly use multivalent logic, rather than the product rule, to justify what they are doing. They require the degree of belief in every link in the chain of inferential reasoning to meet their standard of proof, because the chain is only as strong as its weakest link. If every link meets the scientific standard of proof, the overall belief in the conclusion is acceptable too. In other words, scientists apply the MIN rule when epistemic uncertainty is in play.[31]

6.2.2 Constructive Theorizing

A scientific theory requires linking a number of established but still uncertain conclusions that serve as elemental pixels in a picture of reality. The scientist then forms conjectures, filling the gaps, to explain the varied conclusions.[32]

Again, the MIN rule, not the product rule, applies in creating the complete picture. Any separate and necessary element can be treated as a belief. The MIN conjunction operator handles any set of such beliefs. The picture that connects them will be as strong as the weakest belief in the set. As long as each element meets science's standard of proof, the conjoined picture of elemental reality is acceptable

---

[31] See, e.g., Nichols et al. (2005), p. 653 ("We show that a correct test for a logical AND requires that all the comparisons in the conjunction are individually [statistically] significant. This result [for multiple hypothesis testing] holds even if the comparisons are not independent."). A probabilist would be more conservative when testing each hypothesis, using something like a Bonferroni correction to require that each hypothesis had passed a more demanding *p*-test. The analogy in law to science's conservative probabilism would involve those legal theorists who argue for a higher standard of proof applied to each element, so that the conjunction of the elements meets the usual standard of proof.

[32] See Ben-Ari (2005), pp. 24, 28–29, 50–52; cf. Cooper (2021) (explaining how recent advances in cognitive science sharpen our ability to understand legal synthesis).

too. The MIN rule applies because connecting the separate conclusions is logically no different from combining a chain of inferred beliefs.

The multiple conjectures necessary to fill gaps in a theory would, being beliefs, likewise be subject to the MIN rule when added to form a theory or explanation. However, the conjectures need not meet the same demanding standard of proof applied to the elements, that is, the conclusions from observations. A conjecture is more like a legal fact. The key feature of a legal fact is the need for immediate decision. Conjectures share that need. They are formulated more or less immediately, not as expressions of truth but as theories to guide future thinking and research. The need for immediate decision calls for a standard of comparative beliefs, rather than an absolute standard. Therefore, the test for a conjecture appears to be whether the theorist believes it more than the theorist disbelieves it. This lenient standard of proof must be satisfied before accepting each conjecture.

Scientists can test my assertion of how they deal with epistemic uncertainty by simply asking themselves how often they use the product rule when spinning a theory from their observations. Not often, I would be willing to lay odds!

Still, scientists are likely to respond that they have their own ways of theorizing, which, they feel, prevent their falling into misuse of the product rule—yet their ways make no nod to multivalent logic. Perhaps the method that scientists are most likely to mention would be inference to the best explanation, which is sometimes called abductive inference.[33]

How can they justify the use of IBE in science? Although they do not, they could justify it by showing that, if the pool of explanations is assembled carefully, IBE is equivalent to using multivalent logic.[34] The scientists' aim when employing IBE is to establish their theory as superior to all competing accounts. IBE requires the scientists to formulate their best explanation, which would be as believable as its weakest link. The critics can offer competing explanations, with any one of their explanations being as believable as its weakest link. The careful scientists will then try to show that their best story is superior to the critics' best explanation. If they succeed, they will in fact have shown their explanation to be superior to all the competing accounts, and indeed to all the competing accounts put together. The equivalence at a fundamental level of IBE and multivalent logic proves my point that multivalent logic justifies scientific practices such as IBE.

Truth-seeking at the cutting edge of science is demanding, but I submit that it is not fundamentally different from legal factfinding. Traditional probability has important roles to play, of course, in both science and law. But when thinking about the real world, fraught with epistemic uncertainty, both scientists and lawyers must often reason in the credal terms of multivalent degrees of belief.

[33] See generally Lipton (2004) (providing the best treatment of the use of IBE in science, but looking to justify the method in part by resort to Bayesian analysis); cf. Earman (1992), pp. 163–185 (championing a role for "eliminative induction" in scientific confirmation theory).

[34] See supra Sects. 4.4.4 and 4.4.5 (making this showing).

6.3 Overview

The methods of multivalent beliefs in law and science indeed extend to all areas of inquiry—to all disciplines and to everyday life—that involve persistent epistemic uncertainty.

Once one starts to think in terms broad enough to encompass and distinguish beliefs and probabilities, the number of everyday problems that profit from belief analysis literally produces amazement. For example, a TV pundit opining as to the chances that Donald Trump will be acquitted on every indictment sets one's mind racing as to how accurately to calculate those chances. If the problem involves epistemic uncertainty—and most real problems do—one should turn to beliefs rather than probabilities. The problem will look different when broken down into measures of belief, disbelief, and epistemic uncertainty. And the different look will often yield a different conclusion.

Westerners are so locked into bivalent thinking that most of us never even realize that there is an additional, richer way of analyzing the world. Reconsider legal factfinding. So many bright theorists have argued that a 60% chance of fault and a 60% chance of causation equal a 36% chance of liability. Then, their divinely decreed truth supposedly warrants overhauling the law, because it says otherwise. However, combining beliefs in the presence of epistemic uncertainty works differently from probability, and gives (as the law does) an even more divine measure of liability.

This book has argued that bivalent thinking has its proper realm but also has its limits, and that multivalent thinking operates accurately in the realm beyond those limits. This thesis is no more radical than calling for putting another tool in the toolbox.

In regular life, if you are considering whether a friend did something bad, you do not seek a probability of certainty, assuming you could even imagine what that phrase meant. Instead, you think about whether you believe the act *to a degree* greater than you disbelieve it. We thus think in multivalent terms!

Put more precisely, this book has argued that humans had used degrees of belief long before the French devised probability. Humans still use multivalent beliefs instinctively for finding facts, inferring conclusions, combining conclusions, and making all sorts of decisions. The time has come for recognizing that fact.

References

Alexander L (1992) Proving the law: not proven. Northwest Univ Law Rev 86:905–915

Allen RJ, Pardo MS (2003) The myth of the law-fact distinction. Northwest Univ Law Rev 97: 1769–1807

Anderson T, Schum D, Twining W (2005) Analysis of evidence, 2nd edn. Cambridge University Press, New York

Baade B (2021) Historical truth before the European Court of Human Rights. In: Philipp AH, Esra D-G (eds) The European Court of Human Rights: current challenges in historical perspective. Elgar, Cheltenham UK, pp 221–243
Ben-Ari M (2005) Just a theory: exploring the nature of science. Prometheus Books, Amherst NY
Brewer S (2011) Logocratic method and the analysis of arguments in evidence. Law Probabil Risk 10:175–202
Clermont KM (2020) Rules, standards, and such. Buff Law Rev 68:751–804
Cooper JM (2021) The science of legal synthesis. St John's Law Rev 95:285–318
Curd M, Cover JA, Pincock C (2012) Philosophy of science: the central issues, 2nd edn. Norton, New York
Earman J (1992) Bayes or bust? a critical examination of Bayesian confirmation theory. MIT Press, Cambridge MA
Fedel M (2010) Uncertainty, indeterminacy and fuzziness: a probabilistic approach. In: Hosni H, Montagna F (eds) Probability, uncertainty and rationality. Edizioni Della Normale, Pisa Italy, pp 219–242
Fenoll JN (2023) Requiem for the burden of the proof. Quaestio Facti 4:1–23
Field RH, Benjamin K, Clermont KM, Clopton ZD (2023) Materials for a basic course in civil procedure, 14th edn. Foundation, St Paul MN
Franklin J (2015) The science of conjecture: evidence and probability before Pascal, 2nd edn. Johns Hopkins University Press, Baltimore
Friedman RD (1992) Standards of persuasion and the distinction between fact and law. Northwest Univ Law Rev 86:916–942
Haack S (2014) Irreconcilable differences? the troubled marriage of science and law. In: Evidence matters: science, proof, and truth in the law. Cambridge University Press, New York, pp 78–103
Hans VP (2014) What's it worth? jury damage awards as community judgments. William Mary Law Rev 55:935–969
Jaynes ET (2003) Probability theory: the logic of science. Cambridge University Press, Cambridge
Kolber AJ (2014) Smooth and bumpy laws. Calif Law Rev 102:655–690
Ladyman J (2002) Understanding philosophy of science. Routledge, London
Lawson G (1992) Proving the law. Northwest Univ Law Rev 86:859–904
Lawson G (2017) Evidence of the law: proving legal claims. University of Chicago Press, Chicago
Lindell B (2017) Multi-criteria analysis in legal reasoning. Elgar, Cheltenham UK
Lipton P (2004) Inference to the best explanation, 2nd edn. Routledge, London
Louis MB (1986) Allocating adjudicative decision making authority between the trial and appellate levels: a unified view of the scope of review, the judge/jury question, and procedural discretion. North Carolina Law Rev 64:993–1047
Nichols T, Brett M, Andersson J, Tor W, Poline J-B (2005) Valid conjunction inference with the minimum statistic. NeuroImage 25:653–660
Nunn GA (2021) Law, fact, and procedural justice. Emory Law J 70:1273–1323
Okasha S (2016) Philosophy of science: a very short introduction, 2nd edn. Oxford University Press, Oxford
Resta G, Zeno-Zencovich V (2013) Judicial "truth" and historical "truth": the case of the Ardeatine Caves massacre. Law Hist Rev 31:843–886
Salter M (2017) Countering Holocaust denial in relation to the Nuremberg trials. In: Behrens P et al (eds) Holocaust and genocide denial: a contextual perspective. Routledge, London, pp 21–33
Stein A (2022) Probabilism in legal interpretation. Iowa Law Rev 107:1389–1437
Twining W (2006) Rethinking evidence, 2nd edn. Cambridge University Press, New York
Twining W, Hampsher-Monk I (eds) (2003) Evidence and inference in history and law: interdisciplinary dialogues. Northwestern University Press, Evanston IL
University of California Museum of Paleontology (2021) The logic of scientific arguments. https://undsci.berkeley.edu/article/howscienceworks_07. Accessed 16 Dec 2021

Chapter 7
Conclusion

[W]e are, I know not how, double in ourselves, so that what we believe we disbelieve . . . .
—Michel de Montaigne (Wikiquote, https://en.wikiquote.org/wiki/Michel_de_Montaigne. But cf. Michel de Montaigne, The Complete Works of Michael de Montaigne 289 (William Hazlitt ed., London, John Templeton 1842) (". . . double in ourselves, which is the cause that what we believe we do not believe"). The original French from 1580 was: "Mais nous sommes, ie ne sçay comment, doubles en nous mesmes, qui fait que ce que nous croyons, nous ne le croyons pas . . . .")

Abstract This book has proceeded in five steps that establish these points: (1) The very common sort of uncertainty called epistemic, as opposed to aleatory, requires a special kind of analysis. (2) As many scholars have recognized already, traditional probability systems are incapable of accounting for epistemic uncertainty. (3) Among the numerous systems created to cure traditional probability's shortcomings and handle epistemic uncertainty, multivalent logic is a completely valid and highly developed system, and it becomes especially evocative for legal factfinding when expressed in the image of belief functions. (4) The resultant system of multivalent beliefs makes great sense in explaining current legal practices both for processing evidence by inference and aggregation and also for evaluating proof through the burdens and standards of proof. (5) The application of multivalent beliefs to legal factfinding is generalizable to all areas of inquiry that involve persistent epistemic uncertainty.

The concern of this book has been decisionmaking under uncertainty. The obvious starting point was the nature of uncertainty. The key insight is that uncertainty includes both the aleatory kind and also **epistemic uncertainty**. The former reflects randomness, while the latter comes from the ignorance left by incomplete, inconclusive, ambiguous, dissonant, or unreliable evidence, from the indeterminacy produced by the vagueness of our concepts and expressed perceptions of the real

K. M. Clermont, *A General Theory of Evidence and Proof*, Law and Philosophy Library 148, https://doi.org/10.1007/978-3-031-66552-3_7

world, and from the limits on our imaginative powers as to what we do not know. Both probability and multivalent logic can handle aleatory uncertainty, but traditional forms of probability cannot handle epistemic uncertainty. To understand evidence-based proof, and to perform it accurately, we need to utilize a logical method that can handle all relevant kinds of uncertainty.

Systems of **traditional probability** are built on bivalent logic, so that any proposition must be either true or false. The systems are additive in the sense that the chances of truth and falsity add to one. The most useful of those systems for factfinding is subjective probability, which relies on the image of the factfinder's willingness to bet on the disputed fact. However, because all versions of traditional probability fail to account for epistemic uncertainty, use of any of them for factfinding will run into a number of problems: (1) being unrealistic about how people measure proof, (2) fumbling when there is weak evidence on both sides, (3) opening the door to the rebuttal that infinite possibilities prevent proving anything, (4) lacking accurate tools for combining uncertain evidence or established facts, (5) posing asymmetries in the treatment of plaintiffs and defendants, and (6) failing conceptually to capture what we intuitively think is adequate proof. Today these problems are obvious, leading some probability theoreticians to alter traditional probability in ways that account for epistemic uncertainty. They have produced a variety of brilliant but clumsy ways to do what multivalent logic does easily and clearly. These include **logical, imprecise, and inductive probability** theories.

Systems of **multivalent logic** provide a better way to represent and handle the epistemic uncertainty that prevails in the real world. First, multivalent logic comprises a variety of valid logic systems, such as **fuzzy logic and possibility theory**. They are more general than classical logic, in that they do without the classical assumption that all propositions are either true or not true. Second, as a descriptive and normative matter, the legal factfinder concerns itself with multivalent degrees of belief based on the evidence presented. The law already conforms to this conception, allowing itself to proceed accurately without puzzles or paradoxes in its factfinding and allowing me to avoid calling for radical reform. Third, the theory of **belief functions** delivers a multivalent concept whose imagery best reflects and illuminates legal factfinding. A degree of belief can coexist with a degree of disbelief produced by the evidence, that is, an active belief in the falsification of the fact; and the factfinder, given evidence with various sources of epistemic uncertainty, can reserve some of its belief as uncommitted while forming a degree of belief the fact is true and a degree of belief the fact is false. Fourth, competing theories such as **inference to the best explanation, relative plausibility, and ranking theory** turn out to be largely equivalent to multivalent beliefs. But they lack an equivalent fit to legal imagery, an equivalently strong theoretical foundation, and an equivalent ability to dispel the problems of probability. Fifth, as a marriage of the concept of belief functions with the operators of multivalent logic, my **multivalent belief theory** manages to resolve all of traditional probability's problems that stem from its failure to account for epistemic uncertainty. Multivalent beliefs give a way to represent realistically how people find facts, to handle weak evidence on both sides nimbly, to dissipate the puzzle of infinite possibilities, to provide accurate tools for combining uncertain evidence or established facts, to resolve the seeming asymmetries in the treatment of plaintiffs and defendants, and to capture conceptually what we intuitively think is adequate legal proof. Sixth, multivalent beliefs are the appropriate measure whenever, for the sake of accuracy, the decisionmaker needs to keep track of epistemic uncertainties in addition to any aleatory uncertainty. Legal factfinders, for example, must hold all relevant kinds of uncertainty in mind when making and combining their findings.

Multivalent beliefs can be best understood if seen in action, as the **legal factfinder processes evidence and evaluates proof**. (1) The initial phase of factfinding entails the processing of the evidence in three steps. First, the factfinder should connect each item of evidence to a fact necessary to be proved—a so-called element—by constructing a chain of inferences. Second, the factfinder must aggregate the probative force of all the items of evidence that bear on each element. Third, the factfinder may choose to combine the elements of claim or affirmative defense, but the better approach is to proceed directly by applying the appropriate standard of proof to each element. In sum, the factfinder should construct a chain of inferences to produce a belief function for each item of evidence bearing on an element, and then weight and average those beliefs to produce for each element a composite belief function ready for applying the element-by-element standard of proof. (2) The final phase of factfinding entails evaluating the evidence as proof. The preliminary topics on the **burdens of proof** translate readily into the terms of multivalent beliefs. The burden of production, which effectuates multiple process and outcome values, means that a decisionmaker must patrol the sufficiency of the evidence to ensure that there is rationally enough to warrant the factfinder's applying the burden of persuasion. Any view of the burden of persuasion that rests on probabilities should likewise yield to a reformulation along the lines of multivalent beliefs. Additionally, on the key topic of the **standards of proof**, multivalent beliefs make indispensable contributions to understanding. For example, preponderance of the evidence is best understood as providing that the burdened party should win if and only if $Bel(a) > Bel(not\text{-}a)$. The higher standards of proof demand a greater predominance of belief in relation to disbelief.

This book's point is original and huge, as demonstrated in its argument's fifth step. The point extends far beyond legal factfinding. It reaches a lot of **decisionmaking**. For example, deciding questions of pure law is no different in kind from legal factfinding. For another example, science proceeds not so differently in its pursuit of truth. Multivalent beliefs, rather than traditional probability theory, underlie and justify how scientists most often do and should reason and theorize in the face of epistemic uncertainty. Indeed, the multivalent belief method of decisionmaking in law and science extends to all areas of inquiry that involve persistent epistemic uncertainty, whether inside the academy or in everyday life.

Book's Point—in Nonfrightening Form

A degree of belief or disbelief is the measure of the extent to which you estimate something to be fully proven. If you must decide a disputed question in a situation that is uncertain because of lack of perfect knowledge, you should accept the proponent's position if and only if, based on the evidence, you believe each necessary element of the position perceptibly more (or much more, as in a criminal prosecution) than you disbelieve it. Comfortingly, logic can justify this approach without encountering any of those paradoxes that so disrupt probabilist theories. Astoundingly, this logical approach to evidential proof would so alter our way of thinking about truth-finding that our current practices would finally become understandable and sensible.

PS: In an 1817 letter to his brothers, John Keats championed "*Negative Capability*, that is when a man is capable of being in uncertainties, Mysteries, doubts, without any irritable reaching after fact & reason." This book is not a champion of negative capability.

Instead, multivalent belief theory turns out to be both beautiful and true. Or as Keats' Grecian urn would put it, "Beauty is truth, truth beauty." Multivalent beliefs would allow decisionmaking under epistemic uncertainty to achieve that conjunction of beauty and truth.

Index

K. M. Clermont, *A General Theory of Evidence and Proof*, Law and Philosophy Library 148, https://doi.org/10.1007/978-3-031-66552-3

SPRINGER NATURE

GPSR Compliance

The European Union's (EU) General Product Safety Regulation (GPSR) is a set of rules that requires consumer products to be safe and our obligations to ensure this.

If you have any concerns about our products, you can contact us on ProductSafety@springernature.com

In case Publisher is established outside the EU, the EU authorized representative is:

Springer Nature Customer Service Center GmbH
Europaplatz 3
69115 Heidelberg, Germany

The manufacturer's authorised representative in the EU is Springer Nature Customer Service Centre GmbH, Europaplatz 3, 69115 Heidelberg, Germany. If you have any concerns regarding our products, please contact ProductSafety@springernature.com

Printed and bound by CPI Group (UK) Ltd, Croydon, CR0 4YY
30/09/2026
02225584-0004